*Westerns and American Culture,
1930–1955*

To my mother,
Bertha K. Loy,
and to the memory of my father,
Burton L. Loy.
They always found the money
so I could go to the show.
They are the real heroes
of this book.

Westerns and American Culture, 1930–1955

by R. PHILIP LOY

McFarland & Company, Inc., Publishers
Jefferson, North Carolina, and London

Part of Chapter Four first appeared in *Under Western Skies,* issue #51, and is included here with permission of the World of Yesterday Press

Library of Congress Cataloguing-in-Publication Data

Loy, R. Philip, 1940–
    Westerns and American culture, 1930–1955 / by R. Philip Loy.
       p.   cm.
    Includes bibliographical references and index.

    ISBN-13: 978-0-7864-1076-7
    (softcover : 50# alkaline paper) ∞

    1. Western films—United States—History and criticism.
PN1995.9.W4L69   2001
791.43'6278—dc21   2001031256

British Library cataloguing data are available

©2001 R. Philip Loy. All rights reserved

No part of this book may be reproduced or transmitted in any form or by any means, electronic or mechanical, including photocopying or recording, or by any information storage and retrieval system, without permission in writing from the publisher.

Manufactured in the United States of America

McFarland & Company, Inc., Publishers
   Box 611, Jefferson, North Carolina 28640
      www.mcfarlandpub.com

TABLE OF CONTENTS

Preface   1

CHAPTER 1
Sagebrush Heroes   3

CHAPTER 2
"A Mark to Shoot At"   24

CHAPTER 3
Cowboys and Sky Pilots: Religion in Westerns   47

CHAPTER 4
"Cowboy Patriots: B Westerns and American Politics"   75

CHAPTER 5
"Gunplay Is the Glory of the West"   100

CHAPTER 6
"Friendly Neighbors All Around"   121

CHAPTER 7
"Law Is Law and Property Is Property"   152

CHAPTER 8
A White Range   184

CHAPTER 9
"These Indians Not Such Bad People"   214

CHAPTER 10
"No Business for a Girl"   236

References   263

Index   267

Preface

I can remember my first movie as if it were only yesterday, even though many years have passed since that warm Saturday afternoon of September 2, 1944. The Paramount Theater is now a parking lot, and the years have blurred most other childhood memories, but recollections of my first movie remain remarkably clear. I had turned four years old on August 24, so as a special belated birthday present Mother took me to see *The Yellow Rose of Texas* (Republic, 1944), a Roy Rogers Western.

That Saturday afternoon a love affair began between a boy and cowboy movies, and until I graduated from high school in 1958 I saw Westerns nearly every weekend. However, Westerns gave way to other things during college, graduate school and the early years of marriage. Then, in the mid–1970s, the old Westerns of my youth began to reappear on television and I found myself juggling family responsibilities and my professional schedule to watch them.

I also recognized that Westerns had influenced my value system and behavior. They had been important elements in my socialization. Since I had a very normal childhood, I suspected Westerns played a similar role for other people as well. So I began to gather materials, read books about Westerns, attend film festivals and, above all, watch hundreds of Westerns on television and videocassette. This book is a product of that journey and I invite readers, as they share it with me, to remember those Saturday afternoon matinees they spent watching their favorite cowboy stars gallop across the silver screen.

Books are seldom the product of one person's efforts alone, and this one is no exception. Dr. Robert Pitts, Dr. Richard Stanislaw and Dr. Dwight Jessup, all vice-presidents of academic affairs at Taylor University, encouraged the research and provided money to attend popular culture conferences at which many of the ideas were first aired. My secretaries, Mrs. Lavonna Shockey and Mrs. Darlene Jordan, were always helpful; without them, I would still be working on Chapter One. Ed Breen, Alan Miller, the late Earl Armstrong and Ron and Linda Downey are other individuals who either encouraged the research or provided information which enriched it.

Dr. Raymond White, Professor Emeritus of History, and Gary Kramer of Ball State University were important sources of both encouragement and information. Long drives to film festivals and Popular Culture Association conferences went by quickly as we discussed Westerns.

My wife Janet, daughter Lisa and son-in-law Michael Belcher have lived through and, in some instances, suffered through this project with me. I suspect that only family members can fully appreciate the work that goes into a book!

Chapter One

SAGEBRUSH HEROES

Many individuals now in the sixth decade of life and beyond have fond memories of Friday nights and Saturday afternoons in theaters with names such as Liberty, Lyric, Joy, Alamo or Paramount watching cowboy stars of the 1930s, 1940s, and early 1950s chase villains or help a heroine out of harm's way. Certainly children and adults of that era had ample opportunity to view "cowboy movies" because over 2600 Westerns were produced during those years, and the vast majority of them were B Westerns starring one of the well-known cowboy stars of the era (Adams and Rainey). However, those impressive numbers seem to have little influence on many film critics and historians who dismiss Westerns in general and B Westerns in particular as of little importance (Warshow; Garfield). While that may be the case for those narrowly focused on the history and criticism of film, social scientists and students of popular culture should not dismiss B Westerns so quickly. The importance of attending Western movies as an eagerly awaited weekend ritual suggests that the films held an importance that should not be ignored. The argument of this book is simple: Westerns were significant in the socialization process of youngsters and adults in the middle quarter of the twentieth century. Westerns reflected, reinforced and helped to shape values, attitudes and behavior patterns.

For those not formally schooled in the social sciences, socialization is a strange sounding, even frightening, word. It need not be, for it is simply another way of saying that children didn't just grow up. They had a lot of help along the way. People took the time to teach them correct behavior, to help them distinguish between right and wrong, and to affirm those values that became the focal points of their lives. From the very early days of childhood when parents taught proper manners (to share with friends, to drink milk), through those difficult teenage years when they were an important stabilizing force, parents played a crucial role in helping children to learn proper behavior and responsible values.

In the 1940s it was common for parents to hold up the cowboy stars as role models. If Roy Rogers said it was okay for a little boy to go to Sunday School, then it must be okay. If the Lone Ranger advised his radio listeners to start off each day with a healthy breakfast, including a big bowl of Cheerios, then Mother purchased the Cheerios, Nabisco Shredded Wheat, Quaker Puffed Oats or whatever the cowboy hero of the moment was advertising. Before children were old enough to read by themselves, mothers read stories from juvenile novels or comic books about the cowboy stars. The cowboy hero's influence as a role model was dramatically illustrated when a little boy fell out of a fifth story window and fractured nearly every bone in his body. He bit his lip and said bravely, "Buck Jones wouldn't cry and I am not going to cry either" (Rainey 1975, 91).

When children started to school, teachers became important role models. Teachers taught the necessity of doing one's own work and being responsible for it. Children learned not to speak out of turn and to wait in line at the drinking fountain instead of pushing their way to the front. Other people became influential as well. For some, clergy played a pivotal role and peer groups were very important for all young folks. The gang one ran around with influenced speech, dress, attitudes and a lot of other things.

As children grew older, more abstract ideas such as democracy, justice and equality became meaningful. Again, parents, teachers and friends helped to shape those notions. At home, parents taught equality by treating the children as much alike as possible. Children learned about justice through appropriate punishment. In school, teachers normally let a different child lead the class to lunch and, through that, helped everyone to understand that democracy was somehow related to taking turns. Later on, that idea came alive as teenagers took history and government classes and elected school and class officers by popular vote. All these examples highlight the fact that behavior, attitudes and values didn't just happen. Children didn't just grow up. A lot of people helped, and that process is called socialization.

Movies, and cowboy movies in particular, were important elements in childhood socialization. Movies were not as important as were parents or teachers, but they were important. Three significant aspects of the socialization process stand out in particular. First, Western movies were far more important in childhood socialization of the 1930s and 1940s than most people realize. Second, Westerns were most effective when they reinforced what children learned at home and school. And third, the cowboy heroes influenced values, attitudes and beliefs far more than they impacted behavior.

Popular movies, novels and television entertain but they also teach about one's own and other cultures. Because they entertain, viewers are far more likely to retain their lessons than to remember the things in schoolbooks and dry film documentaries that are supposed to educate. I. C. Jarvie in *Movies as Social Criticism: Aspects of Their Social Psychology* made this point when he wrote that movies have unintended social significance because they tell stories which convey information; information influences what people believe and how they act (Jarvie, IX). As if to reinforce Jarvie's point, Bruce Bennett, one of Republic Studio's leading men, commented, "No one thought of anything but entertainment, but…I can see they were more influential than we realized" (Hurst, 70).

Jon Tuska echoes both Jarvie and Bennett with a specific example. Tuska once taught a class for teachers on the image of Indians in motion pictures. He observed that female teachers, including some members of racial minorities, began to examine real Indian cultures in order to distinguish them from motion picture images. The male students objected; they regarded Westerns as embodying the finest moral values of American society and they did not want those values questioned or challenged. The male students reflected in rather stark fashion the significance of Westerns in their socialization process (Tuska 1985, 262).

The role of Westerns in socialization is impossible to quantify. No studies have done so, nor can people who grew up viewing Westerns verbalize in response to questionnaires the impact Western movies had on them. Personal anecdotes, the continuing popularity of film festivals and the extensive airing of Westerns on television all combine to make a persuasive argument that old Westerns tap sentiments which cannot be passed off as nostalgic longing for childhood. Something more is at work; that "something more" points to the important role that Westerns played in childhood socialization.

That leads to a second point about socialization. Western movies were most effective when they reinforced values, attitudes and behavior patterns taught by family and school. As a personal example, my father was active in labor unions and the Democrat Party. My father was not a socialist, yet I grew up with an abiding distrust of bankers and capitalists. I also grew up believing that the federal government was a dependable ally if common people voted into office good public officials who would protect working people and farmers from those capitalists and bankers who thought only of themselves.

That rather simple and naive view of the political and economic world has long since faded, but it echoes throughout Western films. Bankers are more often than not villains. Fred Scott in *The Roaming Cowboy* (Spectrum, 1937) even proclaimed that he was a Democrat, and Wally Wales in 1934 short *Carrying the Mail* (Imperial, 1934) assured viewers that the government in Washington aims to help them.* The message in those and dozens of other Westerns is too clear to be mistaken. They were reflecting and reinforcing a belief system.

But what did Westerns teach? Here one meets a third important socialization role of Westerns. Certainly Westerns had minimum impact on behavior. Most children did not grow up to be cowboys or bank robbers. Most quickly learned they could not imitate the life of cowboy leisure. One had to work in order to live! It is a mistake, then, to identify the important socializing role of cowboy movies with behavior. That will lead to the unmistakable conclusion that Westerns were distractions, nothing more or less, sidetracks on the way to growing up with little lasting significance.

Socialization, however, deals with more than behavior. It also directs and shapes what people believe, and it is here that one discovers a significant role for Westerns. Westerns projected a number of important beliefs, ones that many adults who spent their youths in darkened theaters still affirm. From Westerns, children learned that most folks were basically honest and brave, but sometimes they needed a good leader to stiffen public resistance to the few who were corrupt and dishonest. One thing was clear, however: Crime does not pay! That sounds strange today, but thousands of people grew up believing it was true.

Westerns also taught that very little in life comes without hard work, but success is sure to follow if one works hard and remains steadfastly committed to one's goals. Who can forget the scenes in *Shane* (Paramount, 1953) in which Van Heflin and Alan Ladd worked so hard at uprooting the large tree stump? In numerous ways, that theme of hard work and commitment played out in countless Westerns.

In striving for success, however, one had to play by the rules. While pragmatism had a limited role in Westerns, sometimes one had to cut corners or play loose with legal procedures; more often that not, those who cheated or sought the easy way to success failed. Fair play was the standard Western set. Those who cheated or who competed unfairly, taking advantage of the less fortunate, did not win in the long run. For many, those

---

*Most production information is taken from Les Adams and Buck Rainey's Shoot-Em Ups: The Complete Reference Guide to Westerns of the Sound Era *(Metuchen, 1985)*. I used Michael R. Pitts' Western Movies: A TV and Video Guide to 4200 Genre Films *(Jefferson, 1986)* for Westerns produced after 1977. I list production information for a film the first time that the film is cited in each chapter.*

lessons carry over today. It is disheartening to discover individuals who cheat in order to win more games, get higher grades or make more money.

Sociologists speak of social roles. Each role a person plays (whether it is as parent or child, employer or employee, teacher or student) has its own particular set of rights and responsibilities as well as expectations about proper behavior. Parents are expected to love and provide for their children. Children in turn are supposed to obey their parents and care for them as they age. Public officials are supposed to be honest public servants dedicated to the welfare of the community. One does not have to see many Westerns to recognize that all of those beliefs, as well as many others, figure prominently in the genre, so prominently that several of them will be explored in depth in the following chapters. Westerns helped to shape and to reinforce what several generations believed.

Westerns played a role in the socialization process of millions of boys and girls growing up between 1930 and 1955; for that, if for no other reason, cowboy movies ought to be taken seriously. But there is another important, equally compelling reason to take a fresh look at Westerns. They are chronicles of the years in which they were produced.

Future historians may well regard the quarter century between 1930 and 1955 as the defining years of the twentieth century; they may even see those years as the golden age of American civilization. There is something compelling about the events of the period, an indefinable quality that draws attention to those years. There is much to lament about the period; continued racial discrimination and admission quotas for Jews in America's best colleges and universities are but two of them. But overall, the 1930s and 1940s were years in which the American people began to achieve mass prosperity and to assert international leadership while maintaining those values on which the country had been built.

The Great Depression of the 1930s still fascinates over 60 years after it began to wind down. Economic hardships, human misery, gangster empires and the voices of domestic demagogues jar the conscience, even of those who did not live through the events. Equally compelling, however, are the stories of millions of people who, in the midst of hardship and misery, affirmed the values of hard work, individual responsibility and the importance of keeping families together, turning to government for assistance only when all else failed. As the twenty-first century opens, those alive today grappling with an economy which seems to discard millions of potentially productive citizens can learn much by studying the values and behavior of that generation which suffered through the Great Depression and World War II.

Contemporary citizens also need to consider carefully the record of the generation of American leaders who ushered the United States to a position of world leadership. As current leaders endeavor to steer the American ship of state through dangerous international waters, lessons can be learned from President Franklin Roosevelt as he educated the American people on the threats from Nazi expansionism and Japanese aggression. Presidents Harry Truman and Dwight Eisenhower created a foreign policy which guided American involvement in world affairs until the Soviet Union and Communism collapsed in the 1980s. Current citizens need to know that history.

The years between 1930 and 1955 were a time of landmark, wholesome movies. The studio system was at its zenith, creating actors and actresses who became idols and role models for Americans of all ages, and churning out hundreds of movies each year that played in thousands of theaters. Current political figures and social critics who lament the level of violence and sexuality in contemporary motion pictures often find themselves talking to an unresponsive industry concerned only with the financial bottom line.

After 1934, however, the Production Code created by the Motion Picture Producers and Distributors of America governed what appeared on the silver screen. It was sensitive to excessive violence, implicit (explicit was surely taboo) sexuality, and religious and ethnic slurs. The Production Code required movies that highlighted family, honored hard work and individual responsibility, downplayed brutal, graphic violence, and held up America as a noble land of equality, fundamental fairness, achievement and decency. Those motion pictures, far from being regarded by the rest of the world as irrelevant and quaint, were eagerly sought by foreign distributors and viewed by millions of Europeans who respected America because of what they saw on the silver screen. Contemporary Americans can learn much from that example as well.

Westerns loomed large in the Hollywood production scheme of that era, and each year they were viewed by millions in the United States and abroad. Movies in general, and Westerns in particular, reflected the values held by millions of Americans living between 1930 and 1955, values respected throughout the world.

Most people forgot quickly the specific Westerns of their childhood years. A few remarkable individuals can remember the plots of many cowboy movies they saw as children, but most people can recall only those few B Westerns that left an indelible imprint on their young minds. A particular song such as "Don't Fence Me In," or an especially funny incident such as the little lamb following Gabby Hayes around in *Roll On Texas*

Moon (Republic, 1946), might make a lasting impression, but they were the exceptions. Most of the specific B Westerns faded from memory; the cowboy stars who appeared in the movies did not. They were childhood heroes and, while contemporary adults no longer believe they were ten feet tall and incapable of doing wrong, they still remember fondly their heroes' names and cherish their memories. Simply put, B Westerns and the cowboy heroes who starred in them left an important legacy that has been ignored far too long.

Not all agree with that assessment. Don Miller and David Rothel, two of the better chroniclers of the cowboy heroes, suggest that they did not have much lasting influence. Westerns were good distractions for a Saturday afternoon, but that is about all (Miller, 8; Rothel 1978, 17). Others are not so sure.

Statistics suggest that the cowboy heroes had widespread appeal. By 1939, Gene Autry (through films and personal appearances) was playing to 40,000,000 people annually (Johnston, 18). In 1945, Roy Rogers averaged 35,000 fan letters a month (Martin, 26). Statistics alone cannot convey the intensity of feeling the cowboy heroes generated in their followers. Jack Nachbar, in the Preface of *Focus on the Western*, catches that intensity as he recalls arriving late for a Saturday matinee, running to his seat, turning toward the screen, genuflecting and making the sign of the cross, all unconsciously, until he saw his buddies giggling in their seats (Nachbar, 1). John Nicholas could recall, some 50 years later, what Tom Mix wore the afternoon Nicholas saw him in person at a Detroit theater. Nicholas' parents had emigrated from Greece. "For us," he said, "Tom Mix was the dream of America" (Nicholas, xi). Charles Silver, author of *The Western Film*, wrote that only a crucial Dodgers game could keep him from his Saturday cowboy movie (Silver, 10).

The author can still remember, as if it were only yesterday, lying on the living room floor, the Thursday evening *Marion Chronicle* spread out in front of him, poring over the movie advertisements. If a Roy Rogers Western was in town that weekend, Friday evening was nailed down. By the time school was dismissed on Friday afternoon, Dad was home from work. A quick change of clothes, maybe supper at home (or better yet, hamburger and french fries at a local restaurant), and then on to town to the show!

In 1995, the author participated in a panel on Roy Rogers at the Popular Culture Association Annual Meeting. He told of being on vacation with his parents when he was 11 or 12 years old. While driving past a fish hatchery, his parents asked if he knew what that was. When he explained to them what a fish hatchery was and what it did, his parents were impressed and asked if he had studied that in school. Although he didn't remember where he had learned about fish hatcheries at that time, he was surprised many years later watching *Susanna Pass* (Republic, 1949) with Roy Rogers and Dale Evans, and hearing Evans deliver much the same lecture he had given his parents. In the discussion that followed the presentations, a lady in the audience told a similar story. She accompanied a group of mothers who were taking a Brownie troop or school class on a tour of a fish hatchery. As the guide explained how it worked, the lady said she replied, before she realized what she was saying, "Oh, just like Roy Rogers and Dale Evans."

As the audience chuckled at the similarity of the two experiences, all realized that they verified a central point of all of the presentations. B Westerns did make an impact. Not only did the cowboy heroes serve as role models, the films themselves contained important lessons and information which young viewers remembered as adults.

Film festivals continue to draw sizable crowds. The ones at Charlotte, North Carolina, and Knoxville, Tennessee, are almost devoted entirely to Western films and old serials. The best known of the festivals at Memphis, Tennessee, gives Westerns high visibility. In addition, there are film festivals honoring individual cowboy heroes such as Tom Mix, Buck Jones and Roy Rogers. Sunset Carson, a cowboy hero of the 40s, did three seasons of *Six Gun Heroes* on the Public Broadcasting System. Cable television has discovered the old Westerns are a mother lode to be mined again. They want for neither viewers nor sponsors. The Encore multiplex even has a channel devoted exclusively to Westerns.

It seems obvious that Westerns and their cowboy heroes did, in some fashion, influence American life, an impact that has yet to be explored fully or appreciated to the extent it ought to be. John H. Lenihan is right on the mark when he writes that the Western film "deserves to be considered as part of the nation's transient mythic baggage even as those who care to confront the substance and flavor of American life...consider such evidence as election statistics, political speeches and intellectual writings" (Lenihan, 9). As a prelude to assessing the impact of B Westerns on American life, one needs to know about the cowboy stars who made the films. Who were those guys anyway?

The Great Train Robbery, made by the Edison Company in 1903, is most commonly regarded as the first Western narrative film. It was a pioneer film in the use of cut-aways, camera placement, and editing to tell a story. And it was immensely popular! Irrespective of whatever place *The Great Train Robbery* merits in film history, it is pivotal in the history of Western film for it demonstrated the immense popularity of Westerns in the United States as well as abroad.

The star system had not developed at the time *The Great Train Robbery* was produced, and would not for about another decade, so it would be inaccurate to associate it with any particular star. However, Gilbert M. Anderson had several roles in *The Great Train Robbery*. For Anderson, movies were love at first sight. Anderson remained with the Edison Company for a time, learning his new trade under the tutelage of Edwin S. Porter, producer and director of *The Great Train Robbery*. After an apprenticeship with Porter, Anderson decided to strike out on his own. He formed a partnership with George K. Spoor to create a new film company, Essanay.

In 1908, Essanay decided to make a Western, and Anderson played the lead role. Later, Anderson developed a screenplay from a *Collier's* short story, "Bronco Billy and the Baby." Unable to find an actor to play the part of Bronco Billy, Anderson decided to do it himself. It was a life-changing decision for Gilbert M. Anderson, as Bronco Billy became an instant success. Over the next decade, America had its first cowboy hero—Bronco Billy.

Just as Edwin S. Porter's *The Great Train Robbery* had demonstrated the American public's love for Western movies, Anderson proved the public was ready to identify with a specific cowboy hero. In that sense, both men helped to establish the Western film genre, and Gilbert M. Anderson in particular headed it down a trail that was to dominate the genre for nearly 50 years; the trail of the cowboy hero.

By the beginning of World War I, Anderson had lost his place to William S. Hart, the man usually regarded as the first real cowboy hero. Anderson's films had been one- and two-reelers designed for nickelodeon audiences. Although he also made one- and two-reel films, Hart quickly molded his efforts to the feature film, then largely a foreign import only beginning to appear in the United States.

Hart was different in several ways from the cowboy heroes who would follow him and who are the primary focus of this book. Hart's Westerns were bigger budget films designed for adult audiences. In fact, little in Hart's films were intended to appeal specifically to children. His film *Hell's Hinges* (Triangle, 1916), for example, is one of the first adult Westerns. Hart plays Blaze Tracy, a hard-drinking, evil gunman. In the film, a saloon girl seduced the town minister and Hart had a romantic interest in the minister's sister. Hardly the stuff associated with later cowboy heroes. The characters Hart portrayed drank, smoked and often shot to kill. His costumes were more nearly like those worn by real cowboys than the colorful dress of the cowboy heroes who would follow him.

A glamorous cowboy hero did follow Hart, and in fact may be credited with hastening Hart's retirement. If Hart dominated the genre from 1915 to the early 1920s, Mix, the glamour cowboy hero who replaced him in American affections, and who was Hart's antithesis, would overwhelm it. Tom Mix was the model cowboy hero and all who followed him, until the demise of the cowboy hero in the early 1950s, had to make their peace with the model Mix created.

By the time he arrived in Hollywood, Mix had had a knock-about life of repeated failures. It was not until 1917 when William Fox signed him to a contract that Mix's film career took off. But take off it did, and by the early 1920s Mix was Hart's serious rival. But he was a rival of a different sort. Mix's films were action-oriented entertainment. Because he sought consciously to attract children, Mix avoided controversial themes. He stressed the dress-up, showmanship side of cowboy life by wearing fancy clothes and ornate holsters. Mix's cowboy hero characters did not smoke or drink and normally they did not shoot to kill.

Mix began a code that characterized nearly all the cowboy heroes who followed him. From Mix to the genre's demise in the mid–1950s, most cowboy heroes avoided drinking, smoking and gambling. They seldom used guns when fists or a rope would do, and when they did use a gun it was rarely to kill. Tom Mix began that code, and in that sense he was the king of the cowboys.

Before the Depression, Mix had been a wealthy man and (like many other movie stars) he lived like a king. Few, however, dominated a genre as did Mix. Mickey Rooney, playing the young king in *My Pal, the King* (Universal, 1932), poignantly symbolized the fact. Mix is sitting on Rooney's throne and remarks all he needs is a crown. Young Rooney takes Mix's white Stetson and places it on Mix's head. If the cowboy heroes had a king, it was Tom Mix, and his crown was a cowboy hat.

By the late 1920s, Mix was being copied by several would-be rivals. Ken Maynard could ride better and he lasted longer than did Mix. Maynard's hot temper and penchant for alcohol, however, repeatedly frustrated his career. Hoot Gibson was a real cowboy as well as a good actor. His humorous, offbeat Westerns have stood the test of time and are yet enjoyable. While Hoot Gibson had a great deal of fan appeal, he was not Tom Mix. Fred Thomson, an ordained Presbyterian minister and a star developed by Joseph P. Kennedy's Film Booking Office, made a good impression. Thomson might have rivaled Mix had early death not tragically ended his film career.

Harry Carey began making Westerns prior to World War I and he continued to star in them up to the mid–1930s. Buck Jones started his film career as a stand-in and stunt man for Tom Mix. In 1920, Fox Studio placed Jones in a series of popular Westerns, and he along with Mix were the studio's main Western stars until both left in 1928. Tim McCoy came to Hollywood as an Indian agent, escorting the Indians who helped to make *The Covered Wagon* (Lasky, 1923). McCoy stayed, and from the mid–1920s until 1943, when he reentered military service, he made over 75 films, most of them Westerns. Tim McCoy, Buck Jones and Harry Carey all combined elements of William S. Hart and Tom Mix into highly successful film careers. But, again, they were not Tom Mix.

The coming of sound films found Mix an aging star. In 1932-33 he made nine sound films for Universal Studio and as a last hurrah appeared in a 1935 Mascot serial, *The Miracle Rider*. By the sound era, however, Mix was clearly past his prime. In those early years of sound Westerns, Jones, Maynard and McCoy occupied Mix's place at the Saturday matinee. Newcomers such as Bob Steele and Tom Tyler also demonstrated their fan appeal. And in 1933, with *Riders of Destiny* (Monogram, 1933), John Wayne began climbing the ladder to movie stardom.

Mix's cowboy kingdom was full of active rivals. While that might have troubled Mix, the genre was facing an even more serious problem. Westerns were losing audience appeal. Not only were gangster movies more exciting and bloody, Westerns were suffering from too much predictability. Audiences simply lost interest. In fact, during 1933-34 both McCoy and Jones made several non–Western films.

Fortunately the decline was short-lived, and by 1935 a Western film revival was underway. The resurgence was fueled by three efforts. Harry Sherman at Paramount Pictures launched his Hopalong Cassidy series starring William Boyd. Then Nat Levine, producer of Mascot Pictures, a Poverty Row studio which specialized in serials and B films, sacked Ken Maynard after he made one feature, *In Old Santa Fe* (Mascot, 1934), and one serial, *Mystery Mountain* (Mascot, 1934). Levine had originally planned to star Maynard in a second serial, *Phantom Empire* (Mascot, 1935), but Maynard was impossible to work with through one more effort. Levine took a chance, instead, on a young unknown actor-singer (Tuska 1982, 136). It proved successful. The actor-singer was Gene Autry and with *Phantom Empire* the singing cowboy was born.

Tuska and others have written about the Sherman-Boyd collaboration on the Hopalong Cassidy series and the surprising popularity of the Autry films. Columbia Pictures mogul Harry Cohn's decision to hire Charles Starrett to replace the departing Tim McCoy has received less comment. Starrett's first Western, *Gallant Defender* (Columbia, 1935), was released four months after Boyd's first Hopalong Cassidy movie and two months after Autry's first starring feature film. While it would be foolish to claim that Starrett was as popular as either Boyd or Autry, his films had good scripts, lots of action and good supporting casts, including the Sons of the Pioneers until 1940. Not surprisingly, Starrett's Westerns quickly developed a loyal following.

The mid- to late 1930s were boom years for Western films. During the first five years of the decade, Columbia had Buck Jones and Tim McCoy, the two most popular cowboy stars of that period, under contract. By 1930, Jones needed work badly. In 1928, he had financed and produced a sound Western, *The Big Hop* (Buck Jones Productions, 1928), which turned out to be a financial disaster, and that failure was followed by an ill-fated wild west show venture which bankrupted Jones. When Sol Lesser approached Jones about making Westerns to be released through Columbia exchanges, Jones jumped at the $300 per week, even though it was a far cry from the four-figure weekly salary he had made at Fox during the 1920s (Tuska 1976, 223).

After Columbia released eight of Lesser's pictures, the company took over production of the series, increasing Jones' salary to $500 per week and raising the budget for each film to $25,000 (Tuska 1976, 226). From 1931 until he left Columbia in 1934, Buck Jones was the most popular of all the silver screen cowboys.

Columbia loaned Jones to Universal to make serials, and Jones' Universal chapter plays were popular with the Saturday matinee crowd. As a result, Universal enticed Jones away from Columbia with an agreement to create a separate Buck Jones production unit, one which Jones would control. Jones jumped at the chance and from 1935 to 1937 he made Westerns at Universal. The first few were excellent films. *Stone of Silver Creek* (1935) and *The Ivory Handled Guns* (1935) are as good as anything he made at Columbia. Unfortunately, Jones was not able to sustain that quality. His later Universal efforts—films such as *Sandflow* (Universal, 1937)— and *Sudden Bill Dorn* (Universal, 1937) are strange, confusing Westerns.

In 1937 the new management at Universal was looking for ways to cut costs so they declined to increase Jones' salary. Jones returned to Columbia and made six pictures for that studio in 1938. By the end of the 1930s, however, Jones' film career was in decline.

Columbia also signed Tim McCoy to a contract in 1930. McCoy first came to Hollywood as an interpreter and agent for the Shoshone Indians appearing in *The Covered Wagon*. MGM was impressed enough with McCoy to put him under contract and he appeared in MGM period pictures and Westerns throughout the 1920s. But like so many other Western stars of the silent era, McCoy's career appeared to be over in 1928, another victim of the talkies.

When sound Westerns began to appear in 1929, Carl Laemmle, owner of Universal Pictures, decreed that the studio would make a serial entitled *The Indians Are Coming*. Universal enticed McCoy back to Hollywood to star in the chapter play. Columbia then jumped at the chance to place McCoy under contract and from 1931 until he left Columbia over a salary dispute in 1935, McCoy appeared in a very popular series of Westerns. In fact, McCoy ranked just below Jones in the affections of the matinee crowd.

After he left Columbia in 1935, McCoy never regained the prominence he had at Columbia. For the rest of the decade, McCoy moved from small production units to even smaller ones. The pictures McCoy made for Puritan, Victory and Producers Releasing Corporation (PRC) are surely not of the same caliber as his Columbia films. By the end of the decade, McCoy's film career too was in decline.

During the 1930s, smaller production companies such as Monogram and Tiffany churned out numerous low-budget Westerns starring Tom Tyler, Bob Steele, Ken Maynard, and Hoot Gibson. When Universal's skepticism about producing sound Westerns caused the studio to close down its Western units, Gibson was unemployed for the first time in over a decade. His name, however, continued to be a big draw so smaller production companies starred Gibson in Westerns well into the 1930s.

Maynard's career was a bit more checkered. Maynard's First National silent Westerns are excellent, among the best he ever made. When First National went bankrupt, Maynard moved to Universal and made a series of entertaining Westerns during the transition to sound. Throughout the 1930s, however, Maynard moved from studio to studio as producers tried to make a few dollars off of his screen popularity before he became too difficult to handle.

Bob Steele was the new kid on the block. Even though he had appeared in a few silents, Steele was in no sense a screen rival of silent screen cowboy stars. During the 1930s, however, Steele became a favorite at the Saturday matinee. Part of Steele's prominence is traceable to the sheer number of Westerns he made for numerous production companies during the 1930s. Between 1930 and the end of 1939, Steele appeared in 65 Westerns, an average of over six films a year, which meant that his films appeared often in those theaters showing cowboy movies. Steele's programmers were ones young boys liked: Non-stop action, hard riding, flying bullets and (above all) exciting chair-crashing, barroom-destroying fights highlighted every Steele Western.

By 1935, Westerns were once again popular and exhibitors were clamoring for more of them. That, in turn, prompted independent producers to make several cheap Westerns with some of the lesser known stars of the silent era, including Buffalo Bill, Jr. (Jay Wilsey), Jack Perrin, Buddy Roosevelt, Rex Lease and Guinn "Big Boy" Williams. In addition, some of the independents tried to develop new stars through a series of Westerns with the likes of Lane Chandler, Kermit Maynard and Reb Russell, a football hero of the 1930s. None of those efforts were particularly successful. Watching those films today, one cringes at the poor acting, implausible stories and shoddy editing. That the films were made at all indicates how popular Westerns had become once again by the mid–1930s.

In 1939, when some of the luster was wearing off and audience interest in Westerns seemed to wane, John Ford's *Stagecoach* (United Artists, 1939) unleashed a new wave of enthusiasm for Western films. It not only helped the movie career of John Wayne by taking him out of series B Westerns into bigger budget B and A films, it also encouraged a number of bigger budget A Westerns. Soon after *Stagecoach*, films such as *Dodge City* (Warner Bros., 1939) with Errol Flynn and *The Westerner* (United Artists, 1940) with Gary Cooper were playing first-run theaters. From 1935 until the late 1940s Westerns were staple Hollywood entertainment. The cowboy hero was America's hero.

Unlike the silent 20s or early 30s, after 1935 the cowboy hero often sang. Gene Autry is, of course, the first genuine singing cowboy, but singing in Westerns preceded Autry. Ken Maynard probably ought to be given credit for introducing music into Western films. His *Wagon Master* (Universal, 1929) featured music and it was followed by other Maynard Westerns which incorporated music, including *Strawberry Roan* (Universal, 1933) and *In Old Santa Fe*. Maynard often sang and accompanied himself on either the guitar or the fiddle. Even John Wayne appeared to sing. His first film for Monogram Pictures, *Riders of Destiny*, introduced the character Singing Sandy. Wayne's voice was dubbed, to be sure, but it continued the gradual movement toward a singing cowboy.

Autry, however, revolutionized Westerns and soon other studios were shopping for singing cowboys. Warner Bros. was the first to follow Republic's lead. Two months after *Tumbling Tumbleweeds* (Republic, 1935), Autry's first feature film, Warner Bros. unveiled Dick Foran in *Moonlight on the Prairie* (Warner Bros., 1935). Universal followed with Bob Baker, 20th Century–Fox starred Smith Ballew, and in 1941 Columbia Pictures placed Tex Ritter under contract. Ritter had started making singing cowboy movies for Grand National in 1936, and when that company went broke, he moved to Monogram before switching to Columbia.

The singing cowboy race was run with gusto by the smaller studios and independents. Fred Scott made several films for Spectrum Pictures. Monogram, which after a brief stint as part of Republic, re-emerged in 1937 as a separate studio, had several singing cowboys at various times, including Tex Ritter, John "Dusty" King in the Range Busters series, James Newill in the Renfrew Royal Mounted series, and Jack Randall. PRC, probably the archetype Poverty Row studio, employed George Houston as a singing cowboy in the Lone Rider Westerns, and both James Newill and Tex Ritter, now as the end of his acting career, in the Texas Ranger series. Before it went bankrupt, Grand National, in addition to Ritter, starred Tex Fletcher, a New York radio personality for one Western, and it was the only studio that featured a singing cowgirl. But after three pictures starring Dorothy Page, Grand National scrapped the endeavor. Richard Kahn, an independent producer, even made a few Westerns with all-black casts in an all-black West. Each film featured Herb Jeffries as a black singing cowboy.

When Autry, dissatisfied with his salary, threatened to strike, Herbert Yates, president of Republic Pictures, decided to find a backup singing cowboy. Thus in 1938 Roy Rogers became Republic's new singing sensation. After the war, Republic developed two more singing cowboys, Monte Hale and Rex Allen. The latter was the last of the breed. When Allen's production unit folded in 1953, there were no more singing cowboys. And only two others appeared in the post-war years. Producers Releasing Corporation starred Eddie Dean in a series of films from 1945 through 1948 and Monogram Pictures featured Jimmy Wakely, the popular radio Western singer, in Westerns from 1946 through 1949.

Clearly, not all who appeared as singing cowboys left the same impressions on either the genre or country-western music. The films of Roy Rogers and Gene Autry stand apart from the rest. Bigger budgets, larger casts and elaborate costuming permitted the Autry and Rogers films to set the standard for singing cowboy Westerns. But their contributions were not limited to film. Autry was a popular recording artist and composer. Rogers, as a founder of the Sons of the Pioneers, helped create one of the best-known of all Western vocal groups.

While the films of Tex Ritter, Eddie Dean and Jimmy Wakely did not reflect the quality of those made by Autry and Rogers, all three contributed to country-western music. Ritter retired from films to become a popular country singer, including a stint with the Grand Old Opry. And, of course, he sang the Oscar-winning title song "High Noon" in that well-known Gary Cooper Western. Both Eddie Dean and Jimmy Wakely were successful composers, and Wakely was a popular recording artist in the 1940s and early 1950s.

When Rex Allen's first film, *The Arizona Cowboy* (Republic, 1950), was released, the singing cowboy was riding into the sunset. It is no surprise, therefore, that Allen made only 19 Westerns. Yet, he enjoyed some success as a recording artist, and he carved out a significant place in motion pictures as the narrator of Disney Productions.

The rest of the singing cowboys appeared briefly, with little background in either films or country-western music, made a few motion pictures and then either dropped from sight or shifted their focus outside the Western genre. Most sources on Western films barely acknowledge their careers.

Singing cowboys were not the only popular Westerns; trigger trios also had a lot of fans. In an era of depression and war, everyone needed a friend and teamwork was necessary for national success. Republic Pictures' Three Mesquiteers and Monogram Pictures' Rough Riders, Range Busters and Trail Blazers are the best known trigger trios. Robert Livingston, John Wayne, Tom Tyler and Bob Steele all played at one time or another in the very popular Three Mesquiteers series. In fact, the last small budget Western in which John Wayne appeared was *New Frontier* (Republic, 1939), a Three Mesquiteers film.

PRC had two different trigger trios. The Frontier Marshals series in 1942 starred Lee Powell, Bill Boyd and Art Davis. The series ended when Powell went into military service. Powell had been popular in the Frontier Marshal series, but whatever acting future he may have had ended when Powell died while in military service. From 1942 through 1945 PRC also produced the Texas Ranger series. Dave O'Brien, James Newill and Guy Wilkerson were the stars from 1942 through six releases in 1944. Tex Ritter replaced James Newill and appeared in the series until it went out of production in 1945.

It was also common in the years before World War II to team actors. James Ellison and Russell Hayden both worked in Hopalong Cassidy Westerns. Tex Ritter rode, at different times, with both William Elliott and Johnny Mack Brown. Later on, in *Bells of Rosarita* (Republic, 1945) and *Trail of Robin Hood* (Republic, 1950), Republic had its numerous studio cowboy heroes make guest appearances with Roy Rogers, by then the biggest box office draw of any of them.

In the six years preceding World War II, Republic and a few other minor studios dominated the B Western boom. Republic had John Wayne, Gene Autry and Roy Rogers under contract. In addition to those three, in 1936-37 the studio released a number of films produced by A. W. Hackel starring Johnny Mack Brown and Bob Steele. During and after World War II, Republic developed new cowboy heroes such as Donald "Red" Barry, Sunset Carson, Monte Hale, Rex Allen and Rocky Lane. The studio also enticed William Elliott to leave Columbia in 1942 for the Republic Eagle, logo for the film company. Gene Autry left Republic to join Columbia Pictures in 1947, but even with that loss Republic remained the best-known producer of B Western movies from 1935 to 1954.

In 1945, Republic's Herbert Yates went shopping for a new cowboy star. Fearful that Roy Rogers would strike for a higher salary — as Autry had done in 1938 — or refuse to sign a new contract with the studio, Yates unveiled Monte Hale as Republic's new singing cowboy. In *Out California Way* (Republic, 1946) Yates used the gimmick that had worked so successfully in *Bells of Rosarita* as Roy Rogers, Dale Evans, Allan Lane and Donald Barry made cameo appearances lending a hand to Monte Hale.

Studios such as Monogram and PRC turned out lesser quality products than did Republic. Yet many of their cowboy heroes are still remembered fondly by B Western fans. Lash LaRue, Whip Wilson, Eddie Dean, Jimmy Wakely, Johnny Mack Brown and George Houston are the best-remembered cowboy heroes who worked for Monogram and PRC. Johnny Mack Brown, William Elliott, Lash LaRue and Allan Lane, cowboys who didn't sing, also had substantial fan appeal in the years after World War II.

Johnny Mack Brown was a football All-American at Alabama in the 1920s and then became a motion picture actor. After some early successes at MGM, Brown settled into B Westerns. In the years prior to World War II he made a few serials, starred in series Westerns for Supreme, and during the early war years made a series of excellent B Westerns for Universal. But in 1943, Johnny Mack took his horse Rebel and his six guns to Monogram Pictures. From that year through 1952, Brown made over 60 Westerns for Monogram.

William Elliott was also very popular from the late 1930s to the early 1950s, although by that time he had left the programmer B's to star in bigger-budget Westerns. Elliott's career as a B Western star began at Columbia in 1938 and lasted at that studio until 1943. He then switched to Republic and made over 20 B Westerns, including several in the popular Red Ryder series. In 1946, Elliott jumped to pricier films at Republic, ones with more adult themes, and he stayed with that type of film, first at Republic, then Monogram and Allied Artists until 1954.

Lash LaRue made far fewer films than either Brown or Elliott, and he had the misfortune of making them for studios that put minimal dollars into their efforts. Yet he was immensely popular. LaRue's first film, *Song of Old Wyoming* (PRC, 1945), had him playing an outlaw, and he literally stole the show from its star, Eddie Dean. In 1946, PRC began LaRue's career as a whipcracking hero dressed in black. LaRue made just over 20 Westerns, but his popularity can't be measured in numbers. His films may have been cheaply made, and at times the acting is not the best, but LaRue was popular.

Allan Lane was perhaps even more popular than Lash LaRue. When Lane began to make B Westerns for Republic in 1944, first as Allan Lane, then as Red Ryder and finally as "Rocky" Lane, he proved both popular and durable; he was one of the last cowboy heroes to hang up his guns and quit programmer Westerns. Until the 1950s, when Republic began to make wholesale use of stock footage, Lane's films were action-filled and well-acted. When you paid a dime to see Rocky Lane and his horse Blackjack, you were sure of 60 minutes of action-filled shooting and fighting entertainment.

While Westerns paid the bills for many smaller studios, major producers did not ignore the genre. The cowboy stars who worked at the better-known studios had a large and loyal following. That is most true of those cowboy heroes who rode RKO's silver screen range from 1930 until 1952. From 1930 to 1933, Tom Keene was RKO's leading cowboy star. His Westerns are fast-paced, action-filled films that hold viewers' attention. Keene, however, just never seemed to understand how to convey believable emotion. Anger, excitement or enthusiasm are too often overplayed by Keene, and as a result his characters lack authenticity. That may explain why RKO stopped production of Keene's programmers in 1933.

After a three-year hiatus, RKO signed George O'Brien to an excellent series of Westerns. O'Brien had starred in the silent Western epic *The Iron Horse* (Fox, 1924), and in the early 1930s appeared in a series of Westerns for Fox, many of which were adapted from Zane Grey novels. At RKO, O'Brien's Westerns were just as fast-paced and action-filled as the ones Keene had made. The major difference is that O'Brien was an excellent actor. He seldom overstated — if anything, he underplayed — his role. O'Brien knew how to use humor subtly, often at his own expense, so his films remain delightful over 60 years after they were first released. And O'Brien's barrel-chested physique added to his believability as a Western hero. O'Brien was both a good actor and a popular star; when he joined the Navy in 1940, RKO had big boots to fill. Fortunately for RKO, Tim Holt filled them quite successfully, and from 1940 to 1952 Holt made excellent B Westerns for RKO. The only years Holt's Westerns were not in production were the years he spent in the Army Air Corps.

Holt's success as a cowboy star is not surprising. His father, Jack Holt, had been a leading cowboy star of the silent era, and after that had been a leading man in sound action films and serials before finishing his career in the early 1950s as a character actor. Tim's sister Jennifer was a Western heroine of the 1940s. Tim Holt was merely one, albeit an important one, of Hollywood's leading motion picture family.

Young Tim went to school at Culver Military Academy in Indiana where he participated in sports and was a member of that school's famed Black Horse Troop. His athletic ability and horsemanship naturally turned him to Westerns (Rothel, 1994). Holt appeared in some George O'Brien and Harry Carey RKO Westerns and then assumed the lead in his own RKO series when O'Brien retired from the screen.

Holt's pre–World War II Westerns had good screenplays, were filmed in varied locations, and included strong supporting casts with Ray Whitley, Lee "Lasses" White and/or Ukulele Ike Edwards. Some of them, most notably *The Fargo Kid* (RKO, 1941), combine action and humor into really enjoyable films.

After Holt returned from the service, RKO teamed him with Richard Martin (as Chito, his sidekick) in a series of films that were produced until 1952. As Series B Westerns were running out of steam, they took on a streamlined look with excess stock footage and hackened plots. Holt's programmers escaped those pitfalls. Their plots remained fresh and the location work in the Alabama Hills around Lone Pine, California, gave the films an appealing quality. It is no wonder that Tim Holt is looked upon by those growing up in the late 1940s as one of the biggest of the cowboy stars.

Charles Starrett is one of the most overlooked cowboy stars of the era. When Starrett began making Westerns at Columbia in 1935, probably neither he nor the studio had any inkling that he would last until 1952. Starrett's father had made a fortune in the Starrett Precision Tool Company, and he sent Charles to Dartmouth where the young man was a football star. Charles forsook his father's business, however, for an acting career. From 1930 to 1935 he knocked around Hollywood, appearing as a support or character actor in numerous non–Westerns.

Starrett appeared in his first Western, *Gallant Defender*, in 1935, and he made over 130 B Westerns before he rode off into a 1952 sunset. Starrett's Westerns were non-stop action programmers. Particularly impressive were the first-rate fistfights which appeared frequently in Starrett's films of the late 1930s and early 1940s. In 1940 Starrett introduced a character called the Durango Kid. The Kid was a Robin Hood–type outlaw dressed in black, wearing a black face mask, and riding a white horse. Between 1935 and 1945, that was the only film in which Starrett appeared as the Durango Kid; however, with the *Return of the Durango Kid* (Columbia, 1945), Starrett appeared only as the Durango Kid until the series ended production in 1952.

Starrett is not as well known as many of his cowboy rivals. But Starrett's sheer number of films—over 130 B Westerns—rank him above both Autry and Rogers, and slightly ahead of Johnny Mack Brown, who made just over 115 B Westerns until he too quit the genre in 1952.

Of all the cowboy stars who worked at major studios, few, if any, were more popular than William Boyd. Boyd's parents died when he was a teenager, so the young man virtually raised himself. After knocking around in several jobs, Boyd found himself in Los Angeles in the 1920s, working in motion pictures. He became both a leading man and a well-known supporting player until another actor named William Boyd nearly ruined his career. The other Boyd was arrested for drugs and illegal alcohol possession and the press got the Boyds confused; as a result, the future Hopalong Cassidy's film career seemed to be finished. Then Harry Sherman, a producer at Paramount Pictures, worked out a deal with Clarence Mulford to adapt the Hopalong Cassidy novels for the screen. For reasons not entirely clear, Sherman asked Boyd to play Hopalong Cassidy (Nevins 1988).

Boyd changed the character from the grizzly old veteran of Mulford's novels to the cowboy hero dressed in black and riding a white horse that became synonymous with William Boyd. Hopalong Cassidy became an overnight sensation and adults looking back to their childhood remember fondly those Saturday afternoons as they watched Hoppy ride to the rescue. In the 1940s, Sherman and Paramount tired of the series so Boyd took over production and continued to release Hopalong Cassidy Westerns through United Artists until 1948.

The popularity of B Westerns from 1930 to the late 1940s is traceable to several factors. As a whole, they reflected the traditional morality and value structures of the American Midwest, South and Southwest, regions in which B Westerns were most popular. Beyond that, a variety of cowboy heroes existed for every viewing taste. If one preferred slick, fancy-dressed singing cowboys, one could watch Gene Autry, Roy Rogers or Eddie Dean. For those who wanted action-oriented Westerns more in the mold of William S. Hart, Lash LaRue, Bob Steele or William Elliott were the cowboy heroes to see.

Not only was there diversity of cowboy heroes but of films as well. Some, particularly the films from PRC starring the likes of Buster Crabbe and Lash LaRue, played the smaller, side-street theaters where the admission price, even in the late 1940s, was only a dime. Roy Rogers, Gene Autry, Tim Holt and others either very popular or under contract to a major studio were more likely to provide weekend entertainment at the main-street theaters where admission price was higher than at the side-street theaters.

Not all Western fans appreciated B Westerns. Some preferred those films occupying that uneasy territory between small-budget B films and super Westerns such as *Shane* (Paramount, 1953) and *Red River* (United Artists, 1948). For the fans of bigger budget B Westerns, variety was again the rule. Randolph Scott, Joel McCrea, John Wayne and Rod Cameron offered a diversity of solid Western entertainment. *The Kansan* (United Artists, 1943), *The Virginian* (Paramount, 1946) and *Rio Grande* (Republic, 1950) are examples of better acted films with more plausible plots which still provide action-oriented entertainment for 75 minutes.

Whether it was the B Western with an identifiable cowboy hero, a bigger budget B or an A film, the Western genre dominated Hollywood from 1930 to 1954. But nothing lasts forever. Death came slowly, so slowly many did not recognize it was happening. Yet, change is normal and by the end of World War II the older generation of cowboy heroes had ridden off into the sunset. Tom Mix was dead, the victim of a highway automobile accident. Buck Jones had perished in the famous 1942 Coconut Grove fire in Boston (Keyes; Loy 1999). Hoot Gibson, Ken Maynard, and Tim McCoy had all retired. For the most part Bob Steele and Don Barry were relegated to minor roles. But none of that seemed to matter. William Elliott, Rocky Lane and Rex Allen appeared to be worthy successors. And, indeed, they probably would have been. So one has to look beyond the cowboy heroes to understand the decline of the B Western, and ultimately of the Western genre.

Television appeared on the American scene in a big way by the late 1940s and literally swept the entertainment industry by 1954. At first, television changed very little. The old movies simply appeared on a smaller screen. The Range Rider, Lone Ranger, Annie Oakley and the Cisco Kid emerged as new television cowboy heroes. Even Roy Rogers, Gene Autry and Hopalong Cassidy just changed media. But it didn't last long. By the late 1950s, the cowboy hero had given way to the adult television Westerns with more talk, less action and controversial themes. Clearly something other than television was happening to America.

It was! Americans had lost their innocence. If the country had come through the gangster-riddled 1920s and the Depression 1930s with a belief that men of ability and good will could shape a world of peace and prosperity, that optimism did not survive much after the end of World War II. On the deserts of North Africa, on Pacific islands, on the beachheads of Normandy, and in air battles in the skies over Europe, in ways not fully understood, Americans changed.

Americans stopped believing that moral virtue was enough or even necessary for the good life, or that men of good will could achieve peace and prosperity. Americans lost their awe at the marvels of the natural world. It didn't happen all at once, but gradually the country became more neurotic and materialistic, more sexually obsessed, and more racially divided. Popular culture as a whole and Western movies in particular were buffeted by those changes.

The cowboy hero had no place on the new American range, so as those now well along in life were discovering him, the cowboy hero was already heading his horse toward the sunset. But just as he had trailed the outlaws by following the dust and hoof prints of their horses, so we can assess the impact of the cowboy hero by examining the imprint his films left on the American people.

Chapter Two

"A Mark to Shoot At"

Those events and forces that dominated the news during its formative years influence any generation's understanding of the United States. For the so-called "baby boomers," Vietnam and Watergate were the salient political events of their formative years. Woodstock, Janis Joplin, inflation, escalating gasoline prices and higher interest rates all impacted their lives. Not surprisingly, the parents and grandparents of "baby boomers" experienced a different set of political, economic and social events. The Great Depression, Dust Bowl misery, World War II and the Cold War left their marks on all who experienced those traumatic events.

Events impact individual lives. That was certainly true for those who searched in vain for a job during the Depression or for those young men and women who had their lives disrupted by World War II. In the 1960s, young men were drafted and sent to Vietnam; in the 1970s, young families struggled with high interest rates as they tried to buy a home. Nonetheless, events take on broader social significance only as they are generalized. The Great Depression did not affect only those who were unemployed or dispossessed; it scarred a whole generation. Vietnam not only influenced those young men who fought there, it shaped the consciousness of an entire generation. Events gain broad social significance in a number of ways. Prominent among them is the infusion of current events into popular culture. Events take on significance, often far greater than the events themselves, as they appear in popular songs, novels, television programs and movies. In short, popular culture generalizes and interprets events for its audience.

The manner in which popular culture deals with historical events is important. Some events are probed in depth, others virtually ignored. Villains and heroes appearing in novels, movies and on television influence the manner in which audiences think about current events. Popular culture has substantial impact on the way Americans understand history. That was not much less true from 1930 to 1955 than it is today.

The 25 years between 1930 and 1954 were among the most tumultuous in American history. The Great Depression made an impact that yet scars the memories of those who lived through it. The 1930s were also years of colorful gangsters and frequent shoot-outs with federal agents. And it was a time of the onward march of totalitarianism, culminating in World War II and the Cold War. The country was buffeted by events that still stagger the imagination, and popular culture could not escape the shock. Westerns certainly did not.

Throughout the period, Western films reflected the trauma of current events and used them as sources for their stores. That was possible because by the 1930s Western films were not limited to an authentic Western setting. Increasingly, Gene Autry and Roy Rogers movies featured airplanes, automobiles and other twentieth century inventions. Even John Wayne and Tim McCoy's Westerns made frequent use of the automobile. It wasn't long until other cowboy heroes were adapting their films to the twentieth century. While that created an inauthentic West, it enriched plots by presenting situations with which audiences of the 1930s and 1940s could readily identify. The Depression era and World War II are good cases in point.

The Depression years are most often associated with enormous unemployment statistics, business closings, and other urban-related economic woes. Westerns, however, were not the best vehicles for commenting on urban-related problems; other Hollywood genres did that better. Westerns, on the other hand, did not totally ignore problems in the cities. Two films come to mind. The opening scenes and dialogue in *Trail Dust* (Paramount, 1936) focus on empty cattle pens and empty cattle cars. Cattlemen won't ship their beef until they get a higher price. They turn a deaf ear to the relief committee's explanation that they are unable to raise money. It makes no difference that the committee needs to feed hungry people in the East. The cattlemen are not sympathetic! For too long, they believe, Easterners have called the shots. Now they are unemployed and hungry. They will either pay higher prices or starve! A more sympathetic Hopalong Cassidy organized a trail herd and began a trail drive to deliver beef to the relief committee. The film then becomes a typical Western; Cassidy, Johnny Nelson and Windy Halliday have to fend off rustlers who try to steal the herd. But those opening scenes with their pointed references to Depression conditions provide an interesting context for the action.

In addition to *Trail Dust*, *Wyoming Outlaw* (Republic, 1939), a film discussed more fully in a later chapter, portrays a family trying to keep itself together even though the father, and family provider, is out of work. Donald Barry, in one of his early roles, plays the son who steals cattle and eventually becomes an outlaw to help feed his family. Clearly, finding sufficient food and employment were problems with which urban viewers were painfully familiar.

The Depression, however, was not confined to urban areas. It had begun on the farm in the early 1920s. World War I ravaged European farmers, and American farmers had increased production in order to export foodstuffs to Europe. After the war, American agricultural production continued at the same level, but now American-grown crops competed with those grown by European farmers who had recovered from the war. The predictable occurred. Vast quantities of grain glutted the international market, pushing down prices. American farmers who had gone into debt to increase their acreage when prices were high found themselves facing tough times, and as the Depression struck urban America in 1930, farm conditions worsened. By early 1932, violent clashes erupted over farm mortgage foreclosures. Hard times on the farm effected the entire rural economy (Schlesinger, 42–44; Kennedy, 195–196). Rural banks were among the first to close, taking down in domino fashion other rural-oriented businesses. In many areas, severe Dust Bowl drought added a new misery to be suffered along with unemployment.

Buck Jones incorporated Dust Bowl conditions into his programmer *Outlawed Guns* (Universal, 1935). The opening frames are of giant clouds of dust (the kind which makes day appear as night and blackens the landscape), ranch buildings half-buried by the blowing dust, and cows standing with their backs to the blowing sand, fighting what viewers know is a losing battle with death. In those frames, one feels the misery experienced by farmers and ranchers who suffered through the 1930s Dust Bowl.

The film then switches to the ranch house where Jones is sitting on the floor repairing his saddle as the wind blows hard against the building. Jones' work is interrupted by a knock on the door; when Jones yells for the person to come in, a dust-covered Frank McGlynn, Sr., playing the character Jingles, blows into the room followed by a mini-cloud of dust. During dust storms, the wind blew hard, driving dust and sand through cracks in walls and around windows so that everything in the house was covered with layers of dust and sand. Jones' ranch house was no exception.

Because severe drought accompanied the dust storms, water was valued highly and ranch animals went thirsty. After Jingles drinks from Jones' indoor pump and washes his face, he asks if he might take some of the water to his horse. Jones' response highlights both the miserable conditions confronting animals and the cowboy hero's special concern for his livestock. Buck tells Jingles that he "ought to be kicked all over for not thinking of your horse." Jingles is so taken by Jones' concern for the animal that he asks if he can shake Jones' hand.

An instant friendship forms between the two men, and Jingles helps Jones and his brother move about 800 head of cattle to Lost Valley and better water. They start the cattle drive in the middle of a raging dust storm, but soon dust and drought give way to sunshine and a more pastoral setting. As the cattle are milling around in the water of Lost Valley, Jones utters what must have been on the minds and hearts of thousands of ranchers and farmers devastated by Dust Bowl drought "Don't this water look swell?"

Hollywood responded to the Dust Bowl by making water conservation a frequent theme in B Westerns. *Under Western Stars* (Republic, 1938), Roy Rogers' first starring role, is about a cowboy who gets elected to Congress in order to get Washington to understand the enormity of the problem and take legislative action on a dam. A review of the film in *The New York Times* observed, "The Dust Bowl film shown to Washington society by Roy after his election to Congress on a free-water platform is a darn good documentary...." Rogers' documentary, however, was not about his Congressional district; when the hoax was discovered, leading congressional power-brokers were angry and even more determined to bottle up his bill in committee. It took a visit to the district and the experience of a real dust storm to change the legislators' minds.

Another Rogers film, *Saga of Death Valley* (Republic, 1939), is also about his opposition to a water baron who uses control of water rights to drive local ranchers into poverty. *Red River Valley* (Republic, 1936), a mid–1930s Gene Autry Western, used a dam and irrigation project as its theme, as did another Roy Rogers movie by that same name (Republic, 1941). The Three Mesquiteers film *Gunsmoke Ranch* (Republic, 1937) opens with newsreel footage of violent floods. The plot centers on a scheme by con men to sell worthless land in the West to flood victims. Not surprisingly, area ranchers fight the influx of indigents into their county. The theme in this film, a double whammy of sorts, was familiar to Californians. Victims of the Great Depression and Dust Bowl were pouring into the Golden Bear State, creating a crisis in both employment and poor relief.

Dust Bowl conditions made a lasting impression on citizens of the Great Plains. It heightened their fear of soil erosion and made them aware of the need for water conservation. It is not surprising that those themes continued in Westerns produced after World War II. For example, *Homesteaders of Paradise Valley* (Republic, 1947), a film Allan "Rocky" Lane made in Republic's successful Red Ryder series, preaches that intelligent damming and irrigation can help ranchers and farmers free themselves from the caprice of nature, at least in part.

Homesteaders of Paradise Valley opens with Red Ryder and Little Beaver riding back to a wagon train. The land ahead, they tell the settlers, is too expensive, but there is plenty of good land in Paradise Valley. Gene Stutenroth, playing Bill Hume, scoffs at the idea of settling in Paradise Valley. Everybody knows, he says, that it floods in the spring and is drought-stricken during the Summer. Undeterred, Ryder tells the settlers they can sandbag the river so it won't flood, and build a dam to store water for summer use. Besides, Ryder argues, Paradise Valley has the only land they can afford to buy.

The settlers go along with Red and settle in Paradise Valley. They build a dam and things seem to be working as Red predicted until land developers in Center City decide they need Paradise Valley for their own water needs. The Center City developers hire outlaws and enlist the aid of Stutenroth, who is as jealous of Red as he is selfish, to help chase the settlers out of Paradise Valley. Red frustrates their efforts and the film closes with water running deep in the irrigation ditches of Paradise Valley. The river has been conquered and the valley will bloom with crops.

Some films after World War II broadened drought issues into larger environmental concerns. Four films are particularly interesting. *Riders of the Whistling Pines* (Columbia, 1949) presents Gene Autry as a ex–forest ranger battling lumber men who try to hide a tree blight that would destroy the forest. In 1949, Roy Rogers, too, played a forest ranger: In *Susanna Pass* (Republic, 1949), he delivered a lecture on the importance of fish hatcheries as a mechanism for ensuring future generations access to bountiful nature.

In an earlier Rogers film, *Springtime in the Sierras* (Republic, 1947), the bad guys kill wild game out of season. The film opens with a narration about the threat to our natural heritage posed by the indiscriminate slaughter of wild game animals. The scene shifts to a courtroom in which a judge sternly lectures two men who sold meat and furs purchased from poachers. The judge tells the men they are as much to blame for destroying America's natural bounty as are the poachers.

Rex Allen's *Colorado Sundown* (Republic, 1951) adds a slight twist to the conservation theme. A logging firm wants to cut timber on the mountain slopes but it can't take the trees because they provide valuable ground cover, preventing soil erosion and flooding of the ranches in the valley during heavy rains. Greed, however, drives the logging firm to illegal activity.

The brother-sister owners of the logging firm fake a serious tree blight, murder the forest ranger sent to inspect the trees, and plant an impostor who claims that the trees are infected. Rex Allen helps the ranchers escape a devastating flood and brings the logging firm to justice. As did other Republic Westerns, *Colorado Sundown* teaches the importance of trees and grass cover for the prevention of soil erosion and flooding.

Just as drought and water conservation were concerns of the 1930s and 1940s, so too were gangsters. And the cowboy heroes fought their share of gangsters. *Gun Smoke* (Paramount, 1931) features Richard Arlen as the cowboy hero who fights Eastern mobsters in Idaho. The film opens with a newspaper vendor hawking the latest edition, whose headlines proclaim, "Gang War Rages." The next scenes depict hitmen from Kedge Darvis' gang killing Happy Keeler, the leader of a rival gang.

The action shifts to a speeding train as Darvis, played by William "Stage" Boyd, explains to his gang that they are going to Bunsen, Idaho, until things cool down, and they are going to act like "capitalists" responding to an advertisement placed in Eastern newspapers by Bunsen leaders. The gangsters will pretend to be looking at investment opportunities while they fish and hunt, and then after a couple of weeks, Darvis assures his men, they will pick Bunsen clean to the bone.

All goes according to Darvis' plan as the unsuspecting people of Bunsen are taken in completely by the crooks. The gangsters behave much like tourists, stopping at the Vancey ranch until an old prospector discovers gold. Darvis kills the prospector and the sheriff when the latter tries to arrest him, takes people at the Vancey ranch prisoner, and threatens the families of Bunsen leaders unless they cooperate with him. Darvis sends for the rest of his mob, who quickly clean out Bunsen.

Richard Arlen plays Brad Farley, a cowboy who earns his living rounding up wild mustangs. Darvis and his gang did not dupe Farley, but when no one in Bunsen would listen to him, Farley and his men went back into the hills to hunt more wild horses. In the meantime, Willie the Vancey cook (Willie Fung) helps Sue Vancey's foreman escape from his cellar prison, and the foreman rides to find Arlen.

Arlen and his cowboys ride into Bunsen and round up Darvis' gang. When Darvis learns what Arlen has done, he takes Sue Vancey hostage. He and his gang, mounted on horses, head over the mountains to safety. Of course, the Eastern mobsters are not good horsemen and they become saddle-sore and frightened as the horses pick their way along narrow mountain trails. In the ensuing shoot-out and landslide, all of the gangsters are killed. *Gun Smoke* is an excellent little Western, suggesting how easily Eastern mobsters could be transferred to a Western setting.

Two films from 1932 are other examples of that trend. Rex Bell's *From Broadway to Cheyenne* (Monogram, 1932) is an interesting film. Bell plays a New York City detective. When gangsters wound him during a nightclub fracas, Bell goes to his father's Wyoming ranch to recuperate. He discovers the same gangsters have relocated and are selling protection to local ranchers. Even in Wyoming, they wear city clothes, carry machine guns and drive automobiles. Bell, of course, opposes their scheme and apprehends them.

That same year, Tom Mix made *Hidden Gold* (Universal, 1932). In the opening scenes, three convicts stage a prison break, and once out of jail head for the stolen money they had hidden. Mix, playing a character pursuing a prizefighting career in order to get enough money to save the ranch, naturally becomes involved in their search for the gold as well as police efforts to capture the escaped convicts. The film has more exciting car chases than horse chases. Mix is able to foil the gangsters' efforts to recover the money, all in the midst of a raging forest fire.

Three Autry films released in 1936 featured gangsters as the bad guys. In *Oh Susanna* (Republic, 1936), Autry is knocked unconscious by a gangster who throws him off a train, leaving him for dead, and assumes Autry's identity. The plot thickens when Smiley Burnette and Earle Hodgins rescue Autry. Autry's job is to convince people that he is not the gangster and to apprehend the real one (who, in the meantime, murdered Gene's best friend).

The Big Show (Republic, 1936), made on the grounds of the Texas Centennial celebration, had Gene assuming the identity of a cowboy hero for whom he stunted. The real star owes money to gangsters who have been searching for him. Naturally they assume Gene is the star and endeavor to collect from him. The end result is the requisite number of fist-fights and shoot-outs until Autry apprehends them and in the process becomes a cowboy star in his own right.

The Old Corral (Republic, 1936) is the best of the three 1936 Autry programmers featuring modern gangsters. Hope Manning, playing the heroine, begins the action when she witnesses a Chicago gangland murder. The authorities want to question her and the gangsters want to kill her so she can't talk. Fearing for her life, Manning flees west, and ends up in Turquoise City where Gene Autry is sheriff. Cornelius Keefe and Lon Chaney, Jr., play small town hoodlums who run a Turquoise City gambling house. Keefe recognizes the girl and, thinking to make some money, tells the Chicago gangsters her whereabouts.

The gangsters, carrying the predictable violin and trombone cases, arrive in Turquoise City to get the girl and to teach Keefe and Chaney, Jr.,

Gaucho Serenade, Republic, 1940; Smiley Burnette, Wendell Niles, Gene Autry and Ted Adams. Autry's pre–World War II films regularly featured twentieth century gangster-like criminals.

not to try to shake down Eastern mobsters. Instead of making the deal, the gangsters tell Keefe if he shows them where the girl is, he might not get hurt. When Smiley Burnette recognizes the gangsters, Autry tells him to take the girl out of town. The gangsters see her leave with Burnette and they follow them. In some exciting action, Autry fights machine gun-carrying gangsters driving an automobile, and with some good old-fashioned Western ingenuity he foils their efforts to capture the girl.

The use of modern gangster-like criminals continued into the 1940s and early 1950s. Now rather than Gene Autry, Roy Rogers was more likely to be pitted against modern day crooks. Any number of Rogers B Westerns employ gangster-like villains. *Don't Fence Me In* (Republic, 1945), *Heldorado* (Republic, 1946) and *Apache Rose* (Republic, 1947) are among them. *The Far Frontier* (Republic, 1948) has an interesting twist: Roy Barcroft leads a gang that is smuggling gangsters into the country. The gangsters had either been chased out of the country by the government during World War II or had fled to avoid the draft. Now, for large sums of money,

Barcroft is smuggling them back into the United States. In *Twilight in the Sierras* (Republic, 1950), Roy foils the effort of a criminal syndicate to sell counterfeit gold certificates to a foreign government.

Of all the Rogers programmers, however, *Idaho* (Republic, 1943) most prominently features gangsters. Harry Shannon plays a judge who is determined to close down a gambling establishment run by Belle Bonner (Ona Munson). Bonner fails in her efforts to bribe the judge by supporting his favorite charity, but then she learns from Spike (Arthur Hohl) and Duke (Dick Purcell), two ex-convicts, that the judge was once a notorious bank robber. He had never been caught, and for years had lived as a respectable citizen — so respectable that he was elected judge. Bonner joins forces with Spike and Duke, but Shannon refuses to submit to their blackmail attempts.

The two gangsters kidnap the judge and frame him in a bank robbery. They plant evidence suggesting that Shannon, the judge, was once the notorious bank robber. The action gets hot and heavy as several efforts to capture Spike and Duke fail. But in the end, the gangsters are apprehended, Bonner is headed for jail and the judge's good name is restored.

Even Gene Autry fought gangsters on occasion after World War II. In *Robin Hood of Texas* (Republic, 1947), Gene and the Cass County boys were set up by bank robbers to provide a musical distraction while they robbed the bank. Naturally the police assume Gene and his friends are allies of the gangsters. When one of the Cass County Boys inherits a ranch, the police release them from jail, expecting them to join the rest of the gang. Once in Texas, Autry and his friends open a dude ranch. In the meantime, the gangsters have started to fighting each other. The scene shifts to the dude ranch where the gangster with the money has fled. Soon the rest follow, and the action becomes heated as Gene clears his name and rounds up the criminals.

Westerns, then, depicted Depression-era phenomena such as economic hardship, drought and gangsters. However, their finest current events hour may have been as Westerns went to war (White; Loy 2000). Two distinct phases are apparent in World War II genre Westerns, and they parallel Southern and Midwestern attitudes on foreign policy. Isolation sentiment was particularly strong in the Midwest. Many Midwesterners believed that the country ought to remain faithful to George Washington's warning to avoid foreign entanglements. Europe and Asia were a long way off, and their wars were of no concern to the United States.

At least three films made prior to Pearl Harbor portray Midwestern isolationist attitudes. *Pals of the Saddle* (Republic, 1938), John Wayne's first Three Mesquiteers film, had a unique opening. The first frames were newspaper headlines of the start of the European conflict and of this country's vow to remain neutral. The plot involves an effort by the Three Mesquiteers to stop unidentified foreign agents (with many German characteristics) from smuggling a scarce, war-related substance out of the United States in violation of American neutrality laws. The film was certainly in keeping with isolationist sentiment that the only way to keep America out of war was through an energetic enforcement of the neutrality acts. *Pals of the Saddle* was released as Congress was debating the wisdom of neutrality legislation.

Two other films tapped concerns to preserve American neutrality in the face of an escalating European conflict. Ken Maynard, in *Death Rides the Range* (Colony, 1940), becomes involved with foreign agents who are trying to steal a ranch which contained a helium gas deposit. Helium was a valuable war material and exporting it would have violated neutrality laws. *Chip of the Flying U* (Universal, 1939) found Johnny Mack Brown fighting to keep foreign agents from sneaking arms and ammunition out of the country.

Two Gene Autry programmers released in 1939 weave the impending war theme into the plots. Gene and Smiley Burnette (Frog) play government agents in *South of the Border* (Republic). They are sent to the Latin country of Palermo to stop the work of unidentified foreign agents with interests hostile to the United States. Foreign agents support a Latin revolutionary who intends to grant the foreign government a submarine base, but Gene and Frog help the citizens of Palermo thwart the revolution. *South of the Border* is not about isolationism or neutrality. Rather, it is about protecting North American interests in Latin America. From 1939, the year in which *South of the Border* was made, until the United States entered World War II, President Roosevelt justified lend lease and other forms of aid to Great Britain and the Soviet Union on the basis of protecting the Western Hemisphere from the Axis powers. The Autry programmer fits that theme very well.

War preparedness was the theme of 1939's *In Old Monterey* (Republic). The Army Air Corps needs to buy ranch land for a bombing range. The ranchers led by George Hayes will not sell; they are unwilling to leave the land they worked hard to develop. Gene, working undercover for the Army, shows the ranchers a film about the threat of high altitude bombing for civilians. He argues the United States could be victimized by such attacks if it doesn't design better weapons. That is why the Army needs the bombing range. Hayes is moved by the film, and by Autry's speech. He confesses he was thinking only of himself and not the 140 million other people in the country. Proclaiming he owes his country an apology, Hayes leads the crowd in singing, "Columbia, Gem of the Ocean."

Arizona Gangbusters (PRC, 1940) starring Tim McCoy had a different twist. Much of the action involved Tim's efforts to stop smuggling by enemy agents along the Arizona-Mexico border. Again the enemy agents were unidentified, but they speak with a heavy German accent; however, the film is most interesting because it too has a theme of preparedness. One scene contained a radio message cautioning listeners to watch for activities by saboteurs and fifth columnists. The message was clear: What happened in Europe through political subversion could also happen in the United States if citizens were not vigilant. *Arizona Gangbusters* played in the Marion, Indiana, LunaLite Theater on the weekend of November 1, 1940. That same weekend the Paramount Theater featured the Johnny Mack Brown Western, *Law and Order* (Universal, 1940) and *Baptism of Fire*, a documentary about Hitler's invasion of Poland. Certainly, McCoy's *Arizona Gangbusters* was as much a current events film as the one about the German invasion of Poland.

Films about saboteurs continued throughout the war. The 1943 movie *King of the Cowboys* (Republic, 1943) found Roy Rogers working for an unidentified governor to infiltrate a group of foreign agents blowing up defense industries and communications systems. The Range Busters' *Cowboy Commandos* (Monogram, 1943) had a similar theme. In this picture, the saboteurs operated a saloon which enticed workers away from a local mine, thus lowering production efficiency. Just as did Roy Rogers, the Range Busters apprehended the saboteurs, now openly identified with Hitler's Germany.

Wild Horse Rustlers (PRC, 1943) starring Robert Livingston and Al St. John is one of the most interesting World War II films. Again the theme was sabotage, an effort by Nazi agents to destroy a horse herd destined for army use. But other elements make this film interesting. One theme focused on the role of women in the war effort. Smoky (Lane Chandler) declined the heroine's offer to help with the horse roundup by telling her he would go to town and get some men. By the film's end, she had helped with the roundup, and in turn had been assured by Livingston that it would take the contribution of lots of women to win the war.

Two scenes with Al St. John, one of the most memorable sidekicks of all times, highlight resource conservation. In one segment he stops a wagonload of hay and when the driver (really a saboteur) objects, St. John responds that the wagoneer might be hoarding sugar. In another scene, St. John is careful to preserve coffee grounds for future use, and he has a sugar cube tied to a string for dipping into the coffee. Slapstick humor to be sure, but humor that pointed to the need for all to participate in rationing.

St. John also helped to highlight the enemy. Near the beginning of

Wild Horse Rustlers, Livingston tells him to stand watch by the roadside and make sure Nazi saboteurs did not go by. St. John responds if any do go by he will plug them, and then points his gun at the audience and steps toward the camera, asserting that the same thing went for "Japs." If any do show up, St. John boasts, "I will blast their teeth into a flock of yellow tombstones." Prior to Pearl Harbor, Hollywood portrayed the enemy as agents of foreign governments. Beginning in 1942, however, there was no need for such subtleties; America's enemies were now Germans and Japanese.

Raiders of Sunset Pass (Republic, 1943) is another interesting World War II Western. In this programmer, the younger cowboys have been drafted, leaving the range open to outlaws who rustle cattle and murder ranchers. The ranchers are forced to hire older cowboys, ones too old for the draft. They are unable to patrol all of the range, so the outlaws are in little danger of being caught. Eddie Dew plays a federal agent sent by Washington to help the ranchers round up the outlaws. He gets them to agree to let their daughters form a range patrol, appropriately named the Women's Army of the Plains. The film's heroine, Jennifer Holt, organizes the women and they ride patrol using walkie-talkies to monitor any suspicious activities and to alert the men to rustlers. Parents of the young women only reluctantly support the WAP. Their traditional views are that young women belong at home, not on the range riding patrol, carrying guns and walkie-talkies. It took all of Dew's persuasive powers to dissuade parental opposition. The patrols work, however, as the WAP make it too hot for the rustlers. The rustlers, in turn, play on parental fears by "creating" several accidents—guns misfire and wagon pins break. The parents are ready to force their daughters out of the WAP, but at the last moment Dew proves the accidents are staged and captures the rustlers. In spite of efforts to sabotage the organization, Women's Army of the Plains patrols help to apprehend the outlaws.

Charles Starrett made three entertaining B Westerns in 1944 that dealt with the war. *Cyclone Prairie Rustlers* (Columbia, 1944) has themes similar to *Wild Horse Rustlers* and *Raiders of Sunset Pass*. Nazi agents destroy produce and rustle cattle in an attempt to create a food shortage and slow down war production. Starrett and sidekick Dub Taylor play rodeo performers who have been successful in war bond drives. The government dispatches them to Cyclone Prairie to track down the Nazi agents. Constance Worth's character makes this programmer a bit unusual. She runs the local cafe and appears to be an All-American girl, but she is a Nazi agent working with the local bootmaker who is head of the spy ring.

In *Sundown Valley* (Columbia, 1944), Starrett and Taylor frustrate

Raiders of Sunset Pass, Republic, 1943; Eddie Dew and Jennifer Holt. Holt's uniform has W.A.P. (Women's Army of the Plains) on the sleeve.

the efforts of saboteurs who use a local saloon and gambling hall to entice workers away from their jobs at a local machine gun gunsight manufacturing plant. Forrest Taylor, owner of the factory, has patented a new gunsight and the Army has given him a contract for it. However, worker absenteeism makes it unlikely that his factory can fulfill the contract. All ends well as Starrett is able to unmask the evil intentions of the owner of the saloon, and the factory earns its Production E banner.

Cowboy Canteen (Columbia, 1944) has Starrett joining millions of other young men and women in the armed services. But before he goes on to war, Starrett hires some cowboys, he thinks, to help run the ranch. The cowboys turnout to be cowgirls in the persons of Jane Frazee, Vera Vague and the Tailor Maids. The all-star cast includes "Big Boy" Williams, Dub Taylor, Tex Ritter, Jimmy Wakely and his Saddle Pals, Roy Acuff and the Smokey Mountain Boys and Girls and the Mills Brothers, among others. The girls quickly convince a skeptical Starrett that they can run the ranch — with Tex Ritter's help — in his absence. They even get the Army to establish a canteen in the barn. Drawing on the popularity of New York and Hollywood canteens in which famous personalities entertained soldiers and sailors, *Cowboy Canteen* is a musical rather than an action Western. In fact, about the only action in this one is the fistfight between Ritter and Starrett over Frazee.

In *Black Market Rustlers* (Monogram, 1943), the Range Busters are commissioned by the United States government to stop a gang of rustlers headed by Glenn Strange. The rustlers steal cattle and murder the ranchers in order to sell the beef on the black market, thus undercutting government efforts to control prices and jeopardizing the war effort.

Soon after World War II ended, the longed-for peace gave way to a Cold War between the United States and the Soviet Union. In turn, Americans became concerned about protecting national military secrets and vital natural resources from foreign agents. Three Roy Rogers Westerns used these Cold War fears in their plots. *Under Nevada Skies* (Republic, 1946) found Roy investigating the death of a friend. He discovers that the friend owned a crest in which was hidden the map of a deposit rich in Pitchblende, a necessary ingredient in making atomic bombs. Roy and some Indian friends prevent the villains from getting the map and selling the Pitchblende to a foreign government.

Uranium also figures in the plot in *Bells of Coronado* (Republic, 1950). Agents for a foreign power steal a shipment of uranium and, when the company tries to collect insurance on the stolen ore, the insurance company sends Roy Rogers to investigate. Roy finds clues hard to come by until he buys a Geiger counter. He shows it to Pat Brady, playing Sparrow

Biffle, an old Rogers friend, in Dr. Harding's office. Mysteriously, the Geiger counter begins to tick, but Dr. Hardy claims it is due to his radium needles.

Dr. Hardy, played by Leo Cleary, is an old family doctor who has known Rogers since the latter was a boy. On the surface, Dr. Hardy is kind, concerned for the welfare of his patients and, one assumes, patriotic. In reality, however, he masterminded the uranium theft and he intends to sell the valuable resource to a foreign power. Rogers was not fooled by Dr. Hardy's disclaimer of radium needles. While searching Hardy's office, he discovers uranium samples. With the help of a government agent who had infiltrated the gang, Roy is able to thwart Hardy's attempts to sell the uranium to a foreign power.

The early years of rocketry figure in the plot of *Spoilers of the Plains* (Republic, 1951). Roy's mission in this film is to prevent enemy agents from destroying an experimental rocket. Grant Withers is the villainous Camwell, who poses as a legitimate oil operator but is actually an agent of a foreign government who wants to steal a highly sophisticated firing mechanism developed by Dr. Manning. When one of the rockets can't be located after it is fired, Frankie Manning, Dr. Manning's daughter and assistant (Penny Edwards), turns to Roy Rogers for help.

An interesting exchange occurs between Rogers and Edwards as they search for the missing rocket. He asks her if anybody would want to steal it and Edwards assures Rogers that several foreign governments would like to have the innovative firing mechanism. But Edwards is puzzled as to who would want to do an awful thing like help a foreign government steal the secret. Rogers' response is straight out of 1951 Cold War America with its fear of political subversives. "You never can tell, it could be your next door neighbor," Rogers tells Edwards.

When a plot to blow up Dr. Manning and the scientific camp is unsuccessful, Roy figures out that Camwell is behind the troubles. He goes to the Camwell Oil Company to apprehend Camwell. The plan doesn't work and Roy is captured. But after several action-filled scenes of fights between running wagons, as only director William Witney could stage them, Roy corners Camwell atop an oil derrick. When Camwell falls to his death, Rogers frustrates another effort to steal American military secrets.

Events of the turbulent 1930s and 1940s provide a good setting in which to highlight one important component of the American belief system of that era, a spirit of optimism. Each of the problems — Depression, drought, gangsters and war — assumed that if men of competence and good will rolled up their sleeves and went to work, solutions could be found for nearly any problem. Periods of flood and drought were inevitable, but

Spoilers of the Plains, Republic, 1951; Penny Edwards, Bullet and Roy Rogers. Rogers helps Edwards find a missing experimental rocket.

proper water management could overcome the caprice of nature. Gangsters would be sent to jail once competent police and honest public servants put their minds to it. Few thought that the United States would not ultimately triumph over the Axis powers. Americans of the period were optimists. They survived two of the greatest crises in American history, the Great Depression and World War II. Not only did Americans survive, they emerged militarily stronger and economically more prosperous than ever before. Later generations might doubt American strength, but it never occurred to those growing up in that era to do so.

Westerns did much more than tell audiences about current events. They also interpreted history. More than one teacher reminded students that it was inaccurate history, but nonetheless Westerns transported viewers back in time, making them aware of the nation's history. Specific events such as the Battle of the Little Big Horn, the shooting of Billy the Kid and the gunfight at the O.K. Corral in Tombstone, Arizona, have been featured in Westerns in nearly uncountable numbers. Places such as Dodge City, Deadwood City and the Cherokee Strip were familiar to Western movie audiences in the 1930s and 1940s. Equally familiar were epoch movements such as building the transcontinental railroad, laying the telegraph and enclosing the open range.

It is not the presentation of factual American history as such which is interesting; rather, it is the manner in which that history was told, the way in which audiences were helped to see America, and the meaning that its history was given. Jim Kitses in *Horizons West* writes about Westerns, "For anyone interested in understanding America and its idea of itself, at corporate and deeply personal levels, the form is indispensable." (Kitses, 175) What did Westerns project? What was the Western's idea of America?

Westerns mirrored America's understanding of itself as a country destined to govern the continent from ocean to ocean. Public figures for much of the nineteenth century advocated this idea called Manifest Destiny. Hollywood simply reflected a process already complete by the time *The Great Train Robbery* (1903) first appeared in nickelodeons.

Three silent epochs, *The Covered Wagon* (Lasky, 1923), *The Iron Horse* (Fox, 1924) and William S. Hart's masterpiece *Tumbleweeds* (United Artists, 1925)—are excellent examples of major Westerns about the expansion of the West. The Oscar-winning *Cimarron* (RKO, 1931) and *The Big Trail* (Fox, 1930), with John Wayne in his first starring role, continued to highlight the drama of westward expansion.

The Big Trail is dedicated "to the men and women who planted civilization in the wilderness and courage in the blood of their children." As if to underscore those sentiments, Wayne delivers a patriotic lecture to settlers who, in the midst of a raging snowstorm, want to turn back. He reminds them of the hardships early settlers from England faced. Those settlers, he argues, suffered to build a nation and now those in the wagon train had to suffer a bit as they carried the new nation to the valleys of Washington.

Even earlier in the film, facing the prospects of hostile Indians, one of the men told Wayne, "Injuns have never yet prevented our breed of men from travelin' into the setting sun." Countless other Westerns after 1930 continued to tell the story of settlers migrating West. Even films sympathetic to Indians defended the reservation system; Indians would have to give up their nomadic existence, and the buffalo would have to be exterminated, for both interfered with a God-ordained mission of American whites to settle the land.

Without ever making the case directly, films such as *In Old Caliente* (Republic, 1939) and *Red River* assume that Anglos have a natural right to Western land first settled by Spanish peoples. Indians and Hispanics were not the only obstacle to Manifest Destiny. Evil men pursuing their own dreams of empire came under attack as well. *Winners of the West* (Universal, 1940), a popular Universal serial, had Harry Woods trying to stop the transcontinental railroad. The hero (Dick Foran) of course foiled his attempt. Roy Rogers as Capt. Colt in *The Ranger and the Lady* (Republic, 1940) and as Bill Hickok in *Young Bill Hickok* (Republic, 1940) frustrated efforts by evil, scheming men to create personal empires in Texas and California, thus preventing their natural linkage with the rest of the United States.

Western films reinforced and mirrored an important American belief. Americans felt they were a people destined for greatness; a people whom God had chosen to populate and rule a continent. Figures as diverse as the novelist Herman Melville and the politician-author Albert Beveridge made that claim. It was reflected in hundreds of Hollywood Westerns from the poorest B to super–Westerns.

Manifest Destiny was closely related to the idea of progress, another concept prominently displayed in Westerns. For audiences of the 1930s and 1940s, progress was unquestionably good. Major medical advances meant that pneumonia, once a dreaded illness, was no longer fatal. People looked forward to the day when polio would be preventable. The Tennessee Valley Authority as well as Western dam projects brought electricity to the South and West and with it convenience appliances. Radio, paved roads and more comfortable automobiles all contributed to the belief that material progress and economic development were unbounded blessings. Progress was inevitable, the product of an aggressive people, a people out to make the world a better place in which to live.

Westerns reflected a commitment to progress in several ways. First, progress was viewed as irreversible. That is, once progress occurred, there would be no relapses, and men and women could get on with other problems. In countless Westerns, that was portrayed as the cowboy hero riding out of town with a friendly wave to the appreciative folks he had just helped. The hero had either been called upon to deal with a problem or he had just happened to stumble onto it; in either case the problem was solved by the film's end and the cowboy hero rode away. While nearly every B Western used that motif, a few examples will help those less familiar with the genre.

William Elliott's Columbia B Westerns from 1938 to 1941 are classic illustrations of the irreversible progress theme. *Taming of the West* (Columbia, 1939), *North from the Lone Star* (Columbia, 1941), and *Return of Daniel Boone* (Columbia, 1941) begin with Elliott entering the town as a stranger unknown to anyone except Dub Taylor, playing his familiar role of Cannonball. Soon Elliott rounds up the bad guys and restores peace and justice to the community. Not surprisingly, the grateful townfolk want Elliott to remain as their sheriff. He never does because, now that the crooks have been apprehended, there is no further need for him. So Elliott rides away with a look back and a wave to a now peaceful community.

In *North from the Lone Star*, for example, Elliott rides into Deadwood and breaks up a rigged auction. Arthur Loft, playing Kirby, the main heavy, makes Elliott the town marshal, fully expecting Elliott to obey orders. Wild Bill, of course, does not do as Kirby expected. Rather he forces Kirby to close down his crooked roulette game, and in a final shootout kills Kirby and most of his men. Cannonball thinks Elliott came to Deadwood as a result of his telegram pleading for help, and he expects Elliott to continue on as marshal even though Deadwood has been cleaned up. Claiming Deadwood doesn't need him any more and making Cannonball the new town marshal, Elliott rides away. The implicit assumption is clear: Deadwood, once freed from its lawless element, will remain a peaceful place no longer in need of men like Wild Bill Elliott.

In their well-received Rough Riders series, Buck Jones, Tim McCoy and Raymond Hatton personify the theme of irreversible progress. As rangers temporarily called out of retirement, they work together, although often secretly, to bring the crooks to justice. With their work finished, the three ride their separate ways, each back to his place of retirement. When they solved the problem that brought them out of retirement, it remained solved.

The theme of the wandering cowboy and irreversible progress that dominated B Westerns from 1930 to 1955 did not continue in many television Westerns. Rather than wandering, the star was often part of a community or a ranch. Television programs such as *Have Gun Will Travel*, *Bronco* and *Cheyenne* continued to star a wandering cowboy, but the long-running television Westerns such as *Gunsmoke*, *The Rifleman*, *The Virginian* and *Bonanza* featured a place in which the cowboy star lived and worked. Even Roy Rogers' television series was located in Mineral City, a town in which the action occurred.

The ranch or town was seldom trouble-free. Matt Dillon of *Gunsmoke* had to continually enforce the law; he had to deal with a constant parade of outlaws and problems. Simply because one gunfighter or one band of outlaws was apprehended did not mean that Dodge City would be peaceful. Progress was not an act, it was a process of being vigilant. Unlike Wild Bill Elliott in *North from the Lone Star*, Matt Dillon could not ride out of town with a friendly wave because if he did, the lawless element would return.

Television Westerns such as *Gunsmoke* reflected a nation in transition. Most Americans still believed in progress during the 1950s and early 1960s. Yet voices of protest were emerging, voices who doubted the benefits of economic development, who claimed the United States was inherently racist, and who alleged the United States had begun the Cold War and threatened the rest of the world with nuclear and environmental annihilation.

Popular literature and television shows and, above all else, colleges and universities began to echo those voices. At first, most Americans paid little heed to them, but by the mid–1960s, after the assassination of President John F. Kennedy and the Americanization of the conflict in Vietnam, it became popular to question progress, indeed to doubt whether much of anything could be changed. Pessimism and cynicism spread rapidly throughout American culture.

Progress, however, was more than bringing the bad guys to justice. It was also the unfolding drama of technology. Western films praised the natural expansion of Western Union, the railroads, stagecoach lines and the Pony Express into the vast uncharted wilderness. Again, the lesson in those Westerns was that no problem was too big for men of vision and daring.

The final reel of the last chapter of the popular serial *Winners of the West* is a paean to those men who linked the West Coast to the rest of the country via rails. Foot after foot, the end of the last chapter recorded, mile after mile, rail after rail, the transcontinental railroad was completed. Blackhawk, the central town, becomes a thriving community, rid of its criminal element. The workers were told, "The work you have done here has brought civilization a long step forward."

Winds of the Wasteland (Republic, 1936) is one of the two or three best series B Westerns John Wayne made in the 1930s. Wayne and Lane Chandler play former Pony Express riders put out of work when the telegraph replaced the Pony Express. Using money Wayne had saved and the horses they received as a gift from the Pony Express, the boys decide to start a stage line. Cal Drake (Douglas Cosgrove), the owner of a large stage franchise, believes he has pulled a first-rate swindle when, for $3,000 he sells Wayne and Chandler a battered old coach and the franchise to a line between Buchanan City and Crescent City. The latter, once a thriving community, is now a ghost town.

However, Wayne and Chandle turn adversity into good fortune as they revive Crescent City, and in a stagecoach race beat Cosgrove for a mail contract. *Winds of the Wasteland* is an excellent B Western showing progress as the result of hard work and determination. Keeping with that spirit, Republic dedicated the film to those whose bravery helped string all forms of communication across the West, linking it to the nation's capital.

Western Union (20th Century–Fox, 1941) even had a bad man, Randolph Scott, reformed by being caught up in a movement as big as America itself, the laying of the telegraph line. Scott died in the end, but he died a redeemed, virtuous man, saved by the very progress he so ably assisted.

In the development of communications systems, conflict was bound to occur. For example, the telegraph hurt the stagecoach lines as well as the Pony Express. The cowboy hero, no matter his vested economic interest, always was on the side of progress. Gene Autry in *Last of the Pony Riders* (Columbia, 1953) was an official of the Pony Express, yet he enthusiastically supported the telegraph because it represented progress. Whip Wilson was a Pony Express rider, but in *Stagecoach Driver* (Monogram, 1951) he defended stage lines as well. After all, the development of the West required multiple forms of communication.

Progress had a human dimension as well. It would lead, or so Westerns asserted, to the end of old prejudices and the acceptance of new lifestyles. Two conflicts are good examples of this understanding of progress, cattle versus sheep and the open range versus farms. Western films used as a frequent theme the clash between cattlemen and sheepherders.

A 1950 Errol Flynn film, *Montana* (Warner Bros., 1950), spoke to that concern. Flynn, playing an Australian-raised man whose father had been killed in Montana by cattlemen, goes back to that state to raise sheep. In the process he convinces most cattlemen that the two animals are not mutually exclusive; to the contrary, when the price of beef drops, cattlemen can maintain profits by switching to sheep. Here, in dramatic fashion, was a film about enlightened progress leading to the benefit of all citizens.

Roll On Texas Moon (Republic, 1946), a Roy Rogers Western, brought cattlemen and sheep herders together by demonstrating that the murders blamed on cattlemen were the work of outlaws. In the process, Roy got the two forces to agree that the range was big enough for both of them. In these films, progress led to a happy ending for both groups were accommodated.

Far less pleasant was the resolution of farm versus open range. Here the lesson was clear: Progress meant the end of a life for the cattlemen.

The Randolph Scott Westerns *Abilene Town* (United Artists, 1946) and *Trail Street* (RKO, 1947) highlight this tension. Both are set in Kansas and both involve the coming of wheat farmers who fenced in the open range to protect their crops from cattle. *Shane* (Paramount, 1953), one of the true super–Westerns, had a similar theme. In all three films, the farmers won. They represented a progressive force, the end of the wild west and the coming of civilization.

The natural outgrowth of Manifest Destiny was to populate the prairie, to make it bloom with crops, to encourage the rise of cities, and to develop commerce. That in a nutshell was the American dream, the idea of progress, indeed, the idea of America that unfolded on silver screens throughout the 1930s and 1940s. It was the dream of a people sure of their destiny. Gene Autry summarized that dream in *The Saginaw Trail* (Columbia, 1953). Autry caught the assuredness of Americans when he said, "In a few years, the Saginaw Trail will become first a road and then a broad highway and it won't just happen here, it will happen all over America. Whenever there is a trail, there will be men to follow. Don't ever try to stop progress, go with it, be a part of it."

Hollywood Westerns then interpreted American history as the unfolding progress of a people populating the North American continent, a destiny bequeathed them by an all-wise God. That same God, however, required that people assigned the task of populating a continent be the sort of folks whom God could bless. Character was a crucial issue in Westerns.

The films projected a noble people, men and women of courage who braved elements and fought Indians within a code of behavior approved by a beneficent God. In the process of creating this character, Hollywood recast Wyatt Earp, Bill Hickok, Annie Oakley, Billy the Kid and dozens of other historical figures so they were no more historically accurate than were the cowboy of Mix's glamour and Autry's Cowboy Ten Commandments.

The purpose, however, was not to recreate historical characters, but to use historical figures to create role models. According to Hollywood Westerns, America was the land of heroes who dared the impossible, and pulled it off. If, to do that, Billy the Kid had to be recast in *The Outlaw* (Howard Hughes, 1943), or if Wyatt Earp and Doc Holiday had to be presented as innocent victims goaded to a fight by evil ranchers in *My Darling Clementine* (20th Century–Fox, 1946), it was a small price to pay.

Certainly the cowboy hero was always aware of his role as model. Tom Mix often said he would tolerate nothing in his films that might embarrass youngsters. Gene Autry, Roy Rogers, Charles Starrett and Buck Jones were quite concerned about their public images. The studios were equally concerned. Rex Allen had to sign a pledge, as part of his contract with Republic, that he would not drink alcohol or smoke in public and that he would always appear in cowboy dress (Hartigan, 2:13). The cowboy hero, then, by way of his films, reached out to assure audiences that hard-working men and women of outstanding character and integrity developed America. Americans were a people, or so the films taught, of God's blessing.

Shyster bankers, usually in league with a gunman, might endeavor to frustrate the onward march of Manifest Destiny, but they were doomed to failure because the efforts of good men win in the end. Audiences of the 1930s and 1940s believed that. It was a time to celebrate America, its future and its men and women of character and integrity.

In the summer of 1985, two of the most popular films were *Pale Rider* (Warner Bros.), and *Silverado* (Columbia). Both were heralded by many as the return of the Western genre. Of the two, *Silverado* is most interesting here, for Lawrence Kasdan, director and co-writer of the film, articulated his purpose in more than nostalgic terms. Kasdan claims he patterned the film on Westerns of an earlier era. He wanted his children to see the moral code of heroism, courage and bravery modeled by cowboy heroes of his childhood. "That is," he told *The New York Times*, "an unabashed embrace of the values of old Westerns" (Darnton).

In Kasdan's remark, one hears the echo of Tim McCoy who (near the end of his life) told James Horowitz, "They say to me how we were their heroes and gave them a mark to shoot at ... you gave us a good example" (Horowitz, 275). Jimmy Wakely was even more direct in his comments to Horowitz. Wakely noted, "If we can be stripped of our historical values, if they can get us to where we don't believe in anything, this whole country will fall apart like a bag of cookies" (Horowitz, 242).

Western films, then, did more than reflect current events, they put those events in a setting. The setting was a progressive America sure of its destiny, sure of the integrity of its leaders, and willing to suffer through a Depression and war as the necessary trials for greatness. It was a pre–Vietnam and pre–Watergate outlook to be sure. And it was one the Western movies helped to fashion.

Chapter Three

COWBOYS AND SKY PILOTS: RELIGION IN WESTERNS

The last chapter detailed how Westerns mirrored the American commitment to individual responsibility, progress and Manifest Destiny. Yet, one misses a significant part of the American experience if one assumes that these were mere human creations; they are more than human. Americans believed that individual responsibility, progress and Manifest Destiny had a divine origin; they were yoked to a belief in an omniscient and omnipotent God who directs the course of nations. Since for most of those living in the United States that God is the Christian God, the country scarcely can be understood apart from Christianity. In ethos and outlook — if not always in behavior — the United States is clearly a Christian nation. Christian presuppositions, symbols and language shaped the country's expansion from the time settlements first appeared along the Atlantic coast.

While not all journeyed to the new land for religious reasons, many did, and Manifest Destiny flowed from an outlook brought by many early English settlers to the North American continent. For example, Puritans and Pilgrims fleeing religious discrimination by the Church of England explained themselves in language laden with Old Testament imagery. They regarded themselves as God's new chosen people, a people entrusted with the true religion, the true knowledge of what God is like, and what He requires of believers. Just as God had promised a land to the first chosen people — the Jews fleeing Egypt for Canaan — so He set aside a new land, the North American continent, for His new chosen people. As hostile as it was, Puritans and Pilgrims regarded New England as the new promised land.

God's gifts, however, were conditional, requiring obedience to His will for their fullest enjoyment. As a result, Puritans and Pilgrims believed personal character was paramountly important; each individual was to live according to the guidelines established by a morally perfect God. Immorality, slothfulness, injustice and atheism were more than individual sins, if widespread they threatened the covenant God made with His new chosen people. A reprobate people could expect the same harsh treatment that befell the ancient Jews when they turned away from God. Americans would enjoy God's blessing on their land only if they were an obedient people.

The themes of chosenness, promised land, obedience and punishment have played out continually in American history ever since the early days of those New England colonies (Bellah). Abraham Lincoln's Second Inaugural address was an noteworthy expression of those sentiments. At Gettysburg, Lincoln reminded his listeners that their forefathers had created a political order based on Christian principles. In March 1865, as the bloody Civil War was winding down, he sought a Biblical setting for the conflict.

Reminding his listeners that both the North and the South read the same Bible and prayed to the same God, Lincoln wondered how anyone who used the sweat of another's face for his own benefit could ask anything from a just God, but he quickly added that God had instructed His people not to judge one another. Lincoln then urged that "this terrible war" had been given to the nation by a just God in order to repay by blood drawn from the sword all of the blood that had been drawn by the bondsman's lash. A disobedient people — of both the North and South — were being punished by a just God (Bellah, 54).

However, the time had come, Lincoln believed, to express contriteness before the Holy God, to bind up the nations' wounds, and to get on with national reunification. God had worked His justice; now it was time for Americans to accept the righteousness of His judgments and to take up anew the great national tasks lying before the people.

Within a decade of its end, the American Civil War had taken on mythic properties, Abraham Lincoln had been assigned a quasi-divine nature, and the United States entered a period of intense westward expansion. The tandem values of obedience and punishment, which Lincoln had articulated so eloquently in his Second Inaugural Address, gave way to a Rudyard Kipling–like white man's burden. The North American continent was no less the promised land given to whites by a beneficent God, but now the emphasis was on spreading the presumed superior white Anglo culture to the assumed inferior Indian and Mexican cultures.

Post–Civil War missionary zeal, the religious component stressed taking white Christian culture to backward peoples and the secular component emphasized expanding the United States as an end it itself, replaced the image of the new promised land as refuge for a faithful people. The North American plains, from the Mississippi River to the Pacific Ocean, now believed to belong to North American whites, supplanted the perspective of land given to a people who obeyed the commandments of a Holy God.

After 1865, Christian concepts were used to justify westward expansion and the treatment of Indians and Hispanics, but now those concepts were tied to right, not obedience. God had given the land to whites; it was their birthright. As the Civil War drew to a close, whites viewed western lands as empty spaces inhabited by Indians and a handful of Mexicans who knew little about their proper use. Only when whites seized their birthright could the land become productive. God had given the land to whites so that it would blossom with crops and domestic animals. It was a right that Indians and Mexicans were obligated to acknowledge. If they failed to do so, morally they could be removed from the land or relegated to second class status. Western films reflected that belief; they employed the language of right, not Lincoln's imagery of obedience.

Chapter Two discussed several Westerns that were cinematic celebrations of Manifest Destiny, and later in the book the theme will reappear in relation to the treatment of Indians and Hispanics in Westerns. But Christianity's influence on American culture reached far beyond Manifest Destiny into every facet of American life. Christianity is so pervasive in the United States that surely one must rate the country as more religious than any other western nation. When compared to Europeans, Americans go to church more, pray more frequently, have a more positive view of the Bible, regard faith more central to their individual lives, and are more prone to base public policy on religious principles.

Bible stories, religious symbols of all types and the language of faith permeate American culture. Frederick Elkin wrote in "The Value Implications of Popular Film" that film contains both implicit and explicit messages (Elkin, 1954). Westerns, as morality plays and as hymns to Manifest Destiny, implicitly presented themes, symbols and characters identified closely with Christianity. But Westerns did more; with surprising frequency, explicitly they mirrored the Christian faith as practiced by millions of adherents throughout Middle America. Employing Elkin's categories, Westerns contain both implicit and explicit themes, symbols and messages aligned closely with evangelical and fundamentalist brands of Christianity. By examining those themes, one gets a clearer understanding of how Westerns projected America as a Christian nation.

Religion often appears in subtle, unobtrusive ways. Quick passing comments, a hymn or gospel song sung over an evening campfire, a church spire rising above a town scene — these are examples of the ways Westerns employed the language and imagery of Christianity so matter-of-factly that viewers passed over them with little thought. That does not mean, however, that religion is unimportant. Quite the contrary, the fact that religion appears so casually in Westerns suggests the extent to which it permeated American culture of the time. Viewers did not take much notice of gospel songs over a campfire, a church spire or graveside prayers because they were so culturally prevalent. The unobtrusive appearance of religion in Westerns signals its importance, not its insignificance. A few illustrations make the point.

In *Colorado Sunset* (Republic, 1939), William Farnum is murdered when he discovers that the town's veterinarian is masterminding the attacks on milk farmers in order to force them to join his protective association. Gene Autry and Smiley Burnette had mistakenly bought a dairy farm; they thought it was a cattle ranch. Gene becomes a local hero when he refuses to give in to the outlaws attacking his milk trucks or to join the protective association. He is asked by grateful citizens to sing at Farnum's funeral. Gene honors their request and croons "Beautiful Isle of Somewhere," a well-known gospel song.

Charles Starrett's Columbia B Westerns featured numerous singing groups. In *West of Sonora* (Columbia, 1948) the Sunshine Boys sang two spirituals, "These Bones Are Going to Rise" and "Glory Train." As was often the case in Starrett programmers, the songs do not flow from the action; rather, the action pauses while the Sunshine Boys perform. Audiences in the late 1940s gave very little thought to spirituals in Westerns. It was simply part of that era's culture.

At the beginning of *Alias Billy the Kid* (Republic, 1947), Tom London visits the sheriff to ask for the body of his son who is about to be hanged. London assures the sheriff that he wants to give the boy "a proper Christian burial." As Red Ryder (Jim Bannon,) is about to fight a duel, Little Beaver (Don Reynolds) tells Bannon he will pray for him. And in *Barbed Wire* (Columbia, 1952), Gene Autry joins the cowboys around the campfire to sing the old spiritual "Ezekiel Saw the Wheel Way Up in the Middle of the Sky." All these examples appear in the films without any fanfare, and are treated as ordinary things which common people do or say. These are but five examples. Westerns are full of them.

Many Westerns also contain very explicit Christian symbols, including churches, priests, preachers, crosses and hymns. Others depict religious behavior such as attending church, praying or reading from the Bible.

Religiously devout persons—often males—who are positive role models do not appear as frequently, but it is nonetheless possible to find them in Westerns. Finally, and maybe most surprising, a few Westerns touch on religious revivals and personal salvation, themes lying at the heart of evangelical and fundamentalist Christianity.

Church buildings are readily visible in many town scenes and in some instances people, mostly women, are seen coming and going from church services. Church is not, however, a place where one often sees the cowboy hero. Ken Maynard's comment in *Six Shooting Sheriff* (Grand National, 1938) that it had been a long time since he had been in church reinforces the popular perception that Westerns have little direct relationship to Christianity. They are about action, much of which is violent, not religion. While it is certainly true the cowboy hero does not go to church in most Westerns, there are notable exceptions—enough to merit comment.

Desert Vengeance (Columbia, 1931) has an interesting religious subtheme. Buck Jones is outlaw Jim Cardew, whose gang hides out in a ghost town. Jones and his men have kidnapped a woman who tried to swindle Jones out of a great deal of money. Keeping the woman as a literal slave, Jones is skeptical of the parson's comment that the woman loves Jones. The parson has lived in the town for 40 years preaching and ministering to whomever happened to be around.

In a sequence of scenes the outlaws have a party and Jones brings the woman from her room so she can dance with him, much against her will. As she suffers through Jones's unwanted attention, the outlaws hear the parson ring the church bell announcing services. Jones and his men abruptly end the dance and dutifully go to church. From the context, one assumes they regularly attend services at the church.

The parson greets them at the door, welcoming each man by name. He opens the service with the hymn "Great Day Coming" and, in a bit of B Western irony, each outlaw sings the refrain, "Are you ready for the judgment day." After the hymn, the men listen to the parson read from the scriptures. In this instance, he chooses passages from the prophets of the Old Testament about how the House of the Lord has been turned into a den of robbers and thieves. The film features common worship elements familiar to anyone who attends a Protestant church service.

A few years later, Jones starred in *Stone of Silver Creek* (Universal, 1935)—a film discussed more fully below—and Jones, again, attends a church service, surprising the lady accompanying him when he knows the congregational hymn. Jones, plays Stone, who owns a saloon in Silver Creek. The perception is clear—saloon owners are not supposed to go to church, let alone know church hymns.

In *Down Dakota Way* (Republic, 1949), Roy Rogers and Dale Evans go to church. Dale plays the church organ and Roy sings a song. And, *In Old Amarillo* (Republic, 1951), Rogers helps Elisabeth Risdon organize a prayer meeting to pray for rain.

These films are exceptions, not the rule. Normally the cowboy hero does not attend church nor engage in worship. Westerns unfold around the saloon, bank and sheriff's office, but there are instances in which religion plays a role. While such films are far from the norm, they should not be ignored.

Because many Westerns have Mexican or Spanish settings, Roman Catholic churches appear frequently in Westerns. Much of the action in *Texas Justice* (PRC, 1942) occurs in a mission. The outlaws have taken over the building, imprisoned the padre in a cellar room, and use it as headquarters for their illegal activities. The outlaws dress in priestly robes and pretend to belong to the religious order. George Houston's Lone Rider fights fire with fire as he impersonates a member of the religious order who comes to visit the padre being held captive.

Any number of Gene Autry films use a mission setting as Gene croons a ballad to the heroine. And, in *The Bells of San Angelo* (Republic, 1947), the priest shows Roy Rogers an inscription on the bells of the mission which helps Roy discover the longlost San Angelo mine and apprehend criminals who use the mine to smuggle silver into the United States.

Christian churches are more than buildings in which religious worship occurs, they are also symbols of reconciliation; warring factions put aside their difference when they enter a church. This view of churches was underscored in *Range Feud* (Columbia, 1931). The opening frames are of a church with its sign proclaiming "Peace Meeting." The preacher delivers a mini-sermon on love and then introduces Buck Jones, playing sheriff Buck Gordon, as "Brother Gordon." Ascending to the pulpit, Sheriff Gordon declares that he is determined to keep the peace between warring cattlemen. He also notes in reference to the preacher's sermon that "the law of God is the law of man, but that law has been abused." When one cattleman accuses another of rustling, a gunfight seems imminent. Jones quickly draws his gun and, pointing it over the top of the pulpit, reminds all in the room that they are in a house of God. The preacher then closes the meeting with prayer. While the meeting did little to reconcile the two sides, the film's depiction of the church as a place of peace and reconciliation is striking.

A church building in a Western town is also a symbol of progress. *My Darling Clementine* (20th Century–Fox, 1946) is an excellent film expression of that theme. The unfinished church structure promises that

Tombstone is not far from being transformed into a peaceful, law-abiding community, a place for families, a civilized place. At least two B Westerns also suggest the importance of a church for a community. In *The Missourians* (Republic, 1950), Monte Hale has to track down a gang of outlaws who steal supplies intended for the construction of a church. The church is a sign of civilization and the outlaws want to thwart the development of the town into a progressive community. Keeping the church from being built is a means to that end. In *Take Me Back to Oklahoma* (Monogram, 1940), Tex Ritter solicits the aid of Bob Wills and the Texas Playboys to help raise money for a new church. They find themselves having to chase the crooks who steal the church benefit profits. But, again, the church is a sign of progress. Westerns are not about churches or going to church. However, both appear frequently enough so that one cannot ignore them, and clergy are more visible than are church building.

Spanish and Mexican influences are prominent in the American Southwest and California, and numerous Westerns are set along the Rio Grande or in Mexico, so it is not surprising that Roman Catholic clergy show up regularly in the genre. It would take a separate volume to examine all the films in which Roman Catholic clergy appear, but a few examples will help to clarify how Westerns treated them.

In the vast number of films, Roman Catholic priests, often called padres, are gentle men who, forsaking personal needs, think foremost of their charges. Padres promote justice, reconciliation and understanding between all persons, and are mindful of those who are less able to protect themselves, particularly Indians and children. The Western priest possesses keen insight into human nature and is able to look beneath the human facade, seeing the worth of each person.

A number of Cisco Kid films highlight the latter characteristic. In *The Cisco Kid Returns* (Monogram, 1945), Chico and Pablo turn for advice to a padre who had known them since childhood. The priest understands that they are not outlaws as many people believe; nevertheless, they have strayed from the church and the padre is dismayed by that. He wants Chico and Pablo to listen to him, as they did when they were children, and he chides Pablo for not attending confession. Clearly, the padre is their friend, one to whom Chico and Pablo can turn for help and refuge.

An understanding priest appears *In Old New Mexico* (Monogram, 1945) as well. When Cisco takes an endangered woman from a stagecoach, he hides her in a mission. The woman is grateful for a place to stay, but she asks the padre why that awful outlaw brought her to the mission. The priest assures the woman that he has known Chico since he was a child and that he is not an outlaw but one who fights for the poor and oppressed.

William Farnum plays the kind Father Domonic in the Gene Autry programmer *Mexicali Rose* (Republic, 1939), and he displays all of the characteristics of a Western film padre. Father Domonic runs a children's home at the mission, but it is in danger of closing because he cannot raise enough money to keep it open. The good Father hopes that a company who has promised revenue from oil located on the property will honor their pledge. The company, however, is swindling the orphanage and Gene Autry has to bring them to justice so that Father Domonic can continue his humanitarian work.

Priests figure prominently in the plots of both *The California Trail* (Columbia, 1933) and *The Bells of San Angelo*. In the latter a priest helps Roy Rogers discover the clue which leads to the San Angelo mine. The padre is dismayed that his Mexican parishioners are being oppressed, even murdered, by a mine owner who accuses the Mexicans of stealing. He aids Rogers as the latter exposes the mine owners as smugglers. In *The California Trail*, a priest risks his life to send a message to the governor, pleading for assistance against the local military commander who is depriving the poor peasants of food. The governor arrived in time to help Buck Jones clean up the situation.

Protestant clergy are treated no less favorably than Roman Catholic clergy. Preachers are brave, sincere men of faith determined to bring the gospel and — implicitly — civilization to the west. Earlier in the chapter, Buck Connors' portrayal of the parson in *Desert Vengeance* was noted. Connors' parson is no namby-pamby. He voices disapproval of Jones' treatment of his female captive and he is not afraid to lambaste the outlaw gang from the pulpit. The same image of a preacher appears again in *Stone of Silver Creek* (Universal, 1935).

Stone of Silver Creek is thought by some film critics to be among Buck Jones' best Westerns, and it requires careful analysis because the religious themes and images in it are instructive of the manner in which religion was treated in 1930s and 1940s B Westerns. Stone (Jones) owns a saloon and gambling hall. Niles Welch portrays Timothy Tucker, the town preacher. Stone believes that a growing town needs a business like his, a place where men can get a drink and engage in "honest" gambling. But he also believes that a progressive community needs a church, so he sends Tucker a $1000 check.

Tucker refuses Stone's money; the preacher's idea of community is not that pluralistic! Stone's money is profit from a despicable business, one Tucker intends to shut down; to accept the money would compromise his position and associate God's work with the fruits of the Devil's business. Tucker returns the money to Stone. A check for such a large sum was surely

Stone of Silver Creek, Universal, 1935; Buck Jones, Murdock MacQuarrie, Niles Welch and Marion Shilling. Welch portrays a brave preacher who is wounded while trying to protect Jones.

tempting, but Tucker is willing to live out the implications of his faith. He is a man true to the word he preaches.

The Sunday after Tucker returns the money, Stone goes to church. Tucker, in turn, digresses from his prepared sermon and delivers a lecture on "Thou shall not kill." Clearly, in Tucker's mind, Stone is also a man of violence. Stone, however, won't be deterred by Tucker's judgments. When the collection plate is passed, he deposits the $1000 check in it.

Tucker intensifies his effort to "save" Stone, to tear him from his saloon and gambling hall, and to turn him toward a "respectable" profession. In the meantime, two crooks who Stone chased out of Silver Creek return, determined to kill him. Tucker overhears their plans while resting on a hill from an afternoon ride. He tries to prevent them from killing Stone; Tucker, after all, wants to protect Stone in hopes that he will see the immorality of his profession and change his way of life. To protect Stone, Tucker buys a gun and goes to visit the two crooks. In the process of trying to reason with them, Tucker is badly shot.

Images of the minister in *Stone of Silver Creek* are all positive. Reverend Tucker is a brave man willing to face killers in order to keep them from murdering Stone. On the other hand, he is equally willing to oppose Stone's business. Tucker will not accept Stone's check for fear it might be misunderstood or compromise his position. Buck Jones is the cowboy hero in this programmer but it is certainly true that Welch's Reverend Tucker is a positive role model for both adults and children. He is a man whose religious faith and beliefs command respect.

The Red Rope (Republic, 1937) does not feature religion nearly as much as Jones' programmer, but it contains an interesting portrayal of a preacher. Villain Lew Meehan, is determined to stop Bob Steele from marrying Lois January. Meehan positions his men at the entrances to Steele's ranch in order to prevent anyone from entering. When they stop preacher Forrest Taylor on his way to the ranch to marry the couple, Meehan's henchmen encounter a preacher they can't bully. Taylor goes on to the ranch in spite of their death threats. When the violence gets out of hand, Taylor the preacher also becomes a United States Marshal. He assures Steele, "I can shoot better than I can preach and that is saying a lot."

Buck Jones Westerns had adult appeal; they were not exclusive fare for the Saturday matinee crowd. Steele's programmers, on the other hand, primarily attracted the younger set. Adults, for example, find Taylor's portrayal of the parson whimsical, not at all believable. It is important to understand, however, that "Parson Pete" is a brave man as well as a preacher. He would not be bullied by Meehan's henchmen, nor was he afraid to strap on a gun and enforce the law. Parson Pete was not a "sissy." Little boys who flocked to see Steele Westerns surely did not overlook that image.

In *The Fabulous Texan* (Republic, 1947), William Elliott and John Carroll return to Texas following the Civil War to find that carpetbaggers have imposed a harsh, lawless rule on the state. Carroll's father is a preacher who forcefully criticizes reconstruction policies and the harsh carpetbagger government. Carroll warns his father to tone down his attacks, but the old man refuses. He believes he has an obligation to defend his flock by speaking out against injustice. The minister is murdered, but while he lived he modeled courageous, self-sacrificing leadership.

Donald "Red" Barry plays Dave Winters, a traveling preacher known as "the fighting parson," in *Fugitive from Sonora* (Republic, 1943). Winters goes to Sonora to establish a church, but once there he discovers that his lookalike brother has become an outlaw. Winters then gets involved in bringing the outlaws to justice and trying to convince his brother to mend his ways. Barry's parson character never carries a gun, yet he shows the sort of courage and resolve one expects from a frontier preacher. Unlike Tim McCoy, who often disguised himself as a Sky Pilot, Barry's character in *Fugitive from Sonora* is a parson bent on establishing a church and preaching God's Word.

The bigger-budget adult Western *Passage West* (Paramount, 1951) is another good film about a devout, resolute and brave preacher. Dennis O'Keefe plays Reverend Jacob Garns, leader of a wagon train which is taken over by a group of escaped convicts headed by John Payne. The predictable clashes occur between the two groups, and at one point O'Keefe warns Payne, "Don't mistake meekness for cowardice." Later in the film, O'Keefe demonstrates his meaning by giving Payne a good thrashing in a fistfight. O'Keefe's success in the fistfight pretty much sums up the image of preachers in Westerns produced between 1930 and 1955. They were depicted as men of both courage and conviction whose faith earned the respect of even hardened criminals.

Few B Westerns cast pastors in a negative light. The Production Code would not permit it in the first place, and audiences conditioned to respect the ministry as a special vocation would not have liked the films. *The Fighting Parson* (Allied, 1932) is an exception. Hoot Gibson and his sidekick Skeeter Bill Robbins lose much of their clothing in a crap game. When they try to cheat to win them back, Gibson and Robbins are forced to flee for their lives. They stumble across the vesture of a preacher who had been waylaid by outlaws and stripped of his garments in order to keep him out of town.

Gibson puts on the preacher's clothes and he and Robbins go into town. Townspeople have been waiting for the preacher to arrive so, as to be expected, they mistake Gibson for the preacher and much of the film centers around Gibson trying to extricate himself from that predicament. It is Robert Frazer's portrayal of the preacher, however, that makes this Gibson programmer noteworthy. Frazer's preacher is a pompous, self-important coward whose main concern is the amount of money in the collection plate, not the souls of his congregation. *The Fighting Parson* stands as a nearly singular exception to the positive image of ministers in B Westerns. Surely preachers were not as important role models as the cowboy heroes, but ministers were portrayed as persons respected by their communities and as ones whose behavior was worth emulating.

Westerns produced between 1930 and 1955 usually associated religion with women. Even in *Stone of Silver Creek*, Buck Jones first goes to church because he is romantically interested in Marion Shilling, and he hopes going to church will make her reciprocate his interest. In other films such as the big budget *Dodge City* (Warner Bros., 1939), women lead crusades against liquor and pray for the souls of violent men who frequent saloons.

In the Rex Allen Western *Colorado Sundown* (Republic, 1951), Louise Beavers plays an African-American woman of faith. When one of the villains attempts to steal an important letter, Beavers resists the thief and is severely wounded. The bad guy then escapes with Manhattan, the heroine's pet dog, giving chase. The villain shoots Manhattan; badly hurt, the dog crawls into the brush. When Manhattan is found after a heavy rainstorm, the prognosis is not good. Beavers, in bed recuperating from her wounds, comforts Manhattan. She tells him it's going to take more than iodine and cotton to make him well. Beavers gets her Bible and reads, "And the prayer of faith will save the sick, and the Lord will raise him up." Of course Manhattan recovers.

Devout, pious males also appear in a few Westerns. *Saddle Buster* (RKO, 1932) and *Home on the Range* (Republic, 1946) are two prominent examples. In the first film, Richard Carlyle plays the character "Bible Jude." Jude lives in the mountains and is a pious individual who quotes from the Bible a great deal, mostly from the Book of Proverbs. He raised the orphan Montana, (Tom Keene) and taught him how to capture and break wild horses. Now Montana wants to become a rodeo rider. Jude takes Montana to Fred Burns' ranch so he can break into the rodeo business.

Robert Frazer, who plays a braggart rodeo star, is Montana's chief adversary at the ranch. He bullies Montana into trying to ride Wild Fury, a man-killer, and just to make sure Montana will fail, Frazer cuts the saddle cinch. Montana is thrown from the horse when the cinch breaks and is nearly killed by the animal. The incident so unnerves Montana that he is unable to ride bucking horses again. He flees back to Bible Jude, who patiently nurses him back to emotional health and prepares him once again to ride bucking horses. On his return to the rodeo outfit, Montana discovers that Frazer has been permanently crippled by a fall from a bucking horse. But Bible Jude's influence carries the day as Montana forgives Frazer for cutting the cinch and the two men are reconciled.

In *Home on the Range*, Tom Chatterton portrays Grizzly Garth, a deeply religious man who has turned his ranch into a game preserve. He believes that God wants people to steward His natural environment by protecting animals as well as his fellow man. Unfortunately for Garth, the bad guys in this Monte Hale programmer know there is oil in a lake Garth owns. They offer to buy the ranch, but Garth won't sell. He wants the ranch to be a perpetual game preserve for wild animals. Grizzly Garth is murdered and it's up to Hale to bring the villains to justice and to help complete Garth's dream of a game preserve. The image of Garth as a deeply religious yet courageous man is a striking legacy of an otherwise pedestrian effort.

Gabby Hayes had an interesting role in *Mojave Firebrand* (Republic, 1944), one of the eight Westerns William Elliott made after coming to Republic from Columbia before he began to appear as Red Ryder in that successful Republic series. The film opens with Gabby Hayes searching for gold, not because he wanted personal wealth, but because he wanted to help his fellow man. The narrator concludes that Hayes believed in the Golden Rule.

When he discovers silver, Hayes founds the town of Epitaph, which he hopes will be devoted to honesty, law and justice. Instead of those values, outlaws led by that ace villain LeRoy Mason turn the town into a den of thieves, gamblers and outlaws. When Elliott rides into town and stops Bud Geary from beating up Harry McKim, Hayes' young ward, Hayes concludes that angels have sent Elliott to clean up Epitaph.

Hayes tells Elliott that he has always tried to live by the Book and that he wanted to make Epitaph a place for the weak, where kids could go to school, and a town in which women would feel safe. Elliott decides to remain in Epitaph to help Hayes unmask the brains behind all the trouble.

After loaning Karl Hackett some marked money, money which Hackett used to buy protection from Mason, Hayes and Elliott win back the money by beating Mason at roulette in his saloon. Mason realizes that Elliott and Hayes are on to him, so he shoots Hayes from ambush. The bullet, however, lodges in the pocket Bible Hayes always carries with him. Hayes admonishes Mason's henchmen, "Stick to the Good Book and you will live for a long while."

Hayes' character in *Mojave Firebrand* is a religious person whose faith has civic overtones. Hayes' faith is expressed as honesty, peace, justice and a concern for the less fortunate. Hayes believed that faith leads to good citizenship and he tried to practice it as he founded the town. That surely was a view of faith that viewers in 1944 understood.

In other films, the cowboy star reinforced the importance of religion by demonstrating familiarity with the Bible. *Rollin' Plains* (Grand National, 1938), a Tex Ritter vehicle, is a particularly good example of the cowboy hero using the Bible to trap the bad guys. In this Western, Hobart Bosworth plays the deeply religious Gospel Moody, a man who owns extensive water rights. Gospel permits both cattle and sheep access to his water, but sheepmen Charles King and Karl Hackett want the water for themselves. Ernie Adams playing the character Cain Moody—note the obvious Biblical imagery—is Gospel's half-brother and a sheepman in cahoots with King and Hackett.

The three sheepmen shoot Gospel Moody. They do not kill him, but

Tex Ritter spreads the word that Gospel is dead. Cain Moody, wasting no time, demands his rightful share of the ranch and water rights. Gospel's daughter invites Cain to the ranch to discuss his claim. When Cain arrives at the ranch to claim his inheritance, Ritter forces him to sit in a darkened room while he reads from I Samuel the passage in which Saul, King of Israel, meets the ghost of the dead prophet Samuel. As Ritter reads, Gospel Moody emerges ghost-like in the darkened room. Cain believes that Gospel has come back from the dead and in terror confesses to the murder.

As with Steele's *The Red Rope*, this Ritter Western was aimed at the Saturday matinee crowd. Adults snicker at the implausible ghost-like appearance of Gospel Moody and Ernie Adams' frightened reaction to it. Equally important, however, is the manner in which the Bible story is treated. Both Ritter and Adams are portrayed as regarding the story as factual history. *Rollin' Plains* projects a Biblical interpretation consistent with Protestant fundamentalism. A factually accurate — and for many a literal — Bible was one of the fundamentals of the faith. If the Bible recorded the ghost of the dead prophet Samuel visiting King Saul, then it must have happened. If it could happen to King Saul, why could it not happen to Cain Moody?

Ritter's knowledge and use of the Bible story fit well the religious faith held by many viewers of his films in the Midwest and South of the late 1930s. When an important cowboy star such as Tex Ritter demonstrated that he knew the Bible, it must be acceptable for boys and men to go to Sunday School and read the Bible!

Fundamentalists of the 1930s also believed the Bible would convict those engaged in unacceptable behavior. *Lightnin' Bill Carson* (Puritan, 1936) is a good film example of this fundamentalist view. The veteran character actor Harry Worth plays a clerk whose brother is wrongly accused of murder and lynched by vengeful citizens. Worth avenges his brother's death by murdering, one by one, those who lynched him. Tim McCoy, the cowboy hero of *Lightnin' Bill Carson*, had no role in the lynching, but Worth nevertheless holds McCoy responsible and intends to make McCoy his last victim.

As Worth prepares to meet McCoy in the inevitable final gunfight, his eyes fall on a Bible opened to Romans 12:19. Worth reads, "...For it is written, Vengeance is Mine; I will repay, sayeth the Lord." Worth, immediately convicted of his sin, empties the shells from his revolver and goes out with an empty gun to face McCoy. Worth's last-minute actions transcend the gunfight or his own death. The film's lasting impression is unmistakable; Worth was redeemed by reading Romans 12:19.

Of all the Western movie cowboys, Gene Autry probably had the greatest number of fans, and he surely had a substantial impact on Western films. He was not only America's first singing cowboy, he also broadened the fan appeal of Westerns. Young women in their late teens and early twenties, the age and gender group which ignored Westerns, flocked to Autry's movies. As a result in the years before World War II, Autry ranked as the premier movie cowboy. While Roy Rogers replaced Autry in the popularity contest during the war and while Rogers maintained his claim to be "King of the Cowboys" until he left Republic and the large screen in 1951, Autry remained the favorite of many fans.

The first two years after World War II, Autry was involved in a protracted lawsuit with Herbert Yates of Republic Pictures over his movie contract. Eventually Autry agreed to make six pictures for Republic to fulfill his contractual obligations with that studio, then he signed a long term contract with Columbia Pictures. Under the terms of his agreement with Columbia, Autry had extensive control over his films, including choice of screenplays, director and producer. Ultimately, Autry's films for Columbia bore the imprint of his own company, Flying A Productions. While at Columbia in the early 1950s, Autry made two movies which have interesting religious overtones.

The Old West (Columbia, 1952) has some of the elements of *Hell's Hinges* and *Hellfire* (Republic, 1948), a film which will be discussed later. In *The Old West*, Autry is ambushed by outlaws and left to die. He is discovered and nursed back to health by Pat Buttram, Gail Davis, and House Peters, Sr., who plays a parson. As Autry regains his health, Peters realizes that he intends to hunt down and take revenge on the men who shot him. Peters begins to preach forgiveness and the need for Autry to make a profession of faith. Autry listens, is convinced and makes a profession of faith which includes forgiving the men who shot him. As a result, later in the film, when the outlaws who shot Gene are about to be lynched by a mob, Autry helps them to escape. Like Blaze Tracy (William S. Hart's character in *Hell's Hinges*), Autry had a lifechanging experience that transformed his perspective on revenge.

The film opens with Autry leading a worship service and singing "Somebody Bigger Than You and I." The narrator then explains how the town of Saddle Rock, and by implication Gene Autry, had not always been that peaceful. It took a religious experience to bring about the change.

In his final movie for Columbia, *Last of the Pony Riders* (1953), Autry once again introduced a religious element. The plot is the often used struggle over the mail contract in which Dick Jones plays a young pony express rider. As the telegraph moves further and further West, Gene realizes that the days of the Pony Express are over, so he buys a stagecoach. His boss

Tom McEwen, (John Downey) won't admit the inevitable and fires Gene, accusing him of betraying the hand that feeds him. In the meantime, local banker Clyde Vesey (veteran character actor Howard Wright) intends to begin a stagecoach line. He hires outlaws to run off McEwen horses and harass and murder his riders.

Dick Jones portrays young Johnny Blair, McEwen's best rider, whom the outlaws thoroughly harass. In an early incident, they string wire across the trail; as Johnny's horse trips over it, he is thrown and loses the pocket New Testament and Psalms all of the riders carry. Autry, who has never given up watching over the Pony Express even though he was fired, finds Johnny Blair's pocket New Testament.

As riders quit, Johnny's route is extended, and he spends more hours in the saddle, all of the time being constantly harassed by outlaws. Blair is physically tired and emotionally drained. When his good friend and fellow rider Yank, (Buzz Henry) is murdered, Johnny Blair refuses to ride. If Johnny doesn't ride, the mail will not go through, McEwen's contract will be nullified and Vesey will get the federal mail contract for his stage line. In a desperate attempt to convince Johnny to ride one last time, Autry plays on his pride, but Johnny's response is to admit that he is a coward. Then Autry reads part of Psalm 91 from Johnny's pocket New Testament. He reminds Johnny of God's promise that he will not be harmed by danger in the night or arrows in the day. Inspired and refreshed by hearing the Bible read, Blair pulls himself together and makes the last ride to save the mail contract.

Progress, however, destroys the Pony Express and the film ends as Gene climbs up on a stagecoach in front of a barn painted **Autry and McEwen Stage Line**. Johnny Blair joins him as shotgun guard. Asked if he has all he needs, Johnny responds that he does, holding up the shotgun in his right hand and pointing to his left pocket which holds the pocket New Testament. "These are all I need," Johnny Blair assures viewers.

By 1953, series B Westerns were declining in quality, and Autry's *Last of the Pony Riders* is a mere shadow of the B films he made in the 1930s and 1940s. Certainly his last efforts no longer appealed to adults to any great extent. Adults regard Dick Jones' newfound strength upon hearing the Bible read too fantastic to believe. But at the same time, in 1953 many fundamentalists and evangelicals believed that the Bible contained supernatural, regenerative powers and that merely hearing the Word spoken could inspire men and women to unusual accomplishments. *Last of the Pony Riders* comports well with that view.

Portrayals of preachers, lay men and women of faith, and cowboy heroes who were knowledgeable about and respectful of religion offered viewers of 1930s and 1940s Westerns positive images of religion, and the

Christian religion in particular. Religion is, however, more than an expression of personal faith. In a broader social context, religion includes structures such as church buildings, religious ceremonies such as burial services and sermons, and acts of worship including prayer and singing hymns. As previously noted, many of these appear in B Westerns.

For example, *Driftin' River* (PRC, 1946), an Eddie Dean programmer, contains a sentimental graveside rite. Dean and his sidekick Roscoe Ates are commissioned by the cavalry to buy a herd of horses from Shirley Patterson. Patterson and her loyal foreman William Fawcett are pleased with the sale for it will save the ranch from bankruptcy.

Outlaws, however, are less pleased. They don't want a railroad completed and they know that without the horses, the cavalry can't protect railroad construction workers. Lee Bennett, one of Patterson's cowboys, is really in league with Dennis Moore, the chief villain. Moore does not want the railroad completed because it will bring people, and people will build churches and schools and that will bring law and order to the town. Saloons and gambling houses—Moore's chief source of income—will be closed down. Bennett, in turn, doesn't want law and order because his face appears on too many wanted posters for cattle rustling.

Bennett and his men rustle the horses, ambush a cavalry unit bringing the money to Patterson, and ultimately murder Fawcett. Dean sings a cowboy spiritual over Fawcett's grave, recites a song-poem about the glories of Heaven and gives thanks to God for Fawcett's life. At the film's climax, Bennett turns on Moore and sides with Dean, who is puzzled by Bennett's sudden reform. Bennett tells Dean it might have been because he was tired of seeing his picture on wanted posters, it might have been because of Fawcett's murder, or it might have been due to the prayer Dean recited over Fawcett's grave.

Hymns or religious songs appear as well in Westerns. A burial service in *Dawn on the Great Divide* (Monogram, 1942) concludes with the mourners singing "The Old Rugged Cross." In *Border Saddlemates* (Republic, 1952), Rex Allen plays a veterinarian doctoring Jimmie Moss' pet fox. Moss is worried that the fox will die, but Allen assures him that God loves animals just as he loves human beings, and then Allen sings a song about the animals going into Noah's Ark.

There are, however, few direct references to Jesus Christ. Roy Rogers and Dale Evans sing "May the Good Lord Take a Liking To You" in *Trigger Jr.*, and some of the hymns sung in Westerns make references to the Cross or other Christian symbols. Most of the time, however, it is the Old Testament not the New Testament which is featured in church services. The Prophets and Psalms are read more frequently than the Gospels.

Other films could be cited but the point is clear enough. Westerns between 1930 and the mid–1950s, but particularly B Westerns, positively portrayed religion. Studio moguls such as Herbert Yates at Republic realized that their films circulated predominately in the South and the small-town Midwest. Audiences in the South and rural Midwest were churchgoers, and often they attended fundamentalist churches. It was just good business sense to build respect for religion, and Christianity in particular, into their products. Culturally it was more than just good business sense, it also reinforced religious tendencies of the American heartland. Religion must be something to respect; after all, youngsters saw their cowboy heroes do it every weekend at the local theater. Richard Hurst's history of Republic Pictures includes a pertinent observation which verifies that point. Hurst wrote, "Movies may have had more importance than ministers in this era" (Hurst, 55). The Lynds, in their famous studies of Middletown, Hurst points out, believed that movies had more influence than the local preacher; and Muncie, Indiana, Lynd's Middletown, is the archetype heartland community (Hurst, 55).

In the post–World War II 1940s, Republic appealed to heartland religious sentiments by producing two Westerns with especially heavy religious themes. If *Hell's Hinges* could have been used at a 1917 Billy Sunday revival, *Angel and the Badman* (Republic, 1947) and *Hellfire* (Republic, 1949) were equally suited for Billy Graham revivals of their time.

John Wayne plays Quirt Evans, a wounded outlaw on the run in *Angel and the Badman*. The wounded Evans is discovered by the Worths, a Quaker family, who nurse him back to health. The Worths are courageous, faithful people willing to live out their pacifistic faith in the midst of a violent frontier. Their pacifism is the product of conviction, not the hiding place of cowardice.

Tom Powers plays Dr. Mangrum, a cynical agnostic who continually baits the elder Worth, shaking his head in disbelief at the Quaker's naive faith. But in those exchanges viewers are drawn to the Quaker's firm convictions rather than the doctor's cynical outlook on life. One admires the Worths; they are determined to live out the implications of their faith no matter what the social cost. Dr. Mangrum, on the other hand, has too easily succumbed to the dominant cultural ethos. One wants him to resist it more than he has. The Worths may be naive and that is troublesome, but Dr. Mangrum is harshly cynical and that is even more troublesome.

As Evans mends from his wounds, he and Prudence Worth (Gail Russell) fall in love. She takes him to a Quaker meeting, but Evans rejects the life she has in mind for him. Fleeing the Worth family, Evans returns to his old way of life, drinking and carousing with dance hall girls. But the memory of Prudence Worth is compelling; Evans can't shake it.

Returning to the Worths, Evans gives Prudence his gun as a token of his intention to reform. Having to choose between the gun and the girl, between a life of faith and a life of violence, Evans chooses faith and the girl. Complications begin immediately. Three outlaws come searching for Evans, intending to kill him.

During a buggy ride, Quirt and Prudence are accosted by the outlaws. In the ensuing chase, Prudence is hurt seriously when the buggy wrecks. When Quirt takes her to town for medical treatment, the outlaws are waiting for him and they call him out. Now Quirt Evans faces one of life's hard decisions: In a moment of crisis, he must once again choose between the gun as a symbol of his old self or faith without the gun as a symbol of his new self. Evans is spared that choice at the last moment by United States Marshal Wistful McClintock (Harry Carey). McClintock, a man of violence, intercedes on Evans' behalf and kills the three outlaws.

The overwhelming impression of the film is the sincerity of the Worths' Quaker faith. Yet the film is full of paradoxes. Early in the film, as Evans recovers from his wounds, he discovers that the Worths can't get water because an irascible rancher has dammed up the creek. Evans, the man of violence, pays a visit to the rancher, who does not want to tangle with a notorious gunfighter like Quirt Evans and readily agrees to make water available to the Worths. It took a man of violence to remedy the water situation so that the Quaker family, a people of peace, could live and thrive. Without the man of violence, the people of peace might have been forced to give up their land.

The film ends on the same note. Evans does not have to make a choice between the gun and the girl, between faith and violence, because Marshal McClintock used the gun to kill the outlaws. Again a man of violence made it possible for a man of peace to remain true to his vow to give up violence. Paradoxically, people who affirm pacifism seem to need men of violence, for without the violence, pacifists could not survive. Religion has wrestled with that paradox for two millenniums, and the American people confronted it afresh in the post–World War II 1940s.

A war-weary country turned to religion to console its grief over the carnage of battlefields, and returning veterans turned to the church as a source of stability for their young families. Church attendance shot up and Billy Graham catapulted into the public spotlight as the best-known evangelist since Billy Sunday. His "crusades" filled stadiums and attracted thousands of viewers who watched on television, frequently placing their hand on top of the television cabinet when Graham issued the call to come forward to the stadium altar.

The Cold War, however, short-circuited the hoped — for peace. Soviet incursions into Iraq, Soviet-inspired coups in Eastern Europe and confrontation in Greece and Turkey reminded Americans that violence was still a necessary ingredient in world affairs. If "godless Communism" was to be thwarted, Americans must be prepared to use violence. Hence common to American post–World War II culture was the marriage between patriotism and religion, between the gun and the Bible. To defend America was to defend faith against "godless Communism." To use the gun was, at times, the only way to defend the Bible. *Angel and the Badman* plays out that theme on the Western frontier. In the final analysis the hero in *Angel and the Badman* is the man of violence, Wistful McClintock, who killed so the man of faith would not have to do so. In that sense, *Angel and the Badman* is unlike *Hellfire*.

Hellfire opens with Zeb Smith (William Elliott), enjoying a poker game while a preacher circulates throughout the saloon pleading for donations to help build a church. Smith's fellow poker players catch him cheating, Trevor Bardette is about to shoot him when the preacher steps between them and is hit by the bullet intended for Smith.

Smith assumes responsibility for the preacher, cares for the dying man and agrees to continue his efforts to build a church. Elliott as Smith cannot comprehend the preacher's actions. He can't understand how reading and believing the Bible caused the preacher to step in front of a bullet. Indebted to the preacher for saving his life, Elliott not only agrees to continue efforts to build the church, he consents to build it by "the rules." The rules are those outlined in the Bible, so Elliott begins to read from it. Gradually Elliott moves from skeptic to believer, coming to believe in the teachings of the Bible. Again, in the language of evangelical and fundamentalist Christians, Elliott is "born again."

In his travels, Elliott meets Doll Brown (Marie Windsor). Windsor is a female outlaw, searching for the man who kidnapped her sister. Early in the film she killed a young no-good, and his brothers begin searching for Windsor in order to kill her. As Elliott and Windsor travel from town to town, she makes fun of his religion. She won't read the book, nor does she have much respect for men who do; she associates religion with the weak and cowardly.

The film's climax is nearly straight out of a religious revival. Marie Windsor is in jail for attempting to kill a sheriff when the brothers find her and break into the jail. Elliott has given her his Bible, and she reads and recites the twenty-third Psalm as the brothers shoot her several times. Windsor dies in Elliott's arms, but she dies a woman who has made her peace with God. She too has been "born again." The Bible she so scorned has

Hellfire, Republic, 1949; William Elliott and Marie Windsor. Elliott gives Windsor a pocket Bible while she is in jail for trying to kill the sheriff.

spoken to her just as it did to Elliott. In the final analysis, the Bible proved more powerful. The gun could kill the flesh, but the Bible preserved her soul. The film does not end with the customary "The End"; rather, "Amen" flashes across the screen as the film concludes.

Elliott, once converted, suffered Windsor's scorn of his faith. But he did not waver from his faith, and while in the end his peaceful demeanor could not save Windsor's life, it did touch her soul. Violence lacks the triumphant note in this film that it had in *Angel and the Badman*. In *Hellfire,* violence seems meaningless when compared to the life of faith. Elliott's faith not Wistful McClintock's carbine carried the day.

The "old time religion" associated with fundamentalists and evangelicals has numerous distinctives which appeared in the films discussed in this chapter. Fundamentalists believe in a literal Bible which can dramatically change lives; they believe that Christians must disavow drinking alcohol, smoking and using profane language; they believe that pastors and preachers are honest godly men because God called them to the pulpit and God would not choose hypocrites to preach His word; and finally, they believe that the Church — that is, the building — is the center of community life, the place where one worships and one is buried. All of these elements appear regularly in 1930s and 1940s Westerns. Can there be much doubt that producers of B Westerns chose consciously to reflect a specific religious perspective in their films?

In the two decades between the early 1930s and the filming of *Hellfire*, Hollywood offered viewers a slanted view of religion. Protestant fundamentalist views of Christianity dominated the Western genre. While no specific religious tenets were prescribed, Jewish and Roman Catholic believers surely recognized that the religion they saw in movie theaters across America had much more in common with Protestant fundamentalism than it did with their own expressions of faith.

Jews and Roman Catholics, however, were more visible and more accepted throughout the country than were Mormons. And no discussion of religion in Westerns is complete without some attention to the manner in which Mormons were treated (Loy, 1990). Mormons, after all, helped to develop the West. When Mormon efforts to live among Americans of other faiths were unsuccessful, Mormons fled physical abuse to the Utah desert. Brigham Young and his band of faithful literally made the desert bloom. Yet, for nearly all of the nineteenth century and the first two decades of the twentieth century, Mormons were controversial. The notion that they constituted an exclusive community of believers whose dominant religious practice — polygamy — was alien to the American way shaped popular perceptions of the religion. When the United States Congress made polygamy illegal, and the Supreme Court upheld the law, Mormons further alienated majority sentiment by continuing the practice. Even though Utah was ready for statehood soon after the Civil War, it was not admitted to the Union until 1896, largely as a result of the controversy over polygamy.

Western films first dealt with Mormons when Fox produced movie versions of Zane Grey's *Riders of the Purple Sage* and *The Rainbow Trail*. Both novels contain harsh descriptions of Mormons. Jane Withersteen, the heroine of *Riders of the Purple Sage*, is a Mormon woman who owns and manages a large ranch she inherited from her father. Withersteen, while a faithful Mormon, nonetheless maintains her independence from church elders. Unwilling to permit her to live as an independent, unmarried woman, the elders drive off her cowboys and enlist Oldring, an outlaw who leads a band of riders (the riders of the purple sage) to rustle her cattle, all to force Withersteen's compliance with the wishes of church elders.

Lassiter, the hero gunman of the novel, stumbles across the Withersteen ranch as he searches for his sister who had been kidnapped and forced into a Mormon marriage. Lassiter and Jane fall in love, and at the novel's climax escape across the sage to a hidden valley with a Mormon mob in hot pursuit. Scaling a mountain wall to enter the valley, Lassiter pushes a giant rock, commencing a landslide that buries their pursuers. It also seals the fate of Lassiter, Withersteen and her young ward Faye, for the rockslide destroyed their only exit from the valley.

The Rainbow Valley continues the saga as the central character, Shefford, learns about the valley and begins a search for its trapped inhabitants. In the course of his search, Shefford hears of the "gilded lily," a young woman who lives with other "Hidden wives." "Hidden wives" are multiple wives hidden away by their Mormon husbands who visit them secretly at night, a scheme designed to frustrate the law against polygamy. The "gilded lily" is none other than Jane Withersteen's young ward Faye, who had been whisked out of the valley by the son of Withersteen's chief protagonist in *Riders of the Purple Sage*. If Faye refused to comply with the man's wishes, he threatened to return to the valley and kill Lassiter and Withersteen.

In 1918, Fox made its initial silent versions of the two novels; based on the continuities, the versions appear to have remained faithful to Grey's novels. They were reproduced in the 1920s starring Tom Mix, in the 1930s with George O'Brien, and *Riders of the Purple Sage* was filmed the last time for the big screen in 1941 with George Montgomery as Lassiter. All of the versions after the initial 1918 efforts eliminated any reference to Mormons.

The Mormon elements were deleted because the Production Code was particularly sensitive to religion. In fact, the eighth "Particular Application" of the code contained some noteworthy restrictions on religion in films. No film could throw ridicule on any religious faith; ministers of religion could not be comic characters or villains; and ceremonies of particular religions had to be dealt with respectfully (Moley, 243). Fox could not have filmed the novels—after the Production Code was established—as Grey wrote them. Mormon elders were the villains; the novels are loaded with anti–Mormon sentiment; and polygamy—a Mormon religious practice—is treated harshly. If Fox had included these element in its filmed versions of the novels, the company would have been denied approval to distribute the films.

In 1940, 20th Century–Fox made *Brigham Young* (1940), a film version of Vardis Fisher's novel *Children of God: An American Epic*. Fisher, like Grey, blends respect with criticisms of Mormons into the long novel. For example, Fisher portrays Joseph Smith's revelations about polygamy as more carnal than spiritual, and she suggests that the so-called meadows massacre in 1857 was a Mormon-inspired raid.

Unlike Fox's later treatment of Grey's novels, 20th Century–Fox could not exclude the Mormon element from *Brigham Young;* the film would have been unintelligible without it. The film is, in fact, remarkable for what it did include. *Brigham Young* forthrightly acknowledges violence against Mormons. The film opens with a vigilante raid on a Mormon household, an attack in which the head of the household is beaten to death. The burning of Nauvoo, Illinois, is depicted as instigated by those determined to destroy the Mormon Church. The film, primarily through a speech delivered by Dean Jagger's Brigham Young argues that the First Amendment of the United States Constitution protects all faiths.

Brigham Young sets Mormonism squarely within the Judeo-Christian religious tradition. Jagger — as he narrates — compares Mormons fleeing from Illinois to Utah to Jews escaping Egypt for Canaan. And, early in the film, when Joseph Smith is asked whether Mormons regard themselves as saints, he replies that Mormons believe all people who obey the Ten Commandments are saints. Polygamy is scrupulously avoided. Brigham Young has a wife, not wives, and Tyrone Power and Linda Darnell — hero and heroine of the film — practice a monogamous marriage. *Brigham Young* presented Mormonism as located securely within the mainstream of American religion.

By 1950, *Wagonmaster* (RKO, 1950) was willing to go further. The film openly acknowledged popular perceptions of Mormons. For example, in an early scene, Russell Simpson and Ward Bond, Mormon leaders, walk down the street as unwelcomed guests in a town whose sheriff has ordered the Mormons to leave by sundown. When Harry Carey, Jr., asks Bond if they are Mormons, Bond replies that they are and tells Carey that he — Bond — keeps his hat on so people won't see his horns. And, Bond adds that he has more wives than Solomon — or, at least, that is what people say. One of the visual images of the film is the large number of women and children, as compared to males, in the wagon train. *Wagonmaster* depicts polygamy as a normal Mormon practice.

Later, when the wagon train, now with Carey and Ben Johnson acting as guides, comes across a troupe of entertainers who had been chased out of the same city and are now stranded in the desert, Russell Simpson, the spiritual leader of the group, wants to leave the troupe to the desert's fate. When Alan Mowbray, leader of the entertainers, takes some of Simpson's water for shaving, Johnson retrieves the water, reminding the entertainer that water is a scarce commodity in the desert. Johnson returns the water to Simpson, but the elder (in a fit of self-righteousness) throws it on the ground.

Wagonmaster is a refreshing film that treats Mormons as Mormons. They are pictured as a gritty people determined to establish homes in the wilderness but they also practice polygamy and can be very intolerant of other people. Which is to say, they are depicted very much like every other group which ventured west in the nineteenth century.

Explicit Christian symbols appear frequently in 1930–55 Westerns, but that does not exhaust the important place of religion in Westerns. Elkins reminds us that themes need not be overtly religious to project values that are peculiarly associated with Christianity. He suggested several such implicit themes: good versus evil, law versus justice, viceless heroes, special care for children and the unfolding of social progress (Elkin, 1954, 321).

Westerns are stories about the clash between good and evil. Probably over 95 percent of all Westerns depicted it in vivid symbol-laden images. Evil in Western films took forms familiar to those reared in an environment of Bible stories and social and political rhetoric laced with Biblical imagery. Consistent with these images, people in Westerns pursued greed, sought power, practiced crooked politics and were motivated by revenge. The Old Testament prophets were no more graphic in their assault on Israel's sins than were Western films in their depiction of the evil forces unleashed on decent men and women of the West. On the other hand, good was associated with hard work, community service and justice. Furthermore, these contrasting sets of values were dichotomous in Westerns, and good won! In spite of temporary setbacks, an unambiguous good won. Just as the prophets knew Israel would be restored and vindicated, so too did Westerns assure audiences that when good men persevered, they would triumph over evil.

The second theme, law versus justice, was less prevalent and less predictable than the clash between good and evil. What happens when legal requirements and justice conflict? Did justice prevail even if it required violating legal procedures or was law upheld even if, for the moment, justice remained undone?

Most Westerns stressed justice over law. Cowboy heroes broke into offices, ransacked desks and entrapped criminals, all to get evidence. By modern day law-enforcement standards, they violated several, if not dozens of legal requirements each film. Of course, many of these legal standards were extended to the states by the Supreme Court after 1962 when cowboy heroes had ridden off into the sunset. Yet, most viewers in the 1930s and 1940s knew it was illegal to break into an office or to break out of jail. Only by appeals to a higher law, the nature of justice itself, could such activities be defended.

Riders of the Northwest Mounted (Columbia, 1943) starring Russell

Hayden is a good example of the tension between law and justice. Hayden plays Lucky Lawson of the Royal Canadian Mounted Police. He is sent to Red River to investigate fur stealing, but his superior warns him that he must work within legal limits. Arriving in Red River, Hayden immediately gets involved with Dub Taylor as they try to recover the latter's stolen pelts. When a suspect runs into Dick Curtis' trading post, Hayden follows him and insists on searching the place. Curtis protests that Hayden has no authority to search. Hayden's replies "I'll take the authority."

Later, when Hayden tries to break down the door to a room in which he suspects stolen furs are hidden, a fracas ensues, and an individual is murdered. Mountie Bob Wills relieves Hayden of his post. Wills tells Hayden, "No one is a criminal until they have been convicted. People have rights you need to respect." The problem is, viewers know Curtis is the culprit and they understand the law is protecting him. Clearly there is tension between law and justice.

The tension between law and justice takes an interesting turn in a 1953 Gene Autry programmer, *Goldtown Ghost Riders* (Columbia, 1953). The films opens with Jim Granby (veteran character actor Carleton Young) being shot by Ed Wheeler (Kirk Riley). Wheeler had been serving a prison sentence for murder and when he got out of parole, he came gunning for Granby.

Wheeler explains to circuit court judge Autry, that he, Wheeler, can't be tried for murdering Granby because that would be trying him twice for the same crime, a practice forbidden by the United States Constitution. Wheeler explains that Granby is really Jim Mears, the man who Wheeler was sent to prison for murdering ten years ago.

The movie then unfolds in flashbacks as Wheeler tells his story. Both Wheeler and Mears had been in the army when they discovered gold and Wheeler had gotten rich by selling phony mining claims. Mears began to blackmail him, and since Wheeler had become a leading citizen in the community, he paid the blackmail money until he got the chance to kill Mears.

An interesting flashback exchange occurs when Gene brings Cathy Wheeler (Gale Davis), Ed Wheeler's daughter, into town. Wheeler tells Gene that the territorial governor has given him the power to select a new territorial circuit court judge and he wants Gene to accept the position. When Gene protests that he is a cattleman and doesn't know anything about law, Wheeler replies, "Law is common sense." And Cathy Wheeler adds, "Binding practices of the community and rules of conduct to enforce." Wheeler makes clear to Gene that he must be prepared to use his guns and fists to bring in witnesses and to enforce his sentences. That is an interesting view of jurisprudence, to say the least.

After Wheeler tells his story and explains why he shot Granby, Gene is not sure what to do, but he decides to put him in jail. Gene's reasons are less legal and more for Wheeler's personal safety. He knows that Granby's gang will try to lynch Wheeler, and that all the miners who bought phony claims from him will probably join them. When Gene's hunch proves accurate, he helps Wheeler escape. However, Granby's men kill Wheeler and then kill each other. Justice B Western–style was realized even though the law was not followed precisely.

On occasion, however, the cowboy hero expressed reverence for law above popular notions of justice and maintained that justice had little meaning outside the legal process. William Elliott in *North from the Lone Star* (Columbia, 1941) makes an excellent statement about the need for a sheriff to treat outlaws and the innocent with equal legal respect. Elliott has just become Marshal of Deadwood when Richard Fiske, the owner of a livery stable, kills an outlaw who is trying to drive him out of business. Elliott arrests Fiske, and when Fiske's sister Dorothy Faye protests, Elliott tells her, "The law has got to be the same for everybody. I've got no choice. I was appointed to enforce the law and that's what I am going to do." Faye points to Arthur Loft, whom everyone knows is the brains behind the outlaws, and demands Elliott arrest him as well. Wild Bill's reply is direct: "I have not seen him break any laws."

In many of his films, Tim McCoy, made similar pleas. In *The Western Code* (Columbia, 1932), McCoy warns a hotheaded young man eager to kill Wheeler Oakman, main villain in the film, "The law, when it comes to killing, generally deals out a prison sentence and in some cases a hanging." Later, when he stops a lynching, McCoy tells the mob leader, "You know, there is a law in this country that gives a break to even confessed killers. You might be glad to know that one of these days."

George O'Brien as a Texas Ranger in *The Renegade Ranger* (RKO, 1938) feels compelled to arrest Rita Hayworth for murder even though he was increasingly convinced of her innocence. Harry Carey, the sheriff in *Wagon Trail* (Ajax, 1935), must jail his only son when the lad is caught as part of a stage holdup in which a guard was killed. The tension then between law and justice, a tension which pervades American law, is reflected in Westerns without much effort to suggest an appropriate resolution.

These two themes, the triumph of good over evil and the tension between justice and law, combine with the nature of social progress, discussed in the last chapter, to focus the major values projected in Western films. All three themes are closely associated in America with the Christian religion. So too were the personal characteristics of cowboy heroes that have been noted throughout. Cowboy heroes did not, for the most part, drink or smoke. Needless to say, obscenity and sex would not have survived the industry's self-imposed censorship of the 1930s and '40s.

Quite to the contrary, the cowboy hero was a model of self-sacrifice, always working for the good and material gain of others. And they respected children! Tom Mix in *The Rider of Death Valley* (Universal, 1932), went into a saloon to remind an errant father that his daughter was waiting patiently for him outside. In *The Gunman from Bodie* (Monogram, 1941), Buck Jones found a baby, left when its parents were murdered, took time to milk a cow so the baby could have breakfast, and found a home for it, all before Jones went about his regular business. Many Roy Rogers and Gene Autry films wove the concerns, hopes and fears of children into the plots. In many ways, then, the cowboy hero was a person whose behavior and character were similar to characters from the Bible, and those Bible characters and stories were very familiar to audiences in the South, Southwest and Midwest.

The values expressed in Westerns, ones which Elkins suggested reflect our Christian society, did not just happen. Herbert Yates, President of Republic Pictures, and executives of other Western production units understood their audiences, and they molded their products to fit audience expectations.

Richard M. Hurst observed that Republic had its greatest impact as it "reinforced the ethical and moral standards of the times" (Hurst, 89). That, Hurst claims, helps to explain the financial success of Republic. Morris R. Abrams, a scriptwriter for Republic, acknowledged Hurst's point and commented, "Virtue triumphant was taken for granted" (Hurst, 71). Hurst provides a fitting summary for this chapter. He wrote that four messages were inherent in B Westerns, but we can expand that to nearly all Westerns produced between 1930 and 1955: a traditional morality play or sermon which reflected the traditional values of the Bible Belt, decency, law and justice, the search for fundamental dignity of all people, and an idealism and optimism which pervaded American life (Hurst, 123).

Chapter Four

COWBOY PATRIOTS: B WESTERNS AND AMERICAN POLITICS

The United States was the first nation to declare its independence from European colonial domination and therefore is rightly regarded as the first new nation. It was also the first country to create a new government. Drawing on practical experience as well as political theories from the ancient Greeks to the eighteenth-century French, America's founding fathers discarded old political arrangements and created a new political structure. The Articles of Confederation were a less-than-successful effort at government building, but the Constitution of the United States hammered out in Philadelphia during the summer of 1787 has existed for over 210 years.

While it is true that no outsider can understand Americans fully without grasping the inherent religious nature of its people, democracy, not religion, is the defining characteristic of the American experience. Foreign visitors do not flock to American cathedrals nor seek out other places of historic religious importance. Instead they visit the United States Capitol, the White House, take the Freedom Walk in Boston or explore famous Revolutionary and Civil War battlefields. For the rest of the world, America's political achievements, not its religious heritage, define the country's importance in world history.

Since 1800, millions of immigrants from all corners of the Earth have flocked to the United States seeking refugee from political, ethnic and religious tyranny. Consequently, Americans have no single racial, ethnic or sectarian quality. Pre–Civil War immigrants, mostly German, Irish, Scotch-Irish or English, were easily assimilated. After 1870, new citizens were Eastern European, Polish, Italian, Russian or other nationalities. They spoke Yiddish, various Slavic languages or Italian, brought with them churches and denominations new to the North American continent, and their diverse customs, including food, enriched American culture.

Post–1870 immigrants came with many understandings of the word freedom, but for all immigrants freedom meant a fresh start in a new land. Freedom, representative government, equality of opportunity and civil liberties became the hallmarks of the American experience as the nineteenth century drew to a close.

Those post–Civil War immigrants sought also to become full-fledged Americans. They struggled to learn the English language, and frequently they modified or changed their names in order to make them appear more "American." In short, they embraced their newly adopted country with relish. Surely large cities of the early twentieth century housed many ethnic enclaves; the word ghetto was first associated with Jews, not African-Americans. While Polish, Yiddish or Italian might have been the dominant language of the neighborhood, its residents actively pursued Americanization. They wanted to become full-fledged Americans rather than preserve their native identity.

The masses of post–Civil War immigrants also became laborers, supplying manpower for the steel mills, slaughtering houses, packing plants and (later) the rapidly expanding automotive industry which made the United States the world's foremost industrial power. Other immigrants were economically more adventurous. Of this group, early twentieth century Jewish entrepreneurs who helped to develop the motion picture industry are most noteworthy. Many of them started out as nickelodeon operators, then began their own exchanges to ensure a steady supply of new films to their nickelodeons, and finally went into production when their exchanges needed new films. Carl Laemmle—founder of Universal Pictures—and William Fried—who changed his name to Fox—are but two prominent examples of early Jewish motion picture pioneers.

Not surprisingly, early films, and most notably Westerns, reflected the dominant American ethos these men so eagerly embraced. Individualism, freedom, self-reliance and a commitment to the democratic creed marked their early Western efforts. However, sentiment shifted somewhat between 1930 and 1945 as the nation grappled with economic depression and then world war. Individualism and self-reliance receded as government became more prominent and important. To understand the significance of that shift, one must consider the insights of another European, one who did not immigrate to the United States, but one who traveled extensively throughout the country and recorded his observations in a remarkable book, *Democracy in America*.

Alexis de Tocqueville, born in 1805, the son of a French aristocrat, witnessed the defeat of Napoleon and the failure of French democracy when the victorious European powers restored the French monarchy at the Vienna Conference of 1816. From a distance, Tocqueville could see that democracy had taken root in the United States, and he was puzzled as to why it had failed in his country. In an effort to find answers to that question, Tocqueville began an extensive tour of the United States in the late 1820s. When he published his observations in the two-volume study *Democracy in America*, Tocqueville quickly was recognized as a keen observer of American life and character. The young French visitor was particularly adept at identifying qualities of American character, relating those qualities to social and political institutions, and anticipating trends that would influence both.

As he observed American life, Tocqueville was struck by its individualism, which he defined as "a calm and considered feeling, which predisposes each citizen to sever himself from the mass of his fellow-creatures; and to draw apart with his family and friends" (Tocqueville, II, 104). Joined to the new nation's democratic creed, Tocqueville thought that individualism predisposed citizens to evaluate public affairs in terms of their immediate impact on self, family and friends and to disregard broader social consequences.

The problem that Tocqueville foresaw was that too often individualism is inadequate because citizens need to pool their collective efforts in order to deal with common problems. But in the 1820s, rather than turn to government to solve common problems, Tocqueville observed that American citizens formed voluntary, private associations. If they needed to raise a school, build a road or provide care for widows and orphans, unlike Europeans, Americans did not rely on government; rather they pooled their efforts in a voluntary association and met the need (Tocqueville, II, 114).

Tocqueville, however, foresaw the day when life would become more complex and problems beyond the capacity of voluntary associations. At that time, Tocqueville argued, government would emerge in the United States as a powerful force. With uncanny accuracy, Tocqueville forecast a time when individuals would be less self-sufficient, unable to produce the necessities of life, and unable to meet complex social problems by voluntary action. At that time, he argued, government would become powerful and voluntary associations less prevalent.

In the century between Tocqueville's visit and the 1953 inauguration of Dwight Eisenhower as President, the United States underwent significant social and economic transformation; the country began to look more and more like the place Tocqueville predicted it would become. Individuals seemed less and less able to control their own destinies and more and more dependent on government. The Great Depression and World War II profoundly changed American attitudes toward government.

By 1929, economic depression had been a stark reality in rural America for nearly a decade. Plummeting grain prices after World War I destroyed the economic prosperity farmers enjoyed during the war years. Individual initiative seemed to have little impact on the overall rural economy. Whether farmers increased or decreased acreage under production, grain prices remained unaffected. And it made little difference how cooperative banks were in restructuring farm debt or how understanding merchants were in expecting payments for merchandise; farmers could not pay their bills or meet mortgage obligations.

Realizing they faced economic problems beyond their individual control, farmers increased their political activity by calling for government assistance to help with their plight. The 1920s paved the way for 1930s New Deal programs which reshaped the economics of American agriculture and made it more dependent on governmental intervention.

As the 1930s dawned, urban populations confronted economic hardships at least equal to those of their rural neighbors. Entire industries shut down, "main street" businesses failed, unemployment rose to staggering numbers and banks collapsed as depositors demanded their money. Contrary to optimistic predictions, the economy did not improve. It got worse! By 1932, Americans were buffeted by economic forces beyond their individual control, forces which seemed to cry out for governmental intervention.

And if rural and urban depression were not bad enough, by the early 1930s it appeared that God was conspiring against Americans as well. Giant clouds of dust, driven by incessant winds, ravaged parts of the drought-plagued Great Plains. Farmers and ranchers who had bravely fought depression, stood by helplessly as their land blew away.

If drought and the Depression were insufficient to provoke calls for increased government action, totalitarian regimes in Europe and Asia asserted their military power in Ethiopia, Manchuria, the Ruhr Valley and Spain. As the 1930s drew to a close, Americans faced the real possibility of war. Those harbingers of war, of course, brought on a two-ocean war late in 1941, a war of such overwhelming magnitude that the mind grapples to understand its dimensions, and a war which added immeasurably to the growth of big government.

Although he had not foreseen the specific events, Tocqueville nonetheless had forecast the future. Complex, disastrous events overtook American individualism, passed by the American love for volunteer collective action, and hauled Americans rudely into the age of big government. The Great Depression and World War II simply overwhelmed American individualism with its bias for voluntary action. After 1945, the debate was no longer about big government as such, but about the relative size of big government, and the implications of big government for civil liberties.

One is amazed at how easily people after 1930 turned to government for help, and how easily they accepted the emergence of big government. Unquestionably movies helped to pave the way as they applauded the New Deal, depicted drought-induced hard times for ranchers, and reinforced the American war effort. B Westerns were no exception. Week after week, viewers watched as ranchers, farmers and entrepreneurs, among the most individualistic of all Americans, turned to Washington for help. Millions of youngsters and adults watching Westerns learned that while local officials might be corrupt, federal agents were honest public servants. B Westerns taught people that when they were in trouble, they could telegraph Washington for help and wait for the fearless man who would be sent to handle the situation.

Those twin themes of popular support for the federal government, and a bias for federal officials either have been ignored entirely or treated too quickly by most books on B Westerns. The rest of this chapter will address that interesting and controversial issue. The political outlook embraced by most Westerns between 1930 and 1955 had four distinct elements. First, the films were patriotic vehicles that encouraged "Americanism" as an appropriate pride in American customs and institutions. Conversely, they were critical of bad men who wanted to build personal political empires at the expense of the nation.

Second, the films urged that federal officials in Washington knew of and cared about the welfare of all citizens, even those with little social influence who lived in remote locations. Citizens facing all kinds of problems could turn to informed and understanding federal officials, usually the President of the United States, for assistance. Third, local politicians, unlike federal officials, often were portrayed as corrupt. Local mayors and sheriffs, usually in cahoots with a banker, were the brains behind the forces oppressing honest, hard-working folks who were trying to make the West a fit place to live. Finally, Westerns between 1930 and 1955 were biased toward the executive and judicial branches of government. Governors, presidents, bureaucrats and judges appear more prominently in the plot of Westerns than do Congressmen or other legislators. Clearly, it is easier to depict on film a president, governor or some other administrator making a decision or giving an order than it is to picture a legislative body formulating laws. That probably accounts for most of the bias toward the executive branch, but part of it is also traceable to the enormous popularity of President Franklin D. Roosevelt with that generation of Americans.

Overall Westerns, as previous chapters have shown, were resounding endorsements of Manifest Destiny. Western films also embraced a strong sense of nationalism as the logical outgrowth of Manifest Destiny. Unlike earlier generations, when Americans of the 1930s and 1940s spoke of "my country" they meant the United States, not their state or region. By 1930 the Pledge of Allegiance, the United States Capitol Dome and political personalities such as Washington, Jackson and Lincoln were powerful national symbols, unifying all sections and regions of the country. Individuals remained sentimentally attached to their states, and regional peculiarities retained their prominence, but more and more national sentiments and symbols cut through regional affections to weld a strong sense of national citizenship.

Both motion pictures and radio programs reinforced that sense of national identity. National radio networks aired programs all over the country. *Amos n' Andy*, Gene Autry's *Melody Ranch, The Shadow, Lum and Abner, Fibber McGee and Molly* and a dozen other popular shows were favorites of listeners. They reflected national traits rather than state or regional peculiarities. Motion pictures, as well, played in theaters all over America. While Westerns were more popular in the Midwest and South than other regions, they still played New York City and Boston theaters. And, like radio programs, they appealed to national sentiments.

Many villains in B Westerns, however, sought to carve out pieces of the North American continent as their personal political empires or they acted as representatives of foreign powers who sought to take advantage of internal strife in order to annex California, Texas, Arizona or some other western state. The cowboy hero as a patriotic American often was called upon to thwart their efforts. Several Roy Rogers programmers of the early 1940s are good examples.

Young Bill Hickok (Republic, 1940) opens with a representative of a foreign power, (John Miljan) joining forces with raider Hal Taliaferro to keep the North from shipping gold from Dakota Territory to California during the Civil War. By prolonging the war, the unnamed foreign power intended to separate California from the union. The polished language and refined culture of the villainous Miljan, representative of the foreign nation, merely enhances ones' dislike of him. Miljan is even too slick for

Taliaferro, who tells him on more than one occasion to stop using fancy language and speak plain American. And, in the end, when it is clear that Miljan was part of the plot to assassinate President Lincoln, ones judgments are validated.

Roy Rogers as young Bill Hickok, on the other hand, embodies patriotism. Working to stop the raiders and save the Union, Roy demonstrates a great deal of self-sacrificing courage. Early in the film, he nearly loses his life in a shootout with the raiders, and then a few minutes later viewers learn that a young woman had broken off their engagement because he remained loyal to the Union. Later in the film, Roy postpones his marriage a second time, and once again jeopardizes his engagement, in order to help get a shipment of gold past the raiders. At the film's climax, when Roy has proof that Miljan is linked to John Wilkes Booth, he stops Miljan before the villain can make good on his plans to take California out of the Union.

Two other Rogers programmers are set during the Civil War and feature villains who try to use the war as an excuse for their own political ambitions. Senator Lassiter (Edward Keane) is the traitor in *Frontier Pony Express* (Republic, 1939). Lassiter dupes honest people who support the Southern cause into siding with him in an effort to get California to secede from the Union. In reality, Lassiter intends to create a Republic of the Pacific with himself at its head rather than join it to the Confederate States of America. Roy is able to stop Lassiter only after the latter shoots Brett Langhorne (Donald Dillaway), a newspaper editor loyal to the South who won't go along with Lassiter's treachery when he discovers the Senator's true intentions. Langhorne as he lays dying, tells his sister (Mary Hart) of Lassiter's ultimate goal. Hart informs Rogers, who is able to keep Lassiter from stealing a million dollars of gold bullion with which to establish his Republic of California.

In *Colorado* (Republic, 1940), Milburn Stone portrays a Confederate sympathizer who is also Roy Rogers' brother. When his legitimate efforts to help the South are thwarted by Rogers, Stone throws in with Arthur Rankin, who has no loyalties outside of his own self-advancement. Rankin and his cohorts intend to take advantage of Civil War urmoil and turn Colorado into their own personal political empire. Even though Stone is Rogers' brother, Roy remains obedient to his orders as an officer in the Union army. He helps to apprehend the culprits, and as an act of kindness to Stone, the film ends when Roy permits his brother to flee on horseback. Roy knows that a member of the posse will shoot Stone and thus spare him the gallows.

Henry Brandon plays the infamous General LaRue in *Ranger and the*

Lady (Republic, 1940). This film is set in the period before Texas was admitted to the Union. Governor Houston is in Washington trying to convince officials to let Texas take its rightful place in the Union. He leaves LaRue in charge of the government, but LaRue has other more personal plans. He intends to build his own individual empire in Texas. As a step in that direction, LaRue imposes high tariffs on traders using the Santa Fe Trail, and when they turn north to Bents Fort, Colorado, to avoid LaRue's tax, he arbitrarily annexes all of New Mexico to Santa Fe. Roy Rogers and sidekick Gabby Hayes are thrown out of the Rangers because they won't do LaRue's bidding. After 59 minutes of action, Houston returns from Washington and helps Rogers and Hayes round up LaRue and his men, thus preventing them from denying Texas its rightful place as one of the United States.

Even earlier than the Rogers Westerns, Republic had used a similar theme in *The Lawless Nineties* (Republic, 1936). John Wayne portrays a government agent sent to Wyoming to help corral a gang raiding the territory. The plot unfolds around efforts by villains Harry Woods and Charles King to keep Wyoming from becoming a state. As long as it remains a territory, they can continue to outwit local law enforcement and carry on their illegal activities. However, Wyoming statehood would mean more effective federal authority and the end to their lucrative reign of terror.

The Lawless Nineties also recognizes freedom of the press as an essential requirement for self-government. George Hayes plays a crusading newspaper editor who migrates to Wyoming, determined to help the cause of statehood. When Hayes launches his newspaper, he declares it to be another star in the bright firmament of liberty for he believes that people can't participate in their own self-government if they don't possess information, and newspapers are essential means of dispensing political information. Hayes' character understands both the importance and obligation of newspapers in a free society and, hence, he spearheads the campaign for statehood.

Woods and King also understand that lesson, but their reaction is to try to shut down the newspaper. When that fails, they murder Hayes. Ann Rutherford, portraying Hayes' daughter, is as determined as her father, so she takes over as editor and continues to advocate statehood.

A final lesson of this film is that "the popular will" ultimately prevails in a democracy. Woods and King try every politically corrupt trick in the book to keep the honest voice of the people from being heard at the polls. They stuff ballot boxes, steal the boxes before the votes are counted, intimidate potential voters, block entrance into voting places and even murder. In the end they fail because the forces of nationalism seeking to join

Wyoming to the rest of the Union are stronger than the efforts of Woods and King to carve out their personal kingdom. Wayne, the government man, stands for the nation while Woods and King stand for themselves, and in Westerns the nation always won.

A similar theme permeates *Son of Davy Crockett* (Columbia, 1941). William Elliott as young Davy Crockett — son of the legendary frontiersman — rides into Yucca Flats only to discover that it lies in no man's land, part of neither state nor Indian territory, and that it is ruled by Kenneth MacDonald, who plays King Canfield, known locally as the King of the Yucca Strip. The citizens of Yucca Strip want to hold an election so they can vote to join the union. King Canfield opposes the effort and makes it clear that he will not give up his personal domain without a fight. Predictably, Canfield resorts to political treachery to prevent an honest vote. He fails, and in the end Elliott kills him in a gunfight. As Elliott and his sidekick Dub Taylor ride out of Yucca Flats, the people raise the American flag to celebrate membership in the Union. Their spirit of nationalism prevailed over King Canfield's efforts to build his own personal political empire.

Westerns were patriotic films that celebrated the expansion of the nation and extolled the deeply felt sense of nationhood embraced by all Americans. In Westerns, the heroes work to preserve or to expand the union. Villains are those who want to sever some state from the rest of the United States in order to fulfill either personal political ambition or to join it to a foreign nation. As various shades of international totalitarianism emerged in the 1930s, it is not surprising that Westerns of the late 1930s and early '40s celebrated American nationhood and democracy.

However, the spirit of nationhood was never as threatened by foreign elements as it was between 1861 and 1865 by the bloody American Civil War. The sense of being one people, to say nothing of the very existence of a United States, was put to the supreme test. When the war ended, most Americans wanted to get on with unifying the nation, in Lincoln's words, "to bind up the nation's wounds." Unfortunately, Congress had other ideas, and the nation entered into a period of political reconstruction in the South. Not surprisingly, Reconstruction was a time of political violence and corruption throughout the South as opportunists took advantage of the political turmoil to get rich by exploiting the defeated states. Texas was emblematic of the period, and one of the last states to see the end of reconstruction policies.

Most Southerners, however, understandably embittered by defeat, wanted to get on with their lives as they reassembled lost fortunes and adjusted to the new social relationship between former slaves and masters, and they wanted eventually to rejoin the Union. Reconstruction policies and predatory politicians often made that impossible. The humiliation of defeat dragged on as the political and civil liberties of Southerners were denied and their economies exploited by reconstruction politicians out for private gain.

Robin Hood of the Pecos (Republic, 1941) portrays vividly all of the atrocities of reconstruction policies in Texas. Roy Rogers as Vance Corbin returns to find his home county in the grips of marshal law. Cy Kendall as Ballard, the carpetbagger politician responsible for the troubles, uses his authority as tax collector to foreclose on the ranchers' property. George Hayes as Gabby Hornaday plays a night rider who opposes Kendall's efforts to grab all the land for himself.

Col. Davis, of the U.S. Cavalry convinces Roy Rogers that Kendall's power can be ended if Rogers and the rest of the men of the county will take the oath of allegiance to the United States Constitution. Once the oath has been taken by a majority of the males, local elections can be held, and local control restored. Rogers convinces Gabby and the rest of the men to take the oath. It is even superimposed on the screen as Gabby swears allegiance to the Constitution and becomes, once again, a full-fledged American citizen.

Col. Davis is murdered when he is about to discover Kendall's secret file containing evidence that Kendall was enriching himself at the ranchers' expense. Using Davis' murder as pretext, Kendall imposes marshal law once again and arrests Gabby. When a jury declares Gabby innocent, Kendall overrules the jury and decrees that Gabby will be hung.

Rogers identifies Davis' real killer as an associate of Kendall and exposes Kendall's guilt to Gen. Wright, a federal officer who brought troops to prevent the town from being sacked by citizens intent on freeing Gabby. Justice is done when Stacy (Jay Novello), the man who murdered Col. Davis and in turn was shot by Kendall in order to keep him quiet, kills Kendall. Gen. Wright lifts marshal law, clears Gabby of any wrongdoing, and restores local authority by making Rogers sheriff.

All elements of reconstruction politics are present in this exciting little Western. Kendall is the evil carpetbagger out to enrich himself at the expense of defeated Southerners. Col. Davis and Gen. Wright are honest federal officials who have a great deal of respect for their former foes and who want only the best for them now that the war has ended. Rogers plays the enlightened Southerner who takes the oath of allegiance to the United States Constitution and encourages Gabby and the other men to do the same, for once they become citizens again they will enjoy the full protection of civil liberties and the right to self-government.

The Lonely Trail, (Republic, 1936) is similar to *Robin Hood of the Pecos* in several respects. John Wayne plays a Texan who fought on the Union side during the Civil War. Returning to Texas, John finds his ranch in shambles from four years of neglect. To make matters worse, a notice has been posted on the ranch house door notifying Wayne that the property will be confiscated unless back taxes are paid. Wayne and his partner Jed (Jim Toney) need to find jobs, so they go to work as members of the State Police, an organization headed by Cy Kendall, (once again cast as an unscrupulous carpetbagger).

John and Jed learn that the State Police is nothing more than Kendall's private band of outlaws, working not for the public interest but for Kendall's personal gain. John and Jed then help Ann Rutherford's brother Terry (Dennis Moore), leader of the local resistance, to escape being shot by the State Police. As a result of their act of kindness to Terry, John and Jed find themselves in a difficult position. Hunted by Kendall's men, yet unaccepted by the locals who assume that John and Jed are part of Kendall's force because they had fought with the Union during the war, John is badly wounded fleeing from the State Police. Terry convinces his sister that John is on their side, and she tries to hide her badly wounded pre-war sweetheart. But the State Police discover his hiding place, arrest him and sentence him to be hung.

The Governor of Texas, accompanied by a United States cavalry officer, arrives to investigate the charges that Kendall is overtaxing the citizens and failing to turn over all the taxes he collects to the rightful authorities. Kendall has nearly convinced the Governor that the charges are groundless when John and Jed, who have broken out of jail, barge into the room. Jed shows the Governor Kendall's secret wall safe in which he keeps the unreported tax monies.

The local resistance led by Terry and his sister ride into the compound intending to rescue John and Jed from jail, but instead they arrive just in time to stop Kendall and his men from escaping. The film ends with the Governor promising fair taxes and due process of law for all Texans.

Neither would-be kings of personal political empires nor good-for-nothing carpetbaggers could prevent the unification or reunification of the union. And once part of the United States, citizens could count on assistance from the federal government if they needed it. B Westerns portrayed public officials in far-off Washington, D.C., responding to citizens pleas for assistance no matter how remote the location or local the problem. Westerns, with few exceptions, projected the federal government as a dependable ally of the average citizen and an unrelenting foe of those who terrorized the common man.

Billy the Kid Returns (Republic, 1938), Roy Rogers' second starring Western, had that theme. Roy, a Billy the Kid lookalike, becomes involved in a ranchers-versus-homesteaders range war. The ranchers use all kinds of tactics, including murder, to keep homesteaders from settling on federally owned land. And since the ranchers control the local courts, efforts to prosecute them are futile.

The town marshal tells Roy that federal authority is the only thing the ranchers fear. That gives Roy an idea. He arranges to have the ranchers steal U.S. Army horses. (The ranchers believe they are rustling horses owned by the homesteaders, but the animals really belong to the army.) When the cavalry catches them stealing the horses, the ranchers are arrested. Since they will be tried in federal courts, their friends who control the local court system are powerless to help them.

Films such as *Billy the Kid Returns* appear to have been in step with public opinion of the 1930s. In 1936, a Gallup Poll question disclosed strong preference for federal action over state action. The Gallup Poll asked respondents, "Which theory of government do you favor—concentration of power in the federal government or concentration of power in state governments?" and 56 percent of those who responded preferred the federal government. Even in the South, the most politically conservative of all regions, 58 percent chose the federal government.

Contemporary public opinion polls reflect a different attitude. Citizens no longer believe that the federal government is trustworthier than state governments. Nor do contemporary Americans believe that federal officials are honest or competent. Public opinion polls measuring the honesty and competence of public officials were rare in the 1930s and 1940s, but if Westerns are good indicators of public sentiment, the evidence is clear. People of those decades had far more confidence in the federal government and federal officials those do citizens at the beginning of the twenty-first century.

The preference for federal authority was buttressed by the depiction of local governmental officials in B Westerns. Often mayors, members of town councils, sheriffs and local judges were corrupt and self-serving. Two versions of the same Western made by differing production companies nearly a decade apart are good film examples of corrupt local officials. *Gun Law* (RKO, 1938) and *The Law Comes to Gunsight* (Monogram, 1947) employ a similar plot, are set in the same town (Gunsight) and use some of the same character names.

In *Gun Law*, George O'Brien, a federal marshal, stumbles across a dying gunman called the Raven. Both O'Brien and Raven are headed for Gunsight. O'Brien is the marshal sent to clean up the town and Raven the gunman hired to kill O'Brien. When O'Brien is mistaken for Raven, he plays along, and learns that Mayor Blaine, ostensibly a rock of integrity to whom the community looks for leadership, is really in cahoots with the saloon owner who bosses the outlaws responsible for all the community's problems.

Johnny Mack Brown is the cowboy hero in *The Law Comes to Gunsight* who rides into Gunsight on the horse of the dead Pecos, a notorious gunman Mayor Blaine has sent for. The mayor assumes that Johnny Mack is Pecos and makes him sheriff with the expectation that the new sheriff will cooperate with the mayor and his allies (the local saloon owner and a prominent member of the town council). As did O'Brien in the early programmer, Brown plays along until he gets enough evidence to reveal his true identity as a United States marshal sent to clean up Gunsight.

Two Three Mesquiteers programmers, *Santa Fe Stampede* (Republic, 1938) and *Wyoming Outlaw* (Republic, 1939), are among the best examples of corrupt local politicians. The latter features that ace movie villain LeRoy Mason as Balsinger, the boss of a local political machine. Before drought-plagued ranchers can get either relief or jobs they had to make a hefty contribution to the Balsinger's "election" campaign!

The Three Mesquiteers learn of Balsinger's racket when Will Parker (Don Barry in one of his early roles) steals and butchers a steer belonging to them. The Mesquiteers intend to prosecute Will for stealing the steer until they learn about the misfortunes of the Parker family. Will's father Luke Parker (played by Charles Middleton, the evil Ming in the Flash Gordon serials) tells the Mesquiteers that the only available jobs are cleaning up the roads after a dust storm. But then pointing to his injured leg, the elder Parker notes he can't even do that. Besides, he continues, he had been fired as foreman of the road crew because he wouldn't collect a weeks pay from each man for Balsinger's "election" campaign.

John Wayne, playing Stony Brooke, goes to the capitol to tell his friend Senator Roberts of the tactics Balsinger employs and the Committee on Public Welfare promises to hold a hearing. Balsinger's men threaten the local residents' families if they testify. When they can't frighten Luke Parker, they shoot and badly injure him as he is hitching up the team of horses to go to the hearing.

In the meantime, Balsinger has the corrupt local sheriff arrest the Mesquiteers for disturbing the peace. (They got into a fight in Balsinger's office and wrecked the place.) The Mesquiteers are not released from jail until after no one shows up at the committee's hearing and Senator Roberts is forced to cancel it.

The Mesquiteers have a permit to graze cattle in a public park and they employ Will Parker to help herd the cattle. But the Park Rangers won't permit the young man in the park — he is suspected of illegal hunting — so the Mesquiteers are forced to let him go. When Will is caught attempting to kill a deer in the park, he is arrested and put in jail, but he kills a deputy and escapes to become an outlaw.

The film ends when Will traps Balsinger in a bank and uses him as a shield. Will has no intention of escaping; knowing that he is about to die, he wants to make sure that Balsinger dies with him. When the two men exit the bank, both of them are shot to death. In an odd sort of way, justice has triumphed. Will Parker, an outlaw who had killed other men, is in turn killed himself and Balsinger, a corrupt political boss who had terrorized local citizens, meets his own violent end.

LeRoy Mason is again the main villain in *Santa Fe Stampede*. As Mayor, Mason runs Santa Fe Junction with an iron fist, controlling the local sheriff and justice of the peace with the aid of a corrupt attorney. The Three Mesquiteers go to Santa Fe Junction to help an old friend (William Farnum) who has discovered a large gold deposit. Not surprisingly, Mason is trying to swindle him out of it.

When the Mesquiteers catch an outlaw — one of Mason's men — stealing Farnum's horse, they take him to Santa Fe Junction for trial. When the man is freed by the justice of the peace, the Mesquiteers realize what they are up against. The attorney, however, is scared when he discovers that they are the Three Mesquiteers. He wonders what they are doing in Santa Fe Junction. The sheriff's reply ("Maybe they're on government business") suggest that federal authority is the one thing corrupt local officials truly fear.

The local citizens are weary of Mason's corruption so they threaten to form a vigilante committee to clean up the town. Stony Brooke talks them out of it with a plea to use their right of appeal under the Constitution. The Mesquiteers head up a petition drive to get a federal investigation. Stony assures the citizens that Mason has had things his own way because no one exercised the courage to report him to Washington.

Mason, however, is determined to retain his power, and he has Farnum and his little daughter killed as they journey to the capitol to deliver the petition. The little girl's death is Mason's undoing: The judge can't live with her death on his conscience so at the film's climax he tells the Mesquiteers that Mason had Farnum and the little girl murdered. Santa Fe Junction is freed at last from the control of a corrupt mayor and his henchmen.

In B Westerns, local citizens living under the iron heel of local politicians could turn to the federal government for help because federal officials were portrayed as incorruptible. Local sheriffs often worked in league with outlaws, were controlled by dishonest mayors, or were simply on the take, for sale to those with the most money. United States marshals, however, were very different. Buck Jones, Tim McCoy and Raymond Hatton — the Rough Riders — and Ken Maynard, Hoot Gibson and Bob Steele — the Trail Blazers — were all U.S. marshals. Lash LaRue usually played a federal marshal, as did Rocky Lane. In fact, nearly every cowboy hero appeared as a U.S. marshal in some of his movies. Viewers understood that the cowboy hero was an honest man so full of integrity he would not even entertain hints of dishonesty. That reinforces the association between the good guys and the federal government.

Roy Rogers seldom played a federal marshal in his popular late 1940s and early 1950s Westerns. Often, however, he did assume the role of a federal official of some sort. He was a forest ranger in *North of the Great Divide* (Republic, 1950), a member of the United States Soil Conservation Service in *Trail of Robin Hood* (Republic, 1950) and a member of the United States Border Patrol in *Pals of the Golden West* (Republic, 1951). All of these programmers continued the trend in B Westerns of a helpful federal government and honest federal employees who took seriously their responsibilities to serve the people.

Rogers and Gene Autry took the theme of responsible federal officials to its logical conclusion when each played a Congressman. *Mr. Smith Goes to Washington* (Columbia, 1939) with Jimmy Stewart portraying the trials of the average man elected to congress was a smash hit in 1939, but few people realize that Herbert Yates at Republic produced a similar movie with a Western setting a year earlier. Yates' original intent was to star Autry — then the most popular star on the Republic lot — in a Western to be called *Washington Cowboy*. Autry, however, chose to go on strike for more money and to protest Republic's film packing arrangement which made Autry films too expensive for many exhibitors (Autry, 59–61). Republic used the opportunity to star Roy Rogers in the projected Autry programmer.

In *Under Western Stars,* the main villains are not the normal run-of-the-mill outlaws, but rather the Great Western Water and Power Company, a large corporation, and the Congressional process. The power company owns the only source of water in the drought-plagued region, and it uses the local Congressman to keep a bill to build a public dam and reservoir bottled up in committee. When local ranchers, desperate for water, attack the dam, Rogers decides to run for office against Congressman Scully, (Tom Chatterton), who does the bidding of the Great Western Water and Power Company. Roy defeats Scully and heads for Washington, D.C., determined to get a public power bill for his district through Congress.

Roy runs into legislative roadblocks at each turn: Committees won't hold hearings on his bill, fellow Congressmen won't return calls, and nobody important pays any attention to freshman Congressman Roy Rogers. Congressman Rogers learns that even without Congressman Scully, lobbyists for the Great Western Power and Water Company still wield a great deal of influence—certainly more influence than does a freshman Congressman.

Carol Hughes, playing the daughter of the owner of the water company, is secretly on Rogers' side and in love with him, so she suggests that Roy hold a party and show a film about the terrible drought conditions in his district. Roy takes her advice and a gains momentary advantage when Congressman Marlowe is persuaded by the film. It appears that Roy will get his bill through the Congress after all. But when Marlowe visits the district and discovers that the drought footage did not come from Roy's district and that Roy's commentary throughout the film identifying specific ranchers with scenes in the film was all fabricated, Marlowe cancels the investigation and vows that the bill will never get out of his committee.

As Congressman Marlowe and his entourage are about to leave the district, Rogers stages fake holdups, leaving the whole group on horseback. When they get caught in a real dust storm, Congressman Marlowe realizes how bad things really are and agrees to report the bill out of his committee. Word comes, however, that the ranchers are riding to blow up the dam. Marlowe warns Rogers that if the ranchers succeed in blowing up the Great Western Power and Water Company dam, there will be no chance of getting a public water bill through Congress. Riding to stop the ranchers before they do anything rash, Roy is able to divert a wagon full of dynamite before it plunges into the dam and blows up. The ranchers get help from Washington as the public water bill is passed, and Rogers and Hughes ride off into the sunset together

Rovin' Tumbleweeds has many of the same characteristics as *Under Western Stars*. The Green River floods the entire Green River Valley but Congressman Fuller, the local congressman, won't help get a flood control bill through Congress because his benefactor the Randville Development Corporation wants to buy all of the ranch land cheap. A flood control bill would make the land valuable and less prone to flood, hence ranchers would decline to sell at cheap prices.

When Douglas Dumbrille, playing the head of the Randville Development Corporation, figures out that Congressman Fuller is a political liability, he entices Gene Autry, a local celebrity, to run for Congress. Autry campaigns for the flood relief bill, pointing out that it would not raise taxes very much even though Congressman Fuller had maintained that it would.

Rovin' Tumbleweeds (the working title was *The Washington Cowboy*), Republic, 1939; Gene Autry and unidentified actors. Congressman Autry addresses a congressional committee.

When Autry is elected, he heads for Washington, expecting that the justice of his cause will be enough to convince Congress. It doesn't turn out that way. Gene's efforts with the Ways and Means and Appropriations committees all fail. He learns that fellow Congressmen won't return his calls. Like Roy Rogers in *Under Western Stars*, Gene learns that freshmen Congressmen have very little influence in the face of seasoned lobbyists who know the legislative ropes.

His last hope is Senator Nolan, played by the veteran actor William Farnum. Senator Nolan is an oldtime westerner who is impressed when Congressman Autry wins several events in rodeo. He stops by to congratulate Autry and the two wind up eating hamburgers together. Hope shines anew when Nolan gives some hint of helping Autry with his flood control bill. But tragically, Senator Nolan is killed in an automobile accident before he can take action, and Gene and Frog head back to Rand City to face their disappointed constituents.

As they return to Rand City, the area is hit by another heavy rainstorm and the entire area is threatened once again with floods. This time, Autry forces Dumbrille and Fuller to help with the sandbagging and both men see the devastating consequences of their actions. The film ends with Dumbrille and Fuller both pledging support for the flood control bill.

Both films suggest a great deal about public perceptions of politics, and they provide important insights into 1930s congressional politics. The villains in both films are corporation leaders who use their influence with politicians to enhance corporate greed at the expense of the public good. Neither the Great Western Power and Water Company nor the Randville Development Corporation care very much that ranchers and farmers are being flooded out of their homes or that their livestock are dying for lack of water. The "politicians" are one in league with powerful interests and only appear to care about common folks.

Autry and Rogers, on the other hand, protest that they are not politicians and know very little about running for public office. Since they are just common folks — like everybody else — if elected they will be obligated not to powerful interests but to the well-being of the people who elected them. A populist strain of politics was pervasive in the 1930s and both films build on that theme. *Under Western Stars* and *Rovin' Tumbleweeds* reflect political populism as least as well if not better than *Mr. Smith Goes to Washington*.

The two cowboy programmers also depict congressional behavior of the late 1930s. In those days, freshman congressmen were of little consequence. They were supposed to be seen and not heard! Widely accepted congressional practice relegated freshman congressmen to unimportant committees and required then to defer to their elders on important legislative issues (MacNeil, 148–49). When a legislator ignored congressional customs, his colleagues punished him by ignoring his telephone calls and killing his bills in committee.

Powerful congressional leaders could enforce accepted legislative customs because Congress was not a very democratic institution. Committee chairmen controlled their committees completely. They, and they alone, decided which bills to act on and which to kill. Other committee members had little say in the matter. So the only hope any member had to get his bill through committee was to convince the chairman or some other member of Congress who had influence with the chairman.

The Senate in the 1930s was run by the so-called "inner club" of very powerful Senators (W. White, 83–86). In *Rovin' Tumbleweeds*, Senator Nolan was surely a member of the "inner club." On the House side an oligarchy of powerful committee chairmen controlled the legislative process. Congressman Marlowe in *Under Western Stars* is representative of that oligarchy.

In neither film does the process change as a result of Rogers and Autry's efforts. Both men failed to convince leadership to support their bills. Success came only after Congressman Marlowe and Dumbrille, head of the Randville Development Corporation, experience first-hand the devastation of drought and flood. The process — unchanged — merely switches sides. Congress remains the same! But even here the lesson is clear. A conservative, elitist Congress inordinately responsive to lobbyists can't hold off the common man forever. If good men such as Rogers and Autry remain determined, Washington sooner or later will discover the justice of their cause and come to the aid of the common people. That is the populist faith of the 1930s so ably expressed in these two films.

Franklin D. Roosevelt was the dominant political personality of the 1930s. Revered by many, hated intensely by others, through his fireside chats and the mass media's extensive focus on him, Roosevelt became for many Americans a symbol of hope for the common man caught up in the devastation of economic depression and world war. Through the New Deal, Roosevelt's extensive domestic program, the federal government grew appreciably and the power of the President increased in ways not thought possible by earlier generations.

Not surprisingly, B Westerns responded to Roosevelt's popularity and the increased power of the presidency by turning mediocre presidents who served between the end of the Civil War and 1900 into nineteenth century versions of Roosevelt. Portrayals of Presidents such as Grant, Garfield, Harrison and McKinley are numerous in Westerns, and with few exceptions the image presented on the silver screen has more in common with the public's perception of Franklin Roosevelt than it has with the real personalities of the presidents being depicted.

One of the B Westerns examined earlier in the chapter, *The Son of Davy Crockett* is a good illustration. Through a surveying error, residents of a small strip of land called Yucca Flats are neither part of the United States nor included in Indian territory. King Canfield treats the territory as his private empire rules them. Eddy Waller, who plays William Elliott's friend, turns to his old friend and former commander, Ulysses Grant, now President of the United States, for help. Grant is painfully aware of the plight of Waller's fellow citizens in Yucca Flats. Grant doesn't even mind when Waller keeps calling him Ulysses instead of Mr. President; after all, what is ceremony between friends? Because Grant cares deeply about the plight of the common citizens who live in Yucca Flats, he commissions Elliott and Waller as his personal representatives, ones empowered to oversee a special election.

The President of the United States possess no constitutional power to oversee local elections, and Congress is given responsibilities for the territories. But those limitations are of little consequence as *The Son of Davy Crockett* assumes a heroic, powerful, activist president committed to the common man. It had little to do with the Grant presidency of history, but the image is one which clearly mirrors public reaction to Franklin Roosevelt.

Arizona Terror (Republic, 1942) presents a similar image of President William McKinley. The story is an oft-told one about a phony Spanish land grant which the imposter uses to claim ownership of the land and to harshly tax the ranchers. Don Barry and his sidekick Al St. John become "ghost riders" who steal the tax monies from the villains and give it back to the ranchers.

Barry realizes, however, that his actions are, at best, temporary. The ranchers' only hope is to bring their plight to the attention of the President, so Barry writes McKinley. His secretary replies to the letter—the president, of course, never sees it—and tells Barry that the President is going on a national tour and does not have time to look into the issue.

Fate intervenes, however. Barry and St. John are on a night ride when the imposter's henchmen chase them. Jumping a train to escape their predicament, Barry and St. John discover they have boarded the train in which McKinley is touring the country. The two men are able to get into the presidential car and present their case to the President. McKinley, as is the case in B Westerns, knows about the land controversy, is concerned about the people being hurt by it, and encourages Barry and St. John to gather evidence. McKinley assures them that when they get the evidence and telegraph it to Washington, he will act to remedy the situation.

Barry and St. John collect evidence and, as the President instructed, telegraph it to Washington. But before he can take any action, McKinley is assassinated. It now is up to Barry and St. John to track down and destroy the imposter, which they do in true B Western fashion. The presidential image is striking in this film. McKinley is a friendly, all-knowing president who does not mind having his private railroad car invaded by two strangers. Once he learns of their mission, he instructs Barry and St. John to furnish evidence on which he, the President, can act.

Cavalry (Republic, 1936), a Bob Steele programmer produced by A. W. Hackel and released through Republic's exchanges, is an interesting example of the manner in which Abraham Lincoln was depicted on screen. The Civil War is nearly over and defeated Southerners are moving west to start life over again. Steele is a Union cavalry officer called to Washington. When Steele is given orders to report to Washington, the camera focuses on the United States Capitol, then Gilbert Stuart's famous picture

Cavalry, Republic, 1936; Bob Steele. Note the Lincoln silhouette.

of George Washington and finally a silhouette of President Lincoln. Viewers then realize that Lincoln has sent for Steele. Lincoln speaks to Steele about a conspiracy of opportunists who want to sever large sections of the West from the United States and create an independent political empire. Steele is to be Lincoln's personal representative as he cooperates with the cavalry to put down the planned insurrection.

Presidents were not the only chief executives to receive favorable treatment in B Westerns. State governors often were portrayed in terms similar to those used for presidents. *King of the Arena* (Universal, 1933) with Ken Maynard and *King of the Cowboys* (Republic, 1943) are excellent examples of films depicting strong gubernatorial leadership.

King of the Arena opens with the governor conferring with police agencies of the state. A new kind of crime wave known as the "black death" (the victims' blood is congealed and the corpses turn black) is inundating the state. The governor is very concerned, and he forces the law enforcement leaders to acknowledge that they are baffled by the crimes and have no good leads on the culprits. The governor's manner is very formal and his tone of voice very harsh as he deals with the bureaucrats who are unable to solve the crime.

When the governor's secretary interrupts to tell him that Ken Morley (Ken Maynard) of the Rangers has arrived, the governor dismisses the others by telling them he is turning the case over to the Rangers. When Ken enters the room, the governor's whole demeanor changes. The governor is friendly, even informal with Ken. Ken, while respectful of the governor, takes a chair immediately next to the governor's desk and converses with him on a more intimate level than did the state bureaucrats.

The governor listens intently as Ken explains why he thinks a connection exists between a traveling circus in which Ken used to be a trick rider and the "black death." Ken even produces a map to demonstrate that the "black death" happens in cities near where the circus has played. Convinced that Ken is on to something, the governor instructs him to join the circus, act undercover as the governor's special representative and catch those responsible for the "black death."

The images in these opening scenes are interesting. State law enforcement agencies using normal police methods and acting as state bureaucracies are unable to stop the "black death." That is not good enough for an activist governor so he turns to a Ranger. The police bureaucrats scoff at the notion that a Ranger could have success fighting modern criminals. The wise governor knows better, however, so he listens to Ken and is persuaded that the circus holds an important clue to the "black death." Presumably if the governor had been less energetic, citizens of the state would have continued to be victimized by the criminals who employed the "black death" and constantly outsmarted state police agencies.

The governor summons Roy Rogers and Smiley Burnette from a wild west show in *King of the Cowboys*. While World War II rages in Europe and the Pacific, saboteurs are blowing up important communications facilities and defense plants in the state. The governor has tried special agents and other means to learn the identity of the saboteurs, but all of his efforts have failed. Beside himself, the governor pleads with Roy to work undercover for him in tracking down the culprits. Roy can't say no to the governor so he agrees to leave the wild west show and to work undercover for the governor.

The governor gives Roy his private number and orders Roy to telephone him only on that line. It is a dangerous assignment and the governor tells Roy that his last agent was killed while trying to telephone the governor. But before the agent was killed, he was able to say "following Mary." Both Roy and the governor believe that expression is an important clue, but neither knows what it means.

Roy and Burnette take jobs as waiters and dishwashers in a small cafe.

When two women from a tent show stop by the cafe for dinner, they tell him that trouble seems to follow the tent show as buildings keep blowing up in cities in which they are playing. One of them uses the expression "following Mary" and Roy realizes that there is a connection between the tent show and the sabotage.

Roy and Frog get jobs with the tent show and quickly learn that one of the acts, Maurice, is really a front for identifying sabotage targets. Roy calls the governor, but his private secretary (Lloyd Corrigan, who seems somewhat miscast as the brains behind the sabotage ring) learns that the governor has agreed to meet Roy, who will disclose the identity of the saboteurs. The secretary arranges to have the governor's car wrecked and the accident nearly kills the governor.

As the governor lies in a coma on the verge of death, Roy and Frog are able to apprehend the saboteurs and stop the destruction of war-related facilities. Clearly Roy Rogers is the hero of this entertaining B Western, but the image of an activist governor who takes a hands-on approach to stopping the saboteurs is a lasting legacy of the film.

Some Westerns made the connection between a trustworthy government working to solve the common person's problems by introducing a federal agency. Normally the hero was either a governmental employee or one called upon by a federal official to engage in a special mission. The films often open with scenes of lawlessness and then make a transition to a building nameplate proclaiming "Department of Treasury" or "Bureau of Indian Affairs." The setting is the office of one who looks like a government official. That person explains the situation to the hero, who is expected to act for the agency. Here is no bureaucrat interested in turf battles and paper shuffling, but rather, a compassionate public servant concerned about the victims of frontier violence.

Three examples will help to illustrate the point. *Dude Cowboy* (RKO, 1941) opens with Byron Foulger as Frank Adams, a Treasury Department engraver, being kidnapped. The next shot shows an office nameplate that reads:

U.S. Secret Service
Treasury Department

Dennis Moore reports to his chief (Earle Hodgins). Hodgins' role is a bit different from the snake oil salesman and con artist characters normally associated with his career. Moore explains that counterfeit five-dollar bills have been circulating in Nevada. Moore is sure that Foulger has turned bad, but Hodgins examines the bills under a microscope and concludes that they contain clues that Foulger is being held against his will.

Hodgins sends Tim Holt to work undercover on a dude ranch as he tries to rescue Foulger and bring the kidnappers to justice. Hodgins makes clear to Holt that he is as concerned for the safety of the engraver as he is in stopping the circulation of counterfeit money. Hodgins' character is certainly a compassionate civil servant.

The Law Rides Again, (Monogram, 1943) begins in a manner not unlike *Dude Cowboy*. The opening scene depicts Indian raids, all observed by Emmett Lynn, a frontier scout who reports to his superior. Viewers are introduced to the superior and his association with federal authority via the sign over his office:

> U.S. Commissioner
> Territory of Arizona

The commissioner is concerned about the raids, and also puzzled about what is causing them. A man of decisive action who takes his governing responsibilities seriously, he dispenses Hoot Gibson and Ken Maynard, the Trail Blazers, to investigate.

Gene Autry uses an interesting device to establish federal authority in *Whirlwind*, (Columbia, 1951). As the film opens, Gene holds up a stagecoach, taking only the mail bag. A mile or so down the road, another gang of outlaws stop the stagecoach only to discover that it had already been robbed. Then after another mile or so, Gene stops it again and returns the mailbag to the coach.

The next scene shows Autry climbing a telegraph pole and tapping out a message. Now a ticker tape rolls across the screen: **Chief Inspector Post Office Department Washington D.C.** The message goes on to explain that he has foiled a stagecoach holdup and will join Burnette at the next location. By that device, viewers realize that Autry works for the post office department and that federal authority is on the trail of a group of outlaws raiding federal mails.

Indian agents are the only notable exception to the dominate positive image of federal officials. Often — maybe even usually — Indian agents are portrayed as corrupt. They sell the Indians rancid beef and inferior goods, and make handsome profits by selling the good beef and quality merchandise to white people at higher prices. Quite often Indian agents were in cahoots with outlaws intent on stealing Indian land and/or ransacking their sacred burial grounds. The theme of corrupt Indian agents will be explored in greater depth in a later chapter, but for the present readers should recognize that corrupt Indian agents are the exception to the otherwise supportive portrayal of federal officials.

Westerns of the 1930s and 1940s are social journals, documentaries which tell us little about the real West of the latter half of the nineteenth century, but ones which are excellent records of American life in the middle quarter of the twentieth century. They helped a receptive public become comfortable with "big government."

B Westerns show frontier Americans—just as those watching them in the theaters—appealing to government for help in solving problems beyond their individual or collective ability. Furthermore, the films reinforced the belief of Americans that the federal government, headed by their champion Franklin D. Roosevelt, cared about them and wanted to help and to protect them.

If Alexis de Tocqueville had been traveling in the United States during the 1930s and '40s, he would have commented about the important place of motion pictures in shaping American attitudes. He might even have speculated about the manner in which Hollywood helped Americans make the transition from a society of individuals who formed private associations to attack common problems to a population which turned quickly to government for assistance with problems which seemed to get more complex—maybe even more intractable—each year.

Those alive at the opening of the twenty-first century are struck by another element. Americans of the 1930s and '40s approached their problems with the optimism that the federal government was a trustworthy ally. Unfortunately, contemporary Americans are no less dependent on "big government," but they are not inclined to share the early generations confidence in Washington, D.C. officialdom.

Chapter Five

"GUNPLAY IS THE GLORY OF THE WEST"

Film critic Robert Warshow observed that both gangster and cowboy movies, American film genres with a large worldwide following, have men with guns as their central focus (Warshow, 135). Warshow was surely correct about the central feature of Westerns: They unfold around the gun, and they are films about violence! Warshow's comments applied only to major Westerns. He dismissed the work of William S. Hart and Tom Mix as of little interest to adults and he confessed he had never seen a Roy Rogers or Gene Autry movie (Warshow, 141). Nevertheless, his comments about the Western's link to guns fit all types of Western movies.

It is hard to find a Western film without numerous violent acts such as fistfights, chases on horseback, gun battles with outlaws and Indians or at least one murder. It is even harder to envision a cowboy hero who did not wear a gun. Hoot Gibson may be the only one who did not consistently carry a revolver; however, he always managed to find one to tuck in his boot or belt at the crucial time. During 1944 and 1945, as Roy Rogers' Westerns became more musical, they downplayed guns, and often Rogers did not wear his double holstered set of pistols. But like Hoot Gibson, Rogers always was able to get a gun in order to bring the bad guys to justice.

While all of the rest of the cowboy heroes carried guns, including Roy Rogers for most of his career, they adhered to an unwritten cowboy code first employed by Tom Mix. The code required the cowboy hero never to use a gun when a rope or fists would do just as well. And, if the cowboy hero did use his gun, it was never to kill; he always tried to wound the villain.

The gun was only an instrument of violence — it was not an end in itself — and the cowboy hero had a varied arsenal of weapons. Always, however, he used violence.

Westerns forthrightly projected violence as a necessary — and generally acceptable — way to solve problems. They taught viewers to admire the cowboy hero who was a man of violence. Between 1930 and 1955, Western films portrayed violence as a tool used by honorable men for progressive purposes. After 1955, Hollywood was less certain about the efficacy of violence, and more inclined to treat heroes as troubled individuals who did not always use violence for noble reasons. But in the previous quarter-century, audiences sat in darkened theaters week after week learning that fistfights and shootouts were necessary, and that a man did what he had to do.

Who in those 25 years prior to 1955 could have doubted the centrality of violence in American life? The 1930s featured gangsters, armed clashes in rural America over farm foreclosures, brutal confrontations between young aggressive labor organizers and leaders of industry determined to thwart the growth of labor unions, and lynchings in the South, Southwest and Border States. It seemed that violence was inherent in the human condition. If good men failed to use violence, evil would surely triumph.

Violence committed by evil men was regarded as part of fallen humanity. Good guys, (it was always clear in Westerns who the good guys were) had to use violence if evil men were to be prevented from corrupting and endangering society. Indeed, good guys were expected to use violence as well as, if not better than, the bad guys in order to stop the evil. Audiences cheered when the good guys won, and they took it as a sign that all was right in the world when the bad guys were lying dead in the street.

Above all, Westerns projected violence as socially necessary — but they also presented it as manly virtue. Ken Maynard declared to his lady boss from the East in the 1932 film *Come On, Tarzan* (Worldwide, 1932), "Gunplay is the glory of the West." She could not understand Ken's hatred for those evil men who were slaughtering wild horses for dog food. When he threatens to shoot the main villain, his boss (in good Eastern fashion) decries the use of violence in the West. Maynard does not defend violence as social necessity, he responds to her by invoking the glory of the West, and, implicitly, violence as a manly virtue. The careers of Billy the Kid, Wyatt Earp and other historical figures were consciously misrepresented so that their violent and often illegal deeds could be cast in the most virtuous light.

Aversion to guns and violence as the means to settle disputes was associated in Westerns with feminine characteristics. It even takes a humorous twist in *Hard Hombre* (Allied, 1931). Hoot Gibson plays the proper son Peaceful Tolliver, who never wears a gun and scrupulously avoids fights, all to please a mother who wants her son to grow up as a peaceful man. Hoot is scorned by the men as a sissy, a mommy's boy who won't behave as a real western man.

In the 1931 Fox version of *Riders of the Purple Sage* Marguerite Churchill makes George O'Brien give up his guns. Even though outlaws have driven off her cattle and killed her cowboys, she doesn't resort to violence until the outlaws kidnap her young ward, Faye Larkin; she then gives O'Brien his guns back as he goes to rescue the young girl. Churchill can't relate to violence as a manly virtue and she won't permit violence to protect her property, but she recognizes that violence is necessary to prevent harm to Faye Larkin.

In *Blue Canadian Rockies* (Columbia, 1952), Gene Autry and Pat Buttram journey to Canada to help dude ranch owner Gail Davis, discover why she is having so much trouble with a nearby lumber company. When they arrive at the ranch, Autry and Buttram learn that "no guns" is one of the ranch rules. Davis takes their rifles and sidearms and locks them in a chest. Buttram's protest that he feels naked without his gun is a good commentary on the close association between the cowboy hero and guns.

As the film reaches its climax, lumberjacks who have been falsely accused of stirring up trouble raid the dude ranch. When Gene, Pat and the other guests try to retrieve their guns from the locked chest, they discover that someone has stolen them. In an effort to prevent violence by confiscating the guns, Gail Davis has simply rendered the ranch unable to defend itself.

All ends well, however, as Autry is able to convince the lumberjacks and Davis that some third party is for unknown reasons stirring up trouble between the lumber camp and the dude ranch. Gene is then able to unmask Tom London, the former partner of Davis's father, who is out to get revenge on his former partner by angering the lumber men so they will destroy the dude ranch. Davis' feminine aversion to guns and violence almost permitted London's scheme to work!

Jean Arthur, who plays Mrs. Starrett in *Shane* (Paramount, 1953), is also opposed to guns. When Alan Ladd as Shane, the ex-gunfighter, comes to live with the Starretts, young Joey Starrett, played so realistically by Brandon De Wilde, is fascinated by Shane and asks him to demonstrate how to use a gun. (Joey's gun is an old rifle which doesn't work!) Shane shows Joey how to wear a gunbelt properly for a fast draw and how to shoot. But Mrs. Starrett asks Shane to quit; she does not want young Joey to learn about guns or to idolize gunfighters.

In a sense, the portrayal of violence in Westerns prior to 1955 is much more harmful than in post–1955 Westerns. Pre–1955 Westerns possess innocence because they lack realism; people did not bleed, even when shot at close range by a .44 caliber handgun. *Shane* was a groundbreaking film in that regard. A.B. Guthrie, the well-known novelist, wrote the screenplay and served as a consultant on the film, and he convinced director George Stevens that if Jack Palance had really shot Elisha Cook, Jr., from close range, Cook would not merely crumple to the ground; he would be blown back several feet by the impact of the bullet. As a result of Guthrie's advice, Stevens had Cook wired so that when Palance fired, Cook went flying backwards and made the scene look real.*

Few believed that violence was any more accurately portrayed than were the many films about Billy the Kid historically accurate. In the youthful innocence of the times, one did not need to see blood splattered over the sidewalk or intestines oozing out of the stomach in order to believe that a person had been shot. Seldom was one asked to consider the physical act of violence, or even the violence itself.

About the same time Edwin S. Porter was cranking out *The Great Train Robbery* (Edison, 1903), the German sociologist Max Weber was trying to make sense out of a rapidly changing modern society (Freund). As the twentieth century dawned, life had become more complex, bureaucracy more pervasive, and government more inclusive; yet, people seemed no less willing to obey authority than in earlier, less complicated times. Weber wanted to understand the casual acceptance of authority. Why, he puzzled, do people so readily acknowledge the authority of other people? Why do most of us, in some fashion, obey those in power.

Karl Marx answered those questions by developing the idea of false consciousness. According to Marx, those who control the means of production on which workers depend for their livelihoods also control government, media and other cultural agents such as the church. Marx believed that social institutions reinforced the property owners' claims to power by creating in the rest of the population a sense that society should be ordered as it is. According to Marx, workers then had a false consciousness and obeyed the ruling class because they didn't know what else to do. Weber thought that Marx's approach was too simple. There was more to modern society than social classes. Marx's simple class model and

---

*Thomas Ford — who was then a member of the English Department at the University of Houston — told me this story (which Guthrie had told him when the two men corresponded) during an annual meeting of the Popular Culture Association in Chicago, April 1994.

impending class conflict which would usher in a new social structure was rejected by Weber, who sought a more complex rationale for authority.

When Weber wrote at the beginning of the twentieth century, governments all over Europe had become larger and more involved in regulating people's lives. Yet Weber understood that government was but one source of authority. Family groups, church and corporations all exercised some form of control over citizens. Each group, he argued, wants habitual obedience; each wants individuals to regard its authority as legitimate and comply with its directives.

The problem Weber sought to understand was how to establish and sustain that authority. Weber did not believe violence could do it; neither did he accept the Marxist explanation of false consciousness. Weber believed that authority required a permanent, ongoing basis which linked it to a habit of obedience. He suggested three distinct sources for habitually obeyed authority: charisma, tradition and rational-legal arrangements (Coser and Rosenberg, 129–134). Although probably most screenwriters and directors of B Westerns had never heard of Max Weber, they incorporated all three types of authority into Westerns as a means of distinguishing legitimate from illegitimate violence.

According to Weber, charismatic authority is one possible reason why people follow a popular leader. In recent years, the term "charismatic" has been associated with religious people who speak in tongues or politicians and entertainers who skillfully use the media to develop a mass following. Citizens are attracted to a charismatic politician because of his or her personality and public image, not necessarily because of widespread public acceptance of the policies they espouse.

That is not exactly what Weber meant by charisma. Rather, he meant that a charismatic person possesses special, even superhuman insights or characteristics. The charismatic leader's insights might stem from other worldly sources such as a religious leader like Jesus, or they might come from special qualities with which only a few human beings were endowed. Clearly the cowboy hero is an example of the latter. He was a charismatic leader whose larger-than-life attributes meant that when he spoke people listened, and when he acted he did so because he saw connections among events and between events and people that less gifted men and women failed to comprehend. When the cowboy hero used violence, he did so with an authority flowing from his charismatic appeal; his use of violence thus was legitimate.

Jon Tuska in *The Filming of the West* devotes two chapters to what he calls the Autry fantasy. Tuska contends that Gene Autry was successful as a cowboy hero not because he looked like a rugged cowboy star as did

Buck Jones or Ken Maynard, but because he created a fantasy world in which a self-assured Gene Autry could nonchalantly sing his way through trouble. In Autry's fantasy world, people instinctively follow Gene's leadership because he is a natural leader who believes in reason, or a song, rather than violence, to settle disputes. But if he has to use violence — and in nearly all of his Westerns he does—Autry can use it better than other men.

While Tuska's claims about the Autry fantasy are accurate, they should not be limited to Gene Autry. Nearly all of the cowboy heroes relied on a similar fantasy. Each developed the image of a bigger-than-life cowboy hero who possessed charismatic qualities similar to those of Gene Autry. The slender frames of Autry, Roy Rogers and Rex Allen, in contrast to the more imposing physical characteristics of Buck Jones, Ken Maynard and Tom Tyler, may have made the fantasy of a charismatic cowboy harder to swallow, but most of the cowboy heroes, in the final analysis, relied on the fantasy of a charismatic leader to whom other people looked for help.

Roy Rogers' films, in particular, are good case studies of the charismatic cowboy. Initially, Rogers was relatively unknown, a slight-of-build, poor imitation of Gene Autry. He was not charismatic, and most of his early films made little pretense that he was. In some of them, *Young Bill Hickok* (Republic, 1940), *Young Buffalo Bill* (Republic, 1940) and *The Ranger and the Lady* (Republic, 1940), for instance, he played historical figures; hence, his charismatic authority came from his character role not his person. Even when he used his own name for the character he played, as in *The Saga of Death Valley* (Republic, 1939), the name Roy Rogers carried no particular meaning. He had to establish his credibility as the plot unfolded.

Gradually his role began to change. By 1941, Rogers had become a popular cowboy hero whose movies were attracting a following. Often his character was Roy Rogers, a nationally known radio singer returning home to be honored as in *Red River Valley* (Republic, 1941) or helping a young fan in trouble as in *Riding Down the Canyon* (Republic, 1942). The movies' plots would then develop from those opening conventions.

From that point, it was easy to make his screen character and his person synonymous. By 1945, he was Roy Rogers, King of the Cowboys. In various Westerns he portrayed a sheriff, an entertainer, a newspaper editor or a rancher, but always he was Roy Rogers, a person respected, trusted and revered by all who knew him. In *Home in Oklahoma* (Republic, 1946), Rogers plays a small town newspaper editor who, along with Dale Evans, proves that Sam Talbot, owner of the Flying T Ranch, was murdered and did not die in an accident as all had supposed. He was a Ranger in *Heldorado*

(Republic, 1946) and a border investigator in *Bells of San Angelo* (Republic, 1947). In both films, however, he is presented as someone who stands apart from the rest of the people, someone they look to for leadership. In *On the Old Spanish Trail* (Republic, 1947), Roy gets involved in the plot because he co-signed a banknote for Bob Nolan and the Sons of the Pioneers. Now he must come up with $10,000 or lose his ranch. Because he is Roy Rogers, the sheriff gives him extra time to raise the money, and the Pioneers look to him as the one to help get them out of the mess. In each of these films, and all others he made from 1945 to the end of his movie career, Rogers' charismatic attractiveness was built into the plot.

In 1948, Rogers' movies, under the direction of William Witney, took a violent turn. Bloody fights, brutal murders and even cruelty to animals were written into the action. Fistfights were particularly realistic and quite graphic. Roy comes out of them the victor, but often with a torn shirt and cut face. Contrast this new trend with the vicious beating he took from David Sharpe in *The Bells of San Angelo*—a beating from which he escaped relatively unscathed. Later on, for example, in *Night Time in Nevada* (Republic, 1948) and *In Old Amarillo* (Republic, 1951), Roy had very brutal, graphic fights with Grant Withers and Roy Barcroft. And, in each case he looked as if he had been in a fight. Now even Roy, on occasion, had to shoot to kill. By that time, however, Rogers had become the best known of all the cowboy heroes. Billed by Republic as the King of the Cowboys, he had become a charismatic figure. When he became more violent, it was within the bounds of his charisma, making the violence legitimate.

Another source of authority, and the one furthest removed from charisma, is rational-legal authority. Bureaucracy, Weber noted, is the predominate form of authority in Europe and the United States. Bureaucracies are structured around rules, offices and positions. Bureaucrats hold positions of authority in a particular office, and they have a right to use that authority as long as it is exercised within the guidelines created by the bureaucracy.

Policemen are employed by a bureaucracy such as a city's police department or the state police organization. Their function is to enforce the law, but they must do so within the rules established by the Congress, state legislatures, city councils or their own organization. Most law enforcement organizations have rules governing the appropriate use of firearms in pursuit of suspected felons. Policemen act legitimately as long as they use their authority—even their firearms—within the rules. Weber called that rational-legal authority.

Rational-legal authority regularly justified the use of violence in Westerns, for quite often cowboy heroes were connected with some organization which gave them a legal right to use violence. They portrayed sheriffs, United States marshals and officials of quasi-public organizations such as the Cattlemen's Protective Association. Because of those formal positions of authority, the cowboy heroes use of violence was legitimate.

Lash LaRue and his sidekick Fuzzy Q. Jones were normally United States marshals, as was Allan "Rocky" Lane in many of his Westerns. More often than not, in his Monogram programmers Johnny Mack Brown was either a federal marshal or an official of some quasi-public association. Unlike Autry, Rogers or William Boyd as Hopalong Cassidy, LaRue, Lane and Brown did not rely on charisma to justify their use of violence; it came from their official position which required them to enforce the law and to use violence if necessary.

Frisco Tornado (Republic, 1950) is one of the best Rocky Lane Westerns. The movie opens with one of the stagecoaches of Eddy Waller— playing his normal character Nugget Clark— being wrecked and the driver and shotgun guard murdered. Waller suspects Stephen Chase, a leading citizen of the town as well as its insurance salesman, of being behind the holdups, but he can't prove it. When the sheriff is murdered, Waller asks the federal government for help and Rocky Lane is sent to look into the situation.

When Waller tells Chase that a deputy federal marshal will be arriving in town the next day, a marshal who has cleaned up several towns, Chase responds that he must be quite a man. But note, it is not Rocky Lane as such who is revered; rather it is Rocky Lane, federal marshal, who draws respect. The name Rocky Lane has no particular meaning to Waller, Chase or anybody else in town. It is Lane's authority as a federal marshal that is sought, not his personal charisma. On his way into town, Lane is bushwhacked by Chase's henchmen, who steal his identification papers. Again, that is a significant point for if Lane's legal authority is valued, he needs the papers to establish his identity as a peace officer, one who has the authority to use violence to rid the town of outlaws.

Chase is temporarily able to use the stolen papers to convince young Paul Ford, an attorney who works for Chase under the mistaken notion that Chase is honest, that Lane is an imposter and probably the brains behind the outlaws. All ends well, however, when Ford discovers the truth and helps Rocky Lane round up Chase and his gang.

Contrast *Frisco Tornado* with 1950s Westerns in which Roy Rogers appeared. In films such as *Bells of Coronado* (Republic, 1950) and *Twilight in the Sierras* (Republic, 1950), Rogers held positions of authority such as a parole officer or insurance company investigator; but his legal authority fades into the background as he becomes Roy Rogers, a charismatic

The Savage Frontier, Republic, 1953; Allan "Rocky" Lane. Lane's marshal's badge denotes his formal authority.

individual known and respected by the community. That element is absent in the Lane programmer. It is Lane's legal authority, not his personal charisma, which gives him the authority to act.

A pattern similar to the one in *Frisco Tornado* can be found in several of Lash LaRue's Westerns. In *Outlaw Country* (Screen Guild, 1949), Lash and his sidekick Fuzzy Q. Jones, played as always by Al St. John, are being chased by a sheriff's posse. After they elude the posse, Lash and Fuzzy discover that Lash looks like an outlaw known as the Frontier Phantom. As United States marshals, Lash and Fuzzy have been ordered to report to their superior at an old ghost town. Once there, Lash has to fight several men who try to block his entrance into the building. His superior has staged the fights in order to see whether or not Lash is the right man to go after the Frontier Phantom.

LaRue has to prove his ability with his fists and his whip; only then is his superior satisfied. The name, Lash LaRue, has no particular charisma attached to it in this film; by whipping the men placed in his way Lash proves he is the man for the job. Nor do the outlaws stand in fear of the name Lash LaRue, they fear his authority as a United States marshal and they try to kill him for that reason.

King of the Bullwhip (Western Adventure, 1951) is a favorite Lash LaRue movie of many B Western fans. Lash and Fuzzy have been ordered to a town terrorized by a whip-carrying outlaw known as El Azote, who is portrayed by Dennis Moore. The newspaper editor publishes the news that two federal marshals are on their way to town and, not surprisingly, outlaws try to bushwhack them.

As the action unfolds, it is clear that the name Lash LaRue carries no special meaning. It is not LaRue the bad guys fear, it is his authority as a marshal. Because no one in the town knows Lash, he is able to join the outlaws and, working undercover, unmask El Azote in a slam-bang bullwhip fight at the film's climax.

Frisco Tornado starring Rocky Lane and the two LaRue Westerns are good examples of the cowboy hero relying on organizational authority and not his personal charisma to justify the use of violence to bring the bad guys to justice. The cowboy hero's use of violence was rooted in his job to protect innocent people. It was a legitimate use of violence because his job required it.

Weber believed that the final source of socially accepted violence was tradition. By tradition, Weber meant an appeal to what had always existed. Social customs, such as the right to protect one's property, or social relationships, such as the important place of the family in American life, are obvious sources of traditional authority. People clearly have a right to use violence to protect their property or their loved ones.

In Westerns, the traditional role of father as an authority figure for the family and defender of the family unit was constantly reinforced. And members of the family unit possessed a legitimate right to seek revenge if a family member was injured or murdered. Many of the films Robert North Bradbury directed for his son Bob Steele and for John Wayne opened with the murder of a parent or brother, and required pursuit of the murderers by the cowboy hero, normally with only marginal reference to lawful procedures for apprehending the guilty person.

Smoky Smith (Supreme, 1935) opens with Steele escorting his parents across a barren desert. When he rides ahead to scout, outlaws led by Warner Richmond attack the wagon and kill Steele's parents. When Steele rides after them, they shoot him and leave him for dead in the desert. But Earl Dwire, who vacates his normal villainous role to play a sheriff in this Steele programmer, rescues Steele. After Dwire nurses Steele back to health, the young man becomes Dwire's deputy and the scourge of every outlaw in the area. Steele, however, is preoccupied with tracking down his parents' killers. He finds Richmond and kills him. In this film, as opposed to *Frisco Tornado* or *Outlaw Country*, Steele's legal authority as a deputy sheriff is secondary; it is the excuse that permits him to search for Richmond. And when Steele finds Richmond, his legal authority becomes secondary to a loyal son's revenge on the one who murdered his parents.

West of the Divide (Monogram, 1934) is an excellent John Wayne Monogram programmer; Robert North Bradbury not only directed, but also wrote the story and screenplay. The film opens with Wayne and George Hayes reminiscing about the conditions under which Hayes found Wayne 12 years before. A man with an unforgettable laugh had murdered Wayne's father and left young Wayne for dead. Hayes rescued the young lad, nursed him back to health and now, 12 years later, both Wayne and Hayes are back looking for the killer and for Wayne's younger brother. By film's end, Wayne has his revenge and discovers that a badly abused young boy was really his kid brother. True to B Westerns and Max Weber's notion that tradition gave Wayne the authority to act, Wayne avenged his father's murder and reunited the family by finding his missing brother.

Buck Jones' *Ivory Handled Guns* (Universal, 1935) pushed the theme of family loyalty to its extreme. Jones's father had been wounded by the Wolverine Kid, played by Walter Miller (the ace villain of Jones' films), and had become a wheelchair-bound cripple. The old man (Carl Stockdale) is obsessed with revenge. He blames Pat Moore, a rival suitor for Jones' mother, for his condition and he won't be satisfied until both Moore and the Wolverine Kid are dead. The Wolverine Kid carries one of two ivory-handled pistols and Jones carries the other one, hence the film's title.

After an interesting story involving a cattle versus sheep feud and the Wolverine Kid's personal vendetta against Jones, the film climaxes with Jones killing the Wolverine Kid in Jones' ranch house while the old man watches. However, instead of rejoicing over the death of an old enemy, Stockdale and viewers are left anxiously suspended as the film ends because Jones has been wounded as well. Will Jones recover? Will he, like his father, be a cripple, another victim of the other ivory-handled gun? The film never answers the question, but it does suggest that revenge — even for the wrongful injury of a family member — has its limits. The gun battle between Miller and Jones at the film's climax exceeded those limits.

An earlier Jones programmer, *The Fighting Ranger* (Universal, 1934) stresses family loyalty as well. Jones and his brother Bob (Paddy O'Flynn) are Texas Rangers in this entertaining Western. When Jones and his pal Thunder, (Frank Rice) leave Bob in town while they go on an assignment, the Cougar kills Bob. When the Cougar escapes over the border, he is

5. "Gunplay Is the Glory of the West" 111

West of the Divide, Monogram, 1933; George Hayes, Blackie Whiteford, John Wayne, Lloyd Whitlock and Billy O'Brien. Wayne finds the man who killed his parents and reunites with his younger brother.

beyond the reach of the Rangers. Jones, however, can't ignore his brother's death or let his killers go unapprehended.

Jones and Rice resign from the Rangers and journey across the border, pretending to be on the run from the law. When Jones tells the Cougar he knows of a rich bank waiting to be plucked, the Cougar takes him into the gang. At film's end, Jones successfully lures the Cougar and his gang back into Texas. The Rangers are waiting for them and round up the entire gang while Jones chases down and captures the Cougar. His brother's death has been avenged, even though Jones had to temporarily leave the Rangers to accomplish his personal mission.

Max Weber's approach is helpful for it offers one possible way in which to distinguish legitimate from illegitimate violence. But it is not enough. Charismatic, legal or traditional authority stress the personal attributes of the cowboy star; they give him the right to use violence. It is personal authority. His charismatic appeal, legal authority or membership in a traditional group, such as a family, made the cowboy hero's use of force defensible. Viewers acknowledge his right to use violence because he possesses unique insights, legal authority or the moral force associated with traditional social roles.

However, violence in Westerns, even B Westerns, is more complex than simply the cowboy hero's use of force. Viewers evaluate violence to a great extent by the way it relates to the situation unfolding on the screen. If a family member is murdered, cattle rustled or a bank robbed, law-abiding folks can use violence to apprehend the bad guys. For example, *The Cimarron Kid* (Universal-International, 1951) has Audie Murphy playing a young Bill Doolin. Doolin joins the infamous Dalton gang as they plan to rob two banks in Coffeyville, Kansas. When the attempted robberies are botched, the town's citizens shoot it out with the Daltons and kill several members of the gang. No one in the audience doubted that the citizens of Coffeyville did the right thing. The situation, or plot, justified their violence as much as did the personal characteristics of the cowboy hero legitimate his use of violence. Violence then must also be understood by how it relates to the plot.

B Westerns used three elements to define the plot and to give the viewer clues as to whether or not the use of violence was legitimate. Those elements are: purpose for which the violence was used, nature of the times in which it was employed, and rules of the game by which the cowboy hero used violence.

The purpose behind violence in B Westerns is very important. Violence used for socially unacceptable goals, usually by evil men, was illegitimate and wrong. Violence was essential to the film, however, for it triggered the plot and the cowboy hero's appearance on the screen. Familiar conventions such as bank robbery, a stagecoach holdup, a sheriff shot or a rancher murdered because of gold or some other precious mineral on his land were used countless times to establish the need for the cowboy hero. Illegitimate uses of violence by the bad guys justified society's use of violence.

In the face of such enemies, the cowboy hero had to use violence, but he used it for a different purpose. He worked for peace and justice. While the cowboy hero's methods differed, purpose ultimately made his use of violence socially acceptable.

Generally, the cowboy hero sought justice by working within a legal framework, and even when he was not a peace officer, the cowboy hero cooperated with them in order to capture the outlaws and to put them in jail, not to work his personal vengeance. Even when the plot is about the murder of a family member and the cowboy hero's determined pursuit of the killers, the hero seldom becomes so obsessed with tracking down the killers that he wantonly disregards their rights to due process of law. He may kill the villain at film's end in a shoot-out, or some accident may happen such as the bad guy falling off of a cliff, but it is always in the context of self-defense. B Western cowboy heroes are not neurotically obsessed with revenge.

Perhaps the best way to understand how the plot justified violence is to examine a Western in which the cowboy hero, driven by revenge, is not a person whom viewers can easily admire because his use of violence is morally tainted. William Elliott plays Shadrach Jones in Republic's bigger-budget *Showdown* (Republic, 1950). The film opens as Jones is digging in a graveyard. Walter Brennan as Capt. MacKellar, owner of a large cattle ranch, and Henry Morgan as gunfighting cowboy Rod Main interrupt his work. In the dialogue that follows, we learn that Jones' brother had come to the area with a large sum of money with which to buy a ranch. Jones was coming to join him when he learned that a person fitting his brother's description had been found on the trail murdered. Jones is digging up the grave to see if his brother is buried in it.

When Jones discovers that it is his brother's grave, he becomes obsessed with finding the murderer. Complicating the plot, Capt. MacKellar's cowboys learn that Jones had been a member of the Texas State Police. Here Republic Studio borrows from its rich film tradition of Westerns in which the state police were pawns of carpetbagger politicians out to rob honest Texans of their property. Even though Elliott assures the cowboys he is no longer a member of the organization nor condoned everything the state police did, the cowboys are not satisfied and a gunfight appears eminent. MacKellar intervenes and saves Jones from certain death.

Two events trigger the plot. First, Jones is forced to kill MacKellar's foreman. The man was wanted by the state police and he disregards Jones' statement that he is no longer hunting him. MacKellar offers the trail boss job to Jones, who declines until he receives change from the bartender for a drink. Part of the money is a bill Jones knew his brother was carrying. Jones quickly agrees to trail boss the herd and forbids any of MacKellar's men to quit. Jones knows the murderer works for the outfit and he intends to find him and kill him.

As the trail drive progresses, Jones' behavior toward the men is harsh. He pushes and goads them to the breaking point. When Dutch, a favorite with the cowboys, becomes ill, Jones seems not to notice. Since Dutch did not tell him he was sick, Jones insists that he ride night herd like everybody else. Dutch's death adds to the hostility existing between the cowboys and Jones.

MacKellar pleads with Jones to give up his search for the killer.

MacKellar assures Jones that there is such a thing as divine retribution. It matters not if Jones finds the killer, God knows who he is and retribution will eventually work out the killer's punishment. Jones is neither persuaded by retribution nor convinced to give up his search, so the trail drive continues from one confrontation to another between Jones and the trail crew.

Jones becomes convinced that Mike Shattay (William Ching) is the murderer. Mike never takes off his boots, and since Jones' brother was killed by a small derringer, Jones assumes that Mike has the weapon hidden in one of his boots. When the cattle reach a deep river, Jones orders the men to strip down to their long johns to swim across. When all of the men except Mike take off their boots, Jones is more convinced than ever that he has found the killer, so he forcibly pulls off Mike's boots. To everybody's horror — including Jones — Mike has a deformed foot and leg. He wears a brace and has learned to walk without a limp, but Mike remains ashamed that he is a cripple. He never removed his boots because he did not want anyone to see the leg brace.

Jones appears sobered by the experience and tells MacKellar he is giving up the search; he is going to let retribution settle the score. MacKellar is pleased and as the trail herd is starting to move, he goes to the aid of a young calf caught in some rocks. The calf's mother — protecting her offspring — gores MacKellar and he knows he is about to die. He pleads with Jones to shoot him and when Jones won't do it, MacKellar shows Jones the derringer with which he killed Jones' brother. They had been playing poker and Jones' brother had won all of MacKellar's money, so MacKellar killed him to get it back. Smiling, MacKellar tells Jones there was more to that retribution business than he had thought. Jones' response is disappointing. He won't kill MacKellar and he won't let MacKellar have whiskey to relieve his suffering. Instead, pointing to the buzzards circling above, Jones tells MacKellar that he is going to leave him to a slow death. Probably, Jones notes, the buzzards won't wait until he is completely dead to start picking over his corpse.

As Jones goes back to his horse, he throws away the derringer with which MacKellar had killed his brother, and he drops a small jeweled cross which had belonged to Dutch. Mike picks up the cross and tells Jones he should throw it away as well. Mike is Jones' conscience, pointing out that Jones' obsession with revenge has made him less than human. There is little noble in Jones' use of violence; he was not much less a murderer than MacKellar. Mike's sermon has its intended impact: Jones gives Mike a bottle of whiskey to take to MacKellar. Whiskey will at least relieve the suffering until he dies from internal bleeding.

By the film's end, Elliott has been saved from his self-destructive mission of revenge. But for most of the footage, his character is not one viewers admire. He is a man insensitive to those around him, a man who pushes the cowboys beyond the limits of human endurance, and a man who shows little concern for the welfare or feelings of anyone. Elliott's pursuit of personal revenge makes this a troubling film, an exception among B Westerns.

Elliott's desire to avenge his brother's murder is a laudable goal and it is one used often in Westerns. Elliott's intent to commit another crime — the murder of the one who murdered his brother — and the harsh manner in which he treats the trail crew makes Elliott's character, Shadrach Jones, less than admirable. The motive for violence, then, looms large in Westerns. Elliott was motivated by revenge, not justice, hence his use of violence is unacceptable. Two bigger-budget Westerns, *The Ox Bow Incident* (20th Century–Fox, 1943) and *The Virginian* (Paramount, 1946) are also good case studies of how motive can make a difference in evaluating the legitimacy of violence.

In *The Ox Bow Incident*, the mob, turned into a posse by a deputy who exceeded his authority, is motivated by revenge for a murder viewers learn later did not happen. Furthermore, the community has a sheriff and judge, but the mob was unwilling to wait for the legal process to run its course, and they hang the wrong three men. At the film's end, Henry Fonda reads from the letter Dana Andrews (one of the lynching victims) wrote to his wife. In it, Andrews expresses the need for all men to respect the law as the core of civilized society. And, he argues, when any group of men take one law into their hands, they have violated the entire law.

In Paramount's 1946 version of *The Virginian*, Joel McCrea, the Virginian, catches Steve, his best friend, with rustled cattle and he hangs him. There were no courts in the territory so even the most respected men in the community condoned the act. At first glance the primary distinction between the two films is that the mob made a mistake. That mistake was not made in *The Virginian;* the guilty man was in fact punished. But probing further, there is even a more basic difference between the two films. Justice motivated the Virginian, revenge the mob. In *The Ox Bow Incident* there was no reason to hang the men. Lawful ways of dealing with them, ways which permitted the accused to establish their innocence, were in place. Those avenues did not exist in *The Virginian*. In that film, the West was depicted as raw frontier without legal structures.

El Paso (Paramount, 1948) illustrates that the line between justice and revenge is not always clear, however. John Payne plays Clay Fletcher, a Charleston, South Carolina, lawyer who goes to El Paso after the Civil War in search of his girlfriend. He discovers that Sterling Hayden, head of the El Paso Land Association, controls the sheriff and judge and rules the town.

Fletcher tries to use the law, but he decides it is a futile effort when the judge is murdered. Gathering together a band of vigilantes, Fletcher tells them that when the scales of justice get out of balance, a gun will help to rectify the imbalance. The vigilantes begin a series of raids and lynchings. But they mistakenly kill an innocent man, a new minister who came to El Paso to open a church. This is too much for Fletcher's grandfather, Judge Fletcher, played by H. B. Warner. The old man had come to El Paso in search of his grandson, and is dismayed to learn of his vigilante activities.

In a moving speech, Judge Fletcher reminds his grandson that as a lawyer he is sworn to uphold the law. The old man scoffs when Clay Fletcher protests that they are upholding the rights of the people. The rights of the people, Judge Fletcher tells his grandson, have been the rallying call for hoodlums throughout history. Judge Fletcher convinces the men to work for legally established courts of justice. He even promises to act as an intermediary with Hayden.

But the old man is murdered, and Fletcher leads the vigilantes on a final showdown with Hayden and his henchmen. Hayden is killed. The henchmen are rounded up and about to be lynched when Fletcher stops the vigilantes. He argues that mob rule is bad, and he asks the vigilantes who or what will try them someday. In the end, Fletcher convinces his men of the need to establish courts that will try the accused in a lawful manner.

In *El Paso*, as in *The Virginian*, justice began as the motivating factor. When it deteriorated into vigilante-driven revenge, Judge Fletcher brought the issue back into perspective. Although the judge was killed, his grandson was able to make a strong case for legal justice at the film's climax. Even on the raw frontier, law and order within a legal system was a goal worth fighting for.

Justice, peace and family revenge, however, were not the only acceptable purposes. Violence was also legitimate if it advanced civilization. Most Westerns are set between 1870 and 1900, a time when the open range began to close, towns emerged and urban values began to displace the more individualistic frontier values. In dozens of Westerns, the hero, while understanding the old ways, sided with the forces of progress against the cattle rancher, the saloonkeeper and the Indian.

Abilene Town (United Artists, 1946) with Randolph Scott portrayed the clash between Kansas wheat farmers and the cattlemen who would not accept closing the cattle trail and a civilized Abilene. The film ended with the saloon and brothel side of the street in shambles, and the cowboys riding away defeated because, as sheriff, Scott had supported the forces of progress. He had defended the wheat farmers in spite of the fact that most of his friends worked on the saloon-brothel side of the street. In addition, what Western movie fan can forget *Shane*, (Paramount, 1953) with Alan Ladd as the gunman who joined forces with the farmers because he recognized in them the future of the West. Progress, expressed as the onward march of American civilization, justified violence.

Personal honor can also justify violence. Violence is legitimate if one's manhood is threatened. A man does what he has to do! How many times has the cowboy hero gone out one more time to meet his adversary in a head-on gunfight because his honor was at stake? Actually, not quite as many as the image suggests. Far more Westerns ended with exciting chase scenes than with one-on-one confrontations between the cowboy hero and the bad guy. Some did, however, end in that fashion and they demonstrate quite vividly the use of violence to protect personal honor and reputation.

The classic main street confrontation may be found in the 1946 *The Virginian*, Brian Donlevy as Trampas gives Joel McCrea, the Virginian, until sundown to get out of town or he will shoot him on sight. McCrea spurns his friends' offer to help, replying that it is between the two of them. When Molly (Barbara Britton) protests that his sense of personal honor is childish and ridiculous. McCrea reminds her that Trampas called him out in front of other people. Trampas has gone too far and if McCrea is to ever again face his friends or even Molly, he will have to meet him on Main Street.

The end of *Shane* is similar to *The Virginian*. Alan Ladd, as Shane, knocks Van Heflin unconscious to keep him from going into town. Ben Johnson had warned Ladd that Ryker has laid a trap for Heflin. Certainly, Ladd took Heflin's place for mixed reasons. He wanted to protect Heflin's family who had been so kind to him, and he was in love with Heflin's wife, played by Jean Arthur. But as the film reaches its climax, it is equally clear that Ladd as Shane went into town for personal honor as well. Jack Palance's character, Wilson, was a gunfighter. A good one! Only Shane could stop him. The farmers were ineffective against Wilson. Shane's personal code required that he act, and for one more time, maybe the last time, Shane followed his code.

William Elliott's *The Savage Horde* (Republic, 1950) makes a similar statement about personal honor. At the film's end, Elliott as Ringo has the drop on the bad guys (including Bob Steele, playing the evil gunfighter, Dancer). Steele's response to Elliott is, "I don't take orders, I give them." At that point, Elliott, holstering his gun, replies to Steele, "I understand you like to count to three" Steele smiles and tells Ringo he might get lucky. Elliott beats Steele to the draw and kills him. Then, as if to further demonstrate his ability, Elliott turns to the rest and asks, "Anybody else?"

One of Lash LaRue's B Westerns has an excellent final confrontation. In *Law of the Lash* (PRC, 1947), LaRue faces the bad guy, Bracken, played by Jack O'Shea, in the final showdown. When Charles King, making a rare appearance as a sheriff, starts to intervene, Al St. John stops him, "Stay out of this Sheriff, this is Cheyenne's fight."

The issue of personal honor is remarkably demonstrated in an outstanding post–1955 Western, *Ride the High Country* (MGM, 1962) with Randolph Scott, in his last film, and Joel McCrea. At the film's end they have the Hammond brothers trapped, but McCrea is wounded and it is not clear how the situation will end until Scott suggests they "call out" the Hammonds face-to-face. They do so, and elder Hammond tells one of his brothers that when Scott and McCrea raise up he will shoot them. He is rebuked by the brother, who invokes family honor and the inevitable face-to-face shoot-out occurs. One even forgets who was right and who was wrong for it had become a point of honor. The violence had been legitimated.

Nature of the times is a second important consideration. The cowboy hero used violence knowing and accepting the fact that his day was ending. He might look forward to settling down on a ranch in Idaho or he might face it with dread, but he accepted his own demise. Hanging up the guns then was important, for only if one desired not to be violent could one use violence legitimately.

Once again that point was classically demonstrated in *Shane*. Alan Ladd, as Shane, killed Jack Palance, the gunfighter hired by the cattlemen. But he killed him only after Shane told Ryker, the cattleman, that the major difference between them was that Shane knew the day of the gunman was over, and that the day of the farmer had begun. Shane, however, could not become a farmer, and as the film ended he rode away in triumph which was really defeat. Triumph, for he had once again practiced his trade as a gunfighter, and he had won, but defeat because it might have been the last time he would do so.

Gregory Peck's role as Johnny Ringo in *The Gunfighter* (20th Century–Fox, 1950) has a theme of time as well. Ringo is 35 years old, an old man for a gunfighter, and a man who cannot escape his reputation. He yearns to see his wife and son and to settle down in a quiet town. But his reputation won't let him.

Peck rides into Cayenne with the three brothers of a kid he was recently forced to kill hot on his trail. He wants to see his wife and son.

The word spreads that Ringo is in town. Skip Homeier, playing the young aspiring gunman Hunt Bromley, who is really nothing more than a small town bully, confronts Ringo. Ringo forces him to back down. After Ringo sees his wife and son and is preparing to leave town, Bromley shoots him from ambush.

The town marshal (Millard Mitchell), a former member of Ringo's gang starts to arrest Bromley, but the dying Ringo stops him. He wants Bromley to carry the reputation of the man who killed Johnny Ringo, to live the rest of his short life as a gunfighter constantly facing drunken cowboys and punk kids. Ringo wants Bromley to suffer through what he, Ringo, has suffered through.

The Gunfighter is clearly a transitional Western. Its slow pace and psychological tension reminds one of later television Westerns. Western film histories treat it as a prime example of the change that took place in the genre in the early 1950s. Yet, there are elements of the classic good-bad man in it. Ringo clearly had committed crimes, but he never shot a man unless he was provoked. And he met them face to face as an honorable man would do. The viewer has sympathy for his plight, wishes Ringo could lay down his guns and walk away from his reputation.

The time theme carried over into many B Westerns. In the Rough Riders Western *Forbidden Trails* (Monogram, 1941), Buck Jones plays Buck Roberts, a retired United States Marshal living peacefully on his Arizona ranch. Two ex-convicts whom he had sent to prison try to kill him; badly hurt, Buck calls for help from his two pals. Tim McCoy as Tim McCall answers the plea for help from his retirement on a Wyoming ranch. Raymond Hatton as Sandy Hopkins leaves his bride standing at a Texas altar. After they help Buck track down the would-be killers, they willingly give up violence and return to a more civilized existence.

Maybe the best representation of the time dimension in any B Western is *The Arizona Ranger* (RKO, 1948), the only film Tim Holt made with his well-known father-actor Jack Holt. Tim plays a young man returning from the Spanish-American War to become an Arizona Ranger. His father Jack was a rough-and-tumble, catch-them-and-hang-them rancher of the old school. The two clash because Tim intends to enforce the law and that means procedural due process of law. Clearly, the times have changed and his father's methods, once legitimate before the law came to Arizona, were now as illegitimate as were the methods and activities of the cattle rustlers.

Finally, the cowboy heroes' methods must be contrasted to the bad guys with whom they do battle. Unlike the heavies, the cowboy heroes observe rules of the game; they fight by rules of fair play. Outlaws not only use violence for socially undesirable and unprogressive ends, they also practice unrestrained violence: outlaws torched buildings at night, they sold whiskey to Indians in order to encourage trouble, they shot from ambush and they carried hidden weapons.

Cowboy heroes, by contrast, obeyed a code that required violence to be restrained. The gun, a central symbol of their violence, was carried openly and visibly. Subtle twists were added as well. In a few early 1930s films, John Wayne played a character known as "Singing Sandy." Before a gunfight, he would sing softly, giving the villain fair warning of what was about to happen. In the Rough Riders series, Buck Roberts, the character portrayed by Buck Jones, would put a stick of chewing gum in his mouth just before he went into action. This too was warning to his adversaries.

Cowboy heroes did not smash barroom chairs over their opponents' heads, they did not gouge eyes and they did not shoot from rooftops. They might plot at night or in secret to trap the bad guys in their evil deeds, but the showdown was a public occurrence played out by the rules of manly conflict. Good could triumph through violence only if the violent act conformed to a code characteristic of honorable men.

In Westerns, violence was legitimate only if it met the criteria just outlined. That seemed to hold for the vast number of Westerns produced between 1930 and 1955. As law enforcement officials fought gangsters, as farmers clashed with sheriffs trying to serve foreclosure notices, and as workers fought with management in often violent confrontations over the right to organize labor unions, to say nothing of the slow, gradual process by which a nation geared itself toward the inevitable showdown with, the Axis powers and later the Soviet Union, American Westerns served up a perspective that is as characteristic of the United States as is the Fourth of July. Those films, even as they entertained, taught us that good men can use violence, and indeed must use it, to thwart evil. And they communicated an even more important fact: There is little need to feel guilty about violence, if it is used at the right time for the right purposes, and if it is used with restraint.

Violence fits well within the American belief system. As a tool of Manifest Destiny, it helped to extend the United States from ocean to ocean. Violence had been indispensable as men of daring and vision raised the telegraph wire and laid rails across vast stretches of prairie and over rugged mountains. Americans thought there was nothing wrong with violence if it was used in the right manner for the right purpose.

CHAPTER SIX

"FRIENDLY NEIGHBORS ALL AROUND"

The three preceding chapters identified several American beliefs. Prominent among these is that the United States is a Christian nation. The word Christian is an elusive notion given shape by nearly countless individual interpretations; nevertheless, Americans took its meaning for granted throughout much of the 20th century, and they assumed that the United States was a Christian nation.

Closely related to that fundamental concept is the idea of Manifest Destiny, or the belief that God gave the North American continent to whites of European descent as a place in which to build a new democratic political order to serve as an example for humankind. Furthermore, to accomplish that task required the legitimate use of violence, for only if virtuous people used violence could they carry out the arduous task of settling a continent.

These beliefs led early nineteenth century settlers to push further West, first into the old Northwest Territory, then Nebraska and finally to settle the Great Plains and the Pacific Coast. Immigrants of differing ethnic backgrounds carried those beliefs as they waited in the long lines at Ellis Island, standing in the shadow of the Statue of Liberty, a universally recognized symbol of American values. Those primary American beliefs dominated American thought from the end of Reconstruction in 1876 through the first half of the 20th century.

To speak of an American belief system that unified a heterogeneous population raises the question of community. Did Americans have a sense of political community and, if so, how was that concept demonstrated in

Westerns? Before examining those questions, the diverse meanings of community need elaboration.

The most common understanding of community is a town. The idealized, traditional image of America is a small town, its streets lined with elm or maple trees, and its residents living cooperatively and harmoniously with their neighbors. Wistful Vista, Fibber McGee and Molly's fictional town, Summerdale, the home of Throckmorton P. Gildersleeve, or Springfield, U.S.A., the location of *Father Knows Best,* are as American as cherry pie and baseball; they are places in which American beliefs are honored. This place, the town, gives meaning and focus to life. One does not merely live in a town, one is involved in its activities. The town is the place where one earns a living, owns a house and raises children, but equally important, it is a place one must nurture. Citizens are supposed to care about how the city is run, and they are obligated to participate in its public life. Community as place, then, presupposes that individuals find meaning in life from where they live and, as a result, they have obligations to the city and to the people who live in the city.

Another, broader meaning of community is Tocqueville's notion of voluntary associations discussed in Chapter Four. People join together in associations to meet common interests and needs. In Westerns, the voluntary association as a community sprang up as local ranchers banded together to stop rustlers, small ranchers and farmers fought for access to water, farmers formed an association to fight cattlemen who were trying to destroy their farms, or miners joined forces to get their ore wagons past outlaws. Whatever the plot, the organization, by meeting common needs, was a type of community.

People who share common beliefs and values also can experience community. People who go to church together share common religious beliefs and they are a community (at least on the Sabbath). Westerns expressed this aspect of community in several ways. The West as a special place, a place distinguished from the East by a unique set of values, figures prominently in the genre. The cowboy hero frequently expressed Western values as he defended them to a skeptical heroine or as he lived them out in his personal activities.

Finally, for many people living in the United States, the country is a community. Americans are proud of the nation's accomplishments, its historic, religious and political values, and its commitment to equal opportunity. Having internalized American ideals, history and culture, most Americans can't imagine living any place else in the world. Patriotic expressions on the fourth of July and Memorial Day are more than jingoism, they reflect strongly held sentiments of people who believe in the United States as a community of values worth dying for. Since this understanding of community has been explored in previous chapters, the present focus will be on the other expressions of community.

The family is a special kind of American community. Certainly other cultures have a stronger sense of class and kinship, and Asians in particular feel strongly the need to honor and care for elderly parents. But from 1930 to 1955 in the United States, the notion of the nuclear family, mother, father and children, was a near-religion in itself. In American culture, the family is the chief instrument of socialization and a major source of meaning in one's life. Historically, the family home, family car, and family vacation were symbols of the important role family played in American culture. In fact, it could be argued that family is the foremost community and through family, community as an ideal, a place or an association takes on meaning.

However, community with its emphasis on group loyalty and traditional authority is only half of the American story. The other half is individualism. After all, the United States government is built on individual consent and protection of the individual's political rights. Free market economics depend on individual ambition and achievement to fuel the economic furnace that has led to an extraordinarily high standard of living for the vast majority of Americans.

In Chapter Four, readers were introduced to Alexis de Tocqueville, a young French observer of Americans who stressed the importance of individualism in American culture. But, Tocqueville noted, the term must be understood within its American context. Individuals were concerned with their own self-interest, but Tocqueville believed that in the United States Americans embrace "self-interest rightly understood," By "self-interest rightly understood" he meant less selfishness than the term "self-interest" normally implies. For example, a businessman respects his customers, does not try to cheat them, and thus assures that his customers will do business with him again. It is self-interest because the businessman wants to get as much business as he can get, but it is also community enhancing because his customers get good products at the lowest possible price.

Tocqueville's observations help us to understand that individualism and community are not contradictory impulses. Yet, there is tension between the two. Nineteenth-century immigrants fled castes and rigid social differentiation of Europe and Asia for a chance at individual achievement. The history of Western expansion in the United States reflects a people in constant geographical motion, individuals breaking free from established communities to seek their fortunes on the frontier.

The historic American social ethic stressed upward mobility and individual responsibility. One was responsible before God to strive for success, and furthermore one was responsible for making do with whatever fortune dictated. Here was a community, but community of a different sort. It was one of autonomous individuals trying to break free from a constraining social order as they pursued individual success. One cannot understand the richness of American life, then, until one comprehends the pull of community and the simultaneous intense sense of individualism that shaped the American experience.

According to the popular view of Western films, the hero is one engaged in a lonely, heroic struggle who stands outside community, and is often rejected by or rejects community. He is a lonely drifter, self-sufficient, yet unfulfilled because he chooses to remain apart from community. That view may describe some pre–1955 Westerns, it may even apply to a few B Westerns and it may increasingly characterize the entire genre after 1955, but it does not describe the vast number of Westerns produced before that year. Traditional Westerns are community-affirming, not community denigrating, and they employ all meanings of community.

In one sense, all pre–1955 Westerns were about community for they presented the American West as a special place with a unique culture. The West was defined by special dress, special skills such as horseback riding and gunmanship, and a practical hard-nosed approach to life. But above all, the Westerns highlighted a particular set of values and attitudes.

Ken Maynard in *Come On, Tarzan* (World Wide, 1932) declares that "gunplay is the glory of the West." He also opposed those trying to destroy the wild horse herds, a symbol of Western independence. And, on at least two occasions, he admonished his lady boss not to cry because "it ain't Western."

George Hayes echoes Maynard's view of the West in *Sons of the Pioneers* (Republic, 1942). Cattle are being rustled and barns burned, but Hayes, sheriff for 30 years, has been unable to apprehend the outlaws. When the people decide to nominate someone to oppose Hayes, they come up with Frank Bennett, played by Bradley Page, newly arrived from the East. Gabby protests, "No Eastern dude, no foreigner for a Western sheriff." He then proposes Roy Rogers, son and grandson of the area's legendary sheriffs.

In the 1935 William Boyd Western *Three on the Trail* (Paramount, 1936), both Buck Peters, owner of the Bar 20, and Hopalong Cassidy, his foreman, know that Kane, owner of a Gunsight saloon, is responsible for cattle rustling and stagecoach robbery. But they are unable to convince Ridley, a transplanted Britisher who believes that both Kane and his puppet sheriff are honest men. At one point, Buck Peters told Ridley, "You have a lot to learn about the West."

Roy Rogers and Dale Evans used variations of the West-as-a-special-place theme in many of their B Westerns. Dale Evans might be an Easterner who had just inherited a ranch or a Wild West show, or a newspaper reporter or writer from the East searching for a story. Whatever variation, until the film's end she was perpetually in trouble because she failed to appreciate and respect the uniqueness of Western culture.

One of Buck Jones' most unusual Westerns, *When a Man Sees Red* (Universal, 1934) underscores differences between East and West. Peggy Campbell plays a young artist who ignores her uncle's pleas to come back to the ranch. She and her Eastern friends view the West with snobbish superiority. However, when her uncle dies, she goes West to take possession of her inheritance. Right away Campbell ignores Jones' advice to be careful with a difficult team of horses. She and the other passengers are in danger of being killed until Jones stops the runaway team. Campbell permits herself to be conned by LeRoy Mason, playing a smooth-talking rustler. She uses him to spite Jones, whom her uncle had appointed as her guardian. Everything turns out all right in the end as Campbell learns that people of the West are not rural bumpkins. She begins to respect their unique culture and even decides to marry Jones.

The big-budget *Billy the Kid* (MGM, 1941) also contains an excellent example of the West as a special place. Ian Hunter plays the Englishman, Keating. Robert Taylor as Billy is amazed that Keating is not afraid of him. But Keating is unarmed and tells Billy, "I am protected by a moral code. Oh, not mine, yours. You wouldn't shoot a man without a gun or if his back was turned. Most men in the West have that moral sense."

Certainly the West as a special culture, a community of sorts, has figured prominently in the American experience since James Fenimore Cooper's Leatherstocking Tales. Hollywood merely highlighted and reinforced that belief. Several of the B Western stars grew up in the East and were attracted to the West because of its special cowboy tradition. Among them were Ken Maynard, Tom Mix, Tim McCoy and Buck Jones. Even Roy Rogers, then Leonard Slye, was drawn to the West at the height of the Depression because it seemed to hold more economic promise than did southern Ohio. The image of the Golden West as a land of promise and excitement has been part of the American experience for some time.

Not only did Westerns reinforce traditional images of the West, they also expressed a bias toward small towns and rural America. Big cities and the East were commonly associated with ugliness, corruption, immorality and economic exploitation. Folks who lived in small towns and rural areas of the American heartland believed they were free from such city problems. To a great extent, Westerns mirrored that belief, because one of the dominant symbols of Westerns is the small town. In fact, traditional Westerns consist entirely of small towns and wide-open landscape.

The typical Western town sat on the edge of the prairie and consisted generally of one busy main street with the requisite saloon, livery stable, general store, bank and sheriff's office. It might also have a few side streets with houses, but, if so, they did not stand out in a noticeable fashion. Action took place on Main Street.

Because the town was small, it was a place where people cared about each other and were involved in community affairs. That Western image of townspeople needs to be underscored. With the exception of the villains, residents were honest, hardworking folks. Usually outlaws and crooks were harassing them, and, more often than not, they were helpless to stop the evil. They were helpless, but hardly ever cowardly!

In confronting whatever evil befell their town, townsfolk needed to identify the source of the evil and then organize to resist it. Often they found it hard to accomplish either task; they were helpless, but they were not cowards. *High Noon* (United Artists, 1952) was a dramatic departure from the typical B Western, not the norm. In *High Noon* the townsfolks were unwilling to confront Frank Miller and his henchmen. They let Marshal Will Kane fight alone. And, in the end, after dispatching the badmen, the marshal rejected the town.

B Westerns presented an entirely different picture of the common man. Ordinary people in 1930s and 1940s B Westerns are brave folks and important allies of the cowboy hero as he fights the bad guys. In *The Riding Fool* (Columbia, 1935), Tim McCoy's ranch allies stop an outlaw gang trying to rob a bank. In *Lawless Nineties* (Republic, 1936) and *Gangs of Sonora* (Republic, 1939), Wyoming citizens work with John Wayne and the Three Mesquiteers to thwart outlaw gangs who want to keep Wyoming being voted into the union. Bob McKenzie steps out of his normal role as buffoon in *Death Valley Outlaws* (Republic, 1941) to help Don Barry round up the crooks. Near the film's climax, as Barry heads off for a final showdown with the bad guys, McKenzie, playing a veterinarian, tells his assistant Snowflake that they are going to help that boy. He then rounds up other townsfolk to stop the local vigilantes from robbing the bank.

Billy the Kid catches the determination of Western settlers to protect their ranches and towns. Keating tries to talk Billy into changing sides. He tells him,

> You know, things are going to happen in this country. Guns and shootings are going out, law and order is on the march. You had better watch out or they will run you over. The good people want to live together as good peaceful citizens and, when they get together, there

isn't a man fast enough on the draw or tough enough to stand against them.

Not only did Westerns depict the average Westerner as brave, he also understood that he was not a solitary individual fighting the world alone. The most effective way to deal with a problem was to form an association of neighbors whose combined resources would be greater than those of any single individual. That theme appears in films such as *Homesteaders of Paradise Valley* (Republic, 1939) and *Saga of Death Valley* (Republic, 1939) in which ranchers pooled their efforts to build dams and irrigation ditches or to fight water barons who were charging outrageous prices.

Normally someone would suggest, "Let's have a meetin' at my place" and the ranchers or farmers—whichever the case—would spread the word about the meetin'. In Red Ryder Westerns, the Duchess' ranch served as the location while in Roy Rogers films it was normally Gabby Hayes' ranch where the meetin' occurred. At the meetin', range patrols would be set up, strategies established and/or resources allocated.

In *Old Amarillo* (Republic, 1951), local ranchers are being destroyed by a prolonged drought. They meet in a local bar to hear William Holmes—playing one of the bad guys—offer to buy them out for a few cents on the dollar. Feeling they have no other option, the ranchers are about to agree to Holmes' offer when Roy Rogers intervenes. He proposes that they raise money and hire an air service to seed the clouds with silver iodide. Roy argues that it has worked other places and it can work for them. The ranchers agree to form an association by pooling their money and hire the air service.

The Salt River Gang, notorious rustlers who steal cattle and then blackmail ranchers into making protection payments so they won't steal more, are the main culprits in *Rustlers* (RKO, 1949), a Tim Holt programmer. The local ranchers are meeting at Frank Abbott's ranch when rustlers throw a note-bearing rock through the front window. They demand $2,000 for 400 head of cattle they had recently stolen from Abbott. The other ranchers advise Abbott to pay the ransom just as they have done. He won't do it, and Abbott tells his friends he is pulling out. That is too much for Martha Hyer, playing Ruth, his daughter. She proposes that they mark the money as a means to tracking down the rustlers. The other ranchers are convinced that it might work and each donates a few hundred dollars.

Frank Abbott initially declines their assistance, responding that this deal is up to him. However, one of the other ranchers reminds Abbott that it is up to all of them. Either they put the Salt River Gang out of business

In Old Amarillo, Republic, 1951; Elisabeth Risdon, William Holmes and Roy Rogers. Ranchers have a meeting to discuss their options in the face of prolonged drought.

or they will all go under. Collective effort was required; the fight was too big for one man. Abbott's response is, "All right. I'll string along."

Both *In Old Amarillo* and *Rustlers* highlight the sense of community that is part of voluntary associations. Some problems are just too big for individuals to handle, but the combined resources and effort of several individuals is a different story. No problem is too big if enough people are willing to tackle it. The old saying "When Americans combine their efforts, the difficult is done quickly, the impossible takes a little longer" was a faith echoed in countless B Westerns.

Involvement, however, had to be modeled. Someone had to stand up to outlaws and serve as a catalyst for the decent folks. Normally the cowboy hero played that role. Sometimes, however, it was a town leader who braved the outlaws' wrath and tried to rally the local population. That person was often the one who called on the cowboy hero for help.

Frequently the local hero was a newspaper editor. In *West of the Law* (Monogram, 1942), a newspaper editor leads the crusade against outlaws even though his printing press had been blown up. The editor is indispensable to the Rough Riders as they learn who was behind the trouble and set out to apprehend the crooks. *The Lawless Nineties* is another example of the important role of a newspaper editor. George Hayes buys the Ponca City newspaper and uses it to crusade for Wyoming statehood. As he launches his paper, Hayes tells his daughter Ann Rutherford, "Another newspaper is about to be born, another star in the bright firmament of Old Glory."

Tim Holt plays the nightrider Mr. Justice in *Red River Robin Hood* (RKO, 1943). Holt and his sidekick Ukulele Ike Edwards return to their Red River ranch only to discover that they and the other ranchers are being forced out by a man who owns a forged Spanish land grant. Holt is the cowboy hero in this one, but the real hero is Otto Hoffman, playing the editor of the *Red River Bugle*. Hoffman stands up to the outlaws, petitions for a new trial and appeals to a higher court when a crooked judge rules in favor of the phony land grant. The newspaper editor is the rallying point for the ranchers. *Red River Robin Hood* also previews an element which became standard in post–World War II Roy Rogers programmers, a lecture within the plot. Hoffman tells Holt that his father once owned a paper mill. He then shows Holt how to identify the manufacturer of any brand of paper and how to distinguish real from forged documents.

On occasion, cowboy heroes even played newspaper editors. At least one Roy Rogers Western, *Home in Oklahoma* (Republic, 1946), opted for that scenario. Randolph Scott is co-owner of the "Fort Worth Star" in *Fort Worth* (Warner Bros., 1951). Scott had left Texas as a gunman to join the Confederate army. He returns a newspaperman! Scott had seen too much violence during the war, and he had seen also how powerful was the press. He became convinced that printer's ink was more important than the gun. When his partner is murdered as he is about to expose Fort Worth's most influential citizen (David Brian), as a crook, Scott takes up the cause and finishes the job.

General Store owners and other small merchants were also prominent as community leaders. Max Terhune and Eddy Waller were often general store proprietors working with Johnny Mack Brown and Allan "Rocky" Lane as those two cowboy heroes fought the bad guys. Al St. John in *The Lone Rider Rides On* (PRC, 1942) played the role of a general store owner, the only man in town who didn't buckle under to the outlaws led by Lee Powell, a bad guy in this one. As a result, he became an important ally of George Houston, the Lone Rider, as the latter endeavored to find out who murdered his parents.

A particularly good film example of Tocqueville's individualism rightly understood is found in *Abilene Town* (United Artists, 1946). Howard Freeman as Ed Balder, owner of the general store, does a great deal of business with the trail crews who drive cattle from Texas to the rail head in Abilene. Balder, one of the town's prominent citizens, was responsible for hiring Dan Mitchell (Randolph Scott) to keep the wild trail crews on the saloon-brothel side of Abilene. Balder wants the cattlemen's business, but when they get drunk and rampage through the town, he does not want them destroying his home or insulting his wife and daughter.

All goes well for Balder and the other merchants until wheat farmers move into the area around Abilene and begin to fence in the open range, blocking the cattle trails. When violence erupts, Mitchell sides with the farmers; Balder protests that the farmers will drive away the cattlemen and businessmen like him will go broke. Mitchell demonstrates to Balder that farmers who live in the area and do business in Abilene stores all year around will bring more business and wealth to the town than trail crews who hit the town once a year. Besides, drunken cowboys also wreck property which must be repaired; farmers build, they do not destroy.

At the film's climax when Mitchell has permitted a drunken trail crew to wreck the saloons and they are about to do the same to the "respectable" side of town, Balder rallies the business community to Mitchell's support. Balder and the other businessmen see that their "self-interest rightly understood" lies with the wheat farmers not the wild trail crews. The film ends with the cowboys riding out of town, and with the promise that Abilene has a bright future as a prosperous farming community.

Both newspaper editors and merchants as community leaders point to an American bias for localism. During the heyday of Westerns, newspapers were normally locally owned and they reflected the concerns of that community. While many people shopped at national chain stores such as A & P, Kroger, Woolworth and Sears Roebuck, it was not uncommon to shop also at locally owned stores. Along with the newspaper editor and owner, local retail merchants were the community leaders. In fact, "the politics of Main Street" was an expression that underscored the crucial leadership role that local businessmen played in small towns of the American heartland.

Although local leaders were indispensable in Westerns, they usually lacked the resources necessary to stop whatever particular evil gripped the community. That task was left to the cowboy hero. The cowboy hero, in turn, related to the community in one of three possible ways: He was not part of the town, but an outsider who rode away when his job was finished; he was a member of the community respected by it and who identified with it; or, he was no longer a member of the community, but a celebrity of some sort who returned for a visit and remained to help his friends.

Quite often the cowboy hero was an outsider who either possessed some legal authority which local officials had requested, or a friend of someone in trouble. He knowingly went to a place of danger because his job required it, or because he felt compelled to assist a friend in trouble. In either case, he went into a community as an outsider.

When the cowboy hero rode into a Western town as a federal marshal or Texas Ranger, obviously he was an outsider. He did not live in the community, and he certainly did not intend to stay after his mission was completed. But even though he was an outsider, the hero was not a maladjusted drifter. More often than not, he worked alone or with a sidekick at a dangerous craft which often resulted in death. While he worked alone, the cowboy hero was not a loner; he made friends easily. Wherever he went, friendly townsfolk accepted him warmly as the answer to their prayers. The B Western cowboy hero was a creature of community. He valued the friendship of his sidekick and comrades and of the people he helped.

Frisco Tornado (Republic, 1950), *King of the Bullwhip* (Western Adventure, 1950) and numerous PRC Buster Crabbe Westerns were set in communities to which Rocky Lane, Lash LaRue and Buster Crabbe came as strangers, and they rode away after law and order had been restored. But they were not maladjusted drifters, loners who rejected community; rather, they were individuals who assisted law-abiding citizens of the community. In the process they became friends with the community's leading citizens, and as they rode away with a friendly wave it was with the promise that they would return someday to visit their newly acquired friends.

While nearly every cowboy hero played the role of a peace officer who rode into a town and rounded up the bad guys, some of the best expressions of that plot are the eight Monogram Westerns in which Buck Jones, Tim McCoy and Raymond Hatton appeared as the Rough Riders. Each man would ride into a small town appropriately named Yucca City, Mesa City or Gold Creek. They appeared as strangers, disguising the fact that they were United States Marshals. Hatton, whose character was called Sandy Hopkins, was the comic of the three who normally played a cook, muleskinner or even an undertaker. McCoy, as Tim McCall, often appeared disguised as a preacher or gambler. Jones, as Buck Roberts, usually played a sheriff or notorious gunman.

In two of the eight films, someone in the town knew Buck Jones; otherwise, they were total strangers to everyone. In *Arizona Bound* (Monogram, 1941), the three men, coming out of temporary retirement, go to Mesa City to investigate a series of stagecoach holdups. Jones volunteers to drive one of the stagecoaches while McCoy plays the role of a parson.

Hatton assumes the role of a cowboy who drives a herd of cattle to Mesa City for Jones.

When Jones' stagecoach is held up, Dennis Moore concludes that Jones is part of the gang and takes him to jail. Tris Coffin, in his often-assumed role as the main brain heavy, convinces the townspeople that Jones is behind all of the holdups and they are about to lynch him when Hatton helps Jones break out of jail. In the meantime, McCoy is able to convince the townspeople that Jones is really a United States Marshall and that Coffin is behind all of their troubles.

Coffin and his outlaws fortify themselves in the saloon for the inevitable shootout while the now-armed townsfolk lay siege to it. In the meantime, Jones, McCoy and Hatton unite as the Rough Riders in the hills outside of Mesa City and ride into town together to round up Coffin and his bunch. In an exciting climax, Jones jumps his horse, Silver, through the window of the saloon and gets the drop on the outlaws. Once the outlaws are rounded up, the three men leave town, each to return to his personal retirement. But they leave Mesa City as friends of the grateful citizens they came to help.

West of the Law is the last Rough Riders film in which the three men appeared together. In this programmer, the local newspaper editor, Rufus Todd, cables Buck Roberts, an old friend, for assistance in stopping an outlaw reign of terror in Gold Creek. Jones poses as an outlaw to get in with the gang that has been stealing ore. Hatton appears as an undertaker while McCoy again plays a preacher.

Hatton smuggles a new printing press in his coffins to replace the one the outlaws had wrecked, and Rufus prints a new edition of his newspaper in which he promises to disclose the name of the brains behind the outlaws. Jones assures Rufus that neither Rand, (Harry Woods) or Ludlow, (Roy Barcroft) are smart enough to run the outfit. Together with Rufus, the Rough Riders discover that Corbett (John Daley) is the main brains heavy. On the surface, Corbett is a respectable mine owner and a pillar of the community, but he is using his worthless mine as a front to ship stolen ore. When Woods, Barcroft and Daley have been rounded up, the Rough Riders leave Gold Creek to return to their own, personal communities. As they ride out of town, the townsfolk are all gathered around the front of the newspaper office to express their appreciation and wave good-bye to the men who saved their community.

The Rough Riders modeled community in several ways. Each man was part of a community that he temporarily left. Jones owned a ranch in Arizona, Hatton ran a hotel in Texas and usually was about to marry a widow lady, and McCoy always returned to his beloved Wyoming. They were not cowboy-lawmen drifting from one town to another, they lived someplace!

The Rough Riders were also a community in themselves. Their longtime association as partners led to trust and camaraderie. For example, in *Forbidden Trails* (Monogram, 1941), Hatton and McCoy readily give up their retirements to help Jones, who had almost been killed by two outlaws bent on revenge. Jones knows all he has to do is cry for help and his old partners would come running. Finally, the Rough Riders make friends and become, temporarily at least, a part of the town they are serving. When they ride away, it is as men who have contributed to the town's peace. They leave as valued friends.

Rocky Lane, Lash LaRue, Buster Crabbe, the Rough Riders and other cowboy heroes who appeared as lawmen may not be the best examples of community affirming B Westerns. They rode into a community because they had a job to do. The town needed to be purged of its lawless element and, after they rid the town of outlaws, the cowboy heroes rode away to another town which needed their special skills. However, it was also common for cowboy heroes to help out because a friend was in trouble. The cowboy hero reflected an important ethic, one helps a friend who is in trouble. Westerns too numerous to count employed this strategy. Prominent among them were Range Buster movies, Johnny Mack Brown, Tim Holt films of the late 1940s and many Hopalong Cassidy Westerns.

In *Rider from Tucson* (RKO, 1950), Tim Holt and his sidekick Chito are appearing in a rodeo in Tucson when they get a letter from Tim's old friend Tug Bailey (William Phipps). Bailey tells Tim that he has discovered gold, plans to get married and wants Tim to be best man at the wedding. Tim and Chito go to Oro Grande for the wedding, but once there, Bailey tells them he has postponed his wedding because outlaws are trying to kidnap him and force him to disclose the location of his claim. As expected of good friends, Tim and Chito jump into the fray to help their friend, and to track down the would-be thieves.

Several Hopalong Cassidy films highlight the value of friendship as well. *Bar 20 Rides Again* (Paramount, 1935) is an excellent little Western which stresses the importance of friendship and loyalty. Jim Arnold writes to old friend Hopalong Cassidy asking for his help in tracking down a gang of rustlers led by an outlaw named Nevada. But Arnold tells Cassidy not to bring Johnny Nelson, who was played skillfully by James Ellison. Nelson and Arnold's daughter had been sweethearts, but she has fallen for Perdue, a neighboring rancher, and Arnold does not want to embarrass Nelson or cause trouble for his daughter or Perdue.

After talking things over with Buck Connors, Cassidy and Connors go to Arnold's ranch, but they order Nelson to remain at the Bar 20. Of course, Nelson does not do as he is told and a subplot has Johnny Nelson trying to win back the affections of his girlfriend. However, the main plot is about Cassidy's efforts to track down the rustlers who are operating from a wilderness of rocks and hidden valleys known as Snake Buttes. Cassidy assumes the disguise of a gambler and rides in the Buttes.

Cassidy and Windy (a role created by Gabby Hayes, much like the one he would make famous in Roy Rogers Westerns) are captured by Nevada's outlaws. Cassidy discovers that the outlaw Nevada — a man with a Napoleon complex — and the rancher Perdue are the same person. Cassidy establishes his skill with both cards and a gun and is readily accepted by Nevada, who sees in Cassidy a cultured man much like himself.

When Cassidy learns of a big cattle raid, he starts a brushfire to alert Connors and Arnold to bring their men and come shooting. They trap Nevada and his outlaws in their stronghold and one of Nevada's gunmen — a man who resents his boss' imperial manner — shoots him. Early in the film, Al St. John, playing one of Nevada's men, had been wounded seriously and Nevada, not wanting to be bothered by a wounded man, kills him, commenting, "You didn't expect to live forever, did you?" The outlaw throws Nevada's words back to him in a sort of B Western sense of justice as the cold, impersonal, would-be Napoleon gets his just deserts.

Cassidy and Buck Connors helped Jim Arnold save his ranch, Johnny Nelson is reunited with his sweetheart, and in Windy the Bar 20 has a new hand and Hopalong Cassidy a new sidekick. The important ingredient in this film, however, is the speed with which Connors and Cassidy responded to a friend's call for help. Part of living together in a community is to help out when the other fellow is in trouble. That is what *Bar 20 Rides Again* is all about.

A similar theme appears in *Three Men from Texas* (Paramount, 1940). When the film opens, Cassidy and Lucky Jenkins (the character played by Russell Hayden who joined the series when James Ellison left it) are Texas Rangers. Hayden, however, has the urge to strike out on his own so he accepts an invitation to become a sheriff of a California town plagued by outlaws. Cassidy remains in Texas, but when the right moment comes, he jumps at the chance to go to California. And, with the smile William Boyd as Hopalong Cassidy made so famous, he acknowledges that part of his reason for going to California is to help Lucky round up the outlaws.

In the first part of *Three Men from Texas*, Cassidy stumbled across a good-hearted, blowhard outlaw named California Carlson. Carlson had been a minor, comical character in Dick Curtis's outlaw band; when the outlaws discover that Cassidy has arrested Carlson, they try to kill both men. Cassidy develops a fondness for Carlson, and California Carlson, the character played by Andy Clyde, became a mainstay as Hopalong Cassidy's comical sidekick until the series came to an end in 1948.

Carlson and Cassidy go to California to help out Lucky. Once there, they discover that the outlaws are part of a land swindle in which the crooks use phony land deeds to drive Mexicans off of their land. At first Lucky is not pleased to see Cassidy; he wants to round up the crooks by himself. But when Lucky is wounded, Cassidy and a small army of dispossessed Mexicans, turned outlaws when they were evicted from their land, round up the crooks in a climactic shootout.

Often Range Busters Westerns involve them in the plot as they aid a friend in need. Forrest Taylor plays a lawyer for Wells Fargo in *Arizona Stagecoach* (Monogram, 1942). When Wells Fargo stages are being held up and the local sheriff can't stop the robberies, Taylor turns to the Range Busters. He observes, "I can't think of anybody better able to help than the Range Busters." They become United States Marshals in *Trail Riders* (Monogram, 1942). Their boyhood friend, a United States Marshal, is murdered and his father, another marshal played by veteran character actor Steve Clark, sends for them. The Range Busters are on their first vacation in five years and are reluctant to give it up. But when they hear that their friend has been murdered, John "Dusty" King says, "Marshal, swear us in." In *Saddle Mountain Roundup* (Monogram, 1941), they track down the killer of an old rancher who was their friend and employer.

Both legal authority and friendship reflect deep-seated American convictions: respect for those in authority because they work for the public good and can be trusted with the right to use violence, and a belief that part of living together in community requires one to help out friends when they need help.

But that is not the whole story! One ought not to wait for the call to be helpful. When one sees trouble, there is an ethical and moral obligation to intervene. Often the cowboy hero was not part of the community nor did anyone ask for his official or unofficial help. He simply saw someone in trouble and stopped to lend a hand. Film examples of this type abound. For example, the film *Way of the West* (Empire/Superior, 1935) opened with Wally Wales helping to stop a runaway buckboard and then rescuing the heroine's small brother from adults who were roughing him up. Even though he was a government inspector sent to protect sheepherders, Wales initially got involved because he saw trouble and went to the aid of those who needed his assistance.

In *Song of the Sierras* (Monogram, 1946), Jimmy Wakely and Lee "Lasses" White are jailed for street fighting. Wakely and his partner Wesley Tuttle arrive in a small town hoping to sell some valuable race horses

Wakely has trained. White, who had previously worked for Wakely, has set up a variety show in town, but the sheriff won't let him put it on until he pays his hotel bill. White explains his predicament to Wakely and the two men are on their way to pay the hotel bill when they observe Zon Murray push an old man to the ground. Wakely tells Murray that he ought to be proud of himself for picking on an old man and White calls Murray a "dirty polecat." When Murray throws a punch at White, Wakely steps in and a fight erupts. The sheriff breaks it up and puts Wakely and White in jail for starting the brawl. Wakely defends his actions by telling the sheriff, "I just couldn't stand by and see an old man pushed around."

But it was not only the cowboy heroes who helped out people in trouble. Sidekicks were just as dependable. For example, Gabby Hayes and Sally Payne reverse roles in *Young Bill Hickok* (Republic, 1940). They hear shooting and ride to help. Roy Rogers, playing Bill Hickok, is badly wounded and pinned down in a stagecoach relay station by raiders bent on destroying the stage line. Only Hayes and Payne, riding to his aid, save Roy from sure death.

Sometimes, however, the cowboy hero helped the wrong people. *Harmony Trail* (Mattox Productions, 1944) was Ken Maynard's last Western. Riding with his pals Eddie Dean and Max Terhune, Maynard sees Bob McKenzie, playing the owner of a medicine show, experiencing car trouble. Maynard says, "Looks like they're in trouble, shall we lend them a hand?" Dean gives the standard cowboy hero reply, "Sure thing." Only later do we learn that McKenzie skipped town without paying his hotel bill. Max Terhune's comment to that is, "Looks like we helped the wrong bird."

John Wayne and Syd Saylor also helped the "wrong bird." *Born to the West* (Paramount, 1937) opens as they ride to assist some men being chased by a gang of riders. The only problem is that Wayne and Saylor pick the wrong side. They wind up helping rustlers elude the posse.

At times, cowboy heroes helped the wrong people and at other times their motive and actions were misunderstood, but that did not excuse them from getting involved. Al St. John captured the spirit of the cowboy hero's concern in *Billy the Kid in Texas* (PRC, 1940). He told Terry Walker and Frank LaRue, "Billy is always helping folks, even goes out of his way to do it." In this film, Bob Steele, as Billy the Kid, watched Charles King rob a wagon. He, in turn, took the money from King in order to give it back to its rightful owners. Again, the assumption was when one sees a problem, one has to become involved.

Quite often the cowboy hero did not ride into a strange situation or ride off at the end of the film because he was part of the community.

Numerous Tim McCoy Columbia Westerns of the early and mid–1930's assigned him the role of a sheriff or some other respected community figure. Instead of riding into the sunset at the film's end, McCoy was often set to marry the pretty girl. *Abilene Town* is also a good example of a hero who identified with a community and endeavored to strengthen it.

The same may be said for several Gene Autry Westerns. In *Rovin' Tumbleweeds* (Republic, 1939) and *Valley of Fire* (Columbia, 1951), Gene is so much part of the community that he is elected to public office as Congressman in the former and mayor in the latter film. In *The Last Round-Up* (Columbia, 1947), Autry is such an integral part of the community his fellow ranchers are convinced to relocate their ranches so Mesa City can build its aqueduct only after Autry leads the campaign for it. In *Stardust on the Sage* (Republic, 1942), his opinion is sought eagerly by cattlemen. Edith Fellows even rigs up a fake radio endorsement by Gene for a gold-mining operation in order to convince cattlemen to buy stock in the mine. After all, if Gene Autry says it is okay, it must be a good investment. Gene plays a local sheriff, a respected member of the community in *The Old Corral* (Republic, 1936). He even kissed the girl at the end of this film.

Throughout his many films, Roy Rogers often played someone with strong community roots, a respected, integral part of the local area. Like Autry in *Rovin' Tumbleweeds*, Rogers was such a natural community leader he got elected to Congress in *Under Western Stars* (Republic, 1938). *Shine On Harvest Moon* (Republic, 1938) and *Wall Street Cowboy* (Republic, 1939) are other early Rogers entries in which he is part of a local community. That tendency continued into the mid–1940s. For example, in *Home in Oklahoma* (Republic, 1946) Roy plays the editor of a small-town newspaper, and in *Don't Fence Me In* (Republic, 1946) he runs a dude ranch and is the son of a respected clergyman.

By the late 1940s and early 1950s, Rogers increasingly identified with a local community. In *Susanna Pass* (Republic, 1949), he is a game warden and in *Trail of Robin Hood* (Republic, 1949), he works for the Soil Conservation Service. In the latter entry, Roy helps Jack Holt harvest his Christmas trees in spite of Clifton Young's efforts to drive Holt into bankruptcy. Roy plays a parole officer in *Twilight in the Sierras* (Republic, 1950). To find one of his missing charges, Roy breaks up a gang of crooks trying to sell forged gold certificates to a foreign syndicate. And, in one of my favorite Rogers Westerns, *Spoilers of the Plains* (Republic, 1951), he stops Grant Withers from stealing American rocket secrets. In all of these films, Rogers identifies with a community. He does not ride in at the beginning of the film or ride off into the sunset as it ends; rather, he is an established member of the community.

The same is true of Rex Allen in *Hills of Oklahoma* (Republic, 1950). The ranchers are being paid low prices for their beef and, in addition, they are being forced to pay higher shipping prices on the one railroad spur line that serves their area. Allen counsels finding another company and, because he is a respected community leader, the other ranchers go along with him. He gets Elisabeth Risdon to agree to buy their cattle, but they will have to drive them to another railroad line. The ranchers are not sure it will work, but they respect Allen and look to him for leadership, so they undertake the drive. As depicted in the film, Allen's family had always been community leaders; therefore, he was following a fine tradition.

Far from being films that personify the lonely struggle of a self-sufficient individual, B Westerns are community affirming. Post–1955 Westerns tended to stress the lonely figure apart from, even denying, community. But that is not the image B Westerns projected. In fact, in some Western programmers the cowboy hero returned to the community in which he had grown up in order to clear up a tarnished reputation.

Buck Jones' *The Throwback* (Columbia, 1935) is a good illustration of that theme. Jones' father had been a social outcast, not well liked by the community's prominent citizens. As a youngster, Jones is shown fighting to uphold his father's name. Then when his father is accused of a crime and killed, Jones leaves the area. Years later he returns as an adult to successfully clear his father's name.

Gene Autry used a similar theme in a couple of his films. In his first feature-length Western, *Tumbling Tumbleweeds* (Republic, 1935), Autry's father banishes him from the ranch because he wrongly thinks his son is a coward. Some years later, Autry returns as part of George Hayes' minstrel show. He discovers that his father has been murdered and Gene cleans up his tarnished reputation by tracking down the killers. Three years later, Republic used a variation of this plot in *The Yodelin' Kid from Pine Ridge* (Republic, 1938). In this entry, Autry is forced to leave home because his father believes he sided with the turpentiners against his own kind, the cattlemen. Once again Gene returns as the star attraction, this time of Smiley Burnette's Wild West Show. He discovers his father murdered, sticks around to track down LeRoy Mason (the killer) and brings peace between the cattlemen and the turpentiners.

One more film convention underscores the important place of community, the return of a community son who has become celebrity, yet remembers his community and comes home to be honored by it. This was a favorite theme in early 1940s Roy Rogers movies such as *Red River Valley* (Republic, 1941) and *The Man from Music Mountain* (Republic, 1943) and in late 1940s films such as *Under California Stars* (Republic, 1949).

Down Dakota Way (Republic, 1949) is particularly interesting. Roy and the Riders of the Purple Sage are on their way to the Cheyenne rodeo. They go through the area in which Roy was raised. He is reminiscing with the Sages when they hear shots. Riding to help, they stumble onto a bus robbery. That reunites Roy with his old school teacher Dolly Paxton (Elisabeth Risdon), a childhood friend Sparrow Biffle (Pat Brady) and the sheriff (Monte Montana). Roy is welcomed back as a renowned son who has done well. In this film, Rogers is not a lonely, heroic individual isolated from his roots, but one who remembers them fondly and shares them with his friends, the Riders of the Purple Sage.

All of the conventions that get the cowboy hero involved in the plot (legal authority, friendship, happenstance or the return of a successful son) reflect individualism. The cowboy hero was one who had made a name for himself. He was successful, and clearly success is an important American attribute. However, another lesson is equally clear: with success comes responsibility to the community. It is popular culture's version of the *noblesse oblige*. For a population which patronized Carnegie-endowed libraries and used other public facilities funded by the generosity of wealthy patrons, it was not so hard to believe that personal success required one to give something back to the community in which one had grown up. B Westerns reflected that assumption quite nicely.

It is time to reconsider how Westerns portrayed individualism and community. B Westerns, far more often than not, are community affirming. They do not portray the cowboy hero as one shaped by a lonely struggle. They picture him as a social being associated with and respected by others as he used his special physical skills in pursuit of social justice.

Community is an important concept transmitted by Westerns to viewers. The ethos of America as a promised land populated by people with a special mission became increasingly important as the twisted cross of Nazism distorted the geography and culture of Europe, and Japan's warlords inched closer to armed conflict with the United States. It is hardly possible to understand the meaning Americans gave to World War II apart from our collective sense of community.

William Elliott's lines in *Prairie Schooners* (Columbia, 1940) serve as a fitting climax for this part of the chapter. Elliott, as Wild Bill Hickok, told Evelyn Young, the film's heroine, "You know, Virginia, I have been listening to the folks as they sat around the fires at night. A man should take root in this land. That is what I am going to do. I will take up a homestead and settle down with friendly neighbors all around me."

If B Westerns affirmed the importance of community, even more so did they reinforce traditional views of family. Gabby Hayes might complain about "durn persnickety women" or proclaim "women, there ought to be a law against them," but overall B Westerns presented marriage as quite normal, and often the cowboy hero got the pretty girl at the film's end.

It is no surprise that Westerns depicted strong family units. Family was too important in the 1930s and 1940s for Westerns to ignore. Two films which have already been commented on extensively demonstrate that. Both *Angel and the Badman* (Republic, 1947) and *Wyoming Outlaw* (Republic, 1939) revolve around families and project family as the normal pattern of living together. The cowboy hero may have been unmarried and, more often than not, gave no indication of intending to get married, but he supported families. Even Raymond Hatton, who was pulled away from a Texas altar on numerous occasions to ride to the aid of Buck Jones and Tim McCoy, seemed to acknowledge the importance of holy matrimony.

Because families were important, plots frequently involved family problems. Included among these were: parent dying to protect child, parent in search of missing spouse or child, the errant son, the strong-willed daughter, revenging the death of a family member, and fighting to save the family home. These are age-old problems that confront families and are thought of as problems because the family unit is important. In that sense, to recognize the problem is to acknowledge the importance of family.

The greatest love a parent can have for a child is to die protecting the child. Westerns modeled that love. For example, in *Between Men* (Supreme, 1935) starring Johnny Mack Brown and William Farnum, Farnum plays the outlaw Rand who fled Virginia believing that he had killed a man. Johnny Mack Brown, the young son Farnum left behind when he fled Virginia, wound up working on Farnum's ranch. While there, Brown fell in love with Beth Marion against the orders of Farnum. That led to a fight between the two men. During the fight, Farnum discovers a birthmark, realizes Brown's identity and puts on Brown's hat so he Farnum, not Brown, will be killed when he leaves the shack in which they had been fighting.

In *Down Dakota Way,* Elisabeth Risdon is especially protective of Byron Barr, the nephew whom she had raised as her own son. He had been involved in a bus holdup and murdered a passenger. But she would not believe he was bad, so she protected him. She helps him escape by holding off the posse after they trail him to her house. Finally, however, she must acknowledge his behavior and no longer protect him. Even then she is visibly torn between her love for him and her commitment to truth and justice.

Between Men, Supreme, 1935; Johnny Mack Brown, Beth Marion and William Farnum. Farnum, playing Brown's father, dies protecting his son.

As a result of mistaken identity, Buck Jones is found guilty of murder in *Boss Rider of Gun Creek* (Universal, 1936). His father (Hainey Clark) knows Buck is not guilty and sets out to clear his son's name. First, he helps Buck escape from the sheriff taking him to prison. Then he arranges to have the real killer meet him. The sheriff, in hot pursuit, arrives in time to shoot and kill the real murderer. Jones assumes the real killer's identity and, with Clark's help, clears himself and assumes his rightful identity. As an aside, on two occasions in the film the father of the murdered girl tries to kill Jones, believing him to be the one who murdered his daughter. He was acting as a father ought to act, taking revenge on the one whom he thought had murdered his daughter.

In other films, the cowboy hero expressed filial affection by unrelentingly searching for a missing spouse or child. In *Rustler's Paradise* (Ajax, 1935), Harry Carey used such a search as the unifying theme of the film. As Cheyenne Kincaid, Carey searches for the man who ran away with his wife and young daughter. Suspecting that the outlaw known as El Diablo may be the man he is looking for, Carey joins El Diablo's gang. When he first meets El Diablo (Theodore Lorch), Carey discovers that a young girl called Connie keeps house for the gang. El Diablo verbally abuses her when he is not pleased with the way she cleans his boots and he threatens to skin her alive if she ever rummages through his old trunk. Carey gets El Diablo to acknowledge that Connie is not his daughter.

When the gang goes on a raid, Carey doubles back to the hideout and goes through the trunk with Connie. Connie shows him a picture of her mother, Carey's wife, and he reads from her diary that his wife recognized her mistake in running away and intended to return to him. Carey learns that El Diablo is really Rance Kimball, the man who forced Carey's wife to go with him.

The gang returns and El Diablo orders Carey tied up and guarded while they raid a prosperous Mexican's ranch. Carey is able to escape his captor and, taking Connie with him, he warns the ranch of the impending raid. A young Mexican rides for help while Carey and the rest fight off El Diablo's gang.

When he sees El Diablo leave the gang, Carey slips out of the ranch house and rides after him. Carey catches El Diablo and takes him back to the hideout in Rustler's Paradise. Stringing him by his hands to a ceiling beam, Carey uses his bullwhip, on the outlaw until El Diablo confesses he forced Carey's wife to run away with him and that he killed her when she threatened to leave him. After El Diablo acknowledges he is Rance Kimball and Carey has beaten him with the bullwhip the outlaw collapses on the rope holding him up, the victim of an apparent heart attack. The sheriff's posse rounds up the gang and Carey and his daughter, reunited, ride off together in search of a new life.

Sometimes, as in *Riders of the Whistling Skull* (Republic, 1937), the roles were reversed and the child, usually a daughter, made a determined search for a missing parent. In this Three Mesquiteers programmer, Mary Russell plays the daughter whose father, a prominent archaeologist, disappeared while searching for valuable Indian artifacts. The Three Mesquiteers help to guide the search party. Outlaws who want the treasure for themselves and fanatical Indians who want to guard their ancient burial grounds can't discourage the faithful daughter from successfully finding her lost father.

The errant son is a common problem in American families and was a familiar theme in Western movies. The young man usually meant no initial harm, but vices such as drinking and gambling or a hot temper got him into trouble and made him vulnerable to crooks who used him for their own purposes. Two John Wayne B's, *The Desert Trail* (Monogram, 1935) and *The Dawn Rider* (Monogram, 1935), and the Range Busters' *Trail Riders* (Monogram, 1942) developed this familiar storyline.

Paul Fix is Mary Kornman's brother in *The Desert Trail*. Young Fix gets involved with bad guy Al Ferguson and together they rob a rodeo promoter. When the old man goes for a gun, Fix kills him. Ferguson then holds the murder over his head in order to force Fix to participate in other holdups. John Wayne and his sidekick Eddie Chandler are accused of the holdup and murder, and they are forced to flee the town. The action is fast-paced as Wayne tries to find the guilty person, romance Kornman and avoid the sheriff who is chasing them.

Fix becomes increasingly disenchanted with Ferguson and wants out, but Ferguson won't permit him to quit. In fact, Ferguson tells Fix they are going to rob the local bank. When Fix tries to warn Wayne of the impending robbery, Ferguson shoots him in the back. Young Fix dies in his sister's arms after he confesses the murder and clears Wayne and Chandler. The young man meant no real harm, he just got mixed up with the wrong person and paid the ultimate price for his mistake.

A similar theme pervades *Trail Riders*. After the Range Busters tell Steve Clark to swear them in, they go gunning for the murderer of their boyhood friend. Their contact is a local rancher (Forrest Taylor). He has a daughter, Evelyn Finely, and an adopted son, Lynton Brent. That Brent is adopted is mentioned several times. When the Range Busters discover he is part of the outlaw gang, Max Terhune wonders how that could happen since he was Taylor's son. John "Dusty" King reminds Terhune that Brent was only an adopted son.

Brent, it turns out, did not want to be mixed up in illegal activity. He joined the vigilantes, run by that ace villain Charles King, because he wanted to help restore law and order. Then, as Brent told the Range Busters, one thing led to another and before he knew it, he was in too deep. He had become part of King's gang and he couldn't get out. However, Brent agrees to work with the Range Busters in the final showdown with King. Brent gets the drop on King, who knocks Brent's gun out of his hand, slugs him and then kills him. B Western justice prevailed. Brent died with a clear conscience trying to do the right thing, but because he had robbed and participated in murders, justice required that he die at film's end.

The Dawn Trail (Columbia, 1930) is an excellent Buck Jones programmer. Jones plays Larry Williams, a sheriff responsible for keeping the peace between cattlemen and sheepmen. He is also set to marry June Denton (Miriam Seeger) daughter of Mart Denton (Charles Morton), a leading cattleman, and sister to Jeff Denton (Erville Alderson). Williams and

Jeff Denton had been friends since boyhood. Unfortunately, Jeff drinks too much and, when drunk, he possesses a violent temper. In a drunken stupor, Jeff kills a sheepman and it's up to Williams to arrest him.

Mart Denton won't believe his son guilty and June tells Williams that if he really loves her he won't arrest her brother. For both father and daughter, loyalty to their brother blinds them to his behavior when drunk, and their hatred of sheepmen makes them believe that Jeff is being framed. Jeff on the other hand remembers killing the sheepman, feels remorseful about it, but is afraid to face the consequences, so he tells his father and sister that he is being framed and that Larry has sold out to the sheepman. His father and other cattlemen help Jeff escape from jail, and they decide to drive their cattle to water in the valley, across land owned by sheepmen. In the end, Mart Denton shoots his son by mistake and Jeff, dying, confesses to the murder, thus vindicating Williams' intention to arrest him.

The Dawn Trail sends mixed signals. On the one hand, viewers understand Mart and June Denton's loyalty to their son and brother. Families, after all, are supposed to support one another in bad times as well as good. Mart Denton's steadfast commitment to his son is admirable, and viewers agonize with June Denton as she is torn between loyalty to her brother and love for the man she intends to marry. Yet, there is something disturbing about their blindness to Jeff's behavior. If they had dealt with his drinking earlier, the murder would not have occurred in the first place. That dilemma of how to love unreservedly but yet confront destructive behavior, so amply expressed in *The Dawn Trail*, is a problem familiar to many families.

Steve Brodie plays Tim Holt's brother in *Brothers in the Saddle* (RKO, 1949). Brodie portrays a compulsive gambler who lies to his fiancée in order to get gambling money from her. Holt tries to keep Brodie from squandering his money, and he hides the truth from Virginia Cox (Brodie's bequeathed). During an all-night poker game, Brodie catches Francis McDonald cheating at cards. Brodie kills McDonald, and Richard Powers accuses Brodie of murdering an unarmed man. Even though McDonald was carrying a gun, Powers and his henchmen testify that McDonald was unarmed. Holt sets out to prove his brother innocent, but before Holt finishes gathering evidence Brodie betrays him. While hiding in the hills, Brodie becomes bitter and disillusioned, so he robs a stagecoach and murders Powers (one of the passengers).

Holt, forced to recognize his brother is an outlaw, tries to capture him. Brodie, however, is shot before Holt can find him and, in the film's climax, Brodie dies in Holt's arms. In *Brothers in the Saddle* the errant brother, while a victim of sorts, also committed serious crimes and, as a result, justice required that he die during the course of the film. But one also wishes Holt had disclosed Brodie's gambling compulsion earlier and maybe saved his brother's life.

The errant son or brother presents unique problems if a family member is a law officer. In *Wagon Trail* (Ajax, 1935), Harry Carey plays a sheriff whose son is found guilty of robbery and murder. The son was guilty, but he had been forced to participate in the robbery because of gambling debts. Carey's obligation to the law requires that he enforce it; however, he helps his son escape a lynch mob and forces Edward Norris, playing the evil Collins, to acknowledge he is the main culprit. Near the end of the film, Carey's son is released from jail and the judge speaks of a new deal for him.

In *Winning of the West* (Columbia, 1953), Gene Autry portrays a Texas Ranger who will not shoot his brother, even though the latter is robbing a bank, and for that Autry is dismissed from the Rangers. He returns to the town and tries to straighten out his brother as well as redeem his own reputation. Quite predictably, Gene exonerates his name, but his brother dies while protecting Gene.

Carleton Young plays Bob Steele's younger brother in *Billy the Kid in Texas*. Young is part of a gang holding up Wells Fargo wagons. Steele becomes sheriff and posts an order against wearing guns in town. Young vows to disobey the order, and he goes gunning for Steele, but at the last second they recognize each other. Steele then talks Young into siding with him in rounding up the outlaws. This one even has a happy ending. As Steele and Al St. John prepare to ride out of town, viewers see that Young is the new sheriff.

One family theme noted in earlier chapters is the drive to avenge the murder of one's parents. John Wayne and Bob Steele used this convention effectively in many of their films, and it was the central focus of George Houston's search in *The Lone Rider Rides On* and of Roy Rogers in *Saga of Death Valley* (Republic, 1939). Jack Randall also used it in *Across the Plains* (Monogram, 1939). White renegades had raided the wagon train and killed his parents. Rescued and raised by Indians, the adult Randall searched for and caught the renegades.

Sierra Passage (Monogram, 1951) is an excellent Wayne Morris Western. In the film, three men murder Morris's father. One of them, Alan Hale, Jr., wore an unusual-looking ring on a stub finger. Taken in and raised by the owners of a traveling minstrel show, Morris becomes an expert shot. But as he travels with the show he is constantly seeking the man with the ring so he can avenge his father's murder. Lloyd Corrigan describes Morris to Lola Albright, the heroine of the film, as a man bothered by a sickness, the need for revenge. When Morris finally confronts

Hale, he is unable to kill him. Instead, Morris shoots him in both hands so Hale will be unable ever again to hold a gun or deal off the bottom of the deck.

Mala Powers plays a white girl raised by Cherokee Indians in *Rose of Cimaron* (20th Century–Fox, 1952). Her foster parents are murdered, and she goes gunning for the killers. Wearing two guns, Powers is every bit the modern woman bent on revenge. When she finds two of the three killers, she calls them out, beats them to the draw and kills both of them. Jack Buetel, as the Sheriff, arrests her for murder. Powers insists, however, that Cherokee justice required her to kill the two and to continue her search for the third killer. Justice (she tells Buetel) must be swift as an arrow. It need not wait for the slow process of courtroom procedure.

Charles Starrett, in one of his pre–Durango Kid films, *Riders of Black River* (Columbia, 1939), returns with Bob Nolan and the Sons of the Pioneers to his hometown. His older brother (Forrest Taylor) rides out to the ranch to put up a welcome sign. Unknown to anyone, the ranch is being used to hide rustled cattle. When Taylor discovers the cattle, Dick Curtis, one of the meanest-looking of all Western villains, kills him. Starrett then must bring his brother's murderer to justice.

Tex Ritter catches the determination of these quests in *Trouble in Texas* (Grand National, 1937). He and his sidekick Horace Murphy ride the rodeo circuit. But Murphy wants them to quit and go back to steady work as entertainers. Ritter won't hear of it. His brother had been killed five years earlier in a faked rodeo accident. Ritter vows to track down his brother's killers even if it takes 50 years.

Whether it was dying to protect one's son, grieving with a family over a prodigal son or seeking revenge for a brother's death, family ties were acknowledged as central to American life. But such ties were also reinforced when the strong-willed daughter entered the scene. Unlike the errant son, she seldom died at the end of the film, and she hardly ever broke significant laws. In some cases she was more exasperating than trouble, while in other films she possessed a strong character and was a real heroine.

One of Dale Evans' most effective film roles was in *My Pal Trigger* (Republic, 1946). She played Gabby Hayes' daughter and was convinced, at least in part, that Roy Rogers did not shoot Golden Sovereign, Gabby's prize palomino horse. She was also concerned that Hayes' mourning for the horse had intensified his hate for Rogers to an irrational level, and that it was leading to excessive gambling and impending financial ruin. On her own initiative, Dale had the charges against Roy dropped, and she confronted Gabby about his drinking and gambling. Because of her efforts, Roy and Gabby were reconciled by the end of the film.

In *Trigger Jr.* (Republic, 1950), Evans played the role of a former circus trick rider. Her mother had been killed in a circus accident and her father, now an embittered cripple, had turned his back on the circus. Dale, on her own initiative, invites Rogers' circus and Wild West show to winter at their ranch. She hopes it will revive her father's sagging spirits as well as their bank account.

Just as often, Evans played a strong-willed daughter who was a source of trouble. For instance, in *Song of Nevada* (Republic, 1944), her character, Joan Barrabee, intended to marry an Easterner who was after her wealth. When she believed that her father had been killed in a plane crash, Evans and her fiancé go to Nevada to run the family ranch. He, of course, ran it for his own advantage and it was up to Roy, in concert with Mr. Barrabee (who had *not* been killed), to straighten out the situation.

Strong-willed daughters were frequently involved in saving the home place after the death of a father. That was the theme in *Ride the Man Down* (Republic, 1953). It was also a part of the plot in *Hawk of Powder River* (Eagle-Lion, 1948), an Eddie Dean Western. The daughter in that film, with the assistance of Dean, refused to sell the ranch even though the Hawk and her outlaws murdered the heroine's father and were trying to run her off the ranch. In another film, *Montana* (Warner Bros., 1950), Alexis Smith was a determined opponent of Errol Flynn. Faithful to her father's teaching that sheep and cattle did not mix, she fought Flynn's efforts to introduce sheep onto Montana grazing lands. Even though by the film's end Smith was a convert to Flynn's perspective, the image she projected was one of a strong-willed daughter intent on preserving her legacy.

If a strong-willed daughter fought to preserve the family homestead, that task was even more incumbent upon the son. Sons, after all, were the most likely to inherit the property and therefore had a greater stake in its preservation. Tex Ritter played such a son in *Raiders of the San Joaquin* (Universal, 1943). After his father's murder, Ritter temporarily became an outlaw, to frustrate outlaws who try to take over ranches so they can sell the right-of-way to a railroad. Ritter's entire purpose was not only to save his own ranch, but those of his neighbors as well. Like Ritter, Fred Scott in an earlier film, *Two Gun Troubadour* (Spectrum, 1937), returned as a masked avenger to reclaim his family home, stolen from him by an uncle who murdered his father.

The Outcast (Republic, 1954) is a bleak Western, much like those which dominated the genre in the middle and late 1950s. John Derek, as Jed Cosgrove, returns to his hometown to reclaim the ranch his uncle (Jim Davis), had stolen from him. Davis had forged a phony will giving Derek only ten percent of the income from his father's ranch. At 15 years of age,

Derek had stood over his father's grave and vowed he would come back and kill a man, his uncle. He returns to kill Davis, and to claim his rightful inheritance.

A line from *Gunman from Bodie* (Monogram, 1941) offered the highest compliment to a strong-willed daughter and one repeated many times about the steadfast son: "She is a chip off of the old block and nobody ever scared the old man out." Family was important in B Westerns, and among the highest praise they could offer a son or daughter was to be a "chip off of the old block." That was particularly true if the "old block" had been a determined community leader or a strong-willed rancher who had carved a home out of the wilderness. Children were supposed to be proud of parents like that and they were supposed to want to carry on the family tradition! That sentiment may seem quaint, even strange and restrictive by contemporary standards, but it struck a responsive chord in the years prior to 1955.

The cowboy hero sided with those forces endeavoring to preserve community and family ties. He fought those who tried to create personal empires and enhance personal wealth at the expense of the community and, ultimately, his hope was to settle down on a small ranch himself, as William Elliott said, "with friendly neighbors all around."

The B Western cowboy hero was not a lonely, isolated individual. Some were important, respected members of their community. However, most were roving ambassadors of peace and justice; they rode into town as the film began and rode away with a friendly wave as the film ended. Even though they were neither married nor lived in the town, they affirmed family and community bonds, important values, ones to be honored and protected.

In that sense, B Westerns fit well the beliefs of mid–twentieth century Americans. But to leave the impression that community monopolized the genre would be a mistake. Individualism is an equally important American belief. Americans have idolized the person who stands apart from society and even flaunts its values. According to the myth of America, the country was populated by nonconformists who had a restless urge to see what lay beyond the next hill. The cowboy hero was an individualist, but one who operated within a community context. His actions were designed to protect and enhance community, not to fulfill personal, selfish desires and ambitions. Bigger-budget Westerns, not the series B films, were films most likely to focus on the individualistic aspect of American beliefs.

Two characters in *Shane* (Paramount, 1953) are excellent examples of American individualism. Alan Ladd as Shane is one of the characters. Not only does he ride in at the beginning of the film and ride away toward the mountains at the end, as the film unfolds he is always on the margin of the community: he stands in the rain as Van Heflin, portraying Joe Starrett, and his friends plot strategy; he remains on the edge of the crowd at Torrey's funeral; and he stays out of Mrs. Starrett's efforts to keep her husband from going to meet Ryker. Ladd does not become involved, except to uphold his personal honor in the saloon fight, until Ben Johnson brings him word of the trap being set for Joe Starrett.

A high moment in the film occurs when young Joey Starrett sees Shane and tells his parents, "Here comes Shane and he is wearing his gun." Here we see not community but an individual, Shane, the gunfighter, estranged from community, preparing to ply his trade. As Shane tells Joey at the film's end, "There is no going back from a killing." So he rides off toward the distant Rockies, the lonely but heroic individual.

In the character Ryker, played by Emile Meyer, we see another side of individualism. Ryker is not a bad man. He is, however, unable to change with the times. The key to understanding Ryker is in the speech he delivers to Joe Starrett. Wilson the gunfighter, so realistically portrayed by Jack Palance, has arrived but he has not yet killed Torrey. Ryker makes one final peace overture to Starrett, but he is rebuffed. Ryker reminds Starrett that he, Ryker, came to the valley when Starrett was no older than young Joey. He fought Cheyenne and still has a stiff shoulder from one of their arrows. He worked hard and fought blizzards and drought to make it outstanding cattle country. Now farmers like Joe Starrett are destroying all he built.

Ryker dies in the end because he cannot or will not adapt to change. He believes he can hold back progress. But that does not change the validity of Ryker's appeal. He had lived out the American dream and he was forced to watch its demise as another dream replaced his. Consistent with American practice, he went down fighting. In *Shane*, Ryker is a tragic figure, an individual who has outlived his era.

We see much of Ryker in John Wayne's character in the earlier film, *Red River* (United Artists, 1948). Wayne, as Tom Dunson, built the Red River D into large cattle empire. He took the land from its Mexican owner and built it up through hard work. No price supports or government assistance; he did it with hard work and perseverance. Then the Civil War comes, and the price of beef plummeted. Facing ruin, Wayne takes another gamble. He starts the cattle toward Missouri and higher-priced markets. Just as Ryker in *Shane* was blinded by his resistance to change, so Wayne as Dunson becomes too single-minded, even cruel, in his determination to take the herd to Missouri. But in spite of these character flaws, both men symbolize the individualistic spirit that helped to build a nation stretching from ocean to ocean.

My Darling Clementine (20th Century–Fox, 1946) also is more representative of the individualistic spirit than community ethos. Henry Fonda as Wyatt Earp is moved by personal considerations, not concern for the town. When he goes into the saloon after the Indian who is shooting up the place, Fonda is not concerned that the Indian might hurt somebody. The shooting has interrupted Fonda's shave and he wants it finished! He does not agree to become marshal until his brother James is murdered and their cattle rustled, and the murder of brother Virgil provokes the final showdown with the Clantons. Even Victor Mature as Doc Holliday joins the Earps for a personal reason. The younger Clanton was responsible, indirectly at least, for the death of Doc's mistress. There is some community sentiment in the film. Cathy Downs, as Clementine, expresses to Fonda the beauty of a Tombstone morning. There is also an interesting interlude in which Fonda accompanies Downs one Sunday morning to the unfinished church. The steeple's skeleton-like appearance holds out the promise of civilization coming to the desert. These are interesting asides, but the film is not about community. It is about personal and family revenge. When the gunfight is over, Clementine remains in Tombstone, Holliday is dead and the Earps head for California. The Earps had revenged the death of their brothers. Tombstone could take care of itself!

There is greater affirmation of community and progress in *Shane* than in *My Darling Clementine*. At least Shane understood the times had changed, that the day of the gunfighter was nearly over. He had used his gun defending the forces of progress. Fonda and Mature used their guns to wreak personal vengeance.

James Stewart may have given the starkest portrayal of the lonely, alienated individual in *The Naked Spur* (MGM, 1953) as he pursued Robert Ryan for the $5,000 reward. When Stewart had returned from the Civil War, he found his girl married to another man, and his property taken from him. Embittered, he is consumed now by the reward money as a way of reclaiming his property. He fights his fellow travelers and himself as he returns Ryan to Kansas.

The film ends with Stewart pulling Ryan's dead body from a raging river. Janet Leigh, the film's heroine, promises to marry him, and to go with him in spite of the fact he is obsessed with returning Ryan for the reward. Amazed that she cares that much for him, Stewart begins to cry, ashamed of his behavior. They bury Ryan by the river and ride off together toward California and a fresh start. There is redemption for Stewart in the end through Leigh's love for him, but throughout the film Stewart's character is a hateful human being, embittered at life and longing for revenge on the entire human race.

Bigger-budget, more adult Westerns, then, offer a correction of sorts to the community-affirming B entries. Taken together, however, the films address the dual strands of community and individualism that permeate American thought. Overall, during the 1930s and 1940s Westerns supported community far more often than they glamorized the exploits of a lonely, heroic and often alienated individual.

Chapter Seven

"LAW IS LAW AND PROPERTY IS PROPERTY"

People in the United States value personal success and hold individuals responsible for their own financial wellbeing. Nowhere is that commitment more apparent than in the American economy. Americans are devoted to free enterprise, and support for free market economics is deeply ingrained in public opinion. Whenever government has intruded into economic relationships, and those have been numerous in the twentieth century, it has done so to even out the balance of employee rights, employer prerogatives and the public good skewed by some malfunction of markets. Socialism has never taken root in the United States.

Support for free market economics is so pervasive that it needs no elaborate explanation or defense. Yet, a paradox exists. Entrepreneurs and businessmen have always been sources of great controversy. Well-known nineteenth and twentieth century entrepreneurs such as Cornelius Vanderbilt, John D. Rockefeller, Andrew Carnegie and Henry Ford helped to create the modern industrial economy and without them the United States' standard of living would be much lower. Yet, historians label some of them "robber barons." Bankers, in particular, are mistrusted, and people seem willing to believe the worst about them. Reflecting that, Walter Isaacson and Evan Thomas in *The Wise Men* suggest that the intense, highly personalized attacks on such political luminaries as Dean Acheson, John McCloy and Robert Lovett by Senator Joseph McCarthy in the early 1950s were as much expressions of populist resentment against Wall Street bankers as they were a concern about Communism (Isaacson, 564). There is a great deal of merit in that argument.

On the one hand, businessmen are respected, but on the other hand they are resented and mistrusted. Americans, in the main, affirm free enterprise and just as eagerly doubt the morality, honesty and civic-mindedness of businessmen. Westerns frequently cast businessmen — saloonkeepers, bankers, shop owners, lumber company owners, lawyers and doctors — as villains. In that way, Western films mirror the paradox existing between widespread belief in free enterprise and populist-driven suspicions of businessmen.

The popular image of a Western outlaw is an uncouth, ill-tempered, greedy and often cowardly person who relied on brawn rather than brain. Within the genre they were called "dog" heavies. Fans recall fondly Bob Kortman, George Chesebro, Charles King, Frank Ellis, Roy Barcroft, Bob Cason, Lane Bradford, Myron Healey and Terry Frost. But "dog" heavies were not the only type of villains. There were also "brain" heavies. As the name implies, these villains bossed the operation, decided which crimes to commit and picked the dog heavies to include in the gang. Usually the brain heavies worked behind the scenes as respected members of the community, but, unknown to most, enriched themselves at the community's expense. Cy Kendall, Arthur Loft, Harry Woods, LeRoy Mason and I. Stanford Jolley are examples of actors who appeared frequently as "brain" heavies. Taken together, "dog" and "brain" heavies personified evil on the silver screen.

Charles King, LeRoy Mason and Harry Woods, three of Western films' best-known villains, played both "dog" and "brain" heavies. As "brain" heavies they often portrayed saloonkeepers. In the eyes of Western film fans, King, Mason and Woods were rough customers and it would have taken a leap of imagination even too great for B Westerns to represent them as pillars of the community, so their characters were seldom reputable community leaders.

Saloonkeepers were natural "brain" heavies because saloons were commonly associated with drunkenness, gambling and prostitution. Many Americans believed saloonkeeping was a sin business; people who made a living off of others people's moral weaknesses were not likely to be honest in other areas of life. That view of saloons did not emerge spontaneously, it was crafted by religious revivalists and social reformers in the United States throughout the nineteenth and early twentieth centuries.

In the 100 years prior to 1920, the United States experienced three waves of protestant religious revivals: the Second Great Awakening, which began in the early 1800s, lasted until the 1840s; the revivals of Dwight L. Moody occurred in the 1880's, and the flamboyant Billy Sunday achieved national prominence in the years prior to World War I. Of the three revival movement, the Second Great Awakening had a varied social agenda.

Charles Finney, the evangelist most closely identified with the Second Great Awakening, believed that, once "saved," regenerate persons ought to demonstrate their newly experienced salvation by working to transform society. Abolition, prohibition and women's rights were all issues energized by revivals of the Second Great Awakening in the years prior to the Civil War. Moody and Sunday, on the other hand, were not social reformers; they eschewed social action in favor of "saving souls." They believed that once persons were "saved" society would be automatically transformed because most social problems would disappear.

The saloon was the one exception to Moody and Sunday's hands-off attitude toward social reform. Both men railed against saloons as they joined forces with the broader anti-saloon movement. Saloons, according to Moody and Sunday, were terrible places where hard-working men gambled away the family income or, worse yet, spent it getting drunk only to go home and abuse the family. People who got "saved" at one of their revivals were expected — almost coerced — to renounce alcohol as one of the sins from which they were saved.

The anti-saloon movement ultimately led to the Eighteenth Amendment of the United States Constitution and the Volstead Act of 1920 as the country began a naive experiment with Prohibition. While Prohibition was relatively short-lived (it ended in 1933), the attitudes promoted by revivalists and social reformers lingered. Saloons simply were not regarded as desirable businesses. Certainly the gangster-ridden "Roaring Twenties" did little to change that image.

People drank liquor in spite of Prohibition and soon speakeasies sprang up throughout the country as places to get otherwise illegal alcohol. When law enforcement agencies seemed to look the other way at these open violations of public law, speakeasies became lucrative businesses. Illegal alcohol became so economically successful by the mid–1920s that urban gangsters warred for control of it. When Prohibition ended, speakeasies were converted to legitimate taverns and nightclubs, but the image of saloons created by evangelists and social reformers, an image reinforced by 1920s gangsters, lingered.

Was it not obvious that the Western outlaw, the gangster's frontier ancestors in crime, would be linked to saloons? Was it such a long step from gambling in a saloon, and usually crooked gambling at that, to defrauding ranchers in order to get their lands? Would people who exploited dance hall girls care about the widow's livelihood? Of course not! Thus emerged the Western film saloonkeeper as villain.

Milburn Morante as Rufus Todd in *West of the Law* (Monogram, 1942), a Rough Riders Western already discussed at length, offers an appropriate introduction to saloons and saloon-keepers. In the opening scenes, Todd prepares a stinging editorial denouncing the crime spree plaguing Gold Creek, and he observes that, none of the crime occurred before the saloon opened. As the action unfolds, Harry Woods, owner of the local saloon, is one of the three men behind the ore robberies. Not only was Woods, whom the audience knew to be a villain, a saloonkeeper, but *West of the Law* associates the coming of the saloon with an increase in crime.

Byron Foulger as the Reverend Henry Lane makes that point emphatically in the Duncan Renaldo Cisco Kid programmer *Satan's Cradle* (United Artists, 1949). The film opens with Foulger addressing a crowd and bemoaning the transformation of Silver City from a nice community into a sin city. Pointing to the Silver Lode Saloon, Foulger observes that the city changed when Ann Savage as Lil arrived and took over the saloon. Now the city was a regular den of gambling, murder and theft.

Bob Steele is a saloonkeeper in the Roy Rogers programmer *The Carson City Kid* (Republic, 1940), and he adds another popular perception to the image of saloons. When Steele sees Rogers' skill with his gun, he decides to offer Rogers a job as bouncer and bodyguard at the Yellowback, his saloon. When Rogers wants to know if Steele is expecting trouble, he replies, "There is always trouble in a place like this." Many Americans in 1940 would have wholeheartedly agreed with Steele's assessment of saloons!

Trouble in the Yellowback happens when Steele cheats Noah Beery, Jr., out of his gold poke in a crooked card game. Beery had struck it rich in the California gold fields but his friendly nature and talkativeness make him easy prey for Steele.

An outlaw known as the Carson City Kid has plagued the area. Since the Kid's identity is unknown, Beery impersonates him and steals back his gold. Roy Rogers is really the Carson City Kid, searching for the man who murdered his brother. Roy has evidence that Steele is Reynolds, the man who killed Rogers' brother.

When Steele's men catch Beery and accuse him of being the Carson City Kid, he goes on trial in the Yellowback. The court proceedings are interrupted by Rogers, dressed as the Carson City Kid. He returns the money belt Beery had stolen and thrown in the bushes right before Steele's men apprehended him.

As Rogers backs through the saloon's swinging doors, he yells "Reynolds!" Steele, who knows the Carson City Kid is after him for murdering his brother, pulls a gun and Roy kills him and then escapes from town. Rogers has his revenge and another Western town is freed of its evil saloonkeeper.

A number of Westerns featuring Charles King as a saloonkeeper "brain" heavy have already been discussed in previous chapters. Among these is *Trail Riders* (Monogram, 1942). King headed the local vigilantes and used them for his own illegal purposes. He was also the local saloonowner, and much of the dialogue occurs in his saloon as he gives orders to his men.

King also played a saloonkeeper in *Rustler's Hideout* (PRC, 1944). Larry "Buster" Crabbe as Billy Carson and his sidekick Al St. John are herding cattle from Wyoming to a Montana market. King is the saloon owner in cahoots with John Merton, the local banker (more about bankers later in the chapter) and the two men try to rustle Crabbe's cattle. They are not successful, and when Crabbe heads to town for the final showdown, Merton, the banker, gets cold feet. Merton is in the process of absconding with the money that he and King have stolen when King catches him emptying the safe. King shoots Merton before he can flee town with the money and Crabbe brings King to justice. But once again the saloon owner is associated with criminal activity.

LeRoy Mason played the role of a "brain" heavy saloonkeeper in *Mojave Firebrand* (Republic, 1944), a Wild Bill Elliott Western. Gabby Hayes discovers a rich vein of silver and he vows to establish a city devoted to peace and justice, a decent town in which God-fearing men and women will live. Unfortunately, Gabby's dream turns to a nightmare as outlaws run rampant in the community. Their base of operation is the Silver King Saloon, owned by Mason (playing the gambler Tracy Dalton). A narrator calls Dalton the "skunk of the frontier and king of thieves," introducing viewers to Tracy Dalton.

Dalton is head of the outlaws who rob and murder, and he uses a young boy who idolizes him to spy on Gabby and Elliott. The young boy, played by Harry McKim, is Gabby's ward. Gabby raised him after the boy's real father was killed in a mining accident. The boy—like many boys his age—doesn't want to go to school or to grow up to be a respectable God-fearing man like Gabby Hayes. McKim wants the glamour and excitement he associates with a man like Tracy Dalton.

McKim won't believe that Dalton is behind the outlaws, and when Dalton realizes how much the boy idolizes him, Dalton uses the boy's trust for his own criminal ends. Dalton shows McKim a roulette wheel, explains how it works and invites McKim to stop by his office whenever he likes. Even when Bud Geary, one of Dalton's hired guns, tries to kill Elliott, McKim won't believe that Dalton is bad. When Dalton tells Elliott that Geary was with him all day, young McKim decides he can't be sure if Geary was the man he saw at the window. Later on, McKim innocently discloses Gabby and Elliott's plans to Dalton, and refuses to believe that his pal Tracy Dalton shot Gabby.

As Gabby and Wild Bill get closer to rounding up Dalton and his cohorts, the mayor (Hal Price), voted into office in an election rigged by Dalton, becomes frightened and decides to leave town. Dalton shoots him with the same high-powered rifle he had used on Gabby. McKim sees Dalton shoot Price and realizes that all the things Gabby and Wild Bill have said about Dalton are true.

In the end, Wild Bill Elliott brings Tracy Dalton to justice and Epitaph, the town founded by Gabby Hayes, becomes a place of peace and justice as Gabby intended. And young Harry McKim learns that saloonkeepers and gamblers are not men of honor and certainly not worthy character models. Tracy Dalton murdered and extorted money, but even more cowardly he used a naive young boy as a tool; he betrayed the wholesome trust of a young person who admired him. Few Westerns have made the saloonkeeper any more despicable than Tracy Dalton in *Mojave Firebrand*.

Saloonkeepers as villains were not limited to B Westerns. *Oh! Susanna* (Republic, 1951) is an example of a bigger-budget film which portrayed the saloonkeeper as a villain. In *Oh! Susanna*, Jim Davis, who in his early years as a Republic contract player frequently appeared as a heavy, operated a saloon and general store from which he sold guns and whiskey to the Indians. Davis' aim was to get the Indians and cavalry fighting each other. Davis knew the cavalry would prevail and drive the Indians from the Black Hills. The Hills would then be open to gold miners and Davis would make a financial windfall selling supplies to them.

James Millican in *Beyond the Purple Hills* (Columbia, 1950) underscores the image of saloonkeepers. In the film, a judge is murdered and his errant son is arrested for the crime. Millican notes the slow progress of justice and observes that if he had committed the crime he would have been swinging from a cottonwood tree because he is a saloonkeeper and gambler.

As Roy Rogers Westerns took on a modern setting, the typical Western saloon became a fancy casino, but little else changed. The casino owner, more often than not, was the brains behind criminal activities. In *Cowboy and the Senorita* (Republic, 1944), the first Rogers entry with Dale Evans, John Hubbard as Craig Allen is both a casino owner and Evans' love interest. Hubbard wants her to transfer a mine to him. Evans believes it worthless, but Hubbard knows it has a rich vein of gold ore. Rogers and his sidekick Guinn "Big Boy" Williams have to prevent Hubbard from defrauding Evans.

Jack Holt in *My Pal Trigger* (Republic, 1946) not only shot Gabby Hayes' prize palomino Golden Sovereign, he also used crooked gambling at his casino to get Hayes heavily in debt. Holt's aim was to gain control of the Golden Horse Ranch, Gabby Hayes' valuable thoroughbred ranch. Roy Rogers saves the day when he allows Dale Evans to win the big horse race. Gabby had bet the ranch against his IOUs and as a side bet, Holt agreed to give him Trigger if Hayes' horse, Golden Empress, won the race. When Holt's men try to bottle in Evans so she can't catch Trigger, Roy draws back to help her. Evans wins the race, Gabby's ranch is saved, Roy gets Trigger and Holt is arrested for shooting the Golden Sovereign.

In *Heldorado* (Republic, 1946), Rogers breaks up a criminal syndicate laundering $1000 bills through a Las Vegas casino and in *Apache Rose* (Republic, 1947) Roy helps his friend Carlos Vega (Russ Vincent) fight George Meeker. Meeker plays the owner of an offshore gambling casino. He holds several thousand dollars of Vincent's IOUs and is using them to force him to deed to Meeker oil drilling rights on Vincent's property. It made little difference whether the action took place in an old-fashioned Western saloon or a modern gambling casino; Hollywood portrayed the owners of such establishments as villains.

On rare occasions, however, Westerns did depict honest saloonkeepers and gamblers. Buck Jones plays the honest owner of a gambling house in *Stone of Silver Creek* (Universal, 1935). Jones' honesty and concern for his establishment's reputation is driven home early in the film. He catches a man who dropped his cards on the floor slipping an extra ace into his hand. Jones exposes the cheat, who is embarrassed and befuddled. A few film feet later, Jones goes into a back room and wins back the deed to a valuable mine from two crooks who had swindled it from a drunken old man in a crooked card game.

Noah Beery was an honest gambler in *Outlaws of Pine Ridge* (Republic, 1942). He chases Emmett Lynn, playing Don "Red" Barry's sidekick, out of the saloon when he catches him cheating at poker. Beery is so impressed by Red Barry's exploits in getting back stolen money from a stagecoach robbery, he offers to make Barry the manager of the casino. Beery expects to be appointed territorial governor, and he will have to move to Pine Ridge. Beery teaches the young Barry all of his card tricks, but warns him against cheating customers. In fact, Beery cautions if he ever catches Barry cheating the patrons, their association will end.

When Barry protests that Noah Beery's son should become manager of the casino, Beery responds that he doesn't want his son (played by a young Clayton Moore), mixed up with gambling and saloons. Even though it is an honest establishment, viewers understand it is still a questionable business, and few fathers want their sons to become saloonkeepers.

A similar theme appears in *Land Beyond the Law* (Warner Bros., 1937). Irene Franklin operates a hotel and saloon, but in letters to her daughter,

Franklin passes off the saloon as a restaurant. When her daughter comes for a visit, Franklin gets Dick Foran and his buddies to convert the saloon to a restaurant. Franklin does not want her daughter to know her mother is a saloonkeeper.

Most of the men who in real life operated saloons, taverns or nightclubs were honest businessmen. Yet they had, and probably still have, unsavory reputations. They were natural heavies and surely few viewers saw an anti-business bias in such portrayals. However, one is struck by the extent to which other businessmen were depicted as heavies.

Bankers and officers of lending agencies were cast as heavies with nearly as much regularity as were saloonkeepers. There were exceptions, of course. Most notable of those exceptions may be Robert Ryan's role as the good banker in *Trail Street* (RKO, 1947). Bankers, however, more often than not fit Berton Churchill's dramatization of the crooked banker, pompous and self-righteous, absconding with the mine payroll in *Stagecoach* (United Artists, 1939). Numerous B Westerns surely cast bankers as heavies.

The Fighting Legion (Universal, 1930) is a transitional Western; while mostly silent, it does have some sound parts. The theme, however, is familiar to all Western fans. Ken Maynard and his sidekick Frank Rice, who is best remembered as Buck Jones' sidekick, stumble across a dying Texas Ranger and agree to take his place in tracking down an outlaw gang operating out of Bowden. The brains of the outfit is a banker who, in league with a saloon owner, keeps Bowden a wide open town dominated by gamblers and gunfighters. All of the time, of course, both men seem deeply concerned about the level of violence and lawlessness in Bowden.

Wheeler Oakman plays a banker, lawyer and Justice of the Peace all rolled into one in Bill Cody's *Frontier Days* (Spectrum, 1934). Oakman bosses a gang that holds up stagecoaches, and he also swindles a family out of its ranch. The father and family provider has been killed and Oakman produces a fake $2,000 note that he claims the deceased borrowed from him. It's up to Cody to expose Oakman as a crook.

Hooper Atchley is the villainous banker in *Scarlet River* (RKO, 1933) starring Tom Keene. Atchley holds a mortgage on Dorothy Wilson's ranch. Her foreman, Lon Chaney, Jr.—in cahoots with Atchley—kills Wilson's cattle so she will be unable to make mortgage payments and lose the ranch. Keene's motion picture company wants to use Wilson's ranch as a movie location. Since the money she receives from the film company can go to mortgage payments, Atchley and Chaney try to stop the filming and Keene, in turn, unmasks the two crooks.

In *Shine on Harvest Moon* (Republic, 1939), Frank Jacquet, a bank president, is the secret partner of Stanley Andrews, the outlaw founder of Jackson's Hole. Jacquet, who is trusted by all the ranchers, keeps Andrews informed about where the cattle are pastured and when they will be moved. Andrews then knows when and where to raid. Roy Rogers finally defeats Andrews and exposes Jacquet as the brains behind the outfit.

Arthur Loft plays banker Sam Wyatt in *Days of Jesse James* (Republic, 1939). Loft convinces Gabby Hayes to put his $40,000 in Loft's bank; Loft and his outlaws then hold up the bank. They make it appear as if Jesse James robbed the bank. Loft even kills the night watchman who recognized him. Roy Rogers unmasks Loft as the culprit and clears Jesse James of the robbery.

The films just discussed and many, many more were produced during the Depression riddled 1930s, but the anti-banker trend continued into the 1940s. A crooked banker who tried to cheat ranchers out of their land triggered the massive migration to Colorado in *Prairie Schooners* (Columbia, 1941). A Roy Rogers Western of the same year, *Jesse James at Bay* (Republic, 1941) depicted bankers as working in concert with crooked railroaders to cheat Missouri farmers out of their land. *Flashing Guns* (Monogram, 1947) with Johnny Mack Brown featured a banker who back-dated a note due him by Raymond Hatton in order to foreclose on Hatton's property which, unknown to Hatton, contained gold.

Nor did the tendency to portray bankers as villains lessen much in the early 1950s. Dennis Moore is a clerk in Jack Holt's bank, and the masked, whip-cracking outlaw leader of a gang terrorizing the area in *King of the Bullwhip* (Western Adventure, 1951). Lash LaRue goes after him, and the film ends with LaRue unmasking Moore in an exciting bullwhip fight. A banker in *Beyond the Purple Hills* was stealing from the judge's estate and he had to kill the judge who had discovered the thefts. Interestingly enough, James Millican — the saloonkeeper — and the man who many suspected of being mixed up in the judge's death was not a crook. However, B Westerns' second-most favorite villain, the banker, was the murderer. In Gene Autry's final outing, *Last of the Pony Riders* (Columbia, 1953), a local banker is trying to destroy the Pony Express so he can get the mail contract for his stage line.

Raymond Massey, the villain in *Dallas* (Warner Bros., 1950), runs a land office and buys up mortgages. While Massey is not, strictly speaking, a banker, one of his lines appears to reflect Hollywood's opinion of bankers. Massey tells one of his brothers, "I don't buy mortgages to get paid back."

Massey's view that he didn't loan money to get paid back was echoed by Grant Withers in *Leadville Gunslinger* (Republic, 1952), an entertaining entry in Republic's Rocky Lane series. By the late 1940s Grant Withers had become one of Republic's leading brain heavies and in *Leadville Gunslinger* he plays the role of Jonathan Graves, a banker and one of Leadville's prominent citizens.

The film opens with a bank robbery. When Sheriff Kenneth MacDonald brings in Chet Yonker, head of the gang which held up the bank, Withers visits the office to express gratitude for the sheriff's fine work, and Withers tells MacDonald he was "glad it was not my bank they picked on." Later viewers learn why the outlaws did not pick on Withers' bank; he is the brains behind their activities! Chet Yonker, played by Republic's well-known heavy Roy Barcroft, is a tough customer and so MacDonald asks for a deputy United States Marshal to come to Leadville and take the prisoner to the county seat. Rocky Lane is the deputy marshal charged with that responsibility.

On his was to Leadville, Lane stops to see his old friend, Eddy Waller, playing his normal role of Nugget Clark. Clark owns a ranch and he tells Lane that a geologist friend recently told him that the ranch probably contained oil. That is Clark's last hope to save the ranch. Withers' bank holds a note on Clark's ranch, and Withers has given Clark two days to pay up. Clark has been unable to pay off the note because outlaws have run off his stock and continued to terrorize the ranch.

Rocky Lane recognized immediately that the two things were interrelated; the outlaws knew about the oil and they were trying to keep Clark from paying off the note. Clark, however, refuses to believe that Withers is behind his troubles. On the day the note is due, Clark goes to see Withers and pleads for more time. He tells Withers that a geologist is coming on the afternoon stage to run tests at his ranch. If the geologist finds oil shale, Clark's neighbors will help him pay off the note, and Clark, in turn, will give his neighbors a share of the oil money.

Withers knows that there is oil on the ranch and he doesn't want Clark to pay off the note, so he orders Yonker and his men to stop the stage and kill the geologist. Withers then has I. Stanford Jolley, a member of the gang, impersonate a geologist and tell Clark that while it looks like oil shale, there is no oil on the property. Clark's neighbors will not give him the money with which to pay off the note; Withers will foreclose and become a rich man.

Lane, in the meantime, has stopped the runaway stage. The driver, who is wounded but not dead as Yonker intended, tells Lane that the geologist had been killed. Lane returns to Clark's ranch in time to hear Jolley tell Clark that there is no oil on the place. Lane realizes that Jolley is a phony geologist who was planted by the gang, so he and Clark prepare a trap to catch the brains behind the gang. Clark goes to town to tell Withers that the geologist said there was oil on the ranch and Lane infiltrates the gang.

The scheme backfires, however, when Yonker orders Lane and two others—including Jolley—to kill Nugget Clark. When Lane shoots one of the outlaws instead and takes Jolley to jail, Withers wanders into the sheriff's office to discover what had happened. He learns that Lane is really a deputy United States Marshal who had fooled Yonker into joining the gang. All ends well, however, as Lane kills Withers in a gun battle and chases down and captures Yonker. Clark's ranch land is full of oil and the scheming banker's efforts to dupe honest people out of their property has been foiled again by the cowboy hero.

A Roy Rogers B Western, *Wall Street Cowboy* (Republic, 1939), offered a backhanded compliment to bankers while questioning the morality of finance agencies. According to the plot, Roy's father had borrowed several thousand dollars from a finance company. When the company refused to extend the time Rogers could pay off the principle (there was, again unknown to Roy, a valuable mineral on the property) he told Niles (Ivan Miller), manager of the finance agency, that his Dad should have gone to a bank. Finance agencies charged such outrageous interest no one could ever pay off a debt.

Clearly, distress over economic conditions may have prompted widespread distrust of bankers throughout the Depression 1930s. Banks and other leading agencies were forced to foreclose on many homeowners, farmers and small businessmen, all victims of the hard times. In fact, a number of Poverty Row studios and independents specializing in Westerns were heavily in debt, and most of them went bankrupt. Animosity toward bankers in the 1930s is neither surprising nor unexpected, but the trend continued into the more prosperous 1940s and 1950s. B Westerns demonstrated a deep-seated suspicion held by many Americans in the middle quarter of the twentieth century that banks and other financial institutions were out to make money any way they could, and often they loaned money in order to foreclose on valuable property. Institutions that loan and invest money and insure property are essential to a modern, complex economy; but they were, and probably still are, resented and mistrusted. B Westerns simply picked up on that fact, incorporated it into plots and reflected it back on the silver screen.

Close behind bankers as villains were those who controlled or sought to speculate in water and good land, the West's two most precious resources. Some speculators were portrayed merely as shysters, playing on the gullibility of those who wanted to get rich quick. For example, the Gene Autry film *The Man from Music Mountain* (Republic, 1938) opened with shots of newly completed Boulder Dam. The plot then unfolded around a con man's scheme to sell property in a ghost town, Gold River, Arizona, on the promise that electricity would be made available as power lines were strung from the dam.

An equally serious theme pervaded Roy Rogers' first movie, *Under the Western Stars* (Republic, 1938). Here, the Great Western Water and Power Company charged allegedly exorbitant water rates. As a result, ranchers were being driven from their land and their animals were dying from lack of water. Working in league with the local congressman, the company had kept a bill authorizing funding for a public dam bottled up in committee.

Near the beginning of the film, Roy rides to the aid of some ranchers who had vowed to open the floodgates of the dam in order to get water for their cattle. When the sheriff arrives to stop the shooting, Roy prevents him from interfering until his (Roy's) sidekick Smiley Burnette opens the floodgates. At one point, as Roy tries to justify his actions, the sheriff replies that "Law is law and property is property." Yet that was not the case because the local judge, after learning what Roy had done, fined him one dollar for trespassing. Law may be law, but clearly property is not property to be protected when it belongs to the Great Western Water and Power Company. An Eastern speculator concerned about his personal wealth, enhanced at the expense of hard-working folk of the heartland, does not merit the law's full protection. His property has an odious taint.

A Gene Autry film, *Red River Valley* (Republic, 1937) combined the natural resource and greedy banker themes. In this film, a banker had loaned money on ranch property so the ranchers could construct dam and irrigation canals to prevent a water shortage. But the banker secretly hired a gang of outlaws to impede construction so the ranchers could not complete the dam in time to stave off drought. Crops would wither, cattle would die of thirst and the ranchers would be unable to repay the loans. The banker would then foreclose, complete the dam and become a wealthy man. Once again we see an unflattering portrayal of bankers.

In *North of the Great Divide* (Republic, 1950), Roy Barcroft plays a cannery operator whose nets trap nearly all of the salmon swimming up to their spawning grounds. Both the salmon and the Indians who depend on them face extinction. Roy Rogers, as an agent of the Bureau of Indian Affairs, unmasks Barcroft as the villain, thus saving the Indians and the salmon. The film ends with the celebration of a treaty regulating the catching of salmon. The moral here is clear: If properly regulated, canneries could fish for salmon and the Indians could continue their way of life. Regulation, however, was necessary because some greedy businessman would try to take more at the expense of others.

June Vincent and Fred Graham are the brother-sister owners of the Hurley Lumber Mill in *Colorado Sundown* (Republic, 1952). The Forest Service will not permit them to cut timber on the mountains because it would cause flooding in the valley during heavy rains. The unscrupulous couple, however, fakes a tree blight known as Beetle Bark, and plants a phony Forest Ranger who orders the trees cut. Rex Allen uncovers their scheme, but not before the valley is seriously jeopardized by a flash flood. Vincent and Graham don't care. After all, they only want to make a financial killing off of the lumber.

Businessmen with unique ties to cattle ranches were often portrayed as villains. In *Racketeers of the Range* (RKO, 1939), the villains worked for the Continental Packing Company. That company was driving smaller firms out of business. Arizona ranchers, therefore, had fewer options; they could either do business with Continental or not sell their beef. Marjorie Reynolds, the heroine, seems to reflect Hollywood's opinion of businessmen. The hero, George O'Brien, pleads with her to think of the Arizona ranchers who have done business with her packing company and not to sell out to Continental. Reynolds replies she does not care about the Arizona ranchers, she is thinking of her own interests. O'Brien is able, however, to protect the Johnson Packing Company and thus ensure an alternative outlet for Arizona beef.

In *Heart of the Golden West* (Republic, 1942), Roy Rogers frustrates the efforts of Ron Lambert (Edmund McDonald), owner of Lambert Cattle and Beef Company. Lambert charges excessively high rates for shipping beef on his trucks. Roy helps the ranchers find an alternative, shipping by steamboat, and stops Lambert when he tries to rustle the cattle.

The image of big businessmen in Westerns is not all bad, however. In *The Singing Cowboy* (Republic, 1936), a businessman turns to television as a new, creative way to advertise his coffee. He hires Gene Autry to star in the programs which his company sponsors. In that manner, he helps Gene make enough money to finance a young girl's needed operation. In *Call of the Canyon* (Republic, 1942), Thurston Hall plays Mr. Johnson of Johnson Packing Company. He goes West to find out why his processing plant is not receiving beef. Hall discovers the local manager is offering much less for the beef than he is supposed to offer. Hall is an honest businessman who believes the ranchers, as well as himself, need to make money. He helps Gene round up the crooks and thus reclaim the good reputation of Johnson Packing Company.

Another Gene Autry Western, *Sunset in Wyoming* (Republic, 1941), opens with scenes of a lumber harvest by Wentworth Lumbering Company, and then shows the flooding caused by the lack of ground cover.

Autry intervenes as irate ranchers attack the lumber camp and he promises to square things with Mr. Wentworth. Asa Wentworth (George Cleveland) has turned the company over to his daughter and her fiancée, but resents being excluded from company decisions. He encourages Autry to confront the young couple. When Cleveland is nearly killed in an automobile accident caused by heavy rains and flooding, his daughter sees the misery her tree harvest has caused the ranchers, and understands that she has placed too much trust in her shyster fiancé. Cleveland resumes control of his company, and he makes restitution to the farmers who have suffered losses.

Even general store owners, the ideal small businessmen, did not escape unscathed. More often than not, they were allies of the good guys — but not always! Several films came to mind in which general store owners were "brain" heavies. In *Texas Bad Man* (Universal, 1932), Tom Mix plays a Texas Ranger who goes undercover to clean up a nest of outlaws. The brains of the outfit is a man who appears to be the mild-mannered proprietor of the local dry goods store. In the film *Under California Stars* (Republic, 1948), Pops (George Lloyd) is the seemingly friendly owner of a local store who masterminds the plot to kidnap Trigger and hold him for ransom. *Riders of the San Joaquin* (Universal, 1941), with Tex Ritter and Johnny Mack Brown, presents the depths of chicanery. A general store owner appears to be an ally of the ranchers who are fighting railroad interests. He even provides free groceries to those ranchers who have been forced off of their land and are unable to pay their bills. All of the time, however, he is the "brain" heavy who directs the outlaw gang. If he can chase the ranchers off of their land, he will make a financial windfall selling right-of-way to the railroad.

A similar image appears in *Law and the Lawless* (Majestic, 1932). The local general store owner-town banker sympathizes with the homesteaders and ranchers who are being driven from their land by a band of night riders who use the symbol and cry of a wolf as their calling card. The store owner-banker extends credit and loans money without demanding collateral or worrying about repayment. When the wolf gang's victims pull up stakes and leave the country, they deed over their property to their friend out of gratitude for what he had done for them. It's up to Jack Hoxie, as the two-gun hero Montana, to bring the wolf gang to justice, and to expose the store owner-banker as the brains behind the operation.

In *The Old Barn Dance* (Republic, 1938), the villains operated a tractor franchise. They convince farmers to convert from horses to tractors purchased on the installment plan. Then they send out outlaws to keep the farmers from harvesting their crops and paying for the tractors. The tractors will be repossessed and the farms purchased at rock-bottom prices.

Gene Autry in his autobiography, *Back in the Saddle Again*, recognized the use of businessmen as villains and he explained it:

> The Wild West of Billy the Kid's day had been done to death. So I came along owing more to Bing Crosby than Bill Hart. My movies offered crimes of cunning, instead of crimes of violence. Dishonest salesmen and financial pirates were my villains. I ran a kind of one-man Better Business Bureau, out in the wide-open spaces [Autry, 50–51].

Autry's comment about his films applies equally to numerous other cowboy heroes.

Generally, however, small businessmen and small ranchers were portrayed in Westerns as American heroes, men and women who embodied the spirit of free enterprise. They were individuals who risked their own, not other people's money, and who fought both nature and the business cycle to create a thriving economy.

Small businessmen were not the only prominent economic heroes in Western movies. Entrepreneurs, closely associated with the spirit of progress, were also heroes. A large part of the American dream affirms the desirability and the inevitability of progress. Not surprisingly, men closely associated with progress were depicted as heroic. The entrepreneurs most often singled out for praise were those men with foresight and courage who developed the West.

Like small businessmen, the entrepreneur risked their own wealth, as well as the wealth of others. But even more than wealth, entrepreneurs risked their reputations and, at times, their lives. They were active, not passive, participants in their grand enterprises. In turn, they had to combat the same elements — weather, natural terrain, Indians and evil-scheming men — as did the small rancher and businessman. Entrepreneurs risked failure in order to build something great. They earned respect, even if only grudging respect, for their efforts. That theme is evident in several films.

Western Union (20th Century–Fox, 1941) with Robert Young and Randolph Scott re-enacted the stringing of the telegraph. The heroes are Young, who is in charge of the project, and Scott, his scout. Scott has a shady past, and in the end is shot by his outlaw brother, played by Barton MacLane. However, the plot is secondary to the great drama of laying the telegraph, and of its praise for the men who made it possible. A similar theme pervades *Wells Fargo* (Paramount, 1937). Joel McCrea, in one of his first starring roles, plays a determined entrepreneur, a man so dedicated to his stage line and to the Union that he risks his marriage for both.

The Pony Express was the subject of numerous Westerns. In 1946,

Republic produced *The Plainsman and the Lady* in which William Elliott plays a wealthy cattleman who decides to risk his money to establish the Pony Express. A later, more fanciful endeavor, *Pony Express* (Paramount, 1953) dealt with the same effort. In the Elliott vehicle, the villain was a stagecoach line concerned with the potential economic damage of the Pony Express. In the 1953 film, the villains are scheming politicians who favor California's independence and who do not want that state linked to the rest of the union.

There are notable differences between businessmen and bankers on the one hand and entrepreneurs on the other. The former were portrayed as using other people's money, as taking little personal risk, and as being individuals who stood to profit from the misfortunes of those who were indebted to them. Entrepreneurs, on the other hand, risked their money as well as that of others, and invested their own efforts in highly dangerous activities such as the Pony Express and the transcontinental railroad. They were major American heroes, portrayed as such in schoolbooks. Bankers and businessmen were simply not regarded that way.

Professionals such as lawyers, medical doctors, veterinarians and teachers do not appear in Westerns as frequently as do saloonkeepers, bankers and businessmen but they do show up as both good and bad guys.

Lawyers know how to fix things! Working closely with bankers and financiers, lawyers can draft documents that make it easy to foreclose legally on valuable land. Lawyers also know how to argue persuasively and they can convince people to do things that might not be in their own personal economic well being. For example, in *Gangster's Den* (PRC, 1945), Al St. John wonders how lawyer I. Stanford Jolley can get by with some of his crooked dealing. Buster Crabbe's response to his sidekick is that "lawyers know how to fix things."

Roy Barcroft plays the crooked lawyer Gil Carse in Tim Holt's *Land of the Open Range* (RKO, 1942). The action opens with the funeral procession of local badman Luke Archer. Carse is part of the procession; Sheriff Walton refers to Carse as a "shyster lawyer." When Holt, Lasses White, Ray Whitley, and Sheriff Walton return to the Sheriff's office, a messenger delivers a note inviting them to the reading of Luke Archer's will.

Archer's will designates that "scoundrel and enemy of the people, Gil Carse" as executor of the estate, including Archer's 64,000-acre ranch. In a final effort to spite the town, Archer decreed that his ranch would be divided into 100 sections and given to the first 100 men who win a land rush race. Archer's only restriction was that only those who had served at least two years in prison were eligible for the land rush.

Not surprisingly, undesirable ex-convicts soon overrun the town.

John Elliott is one of the ex-cons who sees the land rush as an excellent opportunity to start over. He comes to the town with his daughter (Janet Waldo) in hopes of winning one of the tracts of land. They have their eye on a particularly good section by the river. Unfortunately, so does Gil Carse; he intends to build a dam there and control all water in the valley.

Holt and White suspect something is amiss when they suggest to Carse that instead of a land rush, a blind draw be held with the first 100 numbers awarded the corresponding section. That way, Holt argues, nobody will get trampled to death in the land rush. Carse protests that Holt's plan is not legal. Archer's will specifically called for a land rush and as executor of the estate it is Carse's sworn duty to honor the will.

Carse, of course, has an ulterior motive. He wants to stake out the area by the river. When he discovers that Elliott owns a valuable horse that comes from a long line of prize-winning race horses, Carse realizes he can't beat the horse to the section. When his effort to steal the horse fail, Carse has his henchmen set up relays of fresh horses, an illegal tactic, but one designed to ensure that Carse gets the section of land by the river.

Holt, however, discovers the relay strategy and stops Carse from staking out the area. With his gun drawn Holt protects Elliott when he claims the section by the river. Carse and his men engage Elliott in a shootout, but when White and Whitley ride up to help their pal Holt, Carse's men surrender and Carse falls from a cliff as he tries to escape.

Land of the Open Range is a fairly typical B Western of little noteworthiness except the interesting portrayal of the lawyer, Gil Carse. Not only did the sheriff regard him as a shyster, the deceased who made him executor of his estate referred to him as a scoundrel and enemy of the people.

George Carleton plays the crooked lawyer Jason Howley in *Night Time in Nevada* (Republic, 1948) and Grant Withers is the main heavy who had killed his partner in a mine explosion many years before the time of the film. Withers knew that his partner had set up a $50,000 trust fund for his young daughter, but Withers and Carleton had stolen from the fund over the years. Since Carleton was the one responsible for the fund, he and Withers could loot it without anyone suspecting what they were doing.

When the two men learn that the young girl — now a grown woman — is coming West to get the money, Carleton realizes that he and Withers could go to jail for theft. When the woman (Adele Mara) visits the attorney, he assures her everything is in order and suggests she park her trailer near the edge of town overnight while he prepares the necessary paperwork.

That night, Withers tries to murder Mara and her friend by turning on the bottled gas while they sleep in the trailer. Roy catches Withers in the act, and after a brutal fight takes Withers to jail. When Carleton's efforts to get Withers released that night fail, he returns the next morning with a court order directing that Withers be freed. Carleton even has Withers claim to be Mara's father.

Roy discovers that Mara's father had been murdered—the accidental mine explosion had been faked—and he tells Mara the truth. Unfortunately, one of Withers' henchmen overhears Rogers tell Mara that her father had been murdered. At the beginning of *Night Time in Nevada* Withers and Carleton had rustled a herd of Rogers' cattle in order to use the money to replace the funds they had stolen from Mara's trust fund. Now, however, they get greedy. When Mara goes to Carleton's office to get her money, they tie her up in the back room.

Both men realize, however, that a trap has been set for them, and when Carleton becomes frightened, Withers murders Carleton making Mara think it was Rogers who had been killed. The action gets furious as Andy Devine, the Sons of the Pioneers and Mara help Roy round up Withers and his gang.

While Withers was the main villain in *Night Time in Nevada*, George Carleton was no less responsible for pilfering Mara's trust fund. After all, he was the lawyer who was able to hide the crime. And, he successfully got Withers released from jail after Rogers had arrested him on suspicion of attempted murder. Once again, a lawyer was represented as a less-than-honest person.

Not all attorneys in Western films are despicable characters; some of them work for law and order. Smith Ballew plays such a role in *Rawhide* (20th Century–Fox, 1938), a film best remembered as Lou Gehrig's only Western. Ballew is Larry Kimball, a struggling lawyer who opposes Arthur Loft's Cattlemen's Protective Association. Loft had conned an old rancher (Lafe McKee) into hiring him and then, working through a Chicago doctor who had lost his license to practice, kept the old man drugged so he would not learn of Loft's illegal activities.

Loft offers protection against rustlers to the ranchers. But in order to buy the protection, they must pay an entrance fee, a tax on each head of cattle, buy their supplies from the association's store and pay a percentage of their yearly profit to the group. If a rancher doesn't join, he can't buy supplies, and if he tries to bring supplies in from the outside, Loft's henchmen attack the wagons.

Loft's racket worked much like those of Eastern gangsters, a fact brought home to viewers in an exchange between Gehrig and Loft. When Gehrig—who has gone West to help his sister (Evalyn Knapp) run the family ranch—declines Loft's invitation to join the association. Loft menacingly tells Gehrig, "You're not in New York now." Gehrig smiles and replies, "Gee, for a minute I thought I was."

Rawhide, 20th Century–Fox, 1938; Arthur Loft, Dick Curtis and Smith Ballew. Ballew plays an honest lawyer who gets into a fight with Loft and his henchmen.

Soon after his exchange with Gehrig, Loft is playing pool in a pool hall—an establishment which ranked just below taverns for many conservative Americans—when Larry Kimball walks into the establishment. Loft calls Kimball over to his pool table and points out to Kimball, "You're not doing enough business to pay your laundry bill." Then Loft once again offers Kimball a job as lawyer for the Cattlemen's Protective Association. Kimball declines, reminding Loft of an old saying, "If you lie down with dogs, you get up with fleas."

The conversation between Ballew and Loft is interrupted when Gehrig comes into the pool hall to protest that Loft's men shot Si Jenks, foreman on the Gehrig ranch. When Dick Curtis objects to Gehrig calling him a rat, a melee erupts in which Ballew and Gehrig join forces to whip Loft and his henchmen. The film's highlight is surely Lou Gehrig bouncing pool balls off of the villains' heads!

The fight cements a friendship between Ballew and Gehrig, who offers a retainer to Ballew. When Ballew agrees to help Gehrig fight Loft, Gehrig exclaims, "This will be more fun than the World Series." Curtis, who has witnessed the Ballew-Gehrig alliance, tells Loft that they have real problems now with that "smart lawyer butting in."

With Ballew's assistance, the Gehrig ranch fools Loft's men into giving them hay for their cattle but that only starts a new round of violence against the ranch. Knapp — Gehrig's sister — becomes tired of the violence and, unknown to Ballew or Gehrig, she rides to Loft's office to join the association.

In the meantime, Ballew has discovered Loft's scheme to keep Lafe McKee doped up and he rides to the old man's ranch to help him. When Gehrig finds out his sister has gone to join the association, he and Si Jenks ride to town to stop her. Both Ballew and Gehrig are successful and the film ends with Loft apprehended and McKee promising to make restitution to his neighbors.

Paul Hurst, long-time sidekick of Monte Hale, plays John X. Finn, a lawyer and the town's conscience in Hale's last Western, *The Missourians* (Republic, 1950). The action revolves around Hale's efforts to recover $10,000 dedicated to the construction of a church, but stolen by outlaws. However, tolerance is an important subtheme of the movie.

The Kovacs are foreigners living in a small Texas town; Nick Kovacs, the oldest son, is a notorious outlaw. John Hamilton, playing Mayor McDowell, is the most outspoken in his dislike for all the Kovacs, young Steve Kovacs in particular. After a shopkeeper, for no real reason, accuses Steve of stealing, Mayor McDowell tells him, "We don't want foreigners around here. Why don't you go back to the old country?" The mayor wonders why they came to the United States in the first place. Hurst reminds the mayor of his own Irish ancestry and suggests that maybe the Kovacs came to the United States for the same reason as did the mayor's Irish ancestors.

Early in the film, Hurst had described himself to Hale as "a broken-down lawyer who lives on what you pay me for legal fees." Even his daughter has the same opinion. When Hurst tells her he had just about given up practicing law in the town, her response was that was because he took too many unpopular cases that were morally right. Hurst is not a shyster lawyer like Carse in *Land of the Open Range*; he is a man of firm moral convictions that are not always popular.

But Hurst is not the only one who cares about fair play. Hale had tried to talk the mayor into permitting him to resign on a number of occasions, but always the mayor would convince Hale to stay on as sheriff. However, after Hale prevents the shopkeeper from beating up Steve Kovacs and Hurst challenges the mayor's bigotry, the mayor tells Hale that he has been thinking about his desire to resign and has decided to accept Hale's resignation. Hale declines the mayor's not-too-subtle hint and tells him that somebody has to assure equal treatment to all people in the town so he will just stay on as sheriff.

Steve Kovacs also confronts the mayor after the mayor tells him they didn't want foreigners in the town. Steve tells the mayor, "You're a fine Christian, yelling for a church. You hypocrite; you shouldn't be allowed inside a church." When Steve turns away, the mayor tries to shoot him — and would have if a bystander hadn't knocked his gun away.

The mayor and everyone else in town want to believe that Steve Kovacs is a criminal. Nick Kovacs forces Steve to ride along when they raid the wagon train carrying the new church supplies and then pistol-whips his young brother when Steve resists. After the raid, Hale finds the young man wandering dazed in the vicinity of the burned wagons. The mayor and the town quickly conclude that Steve Kovacs is the guilty party and they organize a lynching party.

Again Hurst, as a lawyer, acts as the town's conscience. He tells the lynch mob, "This is a good town. You are all good men. Soon you will have a new church to pray in and a lynching won't bother you much. All they did was steal a little money and all you did was take a man's life." Hurst's sermon and Hale's guns deflect the mob.

When the mayor overhears Nick Kovacs confirm his young brother's story as Nick forces Steve to escape from jail, the mayor knows he had been harsh and wrong in his judgment of the Kovacs. He tells Steve, "It was not so much believing you were guilty that was wrong but believing you were different because you were a foreigner and not as good as we are." Hurst's lectures did some good after all!

In contrast to lawyers, medical doctors are respected and admired by the American public, and it is not surprising that for the most part doctors appear in B Westerns as kind, helping individuals. Doctors usually appear briefly in most Westerns: they deliver a baby, take out a bullet, perform an operation or deliver the bad news to the heroine that her father or brother has died. In some films, however, doctor characters have larger roles, and they appear as both upright citizens and villains.

Roscoe "Soapy" Ates steps outside of his normal sidekick role to play the town doctor in *Renegades of the West* (RKO Radio, 1932). Tom Keene, the cowboy hero in this one, has arranged to spend six months in prison in order to infiltrate a gang he suspects of killing his father. Blackie, his cellmate, tells Keene to look up Curly. When he meets Curly, Keene fakes a bad cough, the B Western symbol of an ex-convict. Curly advises Keene to see a doctor about the cough and sends him to Ates.

Renegades of the West, RKO, 1932; Tom Keene and Roscoe Ates. Ates plays a respected but comical medical doctor.

When Keene arrives at Ates' house, the doctor is not home but his daughter (Betty Furness) invites Keene to wait for him. Keene begins flirting with Furness and after a few minutes she responds. When Ates arrives home and examines Keene, he asks him if he has spent a great deal of time indoors lately. Keene responds that he has. The doctor tells him the cough is nothing to worry about; fresh air and sunshine will cure it.

As Keene leaves, Furness offers him some homemade candy and Ates sees that his daughter is romantically interested in Keene. He calls her into the house to fix dinner and quickly sends Keene on his way. When Furness asks Ates what was the matter with Keene, Ates tells her he has developed a cough from being indoors too much. Furness does not understand until Ates tells her that Keene is an ex-convict.

The rest of the film is routine: Keene infiltrates the gang, develops a friendship with Curly and discovers that the local banker is the brains behind the gang and the one who shot his father. Ates keeps popping up throughout, however, as the comical, stuttering local doctor who nevertheless is a highly valued and respected member of the community.

Roy Rogers plays Stephen Kellog, alias Steve Kells, in *The Border Legion* (Republic, 1940), a film based loosely on the Zane Grey novel of the same title. Kellog is a doctor from Albany, New York, who fled West when he was accused of a crime he did not commit. His fiancée's brother was the real culprit and Kellog did not want to reveal that fact to the authorities, so he left town.

Kellog winds up in Miles City and goes to work in Maude Eburne's saloon. One day the stage comes racing into town and driver Jack Kirk announces that they have been held up by the Border Legion and in the fracas a female passenger was shot. The local doctor is out of town and so Eburne has the girl brought into the saloon. She tells Kellog to take a look at her, and not to ask questions until he is finished. Rogers as Kellog recognizes the girl as his fiancée, Carol Hughes.

After he operates successfully and saves Hughes' life, Eburne shows Kellog a clipping from an Eastern newspaper. It is a story about the authorities' search for Dr. Stephen Kellog. But she promises him to keep the story a secret. Rogers has just bought a stage ticket to leave town when two men from the Border Legion waylay him. They take Rogers to the gang's hideout. Joe Sawyer, head of the Border Legion, has been shot in the leg during a shoot-out in Miles City and he wants Kellog to examine his leg. Rogers removes the bullet and then shows Sawyer the newspaper clipping.

Making Sawyer think he has no other option, Rogers joins the Border Legion in order to work undercover and to help round up the gang. From that point on, the film becomes a typical B Western with lots of action until the legion's crime spree is ended, Hughes' brother confesses to the crime, and Hughes and Rogers are married. But it is Rogers' depiction of a skilled doctor, one who is falsely accused of a crime, which makes this B Western unusual.

Maybe the best characterization of a doctor in any Western is *Hills of Utah* (Columbia, 1951). Gene Autry returns after many years to Coffin Gap, a town being driven to extinction by a feud between the copper mine and large cattle ranchers. The ranchers claim that waste run-off from the copper mine poisons their cattle. Autry's father had been a cattleman and when he was mysteriously shot, Gene rushed him to Coffin Gap only to discover that the town had no doctor. When Gene's father died, Autry vowed to become a doctor. He left the area and went to medical school. Now, years later, Gene returns to Coffin Gap to open a medical practice.

Gene comes back to Coffin Gap, but Bowie French (Denver Pyle), who as a young man had ridden for the elder Autry, does not want a doctor

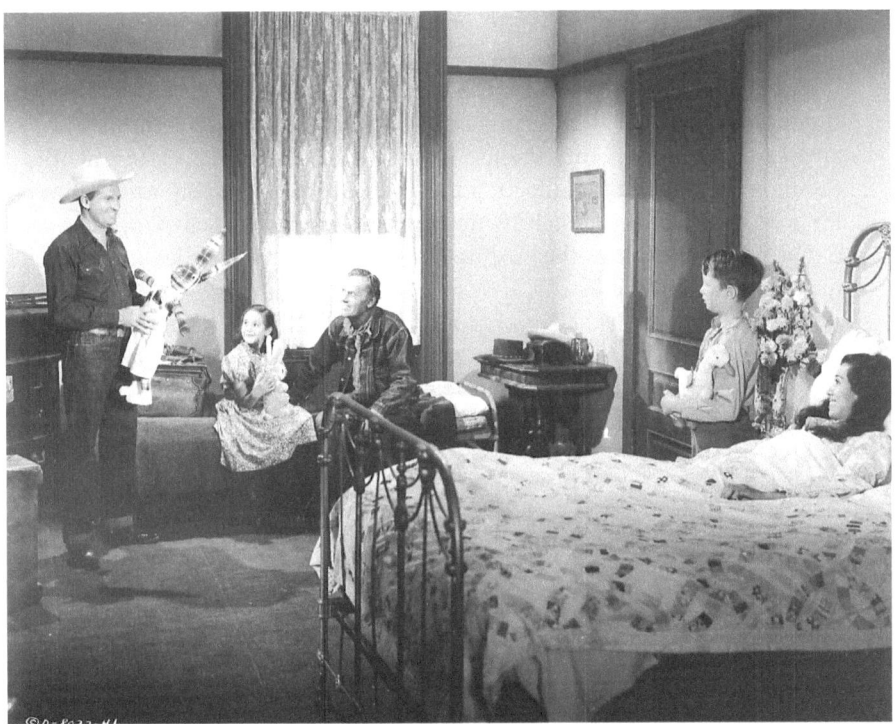

Hills of Utah, Columbia, 1951; Gene Autry, Stanley Price and unidentified players. Autry plays a doctor visiting a sick woman and bringing Easter gifts to the children.

in the town. When two of French's gunmen try to beat up Gene, he and Dusty Cosgrove (played by Pat Buttram one of the best of all sidekicks), whip them in a good old-fashioned fistfight. As Gene treats a wound to Dusty's arm, Elaine Riley, who plays Karen McQueen, rides into town to get Gene to come to the copper mine to look at her little brother who is very ill. Her father Jayde, played by Onslow Stevens, owns the copper mine.

Gene goes with Riley to the mine and, in spite of Jayde's efforts to keep him out of the house, examines the boy. Gene discovers that the boy has an intestinal blockage brought on by too much meat and potatoes and too little exercise. He operates on the boy to relieve the blockage. The operation is successful. As Autry leaves the mine, it appears that he and Jayde McQueen have reconciled.

However, two days later the boy dies, and Jayde McQueen comes gunning for Gene. In the meantime, Gene has met Bowie French and made it clear to him that the fight between the mine and cattlemen is not Gene's fight. He came to Coffin Gap to practice medicine and he will treat anyone in need of medical help.

Gene is able to stave off Jayde McQueen's efforts when Bowie French shoots McQueen in the leg just as McQueen was about to shoot Gene. However, Gene prevents French from killing McQueen. After all this excitement, Dusty puts collection boxes around town to help raise money for a hospital. Nola, French's wife, who has money of her own, buys an old building to serve as the hospital, and Gene orders supplies and equipment for the new facility.

When French discovers what his wife did, he sends his men to intercept the stagecoach bringing the supplies to town. Gene, Dusty and the sheriff's posse ride to stop them. As Gene chases one of French's men, Washoe (William Fawcett) — the cook at the mine — shoots the McQueen rider.

Gene takes the cowboy to the new hospital, but he dies. As French rounds up his gunmen to raid the mine, Nola tells Gene that Bowie French either killed Autry's father or had him killed, and then brought up nearly all of the ranches in the area. Even though he is a wealthy man, French's fear of poverty makes him cruel and heartless.

In an exciting climax, Gene and Dusty ride to warn the miners and fight with them against McQueen and his men. McQueen and Washoe led French and his ace gunfighter (Kenne Duncan), deeper and deeper into the mine. The four men are exchanging shots when Gene joins McQueen and Washoe. Just as Gene arrives, Washoe is hit by one of the slugs. When Gene looks at it, Washoe tells him not to bother; an old miner knows when a vein has been tapped.

Washoe then confesses to have given the boy solid food after the operation even though Gene had left careful instructions that the boy was to have only milk and soup. Washoe realizes he killed the boy. The cook then picks up his gun and starts down the tunnel after Pyle and Duncan. Even though they put three or four slugs in him, Washoe is able to get to them and kill both of the cattlemen.

The final scenes are in Autry's brand new hospital, a visible sign of progress. The death of Bowie French promises to end the war between the mine and cattlemen. One hopes that Coffin Gap will not longer live up to its name. Autry as a compassionate doctor has not only provided medical care for all the citizens, he has also brought peace and reconciliation to the town!

However, even doctors were villains in a few Westerns. Forrest Stanley plays a doctor in *Rider of Death Valley* (Universal, 1933). He and Fred Kohler try to cheat Lois Wilson out of her gold mine. Tom Mix, in his best sound Western, understands what they are up to and frustrates their efforts. Frank LaRue appears to be a helpful doctor in *The Range Busters* (Monogram, 1940). In the end we learn that LaRue is the phantom trying to chase Luana Walters off her ranch so he can get the gold mine.

Karl Hackett plays a doctor in cahoots with Charles King in the Buster Crabbe programmer *His Brother's Ghost* (PRC, 1945). Al St. John has a double role in this one. As a rancher, King's men shoot him while he is trying to organize other ranchers to resist King's efforts to drive them off their land. Later, St. John emerges as a twin brother who pretends to be his murdered brother. Hackett, as the doctor who pronounced St. John dead, can't figure it out.

Perhaps the two best depictions of doctors as villains are *Trail of Kit Carson* (Republic, 1945) and *Bells of Coronado* (Republic, 1950). Rocky Lane, as Bill Haron, goes to California after receiving a letter from his partner Dave McCoy, telling of a rich gold strike. However, when Harmon arrives in California, he discovers that his partner supposedly committed suicide.

Dr. Ryan (Roy Barcroft), the town's foremost citizen, had taken the bullet from McCoy's body. Trigger Chandler (Kenne Duncan), a gunsmith, tested the bullet and testified before a coroner's inquest that the bullet had come from McCoy's gun. In addition, Lane learns that Doc Ryan had bought the mine from McCoy before he died, and he has McCoy's canceled check to verify his claim.

In the meantime, Chandler sends gunman Red Snyder (Bud Geary), to kill Lane. The two men fight in the bar and Sheriff Jack Kirk warns them to leave one another alone. However, as Lane is about to mount his horse, Geary confronts him again and Duncan shoots Geary from ambush. Kirk, believing Lane shot Geary, arrests Lane and they go to Doc Ryan's office to wait for him to remove the bullet. Ryan takes out the bullet, but Geary dies. Ryan and Kirk then accompany Lane to Trigger Chandler's place, where they have Lane fire his gun into a cotton bale. Chandler substitutes the bullet he used to kill Geary for the one Lane fired into the cotton bale, and the sheriff arrests Lane for murder.

In jail, Lane is told that his friend John Benton (Tom London), has been shot. Benton knows that Lane did not shoot Geary and both Ryan and Chandler want him silenced. Lane then realizes that Ryan is mixed up in murder. Lane had learned from the bartender at the saloon that Ryan lost $1000 to McCoy while playing poker and that he wrote a check to cover the loses.

Lane believes that the check Ryan claimed he wrote to buy the mine was really meant to cover his gambling debt. Lane is sure that Ryan, under the pretense of taking out the bullet, will kill Benton. He escapes jail and gets to Benton's in time to stop Ryan from murdering the man. The sheriff's posse arrives at Benton's just as Lane and Ryan are leaving, and Lane heads for town with the sheriff in hot pursuit.

Lane arrives in time to keep Trigger Chandler from destroying the cotton bale. When the sheriff arrives, Lane convinces him that all the bullets had a distinctive marking caused when they penetrated the bale. Chandler, seeing that the game is up, says he will turn state's evidence, but Ryan kills him before he can talk. Lane then chases down Ryan and brings him back to town to stand trial for murder.

Trail of Kit Carson is an exciting little Western with lots of action and unusual twists. One of those twists is Roy Barcroft's able characterization of a villainous doctor who appears to be a leading citizen while committing murder in order to get control of rich gold mines.

Roy Rogers is hired by the Great Southwest Insurance Company to investigate a claim to cover the costs of some stolen uranium ore. He agrees to take the job and heads for Coronado in *Bells of Coronado*. When he arrives in Coronado, Roy stops to see Dr. Frank Harding (Leo Cleary). Dr. Harding was the trusted family physician who had delivered Roy and been his doctor until Roy left Coronado. Harding is removing a mustard plaster from Pat Brady, playing Sparrow Biffle, the role he created for several early 1950s Roy Rogers Westerns. Roy tells them the drought has ruined his ranch so he is looking for work. Dr. Harding helps him get a job as lineman for the Coronado Light and Power Company.

The first morning of work, Roy confides to Brady that he is really an insurance investigator and they ride to the mine. When they discover another ore robbery, Roy and Brady chase after the ore wagon. Shots are fired and Brady is wounded in the arm, but Roy saves the uranium ore and takes it to the warehouse after he drops Brady off at Dr. Harding's.

Dr. Harding, who is really the brains behind the gang stealing the ore, puts Brady under an anesthetic that makes him talk. At Harding's prompting, Brady discloses that Roy is really an insurance investigator. Harding arranges to have his gang cut the power lines that night and steal the ore from the warehouse. A foreign government has made arrangements to buy the ore and Harding needs to deliver.

Rogers, Evans and the Riders of the Purple Sage stop by Dr. Harding's house that evening to check on Brady. Harding gives Roy a package that had come for him; it contains a Geiger counter. As Roy is experimenting with it, the counter begins to tick. When Roy becomes suspicious, the doctor passes it off as radium needles in his desk.

Roy arranges for an examination of the body of the driver who had driven the stolen ore wagon. When he learns that the driver died from poisoning, Roy suspects Dr. Harding is mixed up in the robbery. He goes back to the doctor's office and discovers ore samples stashed behind some books in a bookcase.

When Dr. Harding and Jim Russel, ostensibly one of the gang, catch Roy in the doctor's office, Dr. Harding prepares to shoot Roy, telling him that he brought him into the world and he was going to take him out. Rogers and Russel begin to fight. As the two men roll around on the floor, Russel tells Rogers he is an undercover federal agent.

While Rogers pretends to be knocked out, Dr. Harding is about to shoot again when he gets a telephone call telling him that Jim Russel is a federal agent. Harding turns his gun on Russel and is about to kill him when Roy grabs the doctor. In the ensuing struggle, the gun goes off and Harding is killed. Roy and Jim Russel, with some help from Pat Brady and the Riders of the Purple Sage, prevent the gang from delivering the uranium ore to the foreign agent.

In *Trail of Kit Carson*, Dr. Ryan (Roy Barcroft's character) was a murderer because he was greedy. Greed is an attribute at least as old as the human race itself. Dr. Harding in *Bells of Coronado* was not only greedy, he was a traitor. His willingness to murder to advance his treasonous ends make him a particularly vicious character.

In *Colorado Sunset* (Republic, 1939), a different kind of doctor, the local veterinarian, masterminds a group of outlaws trying to force milk producers to join a protective association. The "vet" also owns a radio station over which he broadcasts helpful animal husbandry information. The messages contain code words that tell his gang where to strike. Gene Autry gets to the bottom of it, and puts the vet out of business.

These film examples of how Westerns treated lawyers and doctors highlight an interesting perspective. While those in the professions did appear as villains on occasion, they were more likely to be treated sympathetically as pillars of the community than were bankers and businessmen. When contemporary businessmen complain about their portrayal in current movies and television shows, contrasting it to the generally positive treatment of lawyers, doctors, and teachers, they are reacting to an element that has characterized popular culture since at least 1930. The anomaly raised earlier in the chapter — respect for, combined with resentment and mistrust of businessmen — seems to permeate American opinion. B Westerns merely reflected that on the silver screen.

Up to this point, this chapter has discussed the image of businessmen in B Westerns and, not surprisingly, found them mixed but largely negative. That, however, is only part of the story; free enterprise also includes employees. How were employees pictured in Westerns? The question is important, for as the 1930s unfolded, labor-management relations went through a profound transformation. At the beginning of the decade, the old outlook of an automatic society largely dominated economic thought (Lowi, 3–13). According to that notion, economic laws that fixed hours, wages and working conditions controlled the business cycle. Those laws were, in turn, beyond human control. The available pool of workers and general economic conditions set wages and hours. Human effort could do little to overcome those elemental forces in the economy.

By 1936, that outlook no longer dominated public policy. Congress and state legislatures had passed hours and wage legislation, taken steps to prop up sagging farm income and granted employees the right to organize industrial labor unions. By the end of the decade, Keynesian economics were in vogue, and major labor unions were important economic and political forces. The American worker had entered his most aggressive and prosperous period in American history, a period that would last for over 30 years.

It is a bit surprising, therefore, to discover that employee rights were largely dismissed by B Westerns, and it is possible to read into those films a not-too-subtle hostility to labor unions. Actually, it may not be all that surprising when one remembers the precarious financial state of many producers. Several smaller studios and a number of independents went bankrupt in the 1930s, and those that remained sought constantly to control costs. One way to contain expenses was to keep the payroll in check. That, in turn, created conflicts with the stars who believed they were worth more than the studio was willing to pay.

Gene Autry's fight with Herbert Yates at Republic over salary is well known. Roy Rogers got his film start when Autry went on strike in 1938. Some believe that Yates began to push the career of Monte Hale in the 1940s because Yates feared Rogers would ask for too much money. And both Autry and Rogers failed, in spite of lengthy court battles, to share in studio profits when their films were sold to television. To compound problems, in the post-war years the Screen Actors Guild had succeeded in recasting the salary structure so walk-ons and support players earned higher salaries. That increased production costs and compromised profit margins. Surely, it must have been tempting for producers to reflect their frustrations in plots and characterizations of employees.

By the mid–1930s, industrial unions, struggling for higher wages and better working conditions for their members, often violently confronted a management hostile to the very existence of unions. The paternalism-loyalty scheme in which employers would watch over their employees as a parent watches over children and employees in turn would be loyal to their employer did not fit labor-management relationships of that era; yet, the inherent conservatism of B Westerns is very evident, for right up to their demise in the 1950s they continued to project the old order as if it still had validity.

A Gene Autry Western, *Red River Valley* (1936), is an excellent example of the old order argument. Gene plays a ditch rider, one who patrols the dam and canal system to make sure the appropriate gates are open to keep each irrigation canal at the necessary water level. At one point in the film, the payroll is stolen; it has been some time since the construction crews have been paid. The crew has an unofficial union headed by George Chesebro with assistance from Charles King, two of Western films' archvillains. Chesebro and King protest — no pay, no work. Autry fights both of them, and with a combination of songs and bullying tactics gets the men to return to work unpaid because the ranchers need the dam finished.

Whatever the screenwriter's intent, the film is anti-worker. There is, at least, a tacit hint that union leaders are, like Chesebro and King, really villains pursuing some ulterior motive, and certainly not men of honesty and integrity. The assumption that workers have an obligation to other sectors of society, in this case the ranchers, is also strange. Construction workers have families to feed and bills to pay. Their wealth is in their labor; they do not have land or livestock to fall back upon. In spite of that, the film suggests that the construction crew has an obligation to work on the promise of some future payday so that the ranchers who have invested in the dam will not lose their ranches.

A corrective of sorts is found in another Autry Western, *Ride, Tenderfoot, Ride* (Republic, 1940). Autry is the heir to a meat packing company. Being a cowboy, he knows little about managing a business, so he agrees to sell his firm to a rival company owned by June Storey. Gene assumes the company he has inherited will continue to operate under new management, and that all employees will keep their jobs. He discovers, however, that Storey has other ideas. The rival firm wants his equipment and has no intention of continuing Gene's firm or retaining the employees. Autry's concern for his employees compels him not to sell. The film portrays Gene as being hurt by the accusation he cares only about himself and does not care about his employees. His motivation, then, is to protect his employees' jobs as well as the financial condition of the packing company.

Tom Mix as Tom Morgan, ranch owner, demonstrated that a ranch owner also has an obligation to care for the cowboys who work for him. He displayed near-parental concern for his employees in *The Rider of Death*

Valley (Universal, 1932). As the film opened, Mix rode into town to rescue his cowboys who were selling their horses, guns and all of the rest of their worldly possessions in order to buy shares in a gold mine. The whole town caught gold fever after gold was discovered in the area. Mix, however, knew better; someone had to prevent his cowboys from being swindled. So he did!

Mix's paternalism is the reverse side of an employee's loyalty to the firm. It suggests a relationship, transcending economics, which cuts to the core of life. In many ways it was a throwback to the old order in which the owners of great landed estates were obligated to care for the peasants tending their fields, and the peasants in turn were to be loyal to the Lord of the Manor. As hard as early nineteenth century utopian reformers tried, similar paternal-loyalty arrangement never made much headway in the English or American factory systems.

B Westerns, it appears, reflected an anachronism, even for their day. Often they portrayed a pastoral setting in which employees and employers lived in harmony. But that bucolic picture failed to mirror the rapid changes taking place in labor-management relations. Because the films ignored those changes, the end result was a not-too-infrequent anti-union bias. Again, producers of B Westerns seemed to know well their audience. Not only did anti-employee biases reflect producers' concern with costs, they also resonated with anti-union sentiment of the South and Midwest.

People in the heartland were individualists with a deep-seated mistrust of labor unions. In addition, unions aroused nativist fears because of their historic ties with immigrants. They also seemed to constrain individual freedom by telling a person how long he could work and at what wage. As unions won the seniority system for lay-offs and job promotions, individual effort seemed to account for less. Certainly Hollywood Westerns with their anti-bank and anti-union themes struck responsive chords in Southern and Midwestern audiences. It follows that this understanding would carry through as Westerns fashioned villains closely associated with the economic institutions most feared and mistrusted by that audience.

Support for free enterprise appears to be cyclical in nature. It waxes and wanes in rather predictable intervals. For example, since the 1980s free enterprise has been widely applauded and college students flock to Business Administration courses. All of that is a far cry from the late 1960s. The period 1930 to 1950 were years in which free enterprise, while not rejected by any stretch of the imagination, was regarded with a great deal of suspicion. Audiences were more likely to respond affirmatively to criticism of business, and to doubt its willingness to consider public need. One must not overstate the case but that attitude was widespread. If so, the anti-banker and anti-union biases in Westerns of that era reflected a general nationwide orientation, one quite compatible with long-standing suspicions of the American heartland.

Richard Hurst, in his excellent history of Republic Studio, offers some support for that conclusion and provide a nice end to this chapter. Hurst quotes from a *New York Post* 1942 review of a Don "Red" Barry film, *The Sombrero Kid*. The reviewer noted the film's anti-banker bias and initially attributed it to Yates' resentment of Eastern financial interests. But continuing, he observed that out in the heartland, the general population likes Westerns. The reviewer concluded, "And since many a Washington legislator hails from those same sticks, the influence of Westerns on banking legislation in the United States is probably greater than you have ever suspected" (Hurst, 10–11). Such a statement ought to be taken with a grain of salt—to use an expression from the sticks—even if it were seriously made. It does, however, help to make an important point. Republic and other producers of Westerns knew their audience and fashioned their films to appeal to that group. Part of that understanding was recognition of the populist streak and anti-union bias within folk of the rural areas and small towns of the heartland. It is evident in their films.

Chapter Eight

A WHITE RANGE

Nearly all persons old enough to remember the thrilling exploits of the cowboy heroes have one thing in common; they grew up in a racially segregated society and Western movies reflected that fact. William S. Hart, Tom Mix, Buck Jones and Roy Rogers all rode a white range. African-Americans and Asians, so visible in the real West, scarcely appear in Hollywood Westerns. Hispanics, even more prevalent in the Southwest and California, fare better, but their portrayal on film more often than not reflects white stereotypes.

Wayne Michael Sarf noted that blacks were treated on the screen in a manner that mirrored the "current formula deemed acceptable to the public." And, he concluded, "More often they were ignored" (Sarf, 224). Writing about post–World War II Westerns, Fenin and Everson point out that there was a marked decrease in the use of blacks in films (Fenin and Everson, 282).

For the most part, Westerns reflected white stereotypes of African-Americans. In B Westerns, four stereotypes are prominent: blacks as loyal servants who want to be cared for by white people, blacks as pursuing menial occupations, blacks as naturally funny and cowardly, and blacks as dancers and entertainers.

Westerns frequently portrayed black people as loyal, dependent servants who were ill equipped to care for themselves. Generally the vehicles through which this image was projected were Westerns set in the Civil War or Reconstruction eras. In *The Lonely Trail* (Republic, 1936), John Wayne plays John Ashley, a Texan who fought for the Union during the Civil War. He returns to Texas to find his friends tyrannized by Cy Kendall, the unscrupulous carpetbagger administrator of the area, who imposes high taxes on the people and then depends on his state police, a bunch of gunmen and outlaws, to collect the money.

The Terry Tavern and plantation are special objects of Kendall's treachery because he suspects Denny Meadows (later Dennis Moore), who along with his sister Ann Rutherford owns the plantation and runs the tavern, is really the leader of the local resistance. Kendall can't catch Terry in any illegal activities, however, because the plantation's loyal black servants—all former slaves—have an elaborate network to warn young Terry when the state police come. When Kendall's gunmen draw near the tavern, the black servants play the harmonica and banjo and sing to alert Meadows and Rutherford of impending danger.

After Wayne enlists in the state police because he needs a job, he realizes Kendall's only intent is to enrich himself at the expense of helpless Texans. Wayne helps Terry escape from the state police and Wayne is badly wounded as the state police chase him and his partner. Wayne seeks refuge at the Terry tavern with the state police in hot pursuit. Rutherford—who had been Wayne's sweetheart before the war—hides him under the bar. She tells the black servants to "act natural," to sing and dance.

The childlike image many whites had of blacks is underscored when Rutherford tells Fred Toones, a black actor who appeared in many Westerns as Snowflake, to drop everything and go for the doctor. Toones, who is holding a tray of glasses, literally does what he is told; he drops the tray full of glasses.

Black stereotypes abound in the film. The servants are musically talented people for whom singing and dancing is natural. They are childlike creatures who must be watched over by white people, and they want to be taken care of by their former masters. All of the black servants continued to live at the Terry plantation even though the war freed them of the need to remain there.

The contrast between good, loyal blacks and those who could not be trusted was highlighted at the beginning of the film. Cy Kendall gives money to a well-dressed, cigar-smoking black male. Obviously the black scalawag was in league with the Northern carpetbagger because the money was to buy black loyalty to Kendall. The film also noted a social distinction between blacks. When Kendall gives his black ally Confederate money, the black man replies that even field hands know "that money is not good." And later, when Toones tells Wayne that Kendall is behind the murders, Wayne replies that Toones has been listening to field hands talk.

The bigger budget *Belle Starr* (20th Century–Fox, 1941) has many of the same racial characteristics as *The Lonely Trail*. In the opening scenes, a black man is plowing in front of a burned-out mansion. His daughter, following along, stoops down to pull an old doll from the ground. The girl shows it to him and he replies it must have belonged to Belle Starr. When the black girl asks about her, he says she was "a mighty fine white lady who lived in the big house."

An unreconstructed Gene Tierney, playing Belle Starr, welcomes her brother home from the Civil War. When they go to town, the streets are full of white politicians assuring freed slaves of full social equality. The camera then pans to show well-dressed black ladies, and black men riding in nice carriages, as well as black people singing and dancing in the street.

Clearly, the film's intent is to show black people rushed into a freedom they do not understand, a freedom manipulated by white politicians for their own advantage. Those scenes are then contrasted with Tierney's loyal black servants, particularly her maid, played by Louise Beavers. These blacks, the film seems to say, are better off because they know that they need to be cared for, and they have remained loyal to the one who has always taken care of them.

Santa Fe Trail (Warner Bros., 1940), the first Western in which Ronald Reagan appeared, makes the same point but even stronger than *Belle Starr*. When Raymond Massey, playing John Brown, realizes that the cavalry, captained by Errol Flynn as Jeb Stuart and Reagan as George Custer, is closing in, he decides to flee Kansas. Massey tells the slaves he has helped to escape from their owners that they are now free and no longer need to be cared for. All of the slaves, except one family, take Brown at his word and go out into the world to enjoy their freedom.

One family realizes it has no way of surviving and remains in the barn. Later Flynn, fleeing a lynch mob, takes refuge in the same barn. After Reagan leads a cavalry charge to rescue Flynn, the black woman tells Flynn, "John Brown gave us freedom, but if this is freedom I don't want any part of it." The black man chimes in, "All I want to do is to get back to Texas and sit on my front porch."

The message in all three films is the same. If left alone, black people are happy serving white people. Freedom is attractive, but it is a burden which former slaves do not understand and are unwilling to bear. The films suggest that racial unrest would not exist if Northern carpetbaggers and Southern black and white scalawags had not stirred up black expectations beyond the level of their natural abilities.

A majority of white Southerners believed that in the 1930s and 1940s, and the same views were expressed by many white adults and children in the Midwest. Sarf, it appears, is correct; Westerns did mirror the social formula deemed most acceptable to the public.

Westerns also reinforced the assumption held by many whites that

Gold Mine in the Sky, Republic, 1938; Fred Toones, Jack Kirk, Gene Autry, Robert Homans, Smiley Burnette, Frankie Marvin and George Lentz/George Montgomery. Fred Toones in his role as "Snowflake," a cook for the cowboys.

African-Americans could perform effectively only in menial, service-type occupations. Fred Toones, who appeared in many Republic Westerns, is a good example of this stereotype. In two films, *Gold Mine in the Sky* (Republic, 1938) and *Bells of San Angelo* (Republic, 1947), he appeared as a cook. In *Hawaiian Buckaroo* (20th Century–Fox, 1938), Toones also plays a cook. This time he is an assistant who alerts the cook to the arrival of the cowboys. Toones is rewarded by being told to quit loafing and get to work. That remark dovetails with another white-generated stereotype, the naturally lazy black person.

In the Gene Autry Westerns *Oh Susanna* (Republic, 1936), *Rovin' Tumbleweeds* (Republic, 1938), *Ride, Tenderfoot, Ride* (Republic, 1940) and *Back in the Saddle* (Republic, 1941), Toones made brief appearances as a railway porter. In the Three Mesquiteers Western *Red River Range* (Republic, 1938), Toones' role is a bit more substantial. He plays the role of a porter at a resort, The Health Hacienda. John Wayne, as Stony Brooke, assumes the identity of a murderer, plants a newspaper with his picture on the front page in his suitcase and registers as a guest. Toones carries the bag to Wayne's room. Toones, of course, sees the newspaper and is told by Wayne to forget what he saw. Toones response is, "Y'sa. I'se forgets awful easy, sir." In *Yodelin' Kid from Pine Ridge* (Republic, 1937), Toones plays a field hand who must tell Gene Autry that his father has been murdered. In all of the films in which Toones appears, he works at a job commonly associated with African-Americans of the era, and speaks in a dialect common to white stereotypes of black speech patterns.

African-American women normally played the role of maid, such Louise Beavers' role as Belle Starr's maid. She plays a similar role in *Colorado Sundown* (Republic, 1952), as maid to Mary Ellen Kay. Beavers is a loyal servant, ever watchful over her mistress. And when a letter from the Forestry Service comes for Rex Allen, Beavers is shot and nearly killed while struggling to keep it from the phony Forest Ranger. In addition, Etta McDaniel — another well-known black actress — played a part much like that of maid in *The Lonely Trail* and in *American Empire* (United Artists, 1942).

Ruby Dandridge's portrayal of Devoria, the black cook in *Home in Oklahoma* (Republic, 1946), is another example of a black character type. When Sam Talbot's horse throws Dale Evans and goes galloping back to the ranch, Dandridge mistakes a train whistle for Talbot moaning from the grave. She claims she heard the same noise the day Sam Talbot died. From that clue, Roy Rogers concludes that Talbot died much earlier than had been reported. Dandridge's behavior also points to another white attitude: blacks are superstitious.

Superstition and cowardice were often tied to the stereotype of a lazy, slow-moving black in order to use that role as the source of humor and comic relief in films. Stepin Fetchit, probably best remembered as one of Shirley Temple's dance partners, portrayed the lazy, slow-moving, funny African-American of racial stereotypes. In *Wild Horse* (Allied, 1932) he plays a ranch flunky completely unable making a stubborn mule obey him. Even simple tasks seem beyond him. At one point Fetchit's job requires him to paste rodeo posters to the barn walls. After Fetchit pastes one poster to a wall he leans against it, and when he walks away the poster sticks to his back. Fetchit, of course, cannot figure out what happened to the poster. In *Wild Horse* his speech pattern is the incomprehensible mumbling slur that Fetchit made so famous in his movies.

Fred Toones had a larger role in *Raiders of the West* (PRC, 1942). Toones plays the wagon driver for Bill Boyd and Art Davis. When the two stars decide to camp for the evening, they choose an abandoned house as

Colorado Sundown, Republic, 1952; Slim Pickens, Rex Allen, Mary Ellen Kay and Louise Beavers. Beavers plays Kay's maid in this Allen film.

a campsite. Toones is sure the house is haunted. Boyd and Davis chide him for believing in ghosts. Toones replies, "Spooks may not bother white folks, but they got a special attraction for us colored folks." In spite of his concern, Toones enters the house — and steps on a cat's tail. Believing the cat's screech to be a spook, he runs out, and keeps running until Boyd and Davis manage to chase him down.

Willie Best's portrayal of Bones in *The Kansan* (United Artists, 1943) captures all of the stereotypes. Best is the porter-handyman in Jane Wyatt's hotel. He is a slow-moving, lazy, cowardly creature. But Bones also likes money, so healthy tips will both energize him and neutralize his cowardice. When the carriage in which Best is riding is captured by the bad guys, Best is pulled shaking and moaning from the floor of the back seat.

Leigh Whipper's role in *Robin Hood of the Pecos* (Republic, 1941) is far more subdued than either Fetchit or Best. Yet in that film, Whipper is the butt of Sally Payne's comic antics. As Belle Starr, Payne wants to sharpen her rifle-shooting and knife-throwing skills. She proposes to knock an apple off Whipper's head, but he won't let her do it. Unlike either

Fetchit or Best, Whipper is as much Payne's guardian and friend as he is her servant. That suggests that in some Westerns, African-American characters did possess a degree of dignity, an element explored later in the chapter. In the meantime, one more stereotype merits consideration: blacks as natural dancers and entertainers.

In *The Lonely Trail,* blacks loyal to the Terry family warned of impending danger by playing musical instruments, singing and dancing. Fred Toones sings a line or two with the rest of the cowboys in *Gold Mine in the Sky.* In Gene Autry's first feature film, *Tumbling Tumbleweeds* (Republic, 1935), Eugene Jackson plays the role of a black song and dance man who dresses like Uncle Sam in George Hayes' minstrel show. And in one of Gene Autry's most unusual films, *The Singing Cowboy* (Republic, 1936), Fred Toones leads a trio of black cowboys who play cow horns. In this film, Autry heads a television program — remember the film was made in 1936 — and Toones' group auditions for a spot on the program. Finally, in two films, *Git Along Little Doggies* (Republic, 1937) and *Round-Up Time in Texas* (Republic, 1937), Autry showcases a troupe of young black singers known as The Cabin Kids.

Many of the racial stereotypes come together in a Gene Autry Western, *Carolina Moon* (Republic, 1940). The film's Southern plantation setting required more black actors and actresses than are found in most Westerns. Etta McDaniel plays Mammy, a loyal black maid of Mary Lee and June Storey. Fred Toones makes a brief appearance as Hardie Albright's house servant, and Paul White plays Billy, the groom for June Storey's prize race horse. In the evening, contented house servants and field hands go about their chores singing Negro spirituals.

Carolina Moon depicts the two races living in harmony with each other because each understood its place in the social arrangement. For example, Toones goes to his boss to get a salary advance so he can bet on the big horse race. Albright chastises Toones, telling him not to waste his money. McDaniel is the protective, loving but excitable mammy of racial stereotyping. And Paul White's Billy is a dependable, conniving, funny groom with a predictable black dialect. *Carolina Moon* brings out all of these racial stereotypes more fully than do most Westerns.

Some B Westerns featured African-American males as sidekicks to the cowboy hero. Three films come to mind: Blue Washington is John Wayne's cook and traveling companion Clarence in *Haunted Gold* (Warner Bros., 1932), Jimmy Robinson plays Pancake, the sidekick of Jack Luden and Art Davis in *Phantom Gold* (Columbia, 1938), and Ernest Wilson is Don "Red" Barry's manservant and sidekick Memphis in *The Phantom Cowboy* (Republic, 1941). The relationship between the cowboy hero and his black sidekick and the characteristics assigned to the sidekick typify racial relationships and stereotypes that existed throughout the 1930s and 1940s. While white sidekicks played second fiddle to the cowboy hero, they always went where the hero went. If the cowboy hero went to a restaurant or the heroine's living room, the sidekick went with him. Black sidekicks did not enjoy that same intimacy.

When Jack Luden and Art Davis go into a restaurant, Jimmy Robinson as Pancake does not go with them and, in fact, in one humor-laden sequence he asks a couple of white men if they know where he can get some hog chitlins. Not only would it have been unthinkable for Pancake to eat in the same restaurant with white people, his exchange with the white men also suggests that white people assumed African-Americans ate different food.

In *Haunted Gold*, John Wayne is invited to spend the night in the only remaining nice home in a once-prosperous community (now a ghost town). Clarence, Wayne's black traveling companion, is told he can sleep in one of the vacant rundown houses across the street. Even though Clarence was a valued traveling companion, a man Friday to Wayne, the racial gap was too great for Clarence to spend the night in the same house with white folks. Clarence is frightened of spooks and goes running to Wayne. When he bursts into the house, wide-eyed and frightened, Wayne calms him down and tells Clarence to wait in the hall. Again, black people did not go into white people's living rooms; they waited in the hall.

Ernest Wilson as Memphis projects the same racial distance in *The Phantom Cowboy*. When viewers first meet Don Barry, he is riding on top of the stagecoach next to the driver, Hank Bell. When outlaws attack, Barry helps Bell fight them off in a running gun battle. When the coach arrives at its destination, Wilson climbs out of the coach. He had not ridden on top with Barry and Bell, nor had Barry ridden in such close quarters with a black passenger, even one who is his manservant.

In all three films, the cowboy heroes address the black characters in a friendly but inferior tone of voice. For example, in *The Phantom Cowboy*, when Ernest Wilson climbs out of the stage, Bell addresses him as "boy" and wonders how he could sleep through all of the shooting. Wayne talks to Blue Washington as if he were a young boy rather than a man considerably older than Wayne. And in *Haunted Gold*, the outlaws make several references to Washington's race by calling him "Smoky" and "watermelon eater."

The three films are full of racial characterizations. The black characters do the menial labor. Pancake cooks and stays with the horses. Memphis' role is never clear, but in one scene he is grooming the horse and in another he shows up dressed as a vaquero and, with a sweep of his hat, announces to Barry, "Boss, your dinner is served." Clarence runs Wayne's errands and even goes back to the ranch to get $1000 that Wayne uses to foil the bad guys.

All three of the black characters are superstitious and afraid of ghosts. *The Phantom Cowboy* has the least of that trait, but at one point when Barry rides up to a hacienda dressed as El Lobo (who all believed had been killed) Memphis says, "Go away, Mr. Ghost; I ain't done nothin'." When Luden tells Pancake they are going to a ghost town to check up on the outlaws, Pancake asks, "Did you say ghost town?" Pancake does not want to go, but he gets on his mule — note Luden and Davis rode horses, Pancake rides a mule — and follows them in order to tend the horses while Luden and Davis investigate.

Wilson as Memphis also fits another racial stereotype: He likes to shoot dice. When Memphis climbs out of the stagecoach at the hacienda, one of the vaqueros comes up to him and Memphis grabs his sombrero. When the Mexican grabs it back, Memphis pulls dice from his pocket and asks the vaquero if he knows what they are. When the Mexican shakes his head, Memphis says, "Well, come on. I have been waiting for you for a long time." The next time we see Memphis, he is dressed in the vaquero's clothes. Unfortunately for Memphis, the next time he appears he is dressed as a poor peasant. When Barry asks Memphis what happened, Memphis shakes his head and tells Barry, "Dice is the devil's invention and I am reformed from now on." But, alas, Memphis is not reformed, for when Barry throws the dice away, Memphis scurries to find them as soon as Barry leaves.

Blue Washington as Clarence combines superstition and gambling. When Clarence is told to go to sleep in the vacant house across the street, he is not sure that is a good thing to do. He tells his horse, "I sure got the creeps; feels like ghosts, spooks and phantoms is all around here." Clarence does not want to go into the house, so he decided to roll the dice. He will try Lady Luck, and if he doesn't role snake eyes, Clarence tells his horse, "I'se don't move another foot."

When Clarence throws snake eyes, he is sure "little Clarence" will be just fine so he goes, slowly to be sure, into the old rundown house. But his troubles have only begun! Wide-eyed, Clarence is looking around when he backs into a cobweb. Certain it is a ghost, Clarence freezes and then he sees a shadow on the wall which he knows is a ghost. At that point, he runs screaming out of the house in search of John Wayne.

Screenwriters even gave Washington dialogue that called attention to his race. At one point, the outlaws have caught Clarence and they force him to lead them through the tunnels of the old mine. When they get to a fork in the shaft, Harry Woods, leader of the outlaw gang, tells Clarence to take the right fork, but Clarence doesn't move. When Woods prods him to move, Clarence replies, "Boss, the spirit is willin', but the feet is stallin'." Later on, when Clarence falls through some floor boards and begins to tumble down the mine shaft, he says, "Bye bye, blackbird." As the film ends, Wayne and heroine Sheila Terry are sitting on a swing about to kiss when Clarence stumbles in. He is carrying flowers obviously intended for Terry, but the film ends with Clarence lying on the ground saying, "Boy, is my face red."

Astute readers may protest that many of the characteristics—fear of ghosts, menial jobs such as cooking and doing the dishes and efforts to get rich quickly—are not racial; white sidekicks such as Smiley Burnette and Al St. John exhibited many of the same traits. That observation is correct, but only to a certain extent. As noted above, white sidekicks went wherever the hero went. They were buddies and social equals. That simply is not the case with black sidekicks. They did not eat or sleep (unless it was outdoors around a campfire) with the hero. The social relationship existing between the cowboy hero and his black sidekick in B Western reflected attitudes and social practices widespread throughout the South and much of the North.

While B Westerns reflected racial attitudes and social practices in the United States during the 1930s and 1940s, there is one notable exception: In a few instances, African-Americans pull guns on white outlaws. Near the beginning of *Haunted Gold*, Harry Woods has the drop on John Wayne, when Clarence pulls his gun and points it at Woods, telling the outlaw, "Y'all better get movin' before I'se loses control." Later Wayne and Clarence get into a brawl with the outlaws with Clarence throwing punches at the white bad guys.

Fred Toones has an interesting role in the Harry Carey programmer *Aces Wild* (Commodore, 1936). Toones plays a horse wrangler who takes care of Carey's horse Sonny. At one point in the film, he even draws his gun and shoots at the white outlaws when one of them is about to shoot Carey. In the end, he is shot by one of the outlaws and dies in Carey's arms. By that time, Toones was a friend and valuable ally.

Fred Toones also has a gun in *Hidden Valley Outlaws* (Republic, 1944). The action opens with John James' father being killed by outlaws illegally homesteading on his property. When a jury declares the men innocent, James takes matters into his own hands. He kills two of the four men who were implicated in his father's murder, and becomes an outlaw in his own right. When his sister (Anne Jeffreys) takes some food to an old mine in which James is hiding, she has to get past Snowflake, who is guarding the entrance to the mine for James. When Jeffreys tells James she is worried he will be discovered, James tells her there is "nothing to worry about with Snowflake out there."

Unfortunately for James, Jeffreys has been trailed by both William Elliott and Gabby Hayes, who have been tricked by a phony telegram into helping to capture James, and by LeRoy Mason, the man who really killed James' father. Gabby Hayes recognizes that they can't get by the rifle-toting Snowflake, but Elliott has an idea — an idea laden with racial stereotypes.

Elliott has Hayes find a chicken, and they turn it loose. Snowflake hears the chicken cackle and thinks of a chicken dinner — a stereotypically favorite food of African-Americans. Snowflake leaves his guard post to catch the chicken, and Elliott and Hayes slip into the cave. But Mason, lurking about, sees Snowflake catch the chicken. When the black guard returns to his guard post, Mason conks him on the head with his pistol and follows Elliott and Hayes into the cave.

In an exchange of gunfire, Mason kills James but Hayes — not knowing that Mason is anywhere around — assumes that one of his bullets ricocheted off of the cave wall. The film then becomes a pretty standard B Western as Elliott and Hayes are accused of murder and must prove their innocence. Roy Barcroft is the real culprit and head of the outlaws while appearing to be an upstanding lawyer, Gilbert Leland, who is working on the side of the ranchers against the illegal homesteaders.

When the ranchers organize a vigilante group to break into jail and lynch Elliott and Hayes, who they believe killed James, Snowflake, his head bandaged from the wound caused by Mason's gun, insists on going along. However, Budd Buster declines Snowflake's request, telling him to stay at the ranch and look after Anne Jeffreys.

Later, as Elliott is digging up a grave which is supposed to contain an innocent homesteader killed by the vigilantes both Hayes and Snowflake are scared. Interestingly, however, Snowflake — and not Hayes — has the dialogue associated with fear of ghosts. When Hayes scoffs at Snowflake for believing in ghosts, the black man replies, "Course I don't, but I could be wrong." And when Elliott tells Snowflake he can leave the grave site, Snowflake says, "Legs, don't fail me now."

Finding that the innocent homesteader is not in the grave, Elliott sends him a fake telegram and then follows Bud Geary, who delivers it. Earle Hodgins is an actor hired by Barcroft to fake the murder. Hodgins does not want implicated in murder and theft so he agrees to confess all. When Elliott takes Hodgins back to Jefferys' ranch to confess to Buster and the rest of the vigilantes, Snowflake sees Hodgins and cries, "Dead man is here." Even when an African-American actor has a relatively strong role — as Toones did in *Hidden Valley Outlaws*—the film still contains numerous racial stereotypes.

Etta McDaniel and Fred Toones offer humorous, yet human, performances in *The Lawless Nineties* (Republic, 1936). Toones plays the loyal servant of George Hayes and Ann Rutherford who accompanies them to Wyoming territory. Toones cleans up the newspaper office and helps with the manual work. One day while sweeping up the office, McDaniel sees him and tries to be friendly. When Toones brushes her aside, McDaniel tells him to be nice to the only woman of his color in the whole town.

After Hayes has been murdered, Toones — again playing Snowflake — spends afternoons at McDaniel's house. She keeps raising the issue of marriage and he keeps resisting the idea. Viewers know, however, McDaniel and Toones are going to get together just as will Wayne and Rutherford.

The Glory Trail (Crescent, 1937) is an interesting Tom Keene programmer because of the mixed racial messages it sends. John Lester Johnson plays Toby, the former slave, and now manservant of Tom Keene. Keene and his small band of Confederate soldiers refuse to surrender even though the war has ended. They want to make new homes—in a community of their own — in Wyoming territory. Toby rides with the soldiers as an equal, and when they sit around the campfire at night, he is in the circle with the rest of the men, not off to one side as would be expected of a black servant.

Yet Toby's understanding of himself is mixed. When Keene sees a union ordnance supply train, he rides down to see if he can buy ammunition. As he leaves, Keene orders his men to remain; he will go alone to see the union officer. Halfway down the trail, however, Toby rides up. Keene tells Toby he left instructions for nobody to follow him. Toby replies, "I ain't nobody, I's just Toby."

Other racial stereotypes surround Toby's character. When Keene camps his outfit near the union supply train for the night, Toby sneaks over and steals a chicken. Keene's breakfast —cooked and served by Toby — is fried chicken. Keene even jokes with Toby by telling him that he understands Washington has passed a law that from now on colored folks get one of the drumsticks. Joan Barclay, the heroine and Keene's love interest in *The Glory Trail*, calls Toby "black boy" as she talks with her maid (Etta McDaniel) as Mandy.

Toby and Mandy develop a romance, just as did McDaniel and Toones in *The Lawless Nineties*. Mandy can't understand, however, why Toby lets Keene treat him as if he is still owned. When she first meets Toby at the ordnance supply train, she asks him why he is hanging around as if he were still owned. Toby has no other explanation other than he has been with Keene since he was a child and, freedom or no freedom, he is going to stay with Keene. At one point in the film, Toby even tells Mandy he had better move along before "Master John tans my hide." Mandy shakes her head in disbelief.

Viewers soon learn, however, that Mandy's relationship with Barclay is certainly no better — and probably worse — than Toby's with Keene. In the evening after Barclay first met Keene and Mandy met Toby, Mandy is combing Barclay's hair and helping her white mistress prepare for bed. When Mandy kids Barclay about Keene, Barclay tells Mandy not to be impudent. Clearly, Mandy had stepped over an invisible boundary separating the two women.

As the film unfolds, Toby and Mandy spend more time together as their romance blossoms. Again, however, viewers are reminded of the racial difference when the white officers have a dance. As the dance breaks up, the camera pans Toby and Mandy standing at the window, looking in at the revelry. In the end, however, the confederates are reunited with their sweethearts, Keene with Barclay and Johnson with McDaniel as a mass wedding concludes *The Glory Trail*.

Willie Best in *The Kansan* was more than a buffoon. After the bad guys capture him and Victor Jory, they overhear plans to raid and burn the town. Someone needs to warn Richard Dix of the impending danger. Out of necessity, Jory turned to a reluctant Best. Best becomes a hero as he first escapes, and then successfully hides from the outlaws trying to find him. Best is thus able to warn Dix, who prevents the outlaws from destroying the town.

The strongest character role for any black actor in pre-1955 Westerns may be Leigh Whipper's performance as Sparks in *The Ox Bow Incident* (20th Century–Fox, 1943). Sparks is a black preacher who accompanies the lynch mob, in part because they may need his services and in part because he hopes to dissuade the mob from its evil course. Sparks explains to Henry Fonda that he saw his little brother lynched, and he hopes the Lord will keep it from happening again. Fonda's response is that he doubts the Lord cares what happens on the mountain that night.

During the course of the film, Whipper does all of those things a preacher does. He prays and sings over the intended victims, and he tries to talk the mob out of lynching the men. His most important moment comes, however, when the mob votes on whether or not to hang the men. Major Tetley (Frank Conroy), invites those opposed to hanging the suspects to step to one side. Whipper is the first man across. He is clearly the conscience of the mob, a remarkable role for a black man in 1943.

The Big Bonzana (Republic, 1944) needs to be considered for it points to a curious element in race relations of the middle quarter of the twentieth century. In this film, Bobby Driscoll, the young actor playing Richard Arlen's kid brother, had a black and a Chinese youngster as his friends. The black boy even runs away with Driscoll when the latter believes his older brother is a coward. Black and white children often played together, and they might even be friends for a while, but only up to a certain age! After that, their personal relationships reflected their places in society.

During the last quarter of the twentieth century, Americans became more aware of Asians than ever before. The opening of the People's Republic of China to American tourists and business offset the bitter memories of Vietnam. Japan, Singapore and South Korea loom as major economic competitors, and their electronics enrich American entertainment. Vietnamese, Laotians and other Asians are now familiar sights in American cities across the continent.

How different all of that is from the middle quarter of the twentieth century. At that time, most Americans could not have located either Korea or Singapore on a world map. China was torn by civil war. Japan had emerged as the Asian military power but few thought war likely between Japan and the United States. Within the United States, Japanese-Americans lived almost exclusively along a narrow strip of the Pacific coast (Daniels, 4). Americans of the heartland seldom came in contact with any Asians.

Of all Asians, Chinese were the most familiar to Americans. North American missionaries returned to tell congregations about the Chinese people and culture, and Pearl S. Buck's *The Good Earth*, published in 1931, became a national best-seller (Kennedy, 401). Chinese had also immigrated to the West as railroad laborers and cooks. They opened small businesses and prospered by hard work. For those reasons, Chinese were regarded in a different light by white Americans than were either blacks or Japanese. Popular culture reflected that distinction. Charlie Chan, a Chinese detective, was an American folk hero of the era. Smiley Burnette, singing "A Defective Detective from Brooklyn" in *Public Cowboy No. 1* (Republic, 1936), even appears dressed as Charlie Chan during part of the song.

However, for the most part Chinese did not have a significant place in Western movies. Michael Wayne Sarf notes that Chinese were neither cowboys nor gunfighters; and with the exception of the Tong wars they were not violent people (Sarf, 224). Sarf is correct that Chinese were not gunfighters, but they do appear in B Westerns as violent people, even villains. Three examples come to mind, and of them *Border Phantom* (Republic, 1937) is the most prominent. This Bob Steele programmer develops around smuggling Chinese women into the country as picture brides for wealthy Chinese males.

Frank Ball plays the role of a scientist using an abandoned hacienda for research on rare butterfly specimens. However, Chan Lee (Miki Morita), also uses the hacienda to hide the picture brides. Karl Hackett, Morita's ally, raises hogs, and several times a week goes across the border to get "soybeans" for his hogs. Of course, instead of soybeans in the barrels, Hackett smuggles Chinese picture brides into the country. When Ball discovers Morita's hideaway and his illegal operation, he tells his niece (Harley Wood) to saddle her horse and take a note to the sheriff. However, as Ball writes the note, Morita shoots and kills him.

Bob Steele and his pal Don Barclay assist Wood in discovering who murdered her uncle. A subplot involves Perry Murdoch's evil intentions on Wood. He loves her but she has no interest in him. Her uncle had even fired Murdoch. When Horace Murphy, playing a bungling, egotistical sheriff, jails Wood, Murdoch has her sprung from jail. He then kidnaps Wood and arranges to have Chan Lee smuggle Wood back across the border in Hackett's wagon rather than go back to jail. His plan almost succeeds until Bob Steele stops both Chan Lee and Murdoch.

The film ends with a less confused Horace Murphy placing Chan Lee under arrest for murder. When Murphy discovers the Chinese picture brides in the hacienda, he orders them detained for deportation back to China. Chan Lee is an exception to Sarf's contention that Chinese were not depicted as violent people in Westerns. Chan Lee was clearly violent; he committed murder to keep Ball from disclosing his illegal business.

Willie Fung — more about him later — plays one of the villains in *Rocky Mountain Mystery* (Paramount, 1935), a film based on a Zane Grey story. Randolph Scott stars as a mining engineer turned detective in this entertaining Western which more closely resembles a "whodunit." Fung as Ling Yat is the Chinese houseboy in cahoots with the Borgs who murdered Jim Ballard (owner of rich radium mine) and then had Mr. Borg impersonate Ballard. Fung, as Ling Yat, appears to be the placid Chinese houseboy, but he is always sneaking around whenever a murder has been committed.

After Scott unmasks Mr. Borg as an impostor by having Ballard's ex-wife come to the mine, he and Tex Murdoch (Charles Sale), round up Fung and the Borgs. The film ends with Murdoch, now sheriff, telephoning the judge to find out the jury's verdict. When Murdoch learns that all of them have been found guilty of murder, he tells the judge not to let anybody talk him into paroling them, "especially that Chinaman. He made a lot of threats agin' me, if I could only have understood 'em."

Chinese also show up as villains in *Cripple Creek* (Columbia, 1952), a bigger budget Western starring George Montgomery. The outlaws in this one add a different twist to robbing gold ore. They hijack the ore wagons, to be sure, but they also process the ore into gold bars. Montgomery, an undercover government man masquerading as an outlaw, infiltrates the gang and discovers the processing is done in an abandoned smelter and the gold is then shipped to San Francisco.

When Montgomery gives that information to his superiors, they station a man at the pier in San Francisco. The processed gold is purchased by a Chinese agent and sent to the Chinese emperor in Peking. When he has the gold crated and stamped "Imperial Palace, Peking, China," he mails a letter to Ah Tong's laundry in Cripple Creek.

The letter gives Ah Tong—who acts as a middleman between the outlaws and the Chinese in San Francisco—instructions to make payment for the gold. Government agents intercept the letter, so they are able to apprehend the outlaws when they try to get their money from Ah Tong.

In the last chapter, Willard Robertson appeared as owner of the dry goods store in *Texas Bad Man* (Universal, 1932), a highly entertaining Tom Mix talkie. In that film, Tet Su Kamal plays Gow, Robertson's house servant. Kamal is always present when Robertson plots new crimes, and the servant seems to be as vicious as his boss. When Robertson asks Gow what he thinks of Bishop, Tom Mix's character in *Texas Bad Man*, Gow gives Robertson an evil smile of approval!

The above films make clear that, on occasion, Chinese are B Western villains. Most of the time, however, there are no Chinese characters in Westerns, and when they do appear, Chinese mirror white stereotypes of them. Stereotypical Chinese engage in service occupations such as cooks, laundrymen, houseboys or day laborers working on railroad construction or in mines. In addition, Westerns portray Chinese as highly excitable people who run around wildly shouting unintelligibly when things go amiss. Chinese characters also display one of two contradictory postures. They are either unskilled in self-defense and easily victimized by the villains, or they are pictured as obstinate, hardheaded individuals moved by neither reason nor circumstance.

Victor Wong plays Iris Meredith's excitable cook in *Taming of the West* (Columbia, 1939), the first entry in the Wild Bill Saunders series starring William Elliott. Wong cooks at Meredith's restaurant, and when he goes outside to watch Dick Curtis and his gang shoot up the town, Curtis throws his lariat around Wong. However, Wong is rescued by Meredith, who shoots Curtis' hat from his head and ridicules him in front of his men for picking on a helpless Chinaman and a woman. Wong was the consummate helpless Chinaman in this episode.

H. T. Tsaing plays Wong's opposite, a independent, strong-willed Oriental, in *In Old Sacramento* (Republic, 1946). William Elliott takes his dinner guests to Tsaing's restaurant. Elliott tells his guests they may order what they wish, but Tsaing will serve whatever he prepared for that day. Even though Elliott will pay for the food, he will get whatever Tsaing wants to serve him!

In other films, Orientals appear briefly as walk-ons with few, if any, speaking parts. Wong Chung made such an appearance in *Forbidden Trails* (Columbia, 1932), a Buck Jones Western, and an unbilled Chinese actor played the owner of a Carson City restaurant in Roy Rogers' *The Carson City Kid* (Republic, 1940). These are but two film examples of the several in which Chinese actors had parts similar to those of Fred Toones. They were walk-ons with, at best, a few lines.

Gene Autry's *Valley of Fire* (Columbia, 1951) is an exception to the otherwise insignificant roles played by Chinese actors. Gene is the mayor of a town without women, so he sends East for women who will come West to become wives. The bad guys in another town learn of Autry's plan, and they scheme to raid the wagon train and whisk the women off to their town to become their wives.

The hero turns out to be Victor Sen Yung, the Chinese launderer in Autry's town. Sen Yung's cousin is a cook for the bad guys, and he overhears their plot to raid the wagon train. He warns his cousin Sen Yung, who in turn alerts Autry to the danger. All ends all as Gene and the other men of the town are able to stave off the attack and win the women for wives.

Chester Gan plays an interesting Chinese character in *Westbound Stage* (Monogram, 1939), a Tex Ritter programmer. A banker hires Ritter to guard a large gold shipment being sent by stagecoach. Gan is one of the passengers. Initially his role is puzzling because viewers cannot figure out why he is in the film; he seems to be included for humorous distraction, but one cannot be sure. When the stagecoach stops overnight at a relay station, the heroine (Muriel Evans) thinks Tex Ritter removed the gold from the strongbox and put it in his saddlebags. She steals the saddlebags, because she had witnessed Tom London and Frank Ellis talk when Ritter left the room with the strongbox.

When London and Ellis steal the strongbox and discover that it is empty, they ambush the stagecoach. In the gunfight that follows, Gan joins the rest of the passengers as he shoots at the bad guys with his ancient rifle. When the outlaws are captured, Evans assures Tex that she has his saddlebags containing the gold safely in her possession.

Tex smiles at her, and then tells Gan to hand him the sack he is carrying. Ritter removes the gold from Gan's sack. He explains that he and Gan always work together, and that Gan had the gold all along. While Gan is not exactly Ritter's sidekick (Nelson McDowell played that role), he was a valuable ally, one Ritter entrusted with an important gold shipment.

Willie Fung is the B Western Oriental counterpart to Fred Toones. Just as Toones' characterization of African-Americans mirrored white perceptions, so do Fung's dramatizations of Orientals. *The Virginian* (Paramount, 1929) and *Hop-A-Long Cassidy* (Paramount, 1935) are good examples of films in which Fung plays an excitable Chinese cook.

Viewers first meet Fung in *The Virginian* when the Taylors' neighbors come from miles around to christen the babies and to meet Molly Stark, the new schoolmarm. Fung complains to Mrs. Taylor that there is too much work and the cowboys she has assigned to help him prepare the food are not working fast enough. One of the white cowboys tells Mrs. Taylor to keep that "slant-eyed muskrat away from me" and refers to Fung as "chink." Fung, in turn, yells incomprehensible Chinese at them.

Fung is Robert Warwick's Chinese cook, Salem, in *Hop-A-Long Cassidy*. Kenneth Thompson is Pecos Jack Anthony, Warwick's ranch foreman, who is in cahoots with a band of outlaws bossed by Ted Adams. The outlaws rustle cattle from both the Bar 20 and Warwick, and Thompson keeps stirring up trouble between the two ranches.

Early in the film, Buck Peters, played by Charles Middleton, rides over to see Warwick in order to straighten out grazing and water rights. Warwick asks Fung to bring them milk. Fung is clearly puzzled. Western ranchers usually drink something stronger than milk! While Fung is getting the milk, Middleton and Warwick are unable to come to any understanding over grazing rights on the open range, so Middleton rides away. When Fung brings the milk, Warwick, clearly upset over the argument, tells Fung he does not want it. Fung walks away, shaking his head and muttering Chinese.

When Hopalong Cassidy and Jimmy Ellison stumble across some old cow hides, Cassidy realizes that the outlaws are changing the brands on cows from both ranches. He and Uncle Ben (George Hayes) ride over to explain to Meeker that both ranches are being victimized by rustlers who are stirring up the water and grazing feud to cover up their rustling.

Fung is hanging out the wash when he sees Cassidy and Uncle Ben ride up. He stops his work and goes to get a shotgun, but when he attempts to shoot at the two Bar 20 hands, the gun's recoil knocks him to the ground. Hayes then ropes him until Meeker comes up to find out what's going on. Hayes sends Fung on his way "Get out of here, you yeller...."

Clearly, Fung's character in B Westerns is a highly excitable Oriental

Call of the Prairie, Paramount, 1936; Willie Fung and William Boyd. Fung often portrayed a highly excitable Chinese cook.

who works at servant-type jobs. When he is overly distraught, Fung spews forth streams of incomprehensible Chinese to all those around him. Furthermore, he is viewed as inferior to whites. The Taylors' cowboy calls him a "slant-eyed muskrat" and "chink." Hayes even gets rid of him by referring to his skin color. Fung's character surely mirrors white stereotypes of Orientals.

Fung has an interesting exchange with Smiley Burnette in the Gene Autry programmer *Git Along Little Doggies* (Republic, 1937), an exchange which plays off of Fung's race. Autry and Burnette treat their cowboys to lunch in Sing Low's restaurant. When Autry tells Burnette to pay, Burnette tells Sing Low to put it on the cuff. However, Sing Low raises both jacket sleeves and shows Burnette his cuffs are full of debts: "No can do, cuffs full already." Burnette responds that Sing Low ought to take that shirt to the laundry, an obvious play on the Chinese laundry so typical of B Westerns. When Burnette tries to get out of paying, Fung begins to mutter in Chinese until Autry pulls off Burnette's boots and pays the restaurant owner. Fung is an enterprising businessman, however. When Autry tries to buy pie for the men, he discovers Burnette is really out of money this time. Seeing a good chance at entertainment, Fung tells Autry he will give them apple pie if Autry and his men will sing for the customers.

Fung had substantial roles in two other Western films. He played the Three Mesquiteers' cook-houseboy in *Come On Cowboys* (Republic, 1937). The Three Mesquiteers become guardians of a small girl. Her governess, however, is convinced that the men are much too violent for such a responsibility, and it appears the judge agrees with her. Fung intervenes with a scheme. If one of the Three Mesquiteers will marry the governess, her fears would be allayed. That duty falls to Ray Corrigan. Fung plays Cupid. He arranges for music, places flowers in key places and does everything in his power to create the proper atmosphere for a marriage proposal.

Some might see his scheming as reflecting the stereotype of a crafty Asian; others might regard his role as houseboy in a similar way. Clearly, the Three Mesquiteers employ Fung, but he is more than an employee. They treat him as an equal, and they listen to his ideas. In that sense, Fung's role is superior to that of any African-American appearing in Western films with the exception of Leigh Whipper in the bigger budget *The Ox Bow Incident*.

Fung also appeared as the cook in *Saddle Mountain Roundup* (Monogram, 1941). He enters the room right after his boss has been murdered, and discovers a partially written letter. Fung is afraid he will be suspected of murdering his boss, so he hides the letter. Just as in *Come On Cowboys*, Fung keeps appearing throughout the film. At one point he is even knocked unconscious by the killer. When Fung shows the letter to the Range Busters, he furnishes them with a valuable piece of information they need to solve the crime.

Eddie Lee is Wong, a Chinese cook, in *The Man from Thunder River* (Republic, 1943). Contrary to stereotypes, Lee is a literate person who quotes Confucius. He even helps catch the crooks by knocking out the general store clerk so William Elliott and Gabby Hayes can get into a gold mine via a secret entrance in the back of the store.

If Chinese seldom had substantial roles in Westerns, Japanese show up even less. By 1940, there were only about 127,000 Japanese living in the entire country. Almost 60 percent of them were native-born and nearly all 127,000 lived in a narrow strip along the California coast (Daniels, 4). Like the Chinese, Japanese were hardworking people who amassed considerable property, but their clannish ways raised local white suspicions and hostility. Always discriminated against, life became even harsher for Japanese-Americans in the days and months after Pearl Harbor.

The Man from Thunder River, Republic, 1943; Eddie Lee, Robert Barron, George Hayes and William Elliott. Lee plays and educated Chinese cook who helps Hayes and Elliott track down the villians.

Chapter Two commented on how the cowboys helped to fight World War II. Interestingly enough, his enemies nearly always were unspecified foreign agents or Nazis. Japanese seldom appear. To be sure, one of the villains in Allan Lane's serial *King of the Mounties* (Republic, 1942) is a Japanese (White, 26). The only other example is found in the Range Busters Western *Texas to Bataan* (Monogram, 1942). This film was released some 11 months after the Japanese attacked Pearl Harbor, and after California's Japanese population had been sent to relocation camps. Escolastico Baucin plays a Japanese cook, Cookie, posing as a Filipino. Cookie is always getting a lot of mail from Japan. When questioned about it, his response is that he has a lot of relatives. However, when the Range Busters escort a herd of horses to Manila for cavalry use, they find Cookie plotting with foreign agents. Of course, the Range Busters put a stop to it. The film fits nicely with popular sentiment that Japanese-Americans could not be trusted. In case of war, they would remain loyal to the Japanese Emperor.

Westerns present Spanish-speaking people differently than they do African-Americans or Orientals. That difference is observable in two distinct ways. First, Anglo actors and actresses play Mexican characters. Blackface, common in other film genres, seldom appeared in Westerns. It was common, however, for Anglo performers to play Mexican characters, particularly wealthy landowners and cantina dancers. Buck Jones even went as far as to assume the role of a Mexican military officer in *South of the Rio Grande* (Columbia, 1932). The film had a complete Mexican setting, yet Anglos played all of the major characters.

Jones also played Joaquin Murietta — the famed Mexican bandit — in *The Avenger* (Columbia, 1931), a film that blames Anglos for chasing Murietta into banditry. Jones, as Murietta, witnesses the murder of his brother, the impending confiscation of the ranch, and he suffers a severe beating with a horsewhip. He vows revenge, but at the film's end Jones realizes his banditry must cease, and he retires to marry Dorothy Revier. The film when taken as a whole is very sympathetic to Hispanics.

The plot of several Westerns required the hero to assume a Mexican disguise. Tim McCoy often used that tactic. In *The Border Caballero* (Puritan, 1936), McCoy plays a Justice Department official who disguises himself as a Mexican and goes after a gang of bank robbers responsible for killing another officer who was working undercover in the gang. In *The Fighting Renegade* (Victory, 1939), McCoy continues his character Lightnin Bill Carson. This time, Carson has been accused of a murder he did not commit. To clear his name, McCoy assumes the disguise of El Puma, a Mexican bandit, and searches for the real killer.

His Mexican caricatures reflect a couple of stereotypes. McCoy's use of stilted English is one. He reverses words, misuses slang and often does not understand the meaning of common phrases. That lends a comical nature to the character he develops, pointing to a second stereotype. Mexicans are often thought of as comical people not alert to what is happening around them. McCoy's Mexican characters reinforce that belief.

Rex Lease in *Fighting Caballero* (Superior Talking Pictures, 1935) is a government agent in Mexican disguise. His portrayal points to other stereotypes. Lease's character is quite a lady charmer, and he usually figures out some way to let other people do his fighting. The stereotypes employed by McCoy and Lease reappear in the Cisco Kid and Pancho characters, but more about them at the end of the chapter.

Another distinctive is that B Westerns could not ignore Hispanic culture as they did blacks and Orientals. Hispanic culture so thoroughly pervaded the Southwest and California, filmmakers as a matter of course integrated it into Westerns. Words with Spanish roots such as lariat, remuda, hacienda, hombre and adios were the language of Western films just as they had been part of the cowboy vocabulary. Customs such as the mid-afternoon siesta and the colorful fiesta to celebrate special events were commonplace in Westerns.

As Roy Rogers Westerns became more musical in the mid-1940s, it was common to rush through the plot and action to get to the film's lavish ending which showcased not only Rogers and Dale Evans but entire choral groups and dance troupes as well. Any number of these lavish endings had a Mexican flavor. Gene Autry frequently acknowledged the influence of Mexican culture by placing several of his films in that setting. Movies such as *Down Mexico Way* (Republic, 1941), *South of the Border* (Republic, 1939) and *Mexicali Rose* (Republic, 1940) permitted Autry to croon Spanish-flavored songs such as "Mexicali Rose" and "South of the Border." And, just as Rogers, Autry's films also incorporated colorful Mexican-like celebrations. *Bells of Capistrano* (Republic, 1942) is a good example.

The cowboy hero's dress and tack also exhibited Mexican influence. The Western saddle with its saddle horn, higher cantle, bigger flaps and silver inlays show a decided departure from the English in favor of the Mexican saddle. The high crown sombrero was influenced by Mexican tradition. In addition, the decorative shirt and ornate gunbelt reflected an Hispanic flavor.

But even the incorporation of Mexican culture into Westerns had its limits. Integration occurred from a position of Anglo dominance. Anglos incorporated Spanish words and phrases, Mexican food, dress and customs, but they also took economic and political control of Mexican land. Subscribing to Manifest Destiny, white North Americans believed God had given them a mission to rule the continent. Allegedly inferior peoples such as Mexicans would have to give way as Anglos asserted claims to the land. Anglos preserved Mexican culture, but it cost Mexicans their land.

Two Western movies in particular depict Manifest Destiny. John Wayne's classic film *Red River* (United Artists, 1948) is one of them. Wayne, as Tom Dunson, leaves a wagon train headed for California to search out good ranch land. South of the Red River in Texas, he stakes out his ranch and its brand the Red River D. Most reviews of the film stress the cattle drive and the ensuing conflict between Wayne and Montgomery Clift. Interestingly, few mention Wayne's seizure of the land (McDonald, 120). He takes it from its Mexican owner, and he kills a caballero just to prove he intends to stay! In this minor, but not very subtle, manner, *Red River* shouts out the case for Manifest Destiny. Wayne is an empire builder, stretching North American claims deep into the Texas plains. But it is only partially an act of self-aggrandizement; he is also a bearer of civilization, one who will make the plains fruitful and productive.

An early Roy Rogers film, *In Old Caliente* (Republic, 1939) concerns the displacement of Hispanics in California. At the beginning of the film, Roy works for Don Miguel Vargas, who owns a large ranch in Southern California. Vargas watches with anger and apprehension as more and more gringo wagon trains come into California. He understands correctly that as more gringos arrive, there will be less room for the Hispanics. Eventually the gringos will push them out. The plot has to do with Rogers rounding up Harry Woods' gang of outlaws. In the end, however, Vargas' concern is not addressed. It could not be, for Vargas had seen the inevitable future. The gringos were coming in large numbers, and they would control California. Just as *Red River*, *In Old Caliente* projects Manifest Destiny as natural; neither film considers the displacement of Mexicans in any moral context. Rather, it is presented as natural consequence of inferior people giving way to a superior culture making its God-given claims to the land.

These two films must be distinguished from other Westerns that portray unjustifiable confiscation of Mexican lands. *California Frontier* (Columbia, 1938) even adds an interesting twist to the idea of Manifest Destiny. That film opens at an unspecified military outpost. Buck Jones is dispatched by his commanding officer to California. The commander reminds Jones that California will soon become a state, and constitutional guarantees will extend to all citizens. But, in California, gold fever had led unscrupulous men to chase Mexicans off their land. Jones apprehended the lawbreakers so that California could be admitted to the Union. Political control of the state might pass from Mexican hands, but under the Constitution of the United States Mexicans possessed rights that had to be protected.

In *The Ranger and the Lady* (Republic, 1940), Roy Rogers opposed Henry Brandon's efforts to establish a personal political empire. While Sam Houston was away in Washington, Brandon had imposed a tariff on all wagon traffic over the Texas portion of the Santa Fe Trail. When the wagons turned north to Bents Fort, Colorado, and then to Santa Fe, they bypassed Texas and Brandon's tax. He directs his henchman Harry Woods to seize all Mexican land between the Texas border and Santa Fe. Unlike Wayne's Tom Dunson who sought personal economic gain, LaRue pursued a personal political empire, one competing with the United States. Here is the opposite of Manifest Destiny. It is a scheme Roy Rogers stops.

Cowboy heroes also rode to the defense of poverty-stricken Mexican peasants unable to defend themselves. Buck Jones in *California Trail* (Columbia, 1933) plays a Yankee scout guarding a wagon train carrying supplies to a hungry Mexican village. When the owner is killed in an Indian attack, Jones and his men escort the wagon train to its final destination. Once there, Jones discovers that the military commandant and his merchant brother are enriching themselves by starving the peasants. Jones assumes the disguise of a black-capped Robin Hood who robs from the rich and gives gold to the peasants so they can buy food.

George O'Brien in *The Renegade Ranger* (RKO, 1938) sets out to arrest Judith Alvarez (Rita Hayworth) for murder and robbery. He learns, however, she is merely responding to a greedy politician who uses his taxing power to bankrupt ranchers and seize their land. Alvarez has surrounded herself with a loyal band of Mexican followers who had been victimized by the tax scheme. Although Mexicans are not the only land-grab victims, they are the primary allies of Judith Alvarez. Even though, as a good Ranger must, O'Brien arrests Alvarez, he also supports the Mexicans who are victims of greedy politicians.

In these Westerns, one particular stereotype appears: the poor defenseless Mexican peasant. But one finds in Westerns other stereotypes as well: the hot-tempered, jealous, independent señorita who is not above flaunting her sexuality; the dashing, romantic caballero; the wealthy landowner; and the sneaky bandit.

Before examining each of these stereotypes, one must consider another peculiarity in the film presentation of Hispanics. For the most part, it was acceptable for an Anglo male, often the cowboy hero, to fall in love with a pretty señorita. Bob Steele in *Oklahoma Cyclone* (Tiffany, 1930) woos a señorita, much to the chagrin of Charles King. Since King plays his usual villain role, Steele gets the girl at the end of the last reel. Hoot Gibson in *Hard Hombre* (Allied, 1931) is the lookalike of a notorious killer. When Gibson becomes foreman on Lina Basquette's ranch, one humorous episode follows another as only the Hooter could play them. But in the end, he and the señorita ride off together! Dorothy Revier plays the Mexican señorita who is Buck Jones' love interest in *The Fighting Ranger* (Columbia, 1934). She helps Jones as he rounds up the gang of outlaws who killed his brother. Lois January is Tim McCoy's señorita in *Lightnin Bill Carson* (Puritan, 1936). The final shootout occurs at her hacienda, as McCoy tries to protect her father from the killer. Later cowboy heroes, following the tradition of Gene Autry and Roy Rogers, forsook love interests. But throughout the 1930s it was common for the cowboy hero to ride off into the sunset with a pretty Mexican señorita.

It was uncommon, however, for an Anglo woman to wed a Hispanic male. It is interesting, for example, that Dorothy Gulliver, the heroine in *Fighting Caballero*, is romantically interested in Rex Lease, who is disguised as the Mexican, Joaquin. But it is only after she discovers he is really a government official, an Anglo, that they are shown romantically involved. At the film's end they ride off together in the back seat of her car. Gulliver scoots close to Lease, and he puts his arm around her shoulder. Clearly there is an implicit double standard in the films. But Westerns merely reflected life, for a great many gender-based double standards typified society of that era.

The pretty señorita in distress is one Mexican character type very evident in the 1930s. As prevalent is the stereotypical independent, hot-tempered señorita who is not above flaunting her sexuality. Several examples from 1930s films come to mind. Anita Camargo plays Julian Rivero's girlfriend, a cantina dancer, in Johnny Mack Brown's *Lawless Land* (Republic, 1937). Nena Quartaro plays the seductive girlfriend of Michael Visaroff, the Mexican outlaw who tends Ken Maynard's wounds in *Arizona Terror* (Tiffany, 1931). As the film unfolds, Quartaro bares a lot of shoulder and leg for a film made in 1931.

Armida plays the role of a jealous cantina dancer in a number of Westerns. In *South of the Rio Grande* (Monogram, 1945), she is jealous of Lillian Molieri. Francis McDonald brought the young girl to the cantina, and Armida believes her man, George Lewis, is paying too much attention to her. Armida is not bashful about venting her anger on him. Even Rita Hayworth, as Judith Alvarez in *The Renegade Ranger*, projects the image of a feisty, independent señorita. However, Estelita Rodriguez best personifies this stereotype.

Her portrayal of Lola the gypsy girl in *On the Old Spanish Trail* (Republic, 1947) is an excellent example of the stereotype Rodriguez expressed so well. Lola is in love with Ricco, played by that handsome Latin Tito Guizar, but she thinks he is in love with Jane Frazee. Rodriguez confronts the unsuspecting Frazee and threatens to kill her if she does not leave Ricco along. Later on, however, when Rodriguez believes Guizar is dying from a gunshot, she brings Frazee to the gypsy camp so he can be with his true love. Words are poor vehicles by which to convey the fire in Rodriguez' eyes as she confronts both Guizar and Frazee.

The same may be said about *The Gay Ranchero* (Republic, 1948). In this film, Rodriguez plays Consuela Belmonte, who runs away from home because she thinks her boyfriend Nicci Lopez, also played by Guizar, is a coward. Nicci has given up bullfighting and Consuela mistakenly assumes he is a coward unworthy of her love. She refuses to return to Mexico with him, and continues to spurn his attention even after he tracks her to a dude ranch run by the Sons of the Pioneers. When Guizar helps Roy Rogers round up the bad guys, Rodriguez sees that he is not a coward and true love wins out in the end.

As Rita in *Susanna Pass* (Republic, 1949), we see more of Rodriguez's temper. Playing the daughter of the jail cook, Rodriguez scoffs at her father's fear of the jailed outlaws. Donning two guns, Rodriguez sings about two-gun Rita from Gower Gulch, and she makes it clear that she can take care of herself. Later in the film, she gives the editor of the local newspaper a tongue-lashing for printing a story critical of Roy Rogers.

In Old Amarillo (Republic, 1951) finds Rodriguez as Pepita Martinez, the hot-tempered, jealous girlfriend of Ken Howell. In this one, she breaks a lot of bottles and furniture as she vents her anger over Howell's philandering ways. Unfortunately, Pinky Lee is standing in the way of most of the flying furniture and bottles. In the last Rogers B Western, *Pals of the Golden West* (Republic, 1951), Rodriguez plays Elena Maderia, owner-operator of a freight line. Pinky Lee is once again the object of her jealous love and wrath.

If Mexican women were normally projected as either pretty señoritas in distress or as feisty wildcats, the image of Mexican males is a bit more complex. The work of four actors highlights the stereotypes most commonly associated with Mexican males. Tito Guizar best represents one stereotype, the handsome Latin who has all the women swooning over him as in the two Rogers Westerns *(On the Old Spanish Trail* and *The Gay Ranchero)* which project Guizar as the romantic swashbuckling hero. Gilbert Roland and Duncan Renaldo, both playing the Cisco Kid, convey the same image.

Martin Garralaga personifies the well-to-do, dignified Mexican leader. Although he played Pancho in a few Cisco Kid Westerns, it was a more subdued, less comical Pancho than the one Leo Carrillo made famous. Often Garralaga was a wealthy Mexican land owner, as in Tex Ritter's initial Western *Song of the Gringo* (Grand National, 1936). Garralaga finances miners caught in hard luck, providing they agree that any profit from their mines be split 50-50 with Garralaga. Unknown to Garralaga, his good friend (Ted Adams) has the miners murdered, and Adams reaps huge profits. Ritter, of course, puts a stop to it. In William Elliott's *The Last Bandit* (Republic, 1949), Garralaga plays a wealthy mine owner whose gold ore is stolen along with Jack Holt's entire train.

In the mid–1940s, Garralaga demonstrated he could play less noble characters as well. In *The Gay Cavalier*, Garralaga is Don Felipe, a land owner living above his means. He wants to marry his youngest daughter to Tristram Coffin, whom Garralaga mistakenly believes is a wealthy gringo. In *South of Monterey* (Monogram, 1946), he is the corrupt commandant of the police who, along with Harry Woods, terrorizes and bankrupts the population.

Charles Stevens played many character roles (Mexican bandit, half-breed and Indian, among others), but he played the poor Mexican peasant better than anyone else. He has a strong sympathetic role as the poor peasant unsuccessfully trying to find food for his family in *California Trail*. He winds up as an important ally of Buck Jones. In *South of the Rio Grande*, Stevens plays Lillian Molieri's father. Because he does not have the means to resist Francis McDonald when he discovers the girl riding in her father's cart, Stevens must consent to his daughter dancing in the cantina.

Julian Rivero played diverse roles. For example, Rivero has an important part in *Arizona Gangbuster* (PRC, 1940) as the Mexican police officer in search of the same foreign saboteurs as Tim McCoy. In fact, Rivero is often the one who rescues McCoy from tight spots. Most people familiar with Westerns, however, associate Rivero with the bragging, sometimes sneaky caballero. He plays the latter in *Lawless Land*. Having brought Anita Camargo to dance in the saloon, he swaggers around demanding that he be treated as an important man and brave gunfighter. In reality he is the sneaky killer who shot the sheriff from ambush. In *Death Rides the Range* (Victory, 1940), Rivero is the comical sidekick of Ken Maynard, not a bandit. Yet the stereotype applies, for Rivero is always bragging about how he is a brave caballero which viewers recognize as more bragging than reality. In a Jack Hoxie programmer, *Law and the Lawless* (Majestic, 1932), Rivero is a two-gun sidekick of the hero. Hoxie introduces Rivero as "the worst caballero in all Mexico" as a way of taking some wind out of Rivero's sails. Thus a stereotype emerges. Mexican males who brag about their bravery are not that brave, and in fact are more likely to shoot from ambush than face their adversary as an honorable man would.

This stereotype filters into a number of Westerns. For example, Jay Novello is an Anglo Wells Fargo agent in *Sheriff of Tombstone* (Republic, 1941). He masterminds stage robberies because he knows what is in the strongboxes. The character he chooses for a disguise is Joe Martinez, a Mexican bandit. Francis Ford as the demented old man in *The Ox Bow Incident* tries to clear himself of the murder for which he is about to be lynched by pointing to Anthony Quinn and crying, "The Mexican did it."

The portrayal of Hispanics in Westerns has much in common with the presentation of blacks and Asians. All reflect white stereotypes. Hispanics were, however, treated somewhat uniquely. As noted above, Westerns utilize Hispanic culture, cowboy heroes disguised themselves as Mexicans, and romantic interludes between Anglo males and Hispanics señoritas were quite common. There remains to be discussed one other way in which Westerns go a step beyond the typical ethnic stereotypes. Unlike blacks, there are Hispanic Western heroes. Zorro and the Cisco Kid are the two most obvious examples.

Republic first discovered that Zorro films attracted audiences when it starred Bob Livingston as a Zorro-like character in *The Bold Caballero* (Republic, 1936). Republic followed immediately with the serial *Zorro Rides Again* (Republic, 1937). On four other occasions, before Republic discontinued its serial unit in 1955, the studio employed the Zorro theme: *Zorro's Fighting Legion* (Republic, 1939), *Zorro's Black Whip* (Republic, 1944), *Son of Zorro* (Republic, 1947) and *Ghost of Zorro* (Republic, 1949). The latter starred Clayton Moore who, of course, became television's best-known Lone Ranger. In addition to the Republic entries, Tyrone Power played Zorro in a big-budget film, *The Mark of Zorro* (20th Century–Fox, 1940). All of these films except the last three Republic serials kept an early California setting. *Zorro's Black Whip* is set in a more modern California, and in this instance Zorro, played by Linda Stirling, is a woman.

The Cisco Kid is probably the best-known Hispanic cowboy hero. Between 1929 and 1955, Warner Baxter, Cesar Romero, Gilbert Roland and Duncan Renaldo all played the Cisco Kid in both the bigger-budget films produced by Fox and the more modest-priced films from Monogram (Nevins, 1998; Loy, 2000). As O. Henry tells the story, the Kid is an Anglo who has killed several people. Fox retained many of the elements of the story when it made the first adaptation of that short story. In *In Old Arizona*, the Cisco Kid is a stagecoach robber who never robs from individuals, only corporations; he is also a cattle rustler, and a murderer who arranges the death of Tonia, his lover, when he discovers she is about to betray him to the army. However, Fox deviated from Henry's story in one important instance: The Kid is Hispanic. That set the trend; the Cisco Kid has remained Hispanic since that film.

By 1939 when Baxter made his last of three Cisco Kid appearances in *The Return of the Cisco Kid* and in Fox's six Cisco Kid Westerns starring Cesar Romero, the Kid is noticeably gentler. By reputation he remains an outlaw, and he even plans some robberies with his sidekicks, but he never follows through on the plans. A pretty girl or a noble cause intervene, and in several instances the Kid winds up helping the local sheriff roundup the bad guys.

When Fox stopped making Cisco Kid films, Monogram purchased screen rights to the character and starred Gilbert Roland and Duncan Renaldo as the Cisco Kid. A bit later, Philip Krasne acquired the rights and released five Ciscos starring Duncan Renaldo through United Artists. The United Artists programmers are the basis for the highly successful Cisco Kid television show in the early 1950s (Nevins 1998).

There are some differences between the ways in which Roland and Renaldo play Cisco. Gilbert Roland's Cisco is more of a bandit, and classic "good bad man." Because of that, Roland's character is a rogue who likes to drink and smoke. And he is inclined to make comments one does not associate with cowboy heroes. In *The Gay Cavalier* (Monogram, 1946), Cisco argues that time is a good thing for it ages wine and mellows women. In *South of Monterey* (Monogram, 1946), he tells Frank Yaconelli to go to sleep and dream of señoritas with nice teeth and pretty legs. In addition, whenever Roland is in jail, he compares that jail with the one in El Paso, his favorite of all the jails he has been in.

Yet even Gilbert Roland's Cisco Kid has much in common with the rest of the cowboy heroes. He always rides to aid the poor and downtrodden, and he never keeps the money he steals; rather, he give it to the poor. Other than his roguish impulse to kiss and run, Roland also shares many of the same values with other cowboy heroes. In *Robin Hood of Monterey* (Monogram, 1947), he promises the sheriff that he will lay his gun on the sheriff's desk if the sheriff will give him time to capture the man who killed his friend. When the sheriff replies he does not believe him, Roland responds that he has never broken his word, for when you break your word you forfeit the most precious thing in life, your honor.

Duncan Renaldo, too, liked the ladies and he was in perpetual trouble with them. Yet his version of Cisco is less roguish than Roland's version. Renaldo's Cisco is often accused of crimes, but mistakenly so. There is much less of the "good bad man" in Renaldo's characterization and more of the typical cowboy hero. And, as was the case with many cowboy heroes, children figure prominently in the plots of his films. In an early one, *The Cisco Kid Returns* (Monogram, 1945), Renaldo searches for the murderer of a little girl's father. In *The Daring Caballero* (United Artists, 1949) he clears a little boy's father who is falsely accused of murder. In an interview with Jon Tuska, Renaldo caught the essence of the character when he said, "When I played Cisco, I wanted to see a different face, a man of generosity. I abhor vengeance, or violence. Cisco was a friend to a better world" (Tuska 1976, 444).

Baxter, Romero, Roland and Renaldo were cowboy heroes, but they also reflected certain stereotypes of Mexicans. All were handsome caballeros with whom women were instantly in love. As a result, they left a trail of broken hearts across Mexico, California and the Southwest. Roland and Romero in particular were sly, carefree creatures who worried little, and were perpetually happy. Renaldo conformed less to this stereotype, but there were certain elements of it in his Cisco. Increasingly, however, in the late 1940s Renaldo began to fashion his character into what it became on television. Cisco became a Hispanic cowboy hero much like any other, and his sidekick Pancho, played by Leo Carrillo, adopted the Smiley Burnette and Al St. John approach as he became the typical sidekick.

Chapter Nine

"THESE INDIANS NOT SUCH BAD PEOPLE"

By 1930, American Indians were something of a dilemma for white Americans. On the one hand, Indians were no longer a threat to white settlement of the continent. They were safely ensconced on reservations, and their great leaders who had led resistance to the whites were long dead. A few older Indians remembered the wild days, days in which they were free to follow the buffalo and to move about at will, but each passing year left fewer and fewer of them. On the other hand, white Americans affirmed a belief system that stressed Manifest Destiny and the inevitability of progress. Indians had been impediments to both.

As white Americans became increasingly sympathetic to the plight of American Indians, they still held an ideology that made Indian suffering inescapable. Anti–Indian sentiment turned into feelings of sorrow and regret, but the result remained unchanged. White Americans were firmly in control of the land and Indians must make do with the little patches of ground left them by the whites. Furthermore, most white Americans knew little about real Indians or Indian culture. They knew about Hollywood Indians, celluloid creations that fit the dominant belief system. But even the depiction of Indians on film changed substantially from the early 1900s to 1954.

Early silent Westerns were less prone to treat Indians sympathetically. They usually employed the stereotype of Indian as savage raider, one who raids and kills because he is an Indian. One-and two-reel silent Westerns such as D. W. Griffith's *The Battle at Elderbrush Gulch* (Biography, 1913) and *In the Days of the Thundering Herd* (Selig, 1914) with Tom Mix employed this stereotype. Later, feature-length Westerns such as the epic *Covered Wagon* (Paramount, 1923) and Ken Maynard's *The Red Raiders* (First National, 1927) continued to present native Americans as savage raiders. There were a few exceptions — the several silent versions of *The Squaw Man*, for instance — but they were few and far between. Overall the image of Indian as savage raider was the dominant one projected on the silent screen.

By 1930, that image had begun to change. For the next 25 years, Hollywood Indians were less inclined to raid and kill in order to satisfy savage instincts. Now they did so because of white treachery. An evil Indian agent might channel medicine and food supplies into more profitable hands and away from the Indians. Outlaws might sell whiskey and guns to Indians and then prod them into war in order to distract from the outlaws' crimes. Whatever the case, after 1930 Westerns were more likely to treat Indians as victims than as savage raiders. There are, of course, some notable exceptions. The film *Geronimo* (Paramount, 1939) comes to mind. Chief Thunder Cloud as Geronimo is unusually, almost pathologically, savage. However, that image is the exception and Westerns produced between 1950 and 1955 were, in most respects. even more supportive of Indians than 1930s and 1940s films. *Broken Arrow* (20th Century–Fox, 1950) and *Fort Osage* (Monogram, 1952) are notable examples of that trend.

Westerns are often criticized for being anti–Indian, but that interpretation needs closer scrutiny. If anti–Indian means portraying Indians as brutal, savage raiders, that assessment does not fit most sound Westerns. The image of Indians as ruthless savages who kill and raid for the joy of it is largely absent from Westerns of the sound era. Quite to the contrary, B Westerns mostly supported Indian claims of white treachery. Tim McCoy's *End of the Trail* (Columbia, 1932) is more sympathetic to the Indian cause than most Westerns. Yet, it is more typical of 1930–1955 Westerns than was *Geronimo*.

In the film, McCoy is court marshaled out of the cavalry because he had been wrongly convicted of selling guns to the Indians. McCoy, in an eloquent speech to his commanding officer (Lafe McKee), defends the Indians. He reminds McKee that because of gold, whites were now breaking the Harney-Sandborn Treaty of 1868 which gave the land to the Indians. McCoy concludes with an unusually strong statement, one very supportive of the Indians:

> We have never kept a single treaty with them. That is why I am for the Indians. Because in every instance, the white man has been to blame. And if these Indians take the warpath now, which they are

surely going to do, then I want to say to you, sir, the bloodshed that results will not be the fault of the Indians. Responsibility must rest entirely with the white man.

That speech is certainly not anti-Indian! Although most Westerns were not that strong in defense of Indians, they were nevertheless sympathetic. But it was sympathy without cost. Indians were not going to get back their lands. The status quo remained. The Indian dilemma was resolved in favor of ambiguity. Whites increasingly felt guilty about history's record of their treatment of Indians, but not guilty enough to make restitution.

Anti-Indian, however, need not be limited to portrayal of Indians as savage raiders; it can also encompass an insensitivity to Indian history and culture. Some writers regard Western movies as anti-Indian because they fail to record accurately the history of Indian-White conflicts or to present Indian culture authentically. Wayne Michael Sarf, Ralph E. and Natasha Friar, Jon Tuska and a number of others have criticized Westerns for their lack of accuracy and authenticity.

That criticism is valid. Westerns did not present true history, and most Indians conformed to the Hollywood image of them. Too often American white viewers mistook Hollywood creations for real Indians, and assumed they knew far more about Indian culture than they knew. If faithfulness to real Indian culture is the benchmark, then Western movies were anti-Indian. But that is not an appropriate standard. Westerns dealt with all facets of the West unauthentically and unhistorically. Who believes that *They Died with Their Boots On* (Warner Bros., 1942) is an accurate biography of George Custer? How many who watch *My Darling Clementine* (20th Century-Fox, 1946) really believe they are viewing an accurate history of the gunfight at O.K. Corral? Some producers, directors and studio publicists might have, on occasion, gotten carried away and claimed too much historical truth, but viewers were not that easily fooled. And most writers, producers, and directors made no grandiose claims to historical accuracy. Why do Indians merit historical and cultural accuracy while Hollywood was recasting the rest of the West?

There is a third sense in which Westerns may be anti-Indian, one related to the lack of historical and cultural authenticity. Westerns were not concerned with accuracy, they were produced to make money. To make money, Westerns had to fit audience expectations. Audiences expected to see Westerns commemorate the coming of civilization to the West. In short, audiences wanted to celebrate the triumph of Manifest Destiny. Indians had to fit white stereotypes associated with Manifest Destiny. Indians had made a noble fight; they simply had been overwhelmed by white numerical superiority, and in many cases duped by white treachery. All of that evoked sympathy, but only within the ideological view that the West belonged to whites and Indians would have to give it up.

Westerns are about the natural extension of the United States across the continent. In a fictionalized manner, Westerns celebrated that part of American history. To be overly concerned with historical accuracy or cultural authenticity is to ask Westerns to be something other than what they are. That is asking too much; Westerns should be accepted or rejected on their own terms.

The ideology underlying Westerns is surely anti–Indian. Westerns, however, did not create the ideology, they merely reflected and popularized a trend first introduced by the early settlers of the North American continent: push on toward the setting sun, move out the indigenous population and claim the land for white settlers. Maybe that practice, and the ideology that underlies it, ought to have been more vigorously challenged than it was. But as Westerns reflected both the practice and the belief they struck a responsive chord in American public taste that made them popular entertainment for 60 years.

By the third decade of the twentieth century, the sense of urgency had gone out of white attitudes toward Indians. It made little sense to be anti–Indian; they no longer posed a threat to white Americans. So whites began to express sympathy and regret. After 1955, it even became fashionable for Westerns to be pro–Indian. But between 1930 and 1955, Westerns — not yet predominately pro–Indian — were more likely to express ambivalence about the treatment of Indians by whites.

Screen images of Indians, just as other ethnic groups, mirror Hollywood stereotypes of them. The stereotypes are apparent in both traits and customs commonly associated with Indians, and in a few character types that appear repeatedly in Western movies. John R. Price summarized best the traits and customs associated with Indians. Westerns, he argues, portrayed Indians as being nomadic peoples who were always opposed to whites. Indians were depicted as preoccupied with war, sexually desiring white women and obsessed with alcohol. Furthermore, they were normally stern, humorless people (Battaille and Silet, 75).

To Price's list of characteristics, Michael Hilger adds the tendency for Hollywood to regard Indians as unimportant in their own right. Hilger argues Indians were often treated as part of the landscape, or as an adversary for the hero with little effort to probe motives for their behavior (Hilger, 51). Jon Tuska adds two other concerns. He notes Indians were frequently victims of Manifest Destiny. In addition, Tuska claims miscegenation was a concern in Westerns. The two races could not intermarry and expect any degree of happiness. Marriage between white women and Indian males was particularly taboo. And, even though white males might take Indian women as wives, the women often were dead at the film's beginning or died during the course of it. Tuska's comment, "The ideology is simple: races should not mix," succinctly describes the relationship between whites and Indians depicted in Westerns (Tuska 1976, 24).

Miscegenation fears permeate *White Eagle* (Columbia, 1932) starring Buck Jones. Jones plays White Eagle, a Bannock Indian who has chosen to live in the white man's world as a Pony Express rider. Barbara Weeks is the heroine who goes West to visit her brother, regional supervisor of the Pony Express and Jones' boss. From the beginning of the film, viewers realize Jones and Weeks are attracted to one another. When someone tells Jason Robards, Weeks' brother, that he ought to be concerned, Robards responds that "White Eagle understands."

War breaks out between the Bannocks and the whites, brought on by white renegades masquerading as Indians. Jones refuses to fight until Robards catches her hugging Jones (when Jones told her he was not going to war, she hugged him). Robards explodes in anger, telling Jones, "I treated you like a white man, but you have forgotten you are an Indian."

Jones, rejected by the whites, joins his people. Later he rescues Weeks from a bad Indian and turns her over to a cavalry patrol. As they part, Jones tells her he would never forget the time their trails rode side by side. Jones' father wearies of war and agrees to peace. He also confesses that Jones is not a Bannock, but rather the son of a dead cavalry officer. Jones, it turns out, had been kidnapped as a baby and, while in fact white, had been raised as a Bannock. Jones was then free to marry Weeks because miscegenation was no longer a concern.

Five distinct Indian character types dominated the genre. Character types are important because the Western, as a film genre, required a high degree of predictability. Indians, therefore, had to be Indians who were recognizable within the contours of the genre. Hollywood Indians, with few exceptions, fit one of the five character types.

The first character type, Indian as savage raider, is one discussed earlier in the chapter. Vicious by nature and white-hating by instinct, this character type dominated the silent screen. It is never entirely absent from sound Westerns, and it even made a minor resurgence in Westerns produced in 1952 and 1953.

The second character type is the helpless Indian. B Westerns often employed this image. Indians are portrayed as simple-minded creatures, unable or unwilling to adapt to change. In addition, they are easily duped and, hence, easy prey for evil white men.

9. "These Indians Not Such Bad People"

White Eagle, Columbia, 1932; Barbara Weeks and Buck Jones. Weeks hugs Jones, playing White Eagle, when he tells her he will not fight the white man.

The third stereotype is the beautiful Indian maiden who is in love with either a white man or one of the Indian braves of her tribe. Above all else, she wants to prevent bloodshed between the races. Better than the rest of her people or the whites—with the exception of the cowboy hero—she sees that peace will lead to harmony and progress for both groups and the lot of her people will improve. Luana Walters plays such a role to Tim McCoy in *End of the Trail*. Debra Paget assumes that role in *Broken Arrow*. She marries James Stewart, and becomes a living symbol of the ability of whites and Indians to live in peace. Quite predictably, however, Paget dies in the film.

The last two character types exist in relationship to one another. The first is the wise old chief who wants to avoid war because he knows it will lead to the destruction of his people. He is almost always opposed by his opposite, the hot-headed young brave who would be chief. The young hothead want to fight or to continue fighting and believes it is better to die resisting the whites than to be cooped up on one of their reservations.

Before examining specific films that employ these stereotypes, two things need clarifying. First, as with Mexicans, it was common for white actors and actresses to play Indians. Jay Silverheels, Iron Eyes Cody, Chief John Big Tree and Chief Yowlachie are just a few of the many real Indians who played Hollywood reel Indians. But as the years wore on, it became more and more common for white actors and actresses to assume Indian roles. Both Debra Paget and Luana Walters played Indian women. Jack Palance was the evil Toriano in *Arrowhead* (Paramount, 1953) and Anthony Quinn played Crazy Horse in *They Died with Their Boots On*. Burt Lancaster, Victor Mature, Rock Hudson, Jeff Chandler and scores of lesser known actors and actresses have also played Indians. No distinction will be made between those films using whites to play Indians from those employing real Indians.

Indian sidekicks are also ignored. Tonto, the Lone Ranger's sidekick, is the best known of these. However, with the exception of two serials in which Chief Thunder Cloud played Tonto, the Lone Ranger and Tonto are creatures of radio and television, not Western films. In fact, it was not until 1956, two years after the demise of series B Westerns, that Clayton Moore and Jay Silverheels made their first full-length feature film, *The Lone Ranger* (Warner Bros., 1956).

Little Beaver was a constant companion to Red Ryder, and on occasion he did help capture the bad guys. Normally, however, Little Beaver was hardly more than a cheerleader for Red Ryder's exploits. The other Indian hero of that era never appeared in films. But many older readers can remember jumping off of the school bus, racing down the driveway and making it to the radio just in time to catch the latest thrilling exploits of Straight Arrow. As a radio character, Straight Arrow is beyond the scope of this book.

John Wayne films are a good starting place to consider Indian stereotypes and character types that appear in both B and bigger-budgeted Westerns. Wayne is unique because he played in both series B and big-budget Westerns, and because his career spanned all of the years 1930–1955. Furthermore, Wayne, as a person, was a living embodiment of the American ideology.

Wayne's early B Westerns follow the pattern of the cowboy hero as a friend to the Indians. The best example is *'Neath Arizona Skies* (Monogram, 1934). Wayne is the guardian of a mixed blood Indian girl (Shirley Ricketts). From her deceased mother she inherits $50,000 in royalties for oil discovered on Indian lands. Wayne protects the girl from the bad guys led by Jack Rockwell and Yakima Canutt who are trying to kidnap her in order to get the money. In the process, Wayne reunites her with her natural white father (Earl Dwire). Dwire dies defending his daughter from the outlaws.

In *The Star Packer* (Monogram, 1934), roles are reversed. George Hayes, seen frequently in Wayne's early Westerns as either his sidekick or friend, is the villain. Yakima Canutt — usually the villain — plays Yak, a friendly Indian who is Wayne's sidekick. Wayne may be the only cowboy hero who had two different minorities as his sidekicks. Blue Washington was his black sidekick in *Haunted Gold* (Warner Bros., 1932) and Canutt played an Indian in *The Star Packer*.

In his later, bigger-budget Westerns, Wayne's relationship to Indians is more complex than it was in his B Westerns. *Stagecoach* (United Artists, 1939) and *Red River* (United Artists, 1948) are among his best-known films. In neither of them are Indians intrinsically important. Rather, to use Hilger's language, they are part of the landscape. They are impediments, obstacles to more important goals. The expected Indian attack heightens the suspense in *Stagecoach*, but the film is not about Indians. In this instance Indians are but one of several obstacles Wayne must overcome on his journey to Lordsburg and revenge on the Plummer brothers. The Indians in *Red River* are, again, mere impediments to getting the herd through to market. They are no more or less important than the weather or dissent among the cowboys. All are hindrances to Wayne's ultimate goal.

Stagecoach also portrays Indians as savages. They attack the stagecoach for no other reason than it is carrying white people. Chris-Pin Martin's wife, an Indian woman, is especially treacherous. She alerts the Indians to the whites' presence at the relay station. The Indians, in turn, attack and drive off the relief horses. The woman then disappears with her Indian relatives, leaving the distinct impression that Indians are sneaky creatures whose words and actions cannot be taken at face value.

In *Fort Apache* (RKO, 1948) and *She Wore a Yellow Ribbon* (RKO, 1949), Wayne plays the Westerner better than in any other films of his illustrious career. Wayne's protagonist in *Fort Apache* is Henry Fonda as Colonel Thursday. Fonda personifies all the Easterners' arrogant ignorance of the West. He regards his assignment to Fort Apache as punishment and he cannot wait to get back East. Thursday is contemptuous of Indians and he regards whites as inherently superior to them, just as he believes the East superior to the West. In one sense, Fonda is a visible symbol of Manifest Destiny. Yet his belief in a class-based society, one in which he is naturally superior, makes him appear un–American. When Thursday is killed with his command, audiences feel he got what he deserved.

Wayne as Capt. Kirby York is the seasoned Westerner who both understands and has sympathy for Indians. Wayne, no less than Fonda, affirms Manifest Destiny, but he does so with a degree of sadness. Wayne

The Star Packer, Monogram. 1934; Yakima Canutt and John Wayne. Canutt plays Wayne's Indian sidekick, Yak.

recognizes and even believes in the eventual triumph of the white superior civilization, but he wants it to come as peacefully as possible. Furthermore, Wayne believes the Indians have legitimate grievances to which the government ought to listen. When Wayne gives his word to the Indians that their concerns will be addressed, he knows they will keep their word and he expects his word to be honored. Fonda disregards Wayne's promise with the remark that a man's word means nothing to savages. He then marches out to destroy them. Because Wayne is under arrest, he escapes the annihilation that follows. The Indians, in this case, are a superior force who outmaneuver Thursday. Wayne's character in *Fort Apache* presents a sympathetic view of Indians. They are worthy opponents, ones to be respected as men and dealt with honorably. In that sense, Wayne's character extends the rules of honorable conflict to Indians as well as white men.

The same view of Indians continues in *She Wore a Yellow Ribbon*.

Even though the film opens with a warning about the gathering of the plains Indians after Custer's defeat, it is not an anti–Indian Western. Indians have left the reservation, Custer has been defeated and the buffalo have returned. Younger braves, particularly Cheyenne Dog soldiers, use these as signs that the time is ripe to push whites from the Indian lands. Wayne, as Capt. Nathan Brittles, about to retire from the Army, wants to get the Indians back on the reservation without bloodshed. At one point Wayne and his column of troopers, escorting two ladies to the stagecoach relay station, encounter a patrol fleeing hostile Indians. Once the patrol is safe, Wayne orders his men to shoot high over the Indians' heads. He wants to scare them off, not kill them.

Near the end of the film, Wayne, accompanied by Ben Johnson as Sgt. Tyree, rides into the Indian camp. He expresses his contempt for the hostile Indians by breaking in two an arrow and then spitting on it. Proceeding on, Wayne is welcomed by his Indian friend Pony-That-Walks (Chief John Big Tree), a chief to whom the young hot-headed braves will no longer listen. Both men lament their old age, and express a desire for peace. But John Big Tree tells Wayne it is too late for peace. Wayne went to the camp to locate the pony herd. Even though he is technically retired, that night Wayne and his troopers run off the Indian ponies. The Indians are left with no option except to walk back to the reservation. Wayne has accomplished his goals. The Indians go back to the reservation and bloodshed is avoided.

She Wore a Yellow Ribbon, however, is a hymn to Manifest Destiny. Wayne sympathizes with the Indians, admires their way of life, and does not want to harm them, but he wants them back on the reservation. Indians must accept the white man's claim to their land. The film ends as troopers ride in front of the camera and the narrator speaks:

> From Fort Reno to Fort Apache, from Sheridan to Starke, they were all the same. Men in dirty shirt blue and only a bold page in history books to mark their passage. But wherever they rode and whatever they fought for, that place became the United States.

The tone in *Rio Grande* (Republic, 1950) is more critical of Indians. Wayne, as Capt. York, is repeatedly frustrated by his inability to follow hostile Apaches across the Rio Grande after they raid American ranchers. In fact, the image of savage raider appears quite regularly throughout the film. Apaches raid the outpost to free Indians Wayne has taken prisoner. They attack a cavalry-escorted wagon train of women and children. Wayne arrives in time to save most of the women, but the Indians escape with one white woman and the children. Wayne pursues. They come across the burned-out wagon and the body of the woman. Viewers are led to believe she was tortured and raped before being murdered. The children, however, were carried across the river. Acting on unwritten orders from Gen. Sheridan (J. Carrol Naish), Wayne crosses the Rio Grande, raids the Indian camp and frees the children.

Rio Grande lacks any empathy whatsoever for the Indians. One does not find in this film a sense of sadness for Indians that characterizes *Fort Apache* and *She Wore a Yellow Ribbon*. The dominant stereotype in *Rio Grande* is Indian as a savage raider who makes war even on women and children. There is no white villain to justify their behavior, nor is there a wise old chief being ignored by the hot-heated young braves. They are just mean by nature!

On balance, however, up to 1954 Wayne's films, while no less stereotypical than other Westerns, are sympathetic to Indians. Indians were portrayed as victims of the gradual expansion of the United States and the inexorable march of progress. The railroad, telegraph, farms and cities required the Indians to be banished from the land, and their free life shackled to the reservation. It was a sad thing to watch, but it was also necessary as one culture gave way to the other one.

Gene Autry moved from Republic to Columbia in 1947 after an out-of-court settlement with the former studio permitted him to make the switch. Of the many Westerns Autry made for Republic, only *Ride, Ranger, Ride* (Republic, 1936) used the Indian story in its plot, and in that picture Indians—Comanches, in this case—are villains. Autry as an army scout understands their treachery and he stops an attack at the beginning of the picture by shooting an Indian trying to signal his comrades. For the rest of the film, Autry works to prevent an Indian attack on army ammunition wagons.

During his six years at Columbia, Autry made four Westerns which incorporated Indians into the plot, five if one counts *The Saginaw Trail* (Columbia, 1953), and Indians are treated sympathetically in all of them. The stereotype in all four films is Indians as victims and Autry as the cowboy hero who is their friend and benefactor. Yet each of these films preaches the need for Indians to adapt to progress and changing times.

The Last Round-Up (Columbia, 1947) projects that attitude better than any of Autry's other films. Indians in this film own dry, arid land. Mesa City wants to build an aqueduct across Indian land to the Big Bend River. Mesa City leaders promise the Indians acre for acre if they will leave their land and move to Cedar Valley. The latter is a beautiful place with abundant water and fertile land. The chief and tribal elders, however, will not go! They want to live where they have always lived, where their fathers are buried.

The head of the water development project responds to the Indians' unwillingness to move to Cedar Valley with the observation that Indians ought to be intelligent enough to know when they are better off. It is up to Gene to convince them to move, and he does by hooking up a television show in which he shows Cedar Valley to the Indians and one of their own, played by Jay Silverheels, who has settled there. The Indians on the old land can talk with Silverheels via a two-way radio and they are convinced to relocate.

There is a healthy dose of paternalism in *The Last Round-Up*. White men know best what is good for Indians because Indians too often are victims of their own ignorance. They remain prisoners to their traditions until a white man shows them the benefits of progress. On the other hand, the film does break through some stereotypes. Because it is set in the modern West, Indians are not presented as savages in feathers, but as peaceful farmers living in harmony with their white neighbors. Furthermore, when they see the economic advantages of Cedar Valley they all agree to move. In *The Last Round-Up,* Indians become like whites. Economic advantage prompted the move. The chief's worry about leaving the bones of their fathers, and his pleas for them to be satisfied with the land on which they have always lived, are ignored after Jay Silverheels' enthusiastic sales pitch over television.

The Cowboy and the Indians (Columbia, 1949) continued the image of Indians as victims of white abuse. A trading post owner conspires with an Indian agent to drive the Indians further into poverty and malnutrition. In fact, the whole theme of the film is the indefensible manner in which reservation Indians were treated. Autry is, of course, their friend and protector. As a secondary interest, the trading post owner works closely with a man who steals Indian artifacts or buys them cheap and then resells them at handsome profits. In one instance, he forces an Indian woman to sell a beautiful blanket that had been in her family for generations in order to buy food for her family. On another occasion, he kills a chief to get a necklace the chief wears, an insignia of his position passed from generation to generation. Here in bold relief is the Indian as victim. *The Cowboy and the Indians* presents the harshness and poverty of life on a reservation, and it highlights the many types of white predators with whom Indians must cope in order to maintain their dignity and preserve their culture. Outside of *End of the Trail,* Hollywood probably never produced a more pro–Indian B Western than *The Cowboy and the Indians.*

In two other Autry Westerns, *Indian Territory* (Columbia, 1950) and

Apache Country (Columbia, 1952), the stereotype of Indian as victim continues. In *Indian Territory,* the villain is the Apache Kid who stirs up renegade Apaches. Working with whites, the Apache Kid wants to keep the valley from being settled. The chiefs oppose the renegades but are powerless to stop the attacks on white wagons. Gene leaves the army to go after the Apache Kid, and when he gets him the trouble stops. The same general theme holds for *Apache Country.* The Indians are blamed for all sorts of things really being done by whites. Autry as a government agent gets to the bottom of it, and clears the Indians of wrongdoing.

In 1953, the last year in which Autry made B Westerns, he starred in one of his most unusual films. *The Saginaw Trail* (Columbia, 1953) was set in Michigan during the 1830s. Indians do not figure directly into the film. But they were blamed for attacks on wagon trains carrying white settlers into the region. The attacks were actually the work of white renegades disguised as Indians. They wanted to preserve the wilderness and thus protect the lucrative fur trade. Again, *The Saginaw Trail* presents the image of Indians as victims of white treachery. As just observed, this image dominated Autry's Columbia Westerns, but it was typical of other cowboy heroes as well.

Generally speaking, B Westerns were sympathetic but paternalistic toward Indians. *Dangerous Venture* (United Artists, 1947) is one of the later entries in the highly successful Hopalong Cassidy series. In this film, William Boyd, Andy Clyde and Rand Brooks go to the aid of Aztec Indians, referred to as ghost Indians because of their hidden location in the mountains. The Indians are determined to keep the whites from robbing the graves of their ancestors. Boyd is sympathetic to that goal and helps them defeat whites who covet the golden treasures. But in the end, Boyd's advice to the Aztec is for them to come out of the mountains and live like white people.

In some B Westerns, Indians are depicted as savage raiders who need to be stirred up by whites. In *Prairie Schooners* (Columbia, 1940), the Pawnee are encouraged to attack a wagon train headed for Colorado. The outlaws assure the Indians that if a few whites get through, soon many more will follow and the hunting and trapping will stop. To protect their fur trade, the outlaws furnish the Indians with guns and they attack the wagons. Only after William Elliott demonstrates to the Pawnee chief that one of the whites is a blood brother to the Sioux, hated enemies of the Pawnee, do the attacks stop.

Riders of the Whistling Skull (Republic, 1937) demonstrates how far white prerogatives could be carried. In this film, a group of scientists are searching for a lost city of golden Indian artifacts. The Three Mesquiteers escort the expedition after the scientist, who discovered the city's location is murdered. The bad guys are the Indians, called fanatics, and a white man whose mother was a member of the tribe. They are trying to protect their treasures, and they are the "bad" Indians! Surely murderers need to be caught, but there is no hint in this picture that there is anything wrong with archaeologists entering tombs and ransacking ancient treasures. White men had done it all over the world, why not to the North American Indians? The Indians, then, are fanatical savages because they resist such white incursions into their sacred treasures. If any B Western can be described as anti–Indian, surely it was this one.

Buck Jones' last film, *Dawn on the Great Divide* (Monogram, 1942) also involves treachery by Harry Woods. Indians are attacking wagon trains along the Oregon Trail and the Rough Riders, with Rex Bell replacing Tim McCoy, are trying to find our why. In the opening scene Bell meets with the Indians, who assure him the attacks are the work of white renegades posing as Indians. Bell gets that message to Jones and Raymond Hatton as they escort a wagon train to Oregon. Renegade whites, led by that ace villain Roy Barcroft who is working for Woods, attack the wagons dressed as Indians. Jones, Hatton and Bell foil Woods' scheme to create a private political empire for himself, and they redeem the Indians' reputation.

Kenneth Harlan plays a crooked Indian agent in *The Law Rides Again* (Monogram, 1943). The film opens with stock footage of Indian attacks on wagon trains which Emmett Lynn, dressed as a frontier scout, observes. Lynn reports the attacks to the Arizona Indian Commissioner and the commissioner sends Hoot Gibson and Ken Maynard, the Trail Blazers, to investigate. It turns out that Harlan has been cheating the Indians. He has not given them a sufficient amount of cattle to feed the tribe so they have gone on the warpath. Hoot visits the Indian tribe, talks to the chief and sees that the Indians are not receiving the cattle Harlan's records show. Gibson and Maynard round up Harlan and his gang and, once the Indians are treated fairly, peace returns to the Arizona frontier.

Richard Powers—as Hutchins, the Indian Agent—is in cahoots with Harry Woods in the Tim Holt programmer *Indian Agent* (RKO, 1948). Woods owns a freight line with a contract to haul supplies to the Indian agency; however, the food and medicine never get to the Indians. Powers gives Woods a receipt verifying delivery, the supplies are then mysteriously stolen and they are sold to prospectors heading for the Black Buttes gold field with Powers and Woods splitting the profit.

The starving Indians led by Red Fox (Noah Beery, Jr.) threaten to go on the warpath. Tim Holt and Chito Rafferty become aware of the Indians' plight when they help rescue Red Fox's young child. The two cowboys realize something is amiss because they had helped to escort Woods' freighters to the agency. Holt and Rafferty snoop around Woods' barn, overhear plans to divert the supplies, and bring the two culprits to justice. *Indian Agent* is another good example of a B Western characterizing Indians as victims of white greed.

In *Snake River Desperadoes* (Columbia, 1951), Monte Blue plays a greedy trader who appears to be a friend of the Indians. But, unknown to both whites and Indians, his gang of outlaws dress as Indians and attack the homesteaders and ranchers. If an Indian war breaks out, Blue will make a huge profit selling supplies, weapons and ammunition to both sides. Charles Starrett, as the Durango Kid, exposes Blue for the crook he is. Even though Blue is killed before Durango can capture him, justice does run its course as Blue is killed in the very Indian raid he tried to foment.

North of the Great Divide (Republic, 1950) features Roy Rogers as an Indian agent. The Oseka Indians need to fish for salmon in order to live. But a cannery, run by Roy Barcroft, has put nets across the river, keeping the salmon from swimming upstream, thus threatening the Indians' livelihood. War is imminent when Rogers is sent by the commissioner to investigate. Nogura, the Oseka chief, is accused of murdering a Mountie, even though Barcroft's henchmen had killed him. In this film, the Indians are victims all around. They are being starved to death because the cannery has blocked the salmon run, and Barcroft's brutality and deceit victimize them.

This Rogers programmer is pro–Indian, but only in a certain sense. The Oseka are already on a reservation when the film opens. They are wards of the United States government and Rogers, as Indian agent, has a duty to protect them. The Indians only want access to the salmon so they can retain some semblance of the old ways. The underlying themes are that both whites and Indians can live in harmony, and a bountiful nature and industry can co-exist side by side if thoughtful men of good will work together. *North of the Great Divide* catches fully the optimistic spirit and undying belief in progress that characterized American public opinion in 1950.

From these examples of B Westerns it ought to be clear Indians were not regarded as savages to be exterminated. Rather, the lesson is: If Indians will recognize the inexorable march of white civilization, make peace with it and adopt white customs, the country is big enough for both races to prosper. Surely such a view is paternalistic, the result of a century of Manifest Destiny. In that sense, Westerns are anti–Indian. But Westerns are against anything that stood in the way of an expansionist nation. Westerns were no more anti–Indian than they were anti–Mexican or anti–cattlemen.

Westerns reflected a belief in Manifest Destiny, progress and the superiority of white North Americans. Contemporary Americans may question those tenets and many even reject them. Earlier generations, ones who flocked to see the cowboy heroes on the silver screen, were less inclined to do so. It is useless to attack Westerns for embodying those beliefs. Nearly all Hollywood genres did it, and popular literature and radio programs echoed them. The belief system simply stood out in boldest relief in Western films and in relationship to American Indians.

In a few films, Indians even rode with the cowboy hero against the villains. Three examples come to mind. In *Across the Plains* (Monogram, 1939), Indians had rescued a young boy from a wagon train raided by white renegades. As an adult, Cherokee (Jack Randall), searches for his parents' murderers, and acts as an intermediary between the United States government and the Indians. He is able to get government protection for Indian lands if the Indians will promise not to make war. At the film's conclusion, the Indians ride to rescue Randall and other men whom the renegades had pinned down behind some rocks. Frank Yaconelli, playing Randall's sidekick Lopez, catches the spirit of the film — and maybe most B Westerns — when he says, "Señor, these Indians not such bad people."

Under Nevada Skies (Republic, 1946), with Roy Rogers, takes this theme even further. Roy is searching for a missing crest, and in the process learns that agents for a foreign government also want it. At the film's end, Rogers enlists the aid of Flying Eagle (George Lewis) and Indians from the Bear Valley Indian Reservation to help him. Although it is the modern West, the Indians attack the ranch by circling around it Hollywood-Indian style. Once he has the crest, Rogers discovers it contains a map with directions to a rich deposit of pitchblende, a necessary substance for making atomic bombs. The Indians in this film are fully acculturated. They live on a reservation and once a year celebrate Pow Wow Days. In the end, they demonstrate their loyalty to the United States by helping Rogers keep a valuable mineral from falling into enemy hands.

Oregon Trail Scouts (Republic, 1947) tells the story of how Little Beaver came to be Red Ryder's ward. Frank Lackteen plays Chief Running Fox, Red Ryder's friend, who permits Ryder and his friends to hunt beaver on Indian land. Roy Barcroft is the outlaw Bill Hunter who tries to kill Ryder and his sidekick Bear Trap (Emmett Lynn) near the beginning of the film in order to get their hunting rights. Ryder and Bear Trap are out of ammunition when a band of Indians ride to the rescue. (One of them had recognized Thunder, Ryder's horse, and knew their friend Ryder was in trouble so they came to help out.) And at the film's exciting conclusion, Hunter and his outlaws engage Ryder and his men in a gunfight when

Running Bear and his Indians arrive in the nick of time. Indians had certainly come a long way in B Westerns. From being chased by cavalry and thought of as a barrier to national progress, in these three films Indians are peaceful citizens who help to catch the bad guys.

Not surprisingly, bigger-budget Westerns present a more diverse picture of Indians than the one found in B Westerns. A few bigger-budget pictures continue to portray the cowboy hero as friend to Indians. That image dominates three Westerns starring Rod Cameron. *Oh! Susanna* (Republic, 1951) has Cameron as a cavalry officer trying to keep gold seeking white settlers out of the Black Hills. He is accused of being an Indian lover by Forrest Tucker, his corrupt commander, and by Jim Davis, playing the role of a saloonkeeper selling whiskey and guns to the Indians. At the film's climax, the Indians have the fort surrounded. However, the wise old chief knows Cameron is a friend of Indians, one who tried to honor the treaty, so he lets those in the fort go free. As the survivors leave, however, they discover the Indians have killed Tucker and his entire command. Tucker had been decoyed away from the fort, and then had led his men into an ambush as he hurried to get back to it in order to battle the Indians.

Even though this film is largely sympathetic to the Indians, there are some negative stereotypes in it. Cameron places the women and children in the powder room so they can be blown up easily in case the Indians overwhelm the fort. Adrian Booth is a saloon entertainer, and a woman of questionable virtue who is scorned by the other women. When the respectable women balk at leaving the chapel for the powder room, Booth reminds them the things she has put up with are nothing compared to what will happen to them should they become captives. Here quite explicitly we see the concern for miscegenation, and the supposed lust Indian males have for white women.

Chill Wills, a sergeant in Cameron's troop, ends the film on an ambivalent note. He recites the Indian fights Cameron had been in since 1872, the year in which *Oh! Susanna* was set. Wills then observes that if people had listened to Cameron in the first place, the bloodshed would have been avoided. Interesting sentiment, but Cameron still played a character who by the film's end was a veteran of the Plains Indian Wars. He may have been the Indian's friend, but he was also one of those responsible for putting them on reservations and keeping them there.

In *Wagons West* (Monogram, 1952), Cameron plays a scout who understands and respects the Indians. Frank Ferguson is the wagonmaster and along with his two sons (Henry Brandon and Riley Hill) appears to hate Cameron and the Indians with equal intensity. Ferguson and his sons, however, are trading guns with Black Kettle and his Cheyenne braves. They find an excuse to leave the wagon train, and Cameron gets suspicious. He follows them, captures Brandon with the wagon containing the guns and takes him back to the wagon train before Ferguson and Hill can bring the Indians to the guns.

In a climactic fight, the Indians kill Ferguson, Brandon and Hill. But they can't get the guns. The wagon train is too strong for them. Cameron fears, however, the Cheyenne will attack as the wagons are spread out over the prairie. So he orders the guns burned, and in a parley with Black Kettle gives the Indians back the furs they traded for the guns as well as the horses and wagon. Black Kettle observes that he has no choice. But he does permit the wagon train to pass through his land unmolested.

In *Fort Osage* (Monogram, 1952), Cameron plays Tom Clay, a wagonmaster. The Osage Indians are making war because Morris Ankrum and Douglas Kennedy have reneged on their treaty commitments to provide food and supplies to the Osage for right of passage through Osage land. Cameron goes to the Osage to find out why they are raiding. As he prepares to go, Cameron tells his white friends that the Osage are human beings like everybody else. He has had a lot of dealings with them and Cameron had always found them to be good and honest people. In the end, Cameron even rides with the Osages as they round up Kennedy and his band of outlaws.

Cameron's three films demonstrate the continuity between small budget programmer B Westerns and the bigger budget B films. The story line is more complex and increased production values are apparent, but Cameron's characters have a great deal in common with the standard cowboy hero.

However, several bigger-budget B Westerns are quite forthright in their treatment of Indians as savages. *Geronimo* is an excellent example. The evil gleam in Chief Thunder Cloud's eye as he shot his pistol into the stagecoach is a striking image. Even in the end, surrounded and about to be captured, Geronimo puts on an army uniform and slips into the cavalry camp to kill just a few more whites. No sympathy here, just a savage Indian, barely above the level of a wild animal.

The same may be said for *Arrowhead* (Paramount, 1953). Jack Palance, playing Toriano, returns from an Indian school in the East. While there he learned the ghost dance. Palance uses that to rally the Apaches for a war to drive out the whites. Charlton Heston, playing an Indian-hating white scout, is vindicated in the end. Heston had preached Indian treachery, a variation of the only good Indian is a dead Indian.

War Paint (United Artists, 1953) adds a new twist to Indian as savage.

Robert Stack, playing a cavalry officer, is determined to take a treaty to Grey Cloud who wants peace. Grey Cloud's son is escorting Stack and his troopers, but the son and his sister oppose the treaty. Together they kill soldiers, run off horses and prevent the men from finding water.

Both Indians prefer war to peace with the whites. The girl had been educated in a white school where she had learned pity, but then white soldiers molested her. She learned that the word of the White Father is not the word of the white people. In the end, the son is killed but his sister is convinced by Stack to help him deliver the treaty. Here is a film with not only a great deal of psychological tension, but one that contrasts the wise old chief with the hotheaded younger generation opposed to peace.

Two other bigger-budget Westerns seem unusually harsh in their portrayal of Indians. In *The Command* (Warner Bros., 1954), Guy Madison plays a doctor thrown into cavalry command when an officer is killed in an Indian attack. Even though the film polishes up the old theme of Plains Indians gathering after Custer's defeat, Indians, Arapahoes in this instance, kill soldiers and attack wagon trains for no apparent reason. And they are pictured as particularly savage. One close-up, for instance, is the screaming distorted face of an Indian as he shoots a flaming arrow into a wagon.

In *Escape from Fort Bravo* (MGM, 1953), Mescalero Apaches have the troopers pinned down in a small gully. The Indians drive four lances in the ground to mark the whites' location, and then using the lances as targets, send rains of arrows down on the troopers. Earlier in the film the Indians had raided a wagon full of guns and tortured the drivers to death. Again, the image is one of inhuman savages making war for the joy of it.

Bugles in the Afternoon (Warner Bros., 1952) is a transition Western as it deals with the Indian theme. Set in Dakota Territory just before the Battle of the Little Big Horn, the film has its share of anti–Indian sentiments. For example, when the cavalry comes across the bodies of some dead miners, one of the troopers remarks that the Indians wiped out the miners just for devilment. Yet there is also a great deal of ambiguity in this film. A cavalry scout surmises at one point that the Indians have decided they will be pushed no further. That comment adds an interpretation to Indian actions more sympathetic to the Indians than the trooper's remark about devilment. When Indians attack a wood detail, they are shown employing battle tactics. After a frontal charge fails, the Indians attack the troopers from three sides. Normally Indians were portrayed as engaging in frontal charges whether or not they worked. *Bugles in the Afternoon* is not particularly sympathetic to the Indians but it does not portray them as ignorant savages fighting for the mere joy of killing.

The Charge at Feather River (Warner Bros., 1953) is more problematic.

Guy Madison leads a troop of reprobate soldiers to rescue two white girls kidnapped by Cheyenne in 1862. Again, this film has its anti–Indian moments. When the troopers come across an old man left to die by his tribe, one of them comments, "No wonder they call them savages," and when the old Indian with his last dying breath shoots an arrow into one of the troopers, the white sentiment is that they must hate us because he had to kill one more of us before he died. There are other anti–Indian sentiments as well. Cheyenne males have raped the older sister. She knows about white attitudes toward miscegenation. She hates the Indians, but yet she does not want to go back into white society. She dreads facing the prissy white women who will stare at her. Her younger sister Jenny (Vera Miles) is a different story. Jenny was going to marry Thunder Hawk, a chief of the Cheyenne. She displays all of the savage hatred associated with Indians. She even shoots her white brother who tries to prevent her escape before she slips on some loose rocks and falls to her death.

Yet the savage theme does not permeate the entire film. Indian behavior is understandable. The time period is the years immediately following the Civil War and the transcontinental railroad is inching across the prairie. The Cheyenne are determined to resist it. Again, they are impediments to both progress and Manifest Destiny, but at least they have motives that make sense. So too is Thunder Hawk's effort to retrieve his bride. Just as the whites had gone after the girls, the Indians wanted to get them back. In the final analysis neither *The Charge at Feather River* or *Bugles in the Afternoon* present Indians as savages in quite the same manner as they appear in *Geronimo*.

Some bigger-budget Westerns even depict Indians acting with honor. *Oh! Susanna* is an example of such a film. *Massacre River* (Allied Artists, 1949) is another one. Iron Eyes Cody, playing Chief Yellow Stone, wants his land protected from buffalo hunters and gold seekers; and, he claims he cannot be responsible for the rebellious deeds of the young men of his tribe who see their lands violated. At the film's end, Cody leads his braves to rescue Guy Madison and Rory Calhoun, who are being attacked by some of Cody's rebellious braves. He tells the two men he is saddened by the bloodshed and gives his word there will be no more fighting. Cody's Chief Yellow Stone is a man of his word, but he is also one who has been shoved back onto a parcel of land, and he is fighting to keep it. He is an honorable Indian, but Manifest Destiny remains triumphant.

The Half Breed (RKO, 1952) continued that theme. Charlie Wolf, played by Jack Buetel, is the mixed blood son of a white father and Apache mother. He tries to live in both worlds, but ultimately decides for the Apache way. The Indians on the reservation are being cheated out of food and supplies until (Robert Young), the hero, intervenes. When Charlie Wolf's sister is killed, war nearly erupts until Young, first a gambler and then an Indian agent, captures the guilty one, kills him and takes the body to Charlie Wolf. At the film's conclusion, Charlie Wolf promises to explain white ways to the Apaches if Young will explain Apache ways to the whites.

In a curious sort of way, *Two Flags West* (20th Century-Fox, 1950) also presents Indians as honorable men. Jeff Chandler plays a hate-filled cavalry commander. He feels exiled, a cripple away from the Civil War in the East. He hates the Confederates who have joined his command on the promise of amnesty, and he hates the Indians. Chandler arrests the son of a chief, and when the latter demands his son's release, Chandler sends the boy's body out to the Indians. Understandably, the Indians attack the fort. After a long day of fighting, ammunition and supplies are running low, and it is obvious that the Indians will overwhelm the fort the next day. However, the chief sends word if the officers responsible for his son's death will surrender to him, he will spare the fort. Chandler, knowing it was his decision, walks out to his death. The Indians, true to their word, leave the fort in peace.

Broken Arrow (20th-Century Fox, 1950) is perhaps the most widely cited Western which portrays Indians as men of honor. The friendship between James Stewart's Tom Jeffords and Jeff Chandler's Cochise caught the imagination of Western moviegoers. The film is indeed important because it fits well within a changing belief system. Racial and ethnic discrimination, far from ending, were at last being challenged. Certainly each year fewer voices were heard defending segregation as an acceptable social arrangement.

Many of these films, including *Oh! Susanna, Fort Osage, The Half Breed* and *Two Flags West,* are either sympathetic to the Indians or at least ambiguous in their view of white treatment of Indians. The new mood, however, did not lead to greater historical or cultural accuracy. Hollywood Indians were made to look better but life was still harsh for real Indians, and they were still subjected to discriminatory treatment. Ambiguity had crept into the American belief system, but that was about all.

Dessert Pursuit (Monogram, 1952) (Wayne Morris) offers a good end to this chapter. The bad guys led by Anthony Caruso are pursuing Morris and the heroine Virginia Grey across the desert. The bad guys are riding camels, and when the pursued and pursuers ride into an Indian settlement on Christmas Eve, the Indians, having never seen camels before, believe the bad guys are the Magi. The view of Indians in *Desert Pursuit* is that they are simple-minded folk, people of literal faith. They are childlike.

Therein lies the dilemma Westerns from 1930 to 1955 never resolved, because American beliefs had not resolved it. Were Indians brutal savages lusting after white scalps and white women, or were they child-like creatures more often than not victims of white treachery? In the silent era, the Indians were more savage, and after 1955 they were more likely to be victims. But in the intervening two decades, the picture was one of ambiguity as white North Americans reassessed the history of the westward movement.

Chapter Ten

"NO BUSINESS FOR A GIRL"

The years 1920 to 1965 were the period between two distinct women's movements. From at least 1870 to 1920, the year the Nineteenth Amendment was ratified, women were engaged actively in social change. The suffragette movement, the push for prohibition and the insistence on legal reforms which changed archaic laws (such as ones excluding women from inheriting real property) were visible demonstrations of an active feminist movement. But it sputtered to an end in 1920. According to traditional interpretations, women then lapsed into quiet acceptance of a male-dominated society, and acknowledged their roles as child-bearers and homemakers. That consensus shattered in the mid–1960s, leading to an aggressive feminism that altered American gender relationships.

Conventional wisdom seems to dictate the substance of this chapter. One should find in Westerns produced between the 1930 and 1955 female characters who are dependent on men, secondary to plot and action, and important only as romantic diversions. However, viewing Westerns from that perspective, one sees quickly that the traditional interpretation is only partially accurate. Women were not nearly as passive, dependent or irrelevant to plot and action as the traditional approach suggests. Their representation on film was as complex and varied as the life experiences of real women.

Just as contemporary women, some women throughout the 1930s and 1940s were wives and mothers who stayed home, kept house and raised the children while the husband worked. Dependent women may even have been the norm, but if so, there were numerous exceptions to it.

Women have always been nurses and teachers. Prior to the mid–1960s, law, business and medicine were generally closed to women, but they dominated the nursing profession, and they made up a large portion of elementary and secondary schoolteachers. Clearly, farm women were important contributors to the family enterprise. They spent long hours in the house, took care of the chickens and tended the garden, and at planting and harvest time frequently worked in the fields alongside their men. Blue-collar wives worked outside the home, in between children, to help supplement limited family income. And younger unmarried women waited tables and manned secretarial desks across America. By contemporary standards women of an earlier generation had an unusually restricted range of opportunities, but one should not confuse limited career possibilities with dependence on men. Women were freer than that.

In reality, women have never been as homebound or as dependent on men as the traditional approach suggests. Real life situations were always mixed. Some women were self-supporting, independent and adventurous. Others were more dependent on men and wanted a husband and family as the ultimate expressions of self-fulfillment.

John Wayne's 1930s Monogram and Republic B Westerns are typical of the latter approach. In most of them, the leading ladies have little to do except to provide the romantic interest. Often the women portrayed daughters or sisters trying to escape the evil clutches of the villains. Examples include *Randy Rides Alone* (Monogram, 1934), in which Wayne helps Alberta Vaughn escape the villainy of George Hayes playing Matt the Mute. In *The Dawn Rider* (Monogram, 1935), Dennis Moore is part of a gang responsible for killing Wayne's father. Marion Burns plays Moore's sister who nurses Wayne back to health after the gang shoots him. Both Vaughn and Burns are typical heroines in Wayne's B Westerns with little to do except smile and look pretty.

Ann Rutherford, however, is an exception. She had a strong role in *The Lonely Trail* (Republic, 1936), a film discussed at length in Chapter Eight. Rutherford is George Hayes' daughter in *The Lawless Nineties* (Republic, 1936). When Hayes is murdered by terrorists trying to keep Wyoming out of the Union, Rutherford assumes responsibility for publishing the newspaper, and she carries on the fight for statehood.

Heroines in 1930s Westerns were often foolish young women, neither good judges of character nor fully appreciative of the dangers they faced. They needed the protective, guiding hand of the cowboy hero, an informed, wise male. Lois Wilson plays a misguided heroine in *The Rider of Death Valley* (Universal, 1932). Wilson goes West to settle her murdered brother's estate that includes the map of a gold mine in Death Valley. Tom Mix forced Fred Kohler and Forrest Stanley, the villains, to divide the map into three parts with each man holding a part. Wilson believes Stanley, playing a doctor, is trustworthy, but she regards Mix as a conceited cowboy.

Stanley, in turn, assumes that when Wilson arrives, each man will turn over his part of the map to her and then Stanley will be able to get it. Mix, wise to the scheme, destroys his critical final part of the map. Without Mix, no one can find the mine's location. Wilson objects to Mix's paternalism, and she resents his high-handedness.

Stranded on the desert at the mine, the four travelers have little water. When Mix beats Tony, trying to get him to go back to the ranch for help, Wilson accuses Mix of being cruel to the animal. Eventually, however, Mix convinces her that he is trustworthy, and Mix sets out across the desert for help. Mix and his men arrive back at the mine just in time to save Wilson. Stanley, now crazed for water, blows up the mine, hoping that the blast will release water from an underground spring.

In the end, Wilson realizes Mix was acting for her own good. For most of the film, however, she is a gullible, shallow woman who does not know her own best interest. Left to her own devices, Kohler and Stanley would have marooned Wilson in Death Valley to die while they took the gold. Only an insightful and paternalistic Tom Mix prevented her from suffering that fate.

Mix's last feature film, *Rustler's Roundup* (Universal, 1933) stars Dianne Sinclair as a misguided heroine. She goes West to sell the ranch after her father is murdered. Convinced by Douglas Dumbrille and Roy Stewart, the villains, that Mix is responsible for her father's death, Sinclair decides to sell the ranch to Stewart. Mix suspects that Dumbrille and Stewart are the real murderers. The ranch contains an underground spring and the two villains want control of the water. Sinclair gives Mix the cold shoulder until her brother (Noah Beery, Jr.) is kidnapped by Dumbrille. At that point, Sinclair realizes Mix is right and that Stewart is really a bad guy who had her father killed to get control of the water. At film's end, Mix and Sinclair ride off together on Tony, Jr.

Two other films from the early 1930s reinforce the image of a confused, victimized female who needs the cowboy hero's protective hand. Rex Bell in *From Broadway to Cheyenne* (Monogram, 1933) shields Marceline Day from Robert Ellis' evil advances. Day plays the daughter of an ex-convict who goes West to make a new life. Ellis is the big city gangster who had clashed with Bell in the city. Ellis, now re-located in Wyoming, tells Day she must submit to his advances or risk having her father's past disclosed. Confused and afraid, Day complies with Ellis' demands. Bell in the meantime has gone to his father's Wyoming ranch to recuperate from gunshot wounds. He recognizes Day's father and learns that Ellis is in Wyoming. Ellis and his gang are selling protection to ranchers. Bell breaks up the racket and protects Day by sending Ellis and his men to jail.

Sheila Terry plays a totally dependent heroine in John Wayne's *Haunted Gold* (Warner Bros., 1932). Terry has been summoned to an abandoned gold mine once owned by her father. Terry's motives for going are unclear. She doesn't know who sent for her, and she believes her father is dead. She also knows that her father lost his share of the mine to Harry Woods before he died. Wayne, playing the son of Terry's father's partner, also received a notice to go to the mine. Like Terry, he has no idea why he has been sent for.

As the plot unfolds, viewers realize the phantom of the mine is really Terry's father, who is trying to get even with Woods for cheating him. During the course of the film, Terry is drawn to Wayne, who protects her, and in the end reunites her with her father. In the film, however, Terry's character is totally dependent on men for protection. She is repeatedly frightened by the spooky nature of her surroundings and is kidnapped by Woods' men. Wayne's role is not only to unmask Woods as the real villain, but also to reassure and protect Terry.

A Ken Maynard Western, *Come On, Tarzan* (World Wide, 1932), adds a different twist to the dependent female. Ken is foreman of the Flying A Ranch. Merna Kennedy, his new boss, arrives fresh from the East. Her uncle had willed her the ranch and she is determined to run it. But to her dismay, Kennedy discovers her uncle had other plans. According to his will, Kennedy was not to manage the spread until Maynard believed she was ready to do so. Until that time he was to act as Kennedy's guardian. Maynard and Kennedy fall in love during the course of the film, and as "The End" flickers across the screen we know Maynard once again has won the pretty girl.

When a Man Sees Red (Universal, 1934) is not an exact remake of *Come On, Tarzan* but the two films have much in common. Peggy Campbell is a conceited Eastern artist who inherits a ranch only to discover that she cannot fire Buck Jones because her uncle had appointed him as her guardian. Yet, she won't listen to him! As a result, LeRoy Mason nearly rustles all of her cattle. In the end, however, Campbell recognizes she needs Jones' strong, guiding hand. Marriage is in the air as the film ends.

Two Fred Scott Westerns from 1937 demonstrate that the image of a dependent female in need of strong male direction lasted beyond the early 1930s. In *The Roaming Cowboy* (Spectrum, 1937), Scott kidnaps Lois January to save her from Forrest Taylor's evil schemes. Taylor is trying to buy up all the ranches, and he needs January's agreement to deed over her share of the ranch. Taylor and his men intend to kidnap January, force her to sign the deed and then kill her. Fred Scott beats them to the punch and kidnaps January before Taylor's man can get to her. January, not realizing that she is in any danger, is understandably indignant, and tries to escape from Scott. By the film's end, however, she knows Scott has her best interest at heart. The picture closes with Scott and January sitting in a swing while Scott sings a love song to her.

Scott helps Victoria Vinton clear her father's name in *The Singing Buckaroo* (Spectrum, 1937). Vinton's father has been accused of embezzling $25,000 from the bank for which he worked. In fact, he took it when he learned that the bank manager was planning to steal it. Scott becomes involved when he rescues Vinton from Dick Curtis, who is trying to get the money from her. Convinced by Vinton that her father is innocent, Scott and his ranch hands help round up the bad guys and clear Vinton's father of any wrongdoing. In this Western, Vinton plays the loyal daughter as well as Scott's love interest.

Any number of actresses comes to mind as ones who specialized in 1930s dependent female roles. Lois January and Virginia Vale are two examples. Maybe Beth Marion did it as well as any, and better than most. Playing the virginal blonde, Marion depended on the protection of an allknowing male. In the film *Between Men* (Supreme, 1935), William Farnum plays the outlaw Rand who protects Marion from the evil intentions of Earl Dwire. Dwire kills Marion's father and she flees to Farnum's ranch seeking protection. There she meets Johnny Mack Brown, and a romance develops. Farnum, however, believes Brown is an outlaw like his other men, so he forbids Brown to see Marion. Farnum's intentions are pure; he wants to protect the innocent Marion from the sort of men attracted to himself.

Tom Tyler is Marion's benefactor in *Phantom of the Range* (Victory, 1936). Marion's uncle owned a sizable ranch on which he buried a large amount of money. Knowing that, Marion goes West hoping to buy the ranch, or at least locate a map to the buried gold. Her uncle's neighbors are searching for the money as well. They use a man dressed in a ghostlike costume who rides the range at night to scare off travelers searching for the buried loot. In addition, Forrest Taylor arranges for his foreman (Charles King) to purchase the ranch at an auction. Tyler foils that plan when he outbids them. Upon learning of Marion's interest in the ranch, Tyler invites her to live there with him. The map, it turns out, was hidden in a picture frame and after 58 minutes of meandering action, Tyler rounds up Taylor and his gang, and Marion gets the treasure. Tyler also got Marion, so the buried treasure becomes marital property.

Marion plays the daughter of the post store clerk in *For the Service* (Universal, 1936). She falls in love with Clifford Jones, the son of the post commander. Jones, as a youngster, witnessed the brutal murder of his

The Fugitive Sheriff, Columbia, 1936; Beth Marion and Ken Maynard. Marion often played the blonde, dependent heroine.

mother by Indians. He never recovered from it. As a result, he is a coward unable to carry out his duties. Marion's role in the film is limited. She is the romantic interest, the dependent female who turns to Buck Jones for help and advice as she frets over her love interest.

Avenging Waters (Columbia, 1936) opens with Ken Maynard rescuing Marion. She is horseback riding when a mountain lion attacks her horse. Maynard kills the mountain lion, but Marion's horse runs away with her. Maynard, on Tarzan, gallops to her aid; when Marion's horse plunges over a cliff into a river, Maynard goes in after her. Once rescued, Marion becomes the object of Maynard's romantic attention. And, of course, he wins her affection.

The view of a dependent woman, one Beth Marion played so well, is probably best summarized in the trial scenes of *Boss Rider of Gun Creek* (Universal, 1936). Buck Jones is on trial, falsely accused of killing a young woman. As another young woman — a friend of the deceased — testifies, two older women in the courtroom note that things like that happen to women who go traipsing around the country instead of staying home where they belong!

Gene Autry wrote in his autobiography *Back in the Saddle Again* that his heroines played "1930s versions of waiting for Gloria [Steinem]" (Autry, 66). Overall that is true, but it is even more accurate for Autry Westerns produced after 1939. Prior to 1939, most of Autry's programmers featured a dependent heroine. In *The Yodelin Kid from Pine Ridge* (Republic, 1937), Gene protects Betty Bronson from a stepfather who beats her. In *The Old Corral* (Republic, 1936), Hope [Irene] Manning plays a vulnerable young woman who runs West after witnessing a Chicago gangland murder. Gene is the sheriff of the Western town to which she flees. It becomes his special responsibility to protect her. In *Public Cowboy No. 1* (Republic, 1937), Autry even kisses Ann Rutherford at the fade.

Autry's Westerns changed the genre to a remarkable extent. Women had bigger and better roles in his films and in the years after 1939, female characters were far more independent and aggressive than were most Western heroines of the 1930s. But even Gene Autry did not change everything at once: His first few films kept within the 1930s tradition, and featured women dependent on men for protection and leadership.

Some films even went so far as to suggest that when a woman forsakes her dependency on men, becomes too independent and assumes she can take charge of her affairs, she is usually in danger of being robbed or swindled. Marjorie Reynolds is the heroine and George O'Brien's nemesis in *Racketeers of the Range* (RKO, 1939). Reynolds plays the owner of a packing company. Her attorney advised her to sell out to a rival firm, but O'Brien prevents the sale because it would make Arizona ranchers too dependent on one packing company. The ranchers would be forced to sell at whatever price that company wanted to pay for their beef. Reynolds believes she can manage her own affairs and that it is in her best interest to sell. The company owes a great deal of money to the ranchers. If she could sell the company, then she could pay off its creditors.

Using his status as a creditor, O'Brien goes to court to prevent Reynolds from selling the company. Reynolds is outraged; she does not realize that her own attorney is on the payroll of the rival company. Her attorney, rather than protecting her interests, is working against them. O'Brien knows that, but Reynolds won't listen to him. Reynolds, the film suggests, is a woman trying to manage her business, but she does not understand how to do it. O'Brien exposes her attorney and saves the packing company for Reynolds as well as for the Arizona ranchers.

When Buck Jones inherits a ranch in *Branded* (Columbia, 1931), his neighbor is Ethel Kenton, a pretty young woman. Kenton objects to Jones fencing in the range, and later is convinced that Jones rustled her cattle. Unbeknownst to Kenton, her foreman is the real villain. *Branded* is another example of a young woman, ostensibly the boss, who is unable to judge accurately the character of the men who work for her. She places her trust in the wrong man until Jones helps her to see the error of her judgments.

In both *Racketeers of the Range* and *Branded*, the heroines mistrust the cowboy heroes and blame them for the bad things happening. In *Clearing the Range* (Allied, 1931), Sally Eilers regards Hoot Gibson as a coward. Gibson returns to his hometown and is friendly to the men everyone in town knows killed his brother. To Eilers' dismay, Gibson won't even stand up to the outlaws who are trying to drive her family off their ranch. Unknown to Eilers, Gibson is the capped rider El Captain who rides at night to bring the villains to justice. Again, we see in Eilers the image of a woman who thought she knew what she was doing — but the truth was exactly the opposite of what she perceived.

Dependent and often misguided women, however, are not the only roles assumed by 1930s leading ladies. Some Westerns depicted women as capable of managing their own affairs. Marguerite Churchill plays Jane Withersteen, heroine of George O'Brien's *Riders of the Purple Sage* (Fox, 1931), a woman more than able to manage her ranch.

Charlotte Wynters has an important role in Buck Jones' *The Ivory Handled Guns* (Universal, 1935). At first, viewers believe Wynters regards Jones as the one who killed her father. But as the film unfolds, it is apparent that she knows the Wolverine Kid (Walter Miller) is the real culprit. Wynters even offers a big reward for Jones' capture in order to encourage her men to find him before the Wolverine Kid does. Throughout the film, Wynters is a strong-willed, thoroughly capable woman up to bossing the ranch.

Lina Basquette plays the rancher's daughter in Ken Maynard's *The Arizona Terror* (Tiffany, 1931). In the end, as in most Maynard Westerns, Basquette succumbs to Maynard's charms. Before that, however, she demonstrates independence and toughness. Two instances stand out in the film. First, she takes a rifle and goes hunting a wolf that has been raiding livestock. Second, her father trusts her to take a large sum of money to the bank. He fears a holdup, but believes Basquette can get the money safely to town.

Claire Rochelle is more than Johnny Mack Brown's love interest in *Guns in the Dark* (Republic, 1937). As owner of the Sundown she is able to boss her men, to earn their respect and to stand up to Dick Curtis and Ted Adams, the villains. Rochelle decides she is going to build a dam across a canyon that Curtis uses. She has a permit from Washington, D.C. to build it, and she tells Curtis—who objects to the dam—he can't stop her. Brown's comment that she is a spunky girl seems to summarize her image throughout the film.

Arizona Terror, Tiffany, 1931; Lina Basquette and Ken Maynard. Basquette portrays an independent woman who gets the drop on Maynard.

Joan Woodbury plays a dance hall girl in *The Eagle's Brood* (Paramount, 1935). After Addison Richards' men murder a young boy's parents, Woodbury finds the boy wandering, lost and frightened. Woodbury then learns that Richards' men are looking for the boy in order to kill him. Woodbury sends word to the boy's grandfather, the Mexican outlaw El Puma (William Farnum), and she hides the boy in a mountain cabin. William Boyd as Hopalong Cassidy promises Farnum he will find the boy after Farnum saves Boyd's life. In the meantime, Richards discovers Woodbury is hiding the boy and kills her when she won't disclose his location. Woodbury portrays a compassionate but brave woman. She dies rather than give into Richards' demand.

The films discussed above are typical of 1930s B Westerns. Ordinarily, the heroine was portrayed as a dependent person who needed male direction and assistance. But there were exceptions to that image. Women were also portrayed as people capable of running the ranch, of thinking for themselves and of acting on their own initiative. In the late '40s early '50s, the latter image became more prevalent. It never became the dominant one, but spunky, independent heroines were far more visible in the '40s and '50s than they had been in the 1930s.

From 1939 until Gene Autry entered the service in 1942, his films presented women in a different light than had his films prior to 1939. By 1939, Autry had deviated from the pattern of the cowboy hero falling in love with the pretty heroine. Autry's early films followed that convention, but by 1939 his role had changed. Increasingly, Gene was a father figure. He might protect the heroine, and frequently he had to teach a haughty young lady a bit of humility for her own good. However, after 1939 Autry almost never rode off into the sunset with the pretty girl. Because of that, the characters Autry's leading ladies played changed.

June Storey appeared with Autry in several 1939 and 1940 films. She played all sorts of characters, but most often a spoiled rich girl. In *Rancho Grande* (Republic, 1940), Storey and her brother inherit a ranch. They exhibit all of the smugness of young Easterners. The ranch becomes a hangout for their hip pals, and they spend too many evenings at the 49 Club, a notorious gambling joint. The villains want to get the ranch as part of an irrigation project. Storey, of course, needs to be saved by Gene from both the outlaws and her own haughtiness.

In *Ride, Tenderfoot, Ride* (Republic, 1940), Storey is the owner of a packing company trying to buy a rival packing firm Autry has inherited. She plays the country club type, totally insensitive to the people who will be unemployed if Gene sells his company. Gene learns that she does not intend to keep his employees. All Storey wants are the customers and plant capacity; Autry therefore refuses to sell. Again we see Storey as a female being duped by Warren Hull, her business manager-boyfriend. Autry not only saves his packing company, he also helps Storey see the error of her ways.

Carol Hughes is Gene's leading lady in *Under Fiesta Stars* (Republic, 1941). In this film, Autry and Hughes co-inherit a ranch and mine. Hughes, from the East, wants to sell out and use the money for luxurious living. Gene knows that if they sell, the Mexicans living on the land and working the mine will be without jobs. Hughes is a bull-headed woman and is conned by a crooked attorney who wants the ranch and mine. Hughes understands her insensitivity in the nick of time when an explosion at the mine kills a Mexican worker and nearly kills Smiley Burnette and his young ward Tadpole.

Fay McKenzie is the heroine in *Home in Wyoming* (Republic, 1942). She plays a newspaper reporter who fails to get a story about Gene. When she scoffs at her failure, telling the editor Autry is a phony, the editor reminds her that Autry is a hero to millions of kids and about two million adults. City sophisticates may not like him, but he is a real hero to people of the heartland. Ordered to Wyoming to get her story, McKenzie gets involved in a Chicago gang war transplanted West. Only after Gene has saved her life does she learn that Autry is not a phony.

Story, Hughes and McKenzie are different from 1930s heroines such as the ones Beth Marion portrayed. They are modern women, headstrong and society-conscious. They still get into trouble, trouble from which Gene Autry must rescue them. But in the end, instead of riding off into the sunset with the cowboy hero, they are better prepared to manage their own affairs. After 1939, Autry's role was not to romance his leading ladies, but to educate them in the ways of the West and to prepare them for responsibility, not to remove them from it. In that sense, Autry's Westerns are a transition into the changed image of women which permeated Westerns during World War II.

During the war years, the image of women in Westerns underwent a substantial transformation. Women became more adventurous, more involved, and less dependent on men. Mona Barrie's role in *Dawn on the Great Divide* (Monogram, 1942) is a good example. Barrie plays the bighearted prostitute, a character as old as the Western film genre. In this instance, she runs saloons and is going to Oregon to open up another one. Totally independent, Barrie projects a tough image. Yet Buck Jones recognizes in her not only independence, but warmth and compassion as well. When a young woman traveling with the wagon train dies during childbirth, Barrie cares for the baby. In the end, Barrie opens up her saloon and helps Buck Jones track down Harry Woods and Roy Barcroft, the real villains who were behind the fake Indian raids on wagon trains.

Jane Wyatt is an interesting heroine in *The Kansan* (United Artists, 1943). The film opens with Richard Dix, the hero, shooting it out with a gang of bank robbers. Dix is badly wounded. The next scene shows him recovering in a hospital. Wyatt comes to visit Dix, and when he asks about the noise on the street below she tells them the town is celebrating his election as sheriff. Clearly, Wyatt had more than a little to do with it.

Later, viewers learn she owns and operates the best hotel and restaurant in town. Wyatt's character is aggressive and independent. She earns a living and has a career of her own. Wyatt even makes clear to Victor Jory, who has long wooed her, that she prefers Dix. In a climactic gun battle, Dix is again wounded. The film concludes with Wyatt visiting him in the hospital. Again Dix asks her what the crowd is celebrating, and she tells him it is celebrating their impending marriage. Wyatt is proposing to Dix!

In *Wild Horse Rustlers* (PRC, 1943), heroine Linda Johnson symbolized the important role women played during World War II. She is running the ranch while her father is gone. Johnson's able foreman Smoky, played by veteran character actor Lane Chandler, tells her he is going to town to get some men to help with the roundup. Johnson replies that she will help. Chandler thanks her, but assures her that he needs men. Robert Livingston, who replaced George Houston as the Lone Rider, has more confidence in Johnson's ability. By the film's end, she has helped with the roundup. Thanking Johnson for her good work, Livingston reminds the audience that it will take the effort of a lot of women to win the war.

Betty Miles adds a new dimension to the heroine in both *The Law Rides Again* (Monogram, 1943) and *Westward Bound* (Monogram, 1944). After Tim McCoy entered military service and Buck Jones died, Monogram's popular Rough Riders series ceased production. To meet their distribution needs, the company coaxed Hoot Gibson and Ken Maynard out of retirement and starred them as the Trail Blazers. Soon Bob Steele joined the other two to form a new trigger trio. Betty Miles appeared as the heroine in a couple of these films.

Miles' character has many masculine qualities in *The Law Rides Again*. Viewers first meet her at a stagecoach relay station as a gun-toting stagecoach driver. Later, she rides to the fort to get the cavalry. When Hank Bell and Chief Thunder Cloud, villains in this movie, pursue her, Miles outrides and outsmarts them. In the exciting climax, she brings the cavalry in the nick of time to rescue Gibson and Maynard, low on ammunition and pinned down by the outlaws.

In *Westward Bound*, the three United States Marshals ride to the aid of ranchers, including Betty Miles who plays one of the ranchers. Two things are striking about her role. First, she is nobody's daughter or niece. She owns and operates her own ranch! Second, just as in *The Law Rides Again*, Miles wears long pants, totes a gun and rides like a man. But this time she is pretty enough to engage the attention of Bob Steele. Maynard and Gibson, late in their careers, were too old and too overweight to become romantically involved, so Steele took their place.

Miles' character suggests a new trend. The tomboy was not unknown in Westerns, but it was uncommon to have a pretty girl — one with romantic appeal — carry a gun, wear long pants and ride a horse. Miles' character was feminine, yet she was independent. She was determined to protect her ranch. It was a new view of women, but it was one that would appear more frequently.

Post–World War II Westerns continued to reflect the new image of women; however, they were called cowboy movies for a good reason. They were films about the cowboy hero and his sidekick. Women normally did not have that much to do with either plot or action. Even in Westerns produced after 1945, women were likely to be nieces or daughters, dependent on males for protection and supervision. Frequently, the cowboy heroes had to rescue them from the bad guys. But moreso than in the 1930s, women after 1945 were depicted as struggling to run the ranch, manage a newspaper or operate a small business. A la Betty Miles in *Westward Bound*, post-war women frequently wore long pants and carried a gun.

Evelyn Finley's portrayed an independent, hard-riding woman who was not afraid to stand up to the bad guys. In *Sheriff of Medicine Bow* (Monogram, 1948), Finley plays Raymond Hatton's daughter. Johnny Mack Brown is the Marshal responsible for sending Hatton, a bank robber, to prison. Finley is bitter; she blames Johnny Mack for sending her father to prison, and she vows to shoot Johnny if he ever sets foot on the ranch.

Finley skillfully runs the ranch in her father's absence, but outlaws who want the property harass her. Knowing of her predicament, Brown arranges to have Hatton paroled so he can come home and help Finley. Even though Finley is glad to see Hatton, she will not permit Brown on the property. It takes a lot of persuasion by Hatton to convince Finley that Johnny Mack was only doing his job. In this film, Finley wears long pants, carries a gun and rides with the men. She is certainly no dependent female.

Gunning for Justice (Monogram, 1948) opens as Johnny Mack Brown comforts a dying Ted Adams. Adams gives Brown a map with instructions to deliver it to Ed in Torre Flats. On his way to Torre Flats, Johnny meets Raymond Hatton and Max Terhune, two old pals, who introduce him to Winnie. Evelyn Finley plays Winnie, a local rancher. The plot thickens as I. Stanford Jolley, the villain, tries to get the map from Johnny Mack. Finley owns her ranch and agrees to sell some stock to Johnny Mack, who is in Torre Flats to buy cattle for an Eastern concern.

On the way to the ranch, Brown and Finley are ambushed. She joins in the fight. Crouching behind a tree, Finley demonstrates she can shoot with the best of men. When Johnny reads the bill of sale, he sees she signed her name Edwina. Brown realizes that Finley is the Ed for whom he is searching. He gives her the map, which identifies the location of buried gold, bullion that Finley's uncle and Jolley had stolen from Confederates during the Civil War. In the end, Johnny Mack Brown saves Finley from Jolley, and helps her to get the gold.

In *Gunning for Justice*, Evelyn Finley portrays a modern woman. She runs her own ranch and is respected by men. For example, at one point the sheriff of Torre Flats is about to run Hatton and Terhune out of town for selling phony tonic water. Finley intervenes and offers them jobs on her ranch. As in other films, she wears long pants (or, at least, a split riding skirt), carries a gun and rides better than most men.

Sheriff of Medicine Bow, Monogram, 1948; Evelyn Finley, Johnny Mack Brown, Raymond Hatton, Max Terhune and Frank LaRue. Finley wears a split riding skirt and totes a gun.

Reno Browne often appeared as a woman who wore long pants and carried a gun. And, like Finley, it was common for Browne's characters to portray an independent woman who ran the ranch. *Fence Riders* (Monogram, 1950) with Whip Wilson and Andy Clyde is typical of those Westerns in which Browne appeared.

She plays the owner of the Lazy T Ranch. Myron Healey, a saloon-keeper "brain heavy," is trying to get the ranch by rustling her cattle. Whip Wilson comes along just in time to break up one rustling attempt. In the gunfight, Browne's foreman is killed so Wilson takes his place. At one important point in the film, Browne rides to warn Wilson that Healey is the real culprit. Later, she goes with her men as they stop Healey and his outlaws in their final rustling effort.

Both Finley and Browne represent a new kind of Western heroine. They are part of the West, at home on a horse, and respected by men. Such heroines are a far cry from the dependent female portrayed by Beth Marion in the 1930s. But Finley and Browne were not alone. Actresses such as Phyllis Coates, Jennifer Holt and Christine Larson all played independent, aggressive women in Monogram Westerns throughout the 1940s.

Several other film examples in the early 1950s of modern women come to mind. Elisabeth Fraser and Elisabeth Risdon have important roles in Rex Allen's *Hills of Oklahoma* (Republic, 1950). Allen heads a group of cattlemen trying to find a buyer who will pay higher prices for their cattle. Risdon is the cattle buyer who decides to buy them, and goes with her secretary (Fraser) to oversee the cattle drive. When a rival company uses an airplane to stampede the cattle, Risdon is nearly killed. Rather than intimidate her, the stampede further strengthens Risdon's determination. During the film she overcomes her bitter memories at being jilted by Allen's grandfather many years earlier. In fact, the film is as much about the businesswoman Risdon as it is about Rex Allen's efforts to get his cattle to market.

Adrian Booth's role in *The Savage Horde* (Republic, 1950) is an interesting mix of old and new images. Booth's character runs a restaurant and has the appearance of being a female entrepreneur. But we learn Grant Withers, the area's biggest rancher who intends to marry Booth, set her up in business. She had been the girlfriend of William Elliott but she broke off her relationship with Elliott because of his gunfighting, outlaw ways.

When Booth can no longer stand Withers' callous disregard for the rights of the small ranchers, she denounces him. Even though Booth realizes she will lose all she has worked for, her sense of right wins out in the end. Her image is one of a woman searching for love and security, but not at the expense of her integrity and in violation of her sense of justice and fair play.

Alexis Smith has a major role in *Montana* (Warner Bros., 1950). Smith plays a woman who inherited the family ranch, a large Montana cattle spread. She is determined to keep Errol Flynn's sheep off the range, just as her father had done to Flynn's father.

Smith's image in the film varies from episode to episode. At points she is a gun-toting female ramrod more than capable of opposing Flynn. Yet, at a party Flynn gives—in order to reason with the cattlemen—Smith shows up as a beautiful woman dressed in a long fashionable gown. Smith as the leading lady is both independent and tough, but she retains her femininity. Modern men and women take such roles for granted. The modern woman can pursue a career in which she competes effectively with men, and still be very feminine. That image in 1950, however, was a long way from common.

Mala Powers' role as a white woman raised by a Cherokee family offers some interesting perspectives in *Rose of Cimarron* (20thCentury–Fox,

1952). When Jack Buetel as the sheriff meets Powers, he takes her to a boarding house so she can be taught to live and act like a white woman. Powers puts on the proper clothing down to corset and pantaloons. But one tea party is one too many. The catty comments and the uppity white women's callous disregard for her feelings prompt Powers to flee their company. So with skirt flying over her pantaloons she runs back to the stable, to her old attire and old ways.

By the film's end she is romantically involved with Buetel, and he saves her from sure death in the final gunfight. Before that, however, Powers demonstrates she is a modern woman who knows how to use a gun and to ride a horse. Recall from the last chapter, she called out two of the three men who killed her Cherokee parents, beat them to the draw, and killed both of them.

Just as this section began with June Storey's roles in Gene Autry Westerns, it seems appropriate to conclude it with some consideration of Gail Davis. From 1950 to 1953, the last year of Gene Autry Flying A productions B Westerns, Davis was his most frequent leading lady. Her roles demonstrate both the change and continuity that typify the images of women in Westerns produced after the 1950s.

Usually Davis played someone's daughter, sister or niece. In both *Sons of New Mexico* (Columbia, 1950) and *Wagon Team* (Columbia, 1952), she is Dick Jones' sister. In the first film, Davis' role is traditional. She is a caring sister who worries about Jones' wild behavior. Autry's solution is to enroll the boy at the New Mexico Military Institute. Jones plays a young outlaw in *Wagon Team*. Davis is the star of their father's medicine show and both she and her father are worried that Jones will be captured and hanged. *Indian Territory* (Columbia, 1950) features Davis as the traditional rancher's daughter as well as Kirby Grant's love interest. She continues as the rancher's daughter in *Texans Never Cry* (Columbia, 1951) but this time she is Gene's love interest.

Bob Steele plays both a Southern sympathizer and Davis' brother in *Silver Canyon* (Columbia, 1952). Davis worries that Steele's behavior will destroy their father, the local union army commander. In this film, Davis shows a great deal of grit as she continually confronts Steele's actions. The same may be said about her role in *Whirlwind* (Columbia, 1951). Davis plays Thurston Hall's niece. Hall is a big rancher whose men rob mail from stagecoaches. At one point early in the film, Hall orders Davis out of the room, telling her this "is no business for a girl." When Davis realizes her uncle's crooked ways, she becomes Gene Autry's ally.

Other films depict Davis as a businesswoman. She runs a Canadian dude ranch in *Blue Canadian Rockies* (Columbia, 1952). Gene and Pat

Buttram go to Canada, at her father's request, to investigate trouble the ranch is having with a local timber company. Gene helps Davis expose Tom London, playing her father's ex-partner, as the real culprit. Davis runs a newspaper in *Winning of the West* (Columbia, 1953) and she operates a toll road in *On Top of Old Smoky* (Columbia, 1953). In the latter film, Gene rescues her from outlaws who discourage stagecoaches from using the road. They want to put her out of business in order to gain control of a valuable mineral deposit on her land.

Davis' films are typical of the early 1950s. Heroines continued for the most part to be dependent on males, and largely marginal to the plot and action. Yet, there are just enough exceptions to remind us that the role of women in American life was undergoing change.

An indication that the status of women had begun to change was the increasing appearance after 1945 of women as villains. During the 1930s, women hardly ever appeared in that role. In 1941, Gene Tierney played *Belle Starr* (20th Century–Fox, 1941). In the film, Tierney marries Randolph Scott, and together they fight Yankee carpetbaggers. Her violence is presented as understandable, and certainly does not reflect the true history of Belle Starr. In fact, it is questionable whether Tierney is a villain in this picture.

In 1942, Lynne Carver was the villainess in Roy Rogers' *Man from Cheyenne* (Republic, 1942). Carver plays the "brain heavy" who bosses a gang of rustlers. On the surface, Carver appears to be a frightened woman from the East, totally out of place in a land as violent as the old West. She seems to belong at a country club, rather than on a ranch. And, she is a bit squeamish. Carver finds murder distasteful, but she is no less reluctant to shoot Rogers when she fears he is about to discover her secret. Roy had emptied a gun and laid it on the table. When Carver tries to shoot him with it, she establishes her own guilt. At the film's end, in the middle of a gun battle, Carver tries to escape in her automobile. Heroines Gale Storm and Sally Payne stop her and apprehend her after Storm has blackened her eye in a fistfight.

Idaho (Republic, 1943) is another Roy Rogers Western featuring a villainess. Ona Munson owns a gambling house which the local judge (Harry Shannon), is trying to close. In the past, the judge had been a notorious bank robber. When two of his former gang members turn up, Munson learns about Shannon's background. She becomes increasingly involved with the two crooks as they try to blackmail Shannon. When a carefully laid scheme to rob an armored car is foiled, Munson is arrested and goes to jail.

After 1945, B Westerns featured women as villainesses more regularly, and Monogram Pictures was one of the leaders. In *The Cisco Kid Returns* (Monogram, 1945), Duncan Renaldo, in his first role as the Cisco Kid, protects a young girl whose father has been murdered. The villains in this case want the ranch, and to get it they must get custody of the girl. Vicky Lane poses as the girl's mother, returned after many years in the East. In reality, the little girl's mother is dead and Lane is an impostor planted by Richard Pryor, the bad guy. Renaldo thwarts their plans by exposing the fake mother.

In *Robin Hood of Monterey* (Monogram, 1947), Evelyn Brent plays the villainess who kills her husband and tries to pin the murder on her stepson. Gilbert Roland, playing the Cisco Kid, is a good friend of the murdered man and knows that Ernie Adams, the accused, is innocent. Roland, as expected, brings Brent to justice.

Jennifer Holt played the Hawk, a vicious leader of outlaws, in *The Hawk of Powder River* (PRC, 1948), a Western starring Eddie Dean. After that movie was released in April 1948, Holt duplicated her villainess role in *Range Defenders* (Monogram, 1948), released in June of the same year, starring Jimmy Wakely. Holt, on the surface, appears to be a respectable community leader who is sweet on the sheriff's son. But in fact, she masterminds a gang of outlaws who rob stagecoaches. Early in the film, Steve Clark asks the sheriff (Frank LaRue) and his son (Riley Hill) to act as guards for his gold ore. Hill rides ahead to scout while LaRue stays with the wagon. Holt fakes a broken wagon wheel, and Hill stops to help her. Holt's men then attack the wagon. Even though they fail to get the gold, they kill the sheriff.

Wakely, much to Hill's displeasure, becomes sheriff. Holt, in turn, plays on Riley's jealousy to drive a wedge between the two men. As Wakely begins to suspect Holt is the culprit, he makes Hill even angrier. In the end, Holt is brought to justice and Hill becomes Marshall. In the process, however, Jennifer Holt plays an unusually realistic villainess.

Christine Larson is Whip Wilson's antagonist in *Crashing Thru* (Monogram, 1949). Although Tristam Coffin appears to be the main heavy, viewers quickly learn that he is a weak man. Larson is the one with the stomach for murder, and the determination to stick it out even though Wilson is a threat to their stagecoach robbery schemes. Wilson assumes the identity of a murdered ranger and rounds up Larson and the rest of her gang.

Roy Rogers' Republic Westerns continued to feature villainesses as well. Stephanie Bachelor and Nana Bryant play vicious killers in two late 40s Rogers Westerns. In *Springtime in the Sierras* (Republic, 1947), Bachelor plays the brains behind a gang of poachers. When Harry Cheshire stumbles onto them in the act of loading dead game, Bachelor kills him in

Range Renegades, Monogram, 1948; Dennis Moore, Jennifer Holt and Riley Hill. Holt, as a villainess, slips a gun to Moore while Hill's gaze is averted.

cold blood. Later, she catches Rogers looking around her barn for a refrigerator plant Andy Devine told him Bachelor had purchased. She and her foreman Roy Barcroft throw Rogers into the unit knowing that he will freeze to death. But Roy escapes, and with Jane Frazee's aid captures Bachelor and Barcroft. Just as in *Man from Cheyenne*, a film in which Gale Storm captures Lynne Carver, Jane Frazee rides down Bachelor after a chase on horseback, pulls her to the ground and knocks her cold.

Nana Bryant is the villainess in *Eyes of Texas* (Republic, 1948). She plays an attorney who, with her henchman Roy Barcroft, uses a pack of killer dogs to murder the owner of a boys' ranch. Bryant wants the ranch and knows that it has been willed to the boys. She hires an impostor to pose as a nephew who was thought killed in the war. In his excitement about discovering his nephew, the old man signs a new blank will. Bryant then fills in the blanks so the impostor inherits the ranch. When Frank Dennis, the impostor, balks at the arrangement, Bryant literally throws him to the dogs. Justice, however, prevails in the end. Bryant dies of a heart attack as she is being assaulted by one of her own dogs.

June Vincent is particularly vicious as the female villain in Rex Allen's *Colorado Sundown* (Republic, 1952). She is the brains of the operation, and the one who does the killing with a quick-acting poison. It is so potent that within seconds the victim is dead. She disposes of two men in that manner, and in the end Vincent tries to use it on herself. Rex Allen arrives just in time to knock the tea cup from her hand.

Gene Autry also featured women as villains in at least three films. Gloria Henry plays Robert Livingston's girlfriend in *Riders in the Sky* (Columbia, 1949). Together they plot Tom London's murder in order to keep him from identifying Livingston as a killer. Sheila Ryan is Keene Duncan's girl friend in *Pack Train* (Columbia, 1953). Duncan's general store charges outlandish prices for merchandise, and when gold is discovered he raises prices twofold. Ryan tends the store and tries to sweet-talk Gene into not siding with the settlers. Mary Castle is her father's ally in *Texans Never Cry* (Columbia, 1951). Castle's father is a printer who supplies the paper on which Richard Powers prints counterfeit Mexican lottery tickets. Castle, actually Powers' girlfriend, is responsible for wooing Gene Autry so he will not uncover the counterfeit ring.

By the 1940s, bigger-budget Westerns also employed women as villains. Jane Greer is a villainess in *Station West* (RKO, 1945). Her gang holds up gold shipments, and on one raid they kill a cavalry patrol escorting the gold. Wells Fargo won't ship out the gold, keeping it stored at the army post. Dick Powell, the hero, plays an army investigator sent to find the cavalry escorts' murderers. Even though Powell falls in love with Greer and she with him, both remain committed to their goals. She wants the gold stored at the army post, and he wants to bring the outlaws to justice. Predictably, Greer dies at the end and the outlaws are captured.

Faith Domergue is an unusually cruel villainess in *The Duel at Silver Creek* (Universal-International, 1952). She and her boyfriend mastermind a gang of silver mine claim jumpers. Near the beginning of the film she strangles to death a wounded man to prevent him from identifying the gang. She then pretends romantic interest in Stephen McNally, playing the role of a famous sheriff, in order to set him up to be killed. At one point Domergue discovers that a bullet wound has damaged McNally's finger. He can't bend it, so it is nearly impossible for him to pull a gun trigger. She tells a young gunfighter of McNally's condition, and only Audie Murphy's intervention saves McNally's life. When McNally and Murphy learn Domergue is part of the gang, they entice her to lead them to the hideout, and in the climactic shootout she is killed.

By 1952, women had come a long way. No longer were they dependent and passive, needing to be continually rescued by the cowboy hero.

Now they were independent, strong-willed people more than capable of making their own way in the world, and frequently cast in the role of villains. Clearly the image of women in Westerns had changed dramatically since 1930.

Unlike the films of most other B Western actors, those of Roy Rogers gave a great deal of visibility to leading ladies. A number of reasons account for this peculiarity. Initially, Rogers was an unknown, untested actor who was not trusted to carry the film by himself. He lacked charisma, and he did not possess many physical attributes one associated with a cowboy star. It was imperative, therefore, to surround him with a strong cast. For example, careful attention was given to a sidekick, so Smiley Burnette or Raymond Hatton accompanied Rogers in early films. In 1939, George Hayes left Paramount and the Hopalong Cassidy series for Republic and the Rogers films. With a few film exceptions, Hayes was with Rogers from 1940 through 1947. By the time Hayes left the series, Rogers was an established star not dependent on a sidekick.

Republic carefully chose Rogers' leading ladies as well. In 1938-39, Mary Hart appeared with Rogers in eight pictures. He claims the studio changed her name from Lynne Roberts in order to have Rogers-Hart, as in the popular composers of Broadway hits, appear on theater marquees, a gimmick no doubt to distract from the star's youthfulness and minimum cowboy qualities (Stern, 108). From 1940 to 1944 several actresses worked in Rogers' films, and it was during this time that Sally Payne offered a tomboy perspective on the heroine.

In 1944, at least according to Rogers, Herbert Yates, owner of Republic, had seen *Oklahoma*, then a smash Broadway hit, and returned to Hollywood determined to incorporate more music into Rogers' Westerns (Hurst, 147, and Tuska 1976, 461). In order to do that he needed a leading lady who could sing. Enter Dale Evans. The combination of Rogers-Evans was successful beyond Yates' wildest expectations or Evans' desire. In spite of the fact she married the star, it took Evans some years to reconcile herself to be a cowgirl (Rogers and Evans 1979, 114–115). Nevertheless, she became one, and with periodic furloughs, Evans starred with Rogers from 1944 through the end of the series in 1951.

Evans' success was reinforcing. Audiences came to expect Rogers' films to have strong leading ladies, and Republic, in turn, felt obligated to provide them. As a result, both Jane Frazee and Penny Edwards stood in for Dale Evans during her time away from the series.

Mary Hart was the first of Roy Rogers' leading ladies. During 1938 and 1939, Hart appeared in seven Rogers' programmers. In all of them she presents a very traditional image. Her roles are that of daughter or niece, one who is dependent on males. Hart worked at an out-of-home job in one film, *Billy the Kid Returns* (Republic, 1938), but it was as a clerk in her father's store. In *Rough Riders Roundup* (Republic, 1939), Hart seems to be more independent, running away from her father to get married. But even there she want to exchange one dependency for another.

With the possible exceptions of *Rough Riders Roundup* and *In Old Caliente* (Republic, 1939), Hart's characters are not central to the plot. For example, in *Shine on Harvest Moon* (Republic, 1938), Hart is listed second on the screen credits, but she played less of a role in the film than did Lulu Belle of Lulu Belle and Scotty, well-known entertainers from the WLS National Barn Dance. Hart was the romantic interest in these early Roy Rogers Westerns who was supposed to glow while Roy Rogers sang. She was the archetype pretty girl who existed for the cowboy hero to woo.

It is interesting to compare the seven early films Hart made with her 1948 appearance as Lynne Roberts, her real name. In *Eyes of Texas*, she plays a nurse who is clearly independent of males. Roberts, in this film, was around to help capture the villains by riding for help. By 1948, then, her role had changed. She was a working woman, self-supporting, and one who could be trusted with a dangerous mission.

Sally Payne was a different sort of heroine than Mary Hart. Payne seldom played the romantic type; her characters were tomboys. And, of course, she brought a great deal of comedy to each role. Even when her roles appeared to be very traditional as in *Robin Hood of the Pecos* (Republic, 1940), in which she played the wife of Sam Starr, or as in a few films in which she appeared as Gabby Hayes' daughter, Sally Payne never portrayed a character very dependent on males. In fact, quite to the contrary, she often helped them out of very difficult situations. For that reason, Payne was involved in the plot more often than Hart or the other actresses with whom she appeared and who are often listed ahead of Payne in the credits.

In *Young Bill Hickok* (Republic, 1940), *Robin Hood of the Pecos* and *Nevada City* (Republic, 1941), Payne was very much the tomboy, wearing men's clothes, carrying weapons and skillfully riding a horse or driving a stagecoach. However, even when she wasn't a tomboy, her characters were tougher, less fragile than Hart's characters or the characters portrayed by the other actresses in Payne's films. Payne's characters related well to men because either as a tomboy she was like them or because as a big sister or buddy they could talk with her and depend on her not to act like a "typical woman." Her parts grew larger as she made more films with Roy Rogers, and by the end of their film association, she often appeared as the first woman listed in the credits. Before that, she was always second behind whichever actress provided the soft, feminine contrast to Payne's tomboy qualities.

The films of Hart and Payne contained an interesting contrast, and it appeared a woman had to choose one of the two. She could be feminine, as was Hart. In that case, she must be dependent on males and leave the world's affairs to them. If she chose the dependent role, her basic pursuit in life was to find the right man, get married and raise children, or more immediately to care for the male in her life, be it father, uncle or boyfriend.

If that seemed less than self-enhancing, the only other option was to become a tomboy accepted by males but not taken seriously by them, or to become a big sister, one to whom males turned for advice and solace but not companionship. That dichotomy began to break down during World War II so as the twenty-first century dawns the concept tomboy seems anachronistic. Many of Dale Evans' films personify this changing state of affairs.

As a general rule, Dale Evans' films reflect post–1940 images, and they involve her in the plot and action. In her first few films, however, Evans assumed the traditional role of one oriented to the home and dependent on males. Then the transition began. In her 1945–46 pictures Evans still played a character normally associated with the home, but at the same time one who asserted her independence from male authority. *My Pal Trigger* (Republic, 1946) is a good film example. Evans plays Gabby Hayes' daughter, but she is also the one who, on her own and without her father's knowledge, drops charges against Rogers, who had allegedly killed Hayes' prize palomino horse. And in one sharp exchange with Hayes, she criticizes him for gambling too much and thus jeopardizing the ranch. In this film, Evans is the ever-faithful daughter, yet she did assert her independence when necessary.

By late 1946, Evans characters were no longer domestic, and they were even more independent. *Home in Oklahoma* (Republic, 1946), *Heldorado* (Republic, 1946) and *Bells of San Angelo* (Republic, 1947) are good film examples of this trend. In the latter film, Evans plays Lee Madison, author of Western novels. Rogers does not believe she knows anything about the real West and, therefore, he regards her as an irritant. Yet, at the film's end, they utilize a trick from one of her books to help catch the villains. Evans' independence continued in the 1947 film *Apache Rose*. She operates a tugboat, wears men's clothing and gets grease on her face.

In 1949's, *Susanna Pass* (Republic, 1949), Evans plays every inch the modern woman. She is Dr. Kay Parker, Ph.D. in marine biology, and a veteran of the Women's Marine Corps. By this time, Rogers films were far removed from Mary Hart's glow-while-he-sang. Evans' character in *Susanna*

Susanna Pass, Republic, 1949; Dale Evans, Robert Emmett Keane and Roy Rogers. Evans plays a former Marine, a Ph.D. in marine biology and a thorough-going independent woman in this Rogers Western.

Pass is very much a lady who is smart and who can take care of herself. Now women, so it seems, could have it all. They could be competitive, independent of men, and yet remain feminine.

Interestingly enough, that emphasis did not continue much beyond *Susanna Pass*. From *Down Dakota Way* (Republic, 1949) through *Trigger, Jr.* (Republic, 1950), Evans' characters are generally bland, in some cases comical, mostly dependent on males, and marginal to the plot. And her last film, *Pals of the Golden West* (Republic, 1951), is not much different from the ones she made in 1949–50. In her later movies, Evans' characters assume more traditional roles. She seems much more dependent on Rogers, and her parts in the films are less central to plot and action.

Evans' 1949–50 films are early examples of the gender reaction that pervaded popular culture, and television in particular, as the 1950s wore on. The popular television shows of the decade such as *Father Knows Best*,

I Love Lucy and *Make Room for Daddy* assume the proper role of woman was that of wife and mother, and the home her proper domain. Evans' Westerns after *Susanna Pass* have more in common with that view than the one projected in her films from 1945 to early 1949.

One of the ways to further explore the change in Evans' roles is to compare her last few films with those in which Penny Edwards appeared. When *Trigger, Jr.* was released on June 30, 1950, Dale Evans did not appear in another film until *South of Caliente* (Republic, 1951) was released October 15, 1951. Edwards appeared in six films during the time Evans was absent from the series. Three of Edwards' films—*Trail of Robin Hood* (Republic, 1950), *Spoilers of the Plains* (Republic, 1951) and *Heart of the Rockies* (Republic, 1951)—involved her in considerable action. But in *North of the Great Divide* her role was minimal, even though she was billed as the leading lady. And her role *In Old Amarillo* (Republic, 1951) is minimal at best.

In all five of the films, however, she projects a modern non-traditional image. For example, in *Spoilers of the Plains*, Edwards played the daughter-assistant of a scientist involved in early rocketry. She is a scientist in her own right with the very important task of plotting the rocket's trajectory so it can be located and recovered. In *Trail of Robin Hood*, Edwards again assists her father, this time protecting his Christmas tree business. And in *Heart of the Rockies*, Edwards, as Ralph Morgan's niece, stands up to her uncle when he tries to stop a road from being constructed through his property. In all five films, while she was closely identified with a male, it was as helper rather than as a dependent. Even in *North of the Great Divide*, her weakest role, Edwards played a public health nurse responsible for the wellbeing of the Indians.

At first glance Edwards' films appear to diverge sharply from the last few films in which Dale Evans appeared. Yet, on closer examination that may not be the case. *Spoilers of the Plains* projects an interesting role conflict. As a scientist and at her father's insistence, Edwards wears horn-rimmed glasses, hair pulled back tightly into a bun, and very plain dresses. But as the film progresses we learn that she longs to let her hair down, literally, and to wear more attractive and stylish dresses. With Rogers' help she musters enough courage to oppose her father and to assert her femininity. She may have been a modern woman of sorts, but at the same time she was a traditional daughter concerned with her father's demands, and a traditional woman who permitted male tastes to dictate what is feminine.

Can the not-too-subtle message of this film be that post-war women really did not know what they wanted? They had been self-supporting and independent during the war because most of the men were gone. But now the men were back and it was time to let the hair shake loose and to wear frilly dresses. It was time to return to the home and to the old ways. Did *Spoilers of the Plains* suggest that the proper role for Dr. Kay Parker, Dale Evans' character in *Susanna Pass*, was no longer to be a Marine Biologist, but to be pretty and to glow while Roy Rogers sang?

Westerns reflected the entire range of gender relationships that characterized the years 1930 to 1955. For the most part, Western heroines were pretty, helpless and dependent in the 1930s. They had little to do in the films, and were included primarily as the love interest for the cowboy hero.

Gene Autry began to change that orientation as the heroines in his movies were often career-oriented, independent women. But even Autry's heroines were frequently misguided ladies who did not know their own good. Autry became less of a lover and more of an educator who had to straighten out the heroine.

World War II revolutionized gender relations. With the men away fighting, women worked in factories, taxied airplanes from factories to military bases, and continued homelife activities such as shopping, balancing the checkbook and raising the children. Divorce rates increased in the years following World War II as husband returned home to find wives able to change flat tires and balance the checkbook, and unwilling to return to a life of dependency. Westerns of the period reflected shifts in gender relations and the tensions between men and women produced by those shifts, just as 1990s Westerns such as *Bad Girls* (20th Century–Fox, 1993) and Sharon Stone's *The Quick and the Dead* (Tri Star Pictures, 1994) represented gender images and relationships of the 1990s.

REFERENCES

Adams, Les, and Buck Rainey. *Shoot-em Ups: The Complete Guide to Westerns of the Sound Era.* Metuchen, N.J.: Scarecrow Press, 1985.
"At the Criterion." *New York Times,* June 25, 1938, 7:3.
Autry, Gene. *Back in the Saddle Again.* Garden City, N.Y.: Doubleday, 1978.
Bataille, Gretchen, and Charles L. Silet, editors. *The Pretend Indians: Images of Native Americans in the Movies.* Ames: Iowa State University Press, 1980.
Bellah, Robert N. *The Broken Covenant: American Civil Religion in a Time of Trial.* New York: Seabury Press, 1975.
Carman, Bob, and Dan Scapperotti. *Roy Rogers, King of the Cowboys.* Privately printed, 1979.
Coser, Lewis, and Bernard Rosenberg, editors. *Sociological Theory: A Book of Readings.* New York: Macmillan, 1964.
Daniels, Roger. *The Decision to Relocate the Japanese Americans.* Philadelphia: J.B. Lippincott, 1975.
Darton, Nina. "Vamoose, You Varmits, the Good Guys Ride Again." *New York Times,* July 7, 1985, 2:1 and 13.
Elkin, Frederick J. "The Psychological Appeal of Popular Film." *Journal of Educational Sociology,* Volume 24 (September, 1950), pp. 72–68.
_____. "The Value Implications of Popular Film." *Sociology and Social Research,* Volume 34 (1954), pp. 320–22.
Fenin, George N., and William K. Everson. *The Western: From Silents to Cinema.* New York: Orion Press, 1962.
Freund, Julien. *The Sociology of Max Weber.* New York: Random House, 1968.
Friar, Ralph E., and Natasha A. Friar, editors. *The Only Good Indian... The Hollywood Gospel.* New York: Drama Book Specialists, 1972.
Garfield, Brian. *Western Films: A Complete Guide.* New York: Rawson Associates, 1982.

Hartigan, Elizabeth. "Popularity of Old Westerns Is Thing of the Past." *The Salt Lake Tribune*, September 2, 1986, 4b.
Hilger, Michael. *The American Indian in Film*. Metuchen, N.J.: Scarecrow Press, 1986.
Horowitz, James. *They Went Thataway*. New York: Dutton, 1976.
Hurst, Richard. *Republic Studio: Between Poverty Row and the Majors*. Metuchen, N.J.: Scarecrow Press, 1979.
Isaacson, Walter, and Evan Thomas. *The Wise Men: Six Friends and the World They Made*. New York: Simon & Schuster, 1986.
Jarvie, I.C. *Movies as Social Criticism: Aspects of Their Social Psychology*. Metuchen, N.J.: Scarecrow Press, 1978.
Johnston, Alva. "Tenor on Horseback." *Saturday Evening Post*, September 2, 1939, pp. 18–19.
Kennedy, David M. *Freedom from Fear: The American People in Depression and War*. New York: Oxford University Press, 1999.
Keyes, Edward. *The Coconut Grove*. New York: Atheneum, 1984.
Kitses, Jim. *Horizons West*. Bloomington: Indiana University Press, 1968.
Lenihan, John H. *Showdown: Confronting Modern America in Western Film*. Urbana: University of Illinois Press, 1980.
Lentz, Harris M., III. *Western and Frontier Films and Television Credits, 1903–1995*. Two volumes. Jefferson, N.C.: McFarland, 1996.
Lowi, Theodore J. *The End of Liberalism: Ideology, Policy and the Crisis of Public Authority*. New York: W.W. Norton, 1969.
Loy, R. Philip. "Buck Jones: An Old-Time Cowboy," in Gary A. Yoggy, editor. *Back in the Saddle: Essays on Western Film and Television Actors*. Jefferson N.C.: McFarland, 1998; pp. 43–58.
_____. "The Cisco Kid: Evolution of a Film Character." *Films of the Golden Age*, No. 19 (Winter 1999–2000), pp. 76–84
_____."Saints or Scroundrels: Images of Mormons in Literature and Film About the American West." *Journal of the American Studies Association of Texas*. Volume 21 (October, 1990), pp. 57–74.
_____. "Soldiers in Stetsons: B Westerns Go to War." Paper presented at the 15th Annual Conference on World War II, Siena College, June. 2000.
_____. "Telegraph Washington for Help," in *Under Western Skies*. #51, (1998), pp. 21–29.
MacNeil, Neil. *Forge of Democracy: The House of Representatives*. New York: David McKay, 1963.
Martin, Pete. "Cincinnati Cowboy." *Saturday Evening Post*, June 9, 1945, pp. 26–27 and 78–81.
Miller, Don. *The Hollywood Corral*. New York: Popular Press, 1976.

Moley, Raymond. *The Hays Office.* Indianapolis: Bobbs-Merrill, 1945.
Nachbar, Jack, editor. *Focus on the Western.* Englewood Cliffs, N.J.: Prentice-Hall, 1974.
Nevins, Francis M. *The Films of Hopalong Cassidy.* Waynesville, N.C.: World of Yesterday Press, 1988.
_____. *The Films of the Cisco Kid.* Waynesville, N.C.: World of Yesterday Press, 1998.
Nicholas, John H. *Tom Mix: Riding Up to Glory.* Oklahoma City: Persimmon Hill Books, 1980.
Pitts, Michael R. *Western Movies: A TV and Video Guide to 4200 Genre Films.* Jefferson, N.C.: McFarland, 1986.
Rainey, Buck. *The Life and Times of Buck Jones: The Sound Era.* Waynesville, N.C.: World of Yesterday Press, 1991.
_____. *The Saga of Buck Jones.* Nashville: Western Film Collectors, 1975.
Rogers, Roy, and Dale Evans; with Jane and Michael Stern. *Happy Trails: Our Life Story.* New York: Simon & Schuster, 1994.
_____; with Carlton Stowers. *Happy Trails: The Story of Roy Rogers and Dale Evans.* Waco, Texas: Word Books, 1979.
Rothel, David. *The Singing Cowboys.* New York: A.S. Barnes, 1978.
_____. *Tim Holt.* Madison, N.C.: Empire Publishing, 1994.
Sarf, Wayne Michael. *God Bless You Buffalo Bill: A Layman's Guide to History and the Western Film.* Madison, N.J.: Fairleigh Dickinson University Press, 1983.
Schlesinger, Arthur M., Jr. *The Coming of the New Deal.* Boston: Houghton Mifflin, 1959.
Silver, Charles. *The Western Film: A Pyramid Illustrated History of the Movies.* New York: Pyramid Publishers, 1976.
Slotkin, Richard. *Gunfighter Nation: The Myth of the Frontier in Twentieth Century America.* New York: Harper Perennial, 1993.
Tocqueville, Alexis de. *Democracy in America.* Two volumes. New York and London: Co-Operative Publication Society, 1900.
Tuska, Jon. *The American West in Film: Critical Approaches to the Western.* Westport, Conn.: Greenwood Press, 1985.
_____. *The Filming of the West.* New York: Doubleday, 1976.
_____. *The Vanishing Legion: A History of Mascot Pictures, 1927–1935.* Jefferson, N.C.: McFarland, 1982.
Variety Film Reviews. 16 volumes. New York: Garland, 1983.
Warshow, Robert. *The Immediate Experience.* New York: Atheneum, 1979.
White, Raymond E. "Hollywood Cowboys Go to War: The B Western Movie During World War II." *Under Western Skies,* No. 25 (September), 1983, pp. 23–66.

White, William S. *Citadel: The Story of the U.S. Senate.* New York: Harper and Row, 1956.

Yoggy, Gary A., editor. *Back in the Saddle Again: Essays on Western Films and Television Actors.* Jefferson, N.C.: McFarland 1998.

INDEX

Abilene Town 45, 116, 130, 137
Abrams, Morris R. 74
Acheson, Dean 152
Across the Plains 229
Acuff, Roy 37
Adams, Ernie 59, 253
Adams, Les 6
Adams, Ted 31, 201, 210, 243, 248
Albright, Hardie 190
Albright, Lola 145
Alderson, Erville 143
Alias Billy the Kid 50
Allen, Rex 17, 18, 23, 28, 29, 46, 63, 105, 138, 164, 188, 189, 250, 255
American Empire 188
Anderson, Gilbert M. 11
Andrews, Dana 115
Andrews, Stanley 160
Angel and the Badman 64, 66, 67, 140
Ankrum, Morris 231
Apache Country 226
Apache Rose 31, 158, 258
Arizona Bound 131
Arizona Cowboy, The 17
Arizona Gangbusters 34, 211
Arizona Ranger, The 119
Arizona Stagecoach 135
Arizona Terror 94, 209, 243
Arlen, Richard 29, 97
Armida 209
Arrowhead 231
Arthur, Jean 102, 117
Atchley, Hooper 159

Ates, Roscoe 63 172, 173
Autry, Gene 9, 13, 16, 17, 18, 21, 22, 23, 27, 28, 30, 31, 32, 33, 44, 45, 50, 52, 54, 60, 61, 62, 72, 73, 74, 80, 89, 90 91, 92, 93, 98, 100, 102, 104, 105, 107, 137, 138, 145, 160, 162, 164, 165, 166, 174, 175, 176, 179, 180, 181, 187, 188, 190, 200, 202,206, 208, 224, 225, 226, 242, 245, 246, 252, 255, 261
Avenging Waters 241

Bachelor, Stephanie 253, 254
Back in the Saddle 187
Bad Girls 261
Baker, Bob 16
Ball, Frank 198
Ballew, Smith 16, 169, 170, 171
Bannon, Jim 50
Baptism of Fire 34
Bar 20 Rides Again 133, 134
Barclay, Don 198
Barclay, Joan 195, 196
Barcroft, Roy 31, 32, 106, 132, 153, 161, 163, 177, 178, 179, 194, 227, 228, 229, 246, 254
Bardette, Trevor 66
Barn Dance, The 165
Barr, Byron 140
Barrie, Mona 246
Barron, Robert 204
Barry, Donald "Red" 18, 19,
23, 26, 56, 57, 87, 94, 126, 158, 183, 191, 192
Basquette, Lina 208, 243, 244
Battle at Elderbrush Gulch, The 214
Baucin, Escolastico, 204
Baxter, Warner 212, 213
Beavers, Louise 58, 188
Bell, Hank 247
Bell, Rex 30, 227, 238
Belle Starr 252
Bells of Capistrano 206
Bells of Coronado 37, 107, 177, 178, 179
Bells of Rosarita 18, 19
Bells of San Angelo, The 52, 54, 106, 187, 258
Bennett, Bruce 5
Bennett, Lee 63
Berry, Noah 158
Berry, Noah, Jr. 155, 227, 238
Best, Willie 189, 190, 196
Between Men 140, 240
Beveridge, Albert 41
Beyond the Purple Hills 157, 160
Big Bonanza, The 197
Big Hop, The 14
Big Show, The 30
Big Trail, The 40
Big Tree, Chief John 220, 223
Billy the Kid 125, 126
Billy the Kid in Texas 136, 145

Billy the Kid Returns 86, 257
Black Market Rustlers 37
Blue, Monte 228
Blue Canadian Rockies 102, 251
Bold Caballero, The 212
Bond, Ward 70
Booth, Adrian 230, 250
Border Caballero, The 205
Border Legion, The 174
Border Phantom 197
Border Saddlemates 63
Born to the West 136
Boss Rider of Gun Creek 141, 241
Bosworth, Hobart 59
Boyd, Bill 18, 188, 189
Boyd, William 13, 21, 22, 23, 107, 124, 202, 226, 244
Boyd, William "Stage" 29
Bradbury, Robert North 109, 110
Bradford, Lane 153
Brady, Pat 37, 139, 178
Branded 242, 243
Brandon, Henry 81, 207, 230, 231
Brennan, Walter 113
Brent, Evelyn 253
Brent, Lynton 143
Brian, David 129
Brigham Young 69, 70
Britton, Barbara 117
Broadway to Cheyenne 30, 238
Brodie, Steve 144
Broken Arrow 215, 219, 234
Bronson, Betty 242
Brooks, Rand 226
Brothers in the Saddle 144
Brown, Johnny Mack 18, 19, 21, 33, 34, 87, 107, 129, 133, 140, 141, 160, 165, 209, 240, 243, 248, 249
Browne, Reno 249, 250
Bryant, Nana 253, 254
Buck, Pearl S. 197
Buetel, Jack 146, 233, 251
Buffalo Bill, Jr. 15
Bugles in the Afternoon 232
Burnette, Lester "Smiley" 30, 31, 33, 50, 96, 98, 138, 163, 187, 193, 197, 202, 203, 245, 256
Burns, Marion 237

Buster, Budd 94
Buttram, Pat 61, 102, 175, 251

Cabin Kids 190
Calhoun, Rory 233
California Frontier 207
California Trail, The 54, 207, 211
Call of the Canyon 164
Camargo, Anita 209, 211
Cameron, Rod 22, 230, 231
Campbell, Peggy 239
Canutt, Yakima 220, 221, 222
Carey, Harry 12, 13, 20, 65, 73, 141, 145, 193
Carey, Harry, Jr. 70
Carleton, George 168, 169
Carlyle, Richard 58
Carnegie, Andrew 152
Carolina Moon 190
Carrillo, Leo 210, 213
Carroll, John 56
Carrying the Mail 6
Carson, Sunset 10, 18
Carson City Kid 200
Caruso, Anthony 234
Carver, Lynn 252, 254
Cason, Bob 153
Cass County Boys 32
Castle, Mary 255
Cavalry 94
Chandler, Eddie 143
Chandler, Jeff 220, 234
Chandler, Lane 16, 34, 43, 44, 247
Chaney, Lon, Jr. 30, 159
Charge at Feather River 232, 233
Chase, Stephen 107
Chatterton, Tom 58, 89
Chesebro, George 153, 181
Chesire, Harry 253
Chip of the Flying U 33
Chung, Wong 200
Churchill, Benton 159
Churchill, Marguerite 102, 243
Cimarron 40
Cimarron Kid, The 112
Cisco Kid Returns, The 53, 213, 253
Clark, Hainey 141
Clark, Steve 143, 253
Clearing the Range 243
Clearly, Leo 38, 178
Cleveland, George 165

Clift, Montgomery 206
Clyde, Andy 135, 226, 249
Coates, Phyllis 250
Cody, Iron Eyes 220, 233
Coffin, Tristram 210, 253
Cohn, Harry 13
Colorado 81
Colorado Sundown 28, 29, 58, 164, 187, 255
Colorado Sunset 50, 179
Come On Cowboys 203
Come On, Tarzan 101, 124, 239
Command, The 232
Connors, Buck 54
Conroy, Frank 196
Cook, Elisha, Jr. 103
Cooper, Gary 17
Corrigan, Lloyd 97, 145
Corrigan, Ray 203
Cosgrove, Douglas 43
Covered Wagon, The 13, 14, 40, 215
Cowboy and the Indians, The 225
Cowboy and the Senorita 157
Cowboy Canteen 37
Cowboy Commandos 34
Cox, Virginia 144
Crabbe, Larry "Buster" 22, 131, 133, 156, 167
Crashing Thru 253
Cripple Creek 198
Curtis, Dick 72, 134, 146, 170, 199, 240, 243
Custer, George 216, 223, 232
Cyclone Prairie Rustlers 35

Daley, John 132
Dallas 160
Dandridge, Ruby 188
Dangerous Venture 226
Daring Caballero, The 213
Darnell, Linda 70
Davis, Art 18, 188, 189, 191, 192
Davis, Gail 61, 72, 102, 251
Davis, Jim 147, 157, 230
Dawn on the Great Divide 63, 227, 246
Dawn Rider, The 143, 237
Dawn Trail, The 143, 144
Day, Marceline 238
Days of Jesse James 160
Dean, Eddie 17, 19, 22, 63, 136, 147, 253

Death Rides the Range 33, 211
Death Valley Outlaws 126
Dennis, Frank 254
Derek, John 147, 148
Desert Pursuit 234
Desert Trail, The 143
Desert Vengeance 51, 54
de Tocqueville, Alexis 77, 78, 79, 99, 122, 123, 129
Devine, Andy 254
Dew, Eddie 35, 36
De Wilde, Brandon 102
Dillaway, Donald 81
Dix, Richard 196, 246
Dodge City 16, 57
Domergue, Faith 255
Donlevy, Brian 117
Don't Fence Me In 31, 137
Down Dakota Way 52, 139, 140, 259
Down Mexico Way 206
Downey, John 62
Downs, Cathy 150
Driftin' River 63
Driscoll, Bobby 197
Dude Cowboy 97, 98
Duel at Silver Creek, The 255
Dumbrille, Douglas 90, 92, 93, 238
Duncan, Kenne 176, 177, 255
Dwire, Earl 109, 220, 240

Eagle's Brood, The 244
Eburne, Maude 174
Edwards, Penny 38, 39, 256, 260
Edwards, Ukulele Ike 21, 129
Eilers, Sally 243
Eisenhower, Dwight 8, 78
El Paso 115, 116
Elkins, Frederick 49, 71, 74
Elliott, John 168
Elliott, William 18, 19, 22, 23, 42, 56, 59, 66, 67, 73, 83, 93, 113, 115, 117, 118, 139, 156, 157, 167, 194, 199, 200, 203, 204, 210, 226, 250
Ellis, Frank 153, 200
Ellis, Robert 238
Ellison, James 18, 133
End of the Trail 215, 219, 225
Escape from Fort Bravo 232

Evans, Dale 10, 19, 52, 63, 105, 125, 146, 147, 157, 158, 188, 206, 256, 258, 259, 260
Evans, Muriel 200
Eyes of Texas 254, 257

Fabulous Texan, The 56
Far Frontier, The 31
Fargo Kid, The 21
Farnum, William 50, 54, 88, 91, 140, 141, 240, 244
Fawcett, William 63, 176
Faye, Dorothy 73
Fellows, Edith 137
Fence Riders 249
Ferguson, Al 143
Ferguson, Frank 230
Fetchit, Stepin 188, 189, 190
Fighting Caballero 205, 208
Fighting Legion, The 159
Fighting Parson, The 57
Fighting Ranger, The 110
Fighting Renegade, The 205, 208
Finley, Evelyn 143, 248, 249, 250
Finney, Charles 154
Fisher, Richard 73
Fisher, Vardis 69
Fix, Paul 143
Flashing Guns 160
Fletcher, Tex 17
Flynn, Errol 44, 147, 250
Fonda, Henry 115, 150, 196, 221, 222
For the Service 240
Foran, Dick 16, 41, 159
Forbidden Trail 200
Forbidden Trails 119, 133
Ford, Francis 211
Ford, Henry 152
Ford, John 16
Fort Apache 221, 222, 224
Fort Osage 215, 231, 234
Fort Worth 129
Foulger, Byron 97, 98, 155
Fox, William 12, 76
Franklin, Irene 158
Fraser, Elisabeth 250
Frazee, Jane 37, 209, 254, 256
Frazer, Robert 57, 58
Freeman, Howard 130
Friar, Natasha 216
Friar, Wayne 216
Frisco Tornado 107, 108, 109, 110, 131

Frontier Days 159
Frontier Pony Express 81
Frost, Terry 153
Fugitive from Sonora 56, 57
Fung, Willie 29, 198, 201, 202, 203
Furness, Betty 173

Gallant Defender 13, 21
Gan, Chester 200, 201
Gangs of Sonora 126
Gangster's Den 167
Garralaga, Martin 210
Gay Cavalier, The 210, 213
Gay Ranchero, The 209, 210
Geary, Bud 59, 156, 177, 194
Gehrig, Lou 169, 170, 171
Geronimo 215, 231, 233
Ghost of Zorro 212
Gibson, Hoot 12, 15, 23, 57, 89, 98, 100, 102, 208, 227, 243, 247
Git Along Little Doggies 190, 202
Glory Trail, The 195, 196
Gold Mine in the Sky 187
Graham, Billy 64, 65
Graham, Fred 164
Grant, Kirby 251
Great Train Robbery, The 10, 11, 40, 103
Greer, Jane 255
Grey, Virginia 234
Grey, Zane 20, 68, 69, 198
Guizar, Tito 209, 210
Gulliver, Dorothy 208, 209
Gun Law 86
Gun Smoke 29
Gunfighter, The 118, 119
Gunman from Bodie 74, 148
Gunning for Justice 248
Gunsmoke Ranch 27
Guthrie, A.B. 103

Hackel, A.W. 18, 94
Hackett, Karl 59, 177, 198
Hale, Alan, Jr. 145, 146
Hale, Monte 17, 18, 19, 53, 58, 171, 172
Half Breed, The 233, 234
Hall, Thurston 164, 251
Hamilton, John 171
Hard Hombre 102, 208
Harlan, Kenneth 227
Harmony Trail 136
Hart, Mary 81, 256, 257, 258

Hart, William S. 11, 13, 22, 40, 61, 100, 184
Hatton, Raymond 42, 89, 119, 131, 132, 133, 140, 160, 227, 248, 249
Haunted Gold 190, 191, 193, 221, 239
Hawaiian Buckaroo 187
Hawk of Powder River 147, 253
Hayden, Russell 18, 71
Hayden, Sterling 115
Hayes, George "Gabby" 8, 33, 59, 82, 84, 110, 111, 124, 127, 129, 134, 136, 146, 156, 157, 158, 160, 190, 194, 195, 201, 202, 203, 204, 221, 237, 256, 257, 258
Hayworth, Rita 73, 208, 209
Healey, Myron 153, 249
Heart of the Golden West 164
Heart of the Rockies 260
Heflin, Van 6, 149
Heldorado 31, 105, 158, 258
Hellfire 61, 64, 66, 67, 68
Hell's Hinges 11, 61, 64
Henry, Buzz 62
Henry, Gloria 255
Henry, O. 212
Heston, Charlton 231
Hidden Gold 30
Hidden Valley Outlaws 193, 195
High Noon 126
Hilger, Michael 217
Hill, Riley 230, 231, 253, 254
Hills of Oklahoma 138, 250
Hills of Utah 174
His Brother's Ghost 177
Hodgins, Earle 97, 98, 194, 195
Hoffman, Otto 129
Hohl, Arthur 32
Holmes, William 127, 128
Holt, Jack 20, 119, 137, 157, 210
Holt, Jennifer 20, 35, 36, 250, 253, 254
Holt, Tim 20, 21, 22, 98, 119, 127, 129, 133, 144, 167, 168, 227, 228
Homans, Robert 187
Home in Oklahoma 105, 129, 137, 258
Home in Wyoming 245

Home on the Range 58
Homeier, Skip 119
Homesteaders of Paradise Valley 27, 127
Hop-A-Long Cassidy 201
Horowitz, James 45
Houston, George 17, 19, 52, 145
Hoxie, Jack 165, 211
Hubbard, John 157
Hughes, Carol 90, 174, 245, 246
Hull, Warren 245
Hurst, Paul 171, 172
Hurst, Richard 5, 64, 74, 183
Hyer, Martha 127

Idaho 32, 252
In Old Amarillo 52, 127, 128, 210, 260
In Old Caliente 41, 207, 257
In Old Monterey 33
In Old New Mexico 53
In Old Sacramento 200
In Old Santa Fe 13, 16
In the Days of the Thundering Herd 214
Indian Agent 227
Indian Territory 225, 226, 251
Indians Are Coming, The 14
Iron Horse, The 20, 40
Ivory Handled Guns, The 14, 110, 243

Jackson, Eugene 190
Jacquet, Frank 159
Jagger, Dean 70
James, John 193, 194
January, Lois 56, 208, 239, 240
Jarvie, I.C. 5
Jeffreys, Anne 193, 194
Jeffries, Herb 17
Jesse James at Bay 160
Johnson, Ben 70, 117, 149, 223
Johnson, John Lester 195
Johnson, Linda 246, 247
Jolley, I. Stanford 153, 161, 162, 167, 248
Jones, Buck 4, 10, 12, 13, 14, 26, 27, 42, 45, 51, 52, 54, 55, 56, 57, 74, 89, 105, 110, 111, 119, 120, 125, 131, 132, 133, 138, 140, 141,

143, 158, 159, 184, 205, 207, 208, 211, 218, 219, 227, 239, 241, 242, 243, 246, 247
Jones, Clifford 240
Jones, Dick 61, 62, 251
Jory, Victor, 196, 246

Kahn, Richard 17
Kamal, Tet Su 199
Kansan, The 22, 189, 196, 246
Kasdan, Lawrence 45
Kay, Mary Ellen 188, 189
Keane, Edward 81
Keane, Robert Emmett 259
Keefe, Cornelius 30, 31
Keene, Tom 20, 58, 172, 173, 195, 196
Kendall, Cy 84, 85, 153, 184, 185
Kennedy, Douglas 231
Kennedy, John F. 43
Kennedy, Joseph P. 12
Kennedy, Merna 239
Kenton, Ethel 242
Keyes, Edward 23
King, Charles 59, 82, 83, 118, 136, 143, 153, 155, 156, 177, 181, 208, 240
King, John "Dusty" 16, 135, 143
King of the Arena 95
King of the Bullwhip 109, 131, 160
King of the Cowboys 34, 95
King of the Mounties 204
Kirk, Jack 177, 187
Kitses, Jim 40
Knapp, Evalyn 169, 171
Kohler, Fred 237, 238
Kornman, Mary 143
Kortman, Robert 153
Krasne, Philip 212

Lackteen, Frank 229
Ladd, Alan 6, 117, 118, 148
Laemmle, Carl 14, 76
Lancaster, Burt 220
Land Beyond the Law 158
Land of the Open Range 167, 168, 171
Lane, Allan "Rocky" 18, 19, 20, 23, 28, 89, 107, 108, 109, 129, 131, 137, 161, 162, 177, 178, 204
Lane, Vicky 253
Larson, Christine 250, 253

LaRue, Frank 136, 177, 253
LaRue, Lash 19, 22, 89, 107, 108, 109, 118, 131, 133, 160
Last Bandit, The 210
Last of the Pony Riders 44, 61, 62, 160
Last Round-Up, The 137, 224, 225
Law and Order 34
Law and the Lawless 165, 211
Law Comes to Gunsight, The 86
Law Rides Again, The 98, 227, 247
Lawless Land 209, 211
Lawless Nineties, The 81, 126, 129, 195, 237
Leadville Gunslinger 160
Lease, Rex 15, 205, 208
Lee, Eddie 203, 204
Lee, Mary 190
Lee, Pinky 210
Leigh, Janet 150
Lenihan, John H. 10
Lesser, Sol 14
Levine, Nat 13
Lewis, George 209, 229
Lightnin' Bill Carson 60, 208
Lincoln, Abraham 48, 49, 81, 83, 94, 95
Livingston, Robert 18, 34, 35, 212, 247, 255
Lloyd, George 165
Loft, Arthur 42, 153, 160, 169, 170
London, Tom 50, 102, 177, 200, 252, 255
Lone Ranger, The 220
Lone Rider Rides On, The 129, 145
Lonely Trail, The 85, 184, 185, 187, 190, 237
Lorch, Theodore 142
Lovett, Robert 152
Luden, Jack 191, 192
Lynn, Emmett 98, 158, 227, 229

McCarthy, Joseph 152
McCloy, John 152
McCoy, Tim 12, 13, 14, 15, 23, 34, 42, 45, 57, 60, 73, 89, 119, 125, 126, 131, 132, 133, 137, 140, 205, 208, 211, 215, 219, 227, 247
McCrea, Joel 22, 115, 117, 118, 166

McDaniel, Etta 188, 190, 195
McDonald, Edmund 164
McDonald, Francis 144, 209, 211
MacDonald, Kenneth 83, 161
McDowell, Nelson 201
McGlynn, Frank, Sr. 26
McKee, Lafe, 171, 215
McKenzie, Bob 126, 136
McKenzie, Fay 245, 246
McKim, Harry 59, 156, 157
MacLane, Barton 166
McNally, Stephen 255
MacQuarrie, Murdock 55
Madison, Guy 232, 233
Man from Cheyenne 252, 254
Man from Music Mountain, The 138, 162
Man from Thunder River, The 203
Manning, Hope 30, 242
Mara, Adele 168, 169
Marion, Beth 141, 240, 241, 249
Mark of Zorro, The 212
Martin, Chris-Pin 221
Martin, Richard 21
Marvin, Frankie 187
Marx, Karl 103
Mason, LeRoy 59, 87, 88, 125, 138, 153, 156, 194, 239
Massacre River 233
Massey, Raymond, 160, 186
Mature, Victor 150, 220
Maynard, Ken 12, 13, 15, 16, 23, 33, 51, 89, 95, 96, 98, 101, 105, 124, 125, 136, 159, 209, 211, 227, 239, 241, 243, 244, 247
Maynard, Kermit 16
Meehan, Lew 56
Meeker, George 158
Melville, Herman 41
Meredith, Iris 199
Merton, John 156
Mexicali Rose 54, 206
Meyer, Emil 149
Middleton, Charles 87, 201
Miles, Betty 247, 248
Miles, Vera 233
Miljan, John 80, 81
Miller, Don 9
Miller, Ivan 162
Miller, Walter 110, 243

Millican, James 157
Mills Brothers 37
Miracle Rider, The 13
Missourians, The 53, 171
Mr. Smith Goes to Washington 89, 92
Mitchell, Millard 119
Mix, Tom 10, 11, 12, 13, 23, 30, 45, 69, 74, 100, 125, 165, 177, 181, 182, 199, 237, 238
Mojave Firebrand 59, 156, 157
Molieri, Lillian 209, 211
Montana 44, 147, 250
Montana, Monte 139
Montgomery, George 69, 187, 199
Moody, Dwight L. 153
Moonlight on the Prairie 16
Moore, Clayton 158, 212, 220
Moore, Dennis 63, 85, 97, 132, 160, 185, 237, 254
Morante, Milburn 154
Morgan, Ralph 260
Morita, Miki 198
Morris, Wayne 145, 234
Morton, Charles 143
Moss, Jimmie 63
Mowbray, Alan 70
Mulford, Clarence 22
Munson, Ona 32, 252
Murdock, Perry 198
Murphy, Audie 112, 255
Murphy, Horace 198
Murray, Zon 136
My Darling Clementine 45, 52, 150, 216
My Pal the King 12
My Pal Trigger 146, 157, 258

Nachbar, Jack 9
Naish, J. Carrol 224
Naked Spur, The 150
'Neath Arizona Skies 220
Nevada City 257
New Frontier 18
Newill, James 16, 17, 18
Nicholas, John 9
Night Time in Nevada 106, 168, 169
Niles, Wendell 31
North from the Lone Star 42, 43, 73
North of the Great Divide 89, 163, 228, 260

Norris, Edward 145
Novello, Jay 84, 211

Oakman, Wheeler 73, 159
O'Brien, Billy 111
O'Brien, Dave 18
O'Brien, George 20, 69, 73, 86, 87, 102, 164, 208, 242, 243
O'Flynn, Paddy 110
Oh Susanna 30, 187
Oh! Susanna 157, 230, 233, 234
O'Keefe, Dennis 57
Oklahoma Cyclone 208
Old Corral, The 30, 137, 242
Old West, The 61
On the Old Spanish Trail 106, 209, 210
On Top of Old Smoky 252
Oregon Trail Scouts 220
O'Shea, Jack 118
Out California Way 19
Outcast, The 147
Outlaw Country 108, 110
Outlawed Guns 26
Outlaws of Pine Ridge 158
Ox Bow Incident, The 115, 196, 203, 211

Pack Train 255
Page, Bradley 124
Page, Dorothy 17
Paget, Debra 219, 220
Palance, Jack 103, 117, 118, 149, 220, 231
Pale Rider 46
Pals of the Golden West 89, 210, 259
Pals of the Saddle 32, 33
Passage West 57
Patterson, Shirley 63
Payne, John 57, 115
Payne, Sally 136, 189, 252, 256, 257, 258
Peck, Gregory 118
Perrin, Jack 15
Peter, House, Sr. 61
Phantom Cowboy, The 190, 191, 192
Phantom Empire 13
Phantom Gold 190
Phantom of the Range 240
Phipps, William 133
Pickens, Slim 189
Pitts, Michael R. 6
Plainsman and the Lady, The 167

Porter, Edwin S. 11
Powell, Dick 255
Powell, Lee 18, 129
Power, Tyrone 70, 212
Powers, Mala 146, 250, 251
Powers, Richard 144, 227, 255
Powers, Tom 64
Prairie Schooners 139, 160, 226
Price, John R. 217
Price, Stanley 175
Pryor, Richard 253
Public Cowboy No. 1 197, 242
Purcell, Dick 32
Pyle, Denver 174, 176

Quartaro, Nena 209
Quick and the Dead, The 261
Quinn, Anthony 211, 220

Racketeers of the Range 164, 242, 243
Raiders of Sunset Pass 35
Raiders of the San Joaquin 147, 165
Rainey, Buck 6
Rancho Grande 245
Randall, Jack 16, 145, 229
Randy Rides Alone 237
Range Busters 18, 34, 37, 135, 143, 177, 203, 204
Range Busters, The 177
Range Defenders 253
Range Feud 52
Ranger and the Lady 81, 105, 207
Rankin, Arthur 81
Rawhide 169
Reagan, Ronald 186
Red Raiders 215
Red River 22, 41, 149, 206, 207, 221
Red River Range 187
Red River Robin Hood 129
Red River Valley 27, 105, 138, 163, 181
Red Rope, The 56, 60
Renaldo, Duncan 210, 212, 213, 253
Renegade Ranger, The 208, 209
Renegades of the West 172
Return of Daniel Boone 42
Return of the Cisco Kid, The 212

Return of the Durango Kid 21
Revier, Dorothy 205, 208
Reynolds, Don 50
Reynolds, Marjorie 164, 242
Rice, Frank 110, 111, 159
Richards, Addison 244
Richmond, Warner 109, 110
Ricketts, Shirley 220
Ride, Ranger, Ride 224
Ride, Tenderfoot, Ride 181, 187, 245
Ride the High Country 118
Ride the Man Down 147
Rider from Tucson 133
Rider of Death Valley, The 74, 176, 181, 237
Riders in the Sky 255
Riders of Black River 146
Riders of Destiny 13, 16
Riders of the Northwest Mounted 71
Riders of the Purple Sage 69, 102, 178, 243
Riders of the Whistling Pines 28
Riders of the Whistling Skull 142, 226
Riding Down the Canyon 105
Riding Fool, The 126
Riley, Elaine 175
Riley, Kirk 72
Rio Grande 23, 223, 224
Risdon, Elisabeth 52, 128, 138, 139, 140, 250
Ritter, Tex 16, 17, 53, 59, 60, 146, 147, 165, 200, 201, 210
Rivero, Julian 209, 211
Roaming Cowboy, The 6, 239
Robards, Jason 218
Robbins, "Skeeter" Bill 57
Roberts, Lynne 257
Robertson, Willard 199
Robin Hood of Monterey 213, 253
Robin Hood of Texas 32
Robin Hood of the Pecos 84, 257
Robinson, Jimmy 190, 191
Rochelle, Claire 243
Rockefeller, John D. 152
Rockwell, Jack 220
Rocky Mountain Mystery 198
Rodriguez, Estelita 209, 210

Rogers, Roy 4, 9, 10, 17, 18, 21, 22, 23, 27, 28, 31, 32, 34, 37, 38, 39, 41, 42, 44, 45, 52, 54, 61, 63, 74, 80, 81, 84, 85, 89, 90, 91, 92, 93, 96,100, 105, 106, 107, 124, 125, 127, 128, 129, 134, 136, 137, 138, 139, 145, 146, 155, 158, 160, 162, 163, 164, 168, 174, 178, 179, 180, 184, 200, 206, 207, 208, 209, 210, 228, 229, 252, 253, 254, 256, 257, 258, 259, 261
Roland, Gilbert 210, 212, 213, 253
Roll On Texas Moon 8, 44
Rollin' Plains 59, 60
Romero, Cesar 212
Rooney, Mickey 14
Roosevelt, Buddy 15
Roosevelt, Franklin D. 8, 33, 80, 93, 99
Rose of Cimarron 146
Rothel, David 9
Rough Riders 18, 42, 98, 119, 120, 129, 131, 132, 133, 154, 227
Rough Riders Roundup 257
Round-Up Time in Texas 190
Rovin' Tumbleweeds 90, 92, 137, 187
Russell, Gail 64
Russell, Mary 142
Russell, Reb 16
Rustlers 127, 128
Rustler's Hideout 156
Rustler's Paradise 141
Rustler's Roundup 238
Rutherford, Ann 82, 85, 129, 185, 195, 237, 242
Ryan, Robert 150, 159
Ryan, Sheila 255

Saddle Busters 58
Saddle Mountain Roundup 135, 203
Saga of Death Valley, The 27, 105, 127, 145
Saginaw Trail, The 45, 224, 226
St. John, Al 34, 35, 94, 129, 134, 136, 145, 156, 167, 177, 193
Sale, Charles 198
Sandflow 14
Santa Fe Stampede 87, 88

Santa Fe Trail 186
Sarf, Wayne Michael 184, 186, 197, 216
Satan's Cradle 155
Savage, Ann 155
Savage Horde, The 117, 250
Sawyer, Joe 174
Saylor, Syd 136
Scarlet River 159
Scott, Fred 16, 147, 239, 240
Scott, Randolph 22, 44, 45, 116, 117, 118, 129, 130, 166, 198, 252
Seeger, Miriam 143
Sen Yung, Victor 200
Shane 6, 22, 45, 102, 103, 117, 118, 148
Shannon, Harry 32, 252
Sharpe, David 106
Shattay, Mike 114
She Wore a Yellow Ribbon 221, 222, 223, 224
Sheriff of Tombstone 211
Sherman, Harry 13, 22
Shilling, Marion 55, 57
Shine On Harvest Moon 137, 159, 257
Showdown 113
Sierra Passage 145
Silver, Charles 9
Silver Canyon 251
Silverado 46
Silverheels, Jay 220, 225
Simpson, Russell 70
Sinclair, Dianne 238
Singing Buckaroo, The 240
Singing Cowboy, The 164
Six Shooting Sheriff 51
Smith, Alexis 147, 250
Smoky Smith 109
Snake River Desperadoes 228
Sombrero Kid, The 183
Son of Davy Crockett 83, 93, 94
Son of Zorro 212
Song of Nevada 147
Song of Old Wyoming 19
Song of the Gringo 210
Song of the Sierras 135
Sons of New Mexico 251
Sons of the Pioneers 13, 17, 124, 146
South of Caliente 260
South of Monterey 210, 213
South of the Border 33, 206
South of the Rio Grande 205, 209, 211

Spoilers of the Plains 38, 137, 260, 261
Spoor, George K. 11
Springtime in the Sierras 28, 253
Squaw Man, The 215
Stack, Robert 232
Stagecoach 16, 159, 221
Stagecoach Driver 44
Stanley, Forrest 176, 237, 238
Star Packer 221
Starrett, Charles 13, 21, 35, 36, 45, 50, 146, 228
Station West 255
Steele, Bob 13, 15, 18, 22, 23, 56, 60, 89, 94, 109, 110, 117, 118, 145, 155, 197, 208, 247, 251
Stevens, Charles 210
Stevens, George 103
Stevens, Onslow 175
Stewart, James 89, 150, 219, 234
Stewart, Roy 238
Stirling, Linda 212
Stockdale, Carl 110
Stone, Milburn 81
Stone, Sharon 261
Stone of Silver Creek 14, 51, 54, 55, 56, 57, 158
Storey, June 181, 190, 245, 246, 251
Storm, Gale 252, 254
Strange, Glenn 37
Strawberry Roan 16
Stutenroth, Gene 28
Sudden Bill Dorn 14
Sunday, Billy 153
Sundown Valley 35
Sunset in Wyoming 164
Sunshine Boys 50
Susanna Pass 10, 28, 137, 210, 258, 259, 260

Tailor Maids 37
Take Me Back to Oklahoma 53
Taliaferro, Hal 80, 81
Taming of the West 42, 199
Taylor, Dub 35, 37, 42, 72, 83
Taylor, Forrest 36, 56, 135, 143, 146, 239, 240
Taylor, Robert 125
Temple, Shirley 188
Terhune, Max 129, 136, 143, 248, 249

Terry, Sheila 193, 239
Texans Never Cry 251, 255
Texas Bad Man 165, 199
Texas Justice 52
Texas Rangers 18
Texas to Bataan 204
They Died with Their Boots On 216, 220
Thompson, Kenneth 201
Thomson, Fred 12
Three Men from Texas 134
Three Mesquiteers 18, 27, 33, 87, 88, 142, 187, 203, 226
Throwback, The 138
Thunder Cloud, Chief 215, 220, 231, 247
Tierney, Gene 186, 252
Tocqueville, Alexis de 77, 78, 79, 99, 122, 123, 129
Toney, Jim 85
Toones, Fred 187, 188, 190, 193, 195, 200
Trail Blazers 18, 89, 98, 227
Trail Dust 25
Trail of Kit Carson 177, 178, 179
Trail of Robin Hood 18, 89, 137, 260
Trail Riders 156
Trail Street 45, 159
Trigger Jr. 147, 259, 260
Trouble in Texas 146
Truman, Harry S. 8
Tsaing, H.T. 200
Tucker, Forrest 230
Tumbleweeds 40
Tumbling Tumbleweeds 16, 138, 190
Tuska, Jon 5, 13, 14, 104, 213, 216, 217
Tuttle, Wesley 135
Twilight in the Sierras 32, 107, 137
Two Flags West 234
Two Gun Troubador 147
Tyler, Tom 13, 15, 18, 240

Under California Stars 138, 165
Under Fiesta Stars 245
Under Nevada Skies 37, 229
Under Western Stars 27, 89, 91, 92, 163

Vague, Vera 37
Vale, Virginia 240

Valley of Fire 137, 200
Vanderbilt, Cornelius 152
Vaughn, Alberta 237
Vincent, June 164, 255
Vincent, Russ 158
Vinton, Victoria 240
Virginian, The 23, 115, 116, 117, 201
Visaroff, Michael 209

Wagon Master 16
Wagon Team 251
Wagon Trail 73, 145
Wagonmaster 69
Wagons West 230
Wakely, Jimmy 17, 19, 37, 45, 135, 136, 253
Waldo, Janet 168
Wales, Wally 135
Walker, Terry 136
Wall Street Cowboy 137, 162
Waller, Eddy 93, 107, 129, 161
Walters, Luana 177, 219, 220
War Paint 231
Warner, H.B. 116
Warshow, Robert 100
Warwick, Robert 201
Washington, Blue 190, 192, 221
Way of the West 135
Wayne, John 13, 16, 18, 22, 32, 40, 43, 44, 64, 82, 87, 109, 110, 111, 120, 126, 136, 143, 145, 149, 184, 185, 187, 188, 190, 191, 192, 193, 206, 220, 221, 222, 223, 224, 237, 239
Weber, Max 103, 104, 106, 109, 110, 119
Weeks, Barbara 218, 219
Welch, Niles 54, 55, 56
Wells Fargo 166
West of Sonora 50
West of the Divide 110, 111
West of the Law 128, 132, 154
Westbound State 200
Western Code, The 73
Western Union 166
Westerner, The 16
Westward Bound 247, 248
When a Man Sees Red 239
Whipper, Lee 189, 196
Whirlwind 98, 251
White, Lee "Lasses" 21, 135, 136, 167, 168

White, Paul 190
White Eagle 218
Whiteford, Blackie 111
Whitley, Ray 21, 167
Whitlock, Lloyd 111
Wild Horse 188
Wild Horse Rustlers 34, 35, 246
Wilkerson, Guy 18
Williams, Guinn "Big Boy" 15, 37, 157
Wills, Bob 53, 72
Wills, Chill 230
Wilson, Dorothy 159
Wilson, Ernest 190, 191, 192
Wilson, Lois 176, 237, 238
Wilson, Whip 19, 44, 249, 253
Winds of the Wasteland 43
Windsor, Marie 66, 67
Winners of the West 41, 43
Winning of the West 145, 252
Withers, Grant 38, 106, 137, 160, 161, 162, 168, 169, 250
Witney, William 38
Wong, Victor 199
Wood, Harley 198
Woodbury, Joan 244
Woods, Harry 41, 82, 83, 132, 155, 193, 207, 210, 227, 228, 239, 246
Worth, Constance 35
Worth, Harry 60
Wright, Howard 62
Wyatt, Jane 189, 246
Wynters, Charlotte 243
Wyoming Outlaw 25, 87, 140

Yaconelli, Frank 213, 229
Yates, Herbert 17, 18, 19, 61, 64, 74, 89, 180, 183, 256
Yodelin' Kid from Pine Ridge, The 138, 188, 242
Young, Carleton 72, 145
Young, Clifton 137
Young, Robert 166, 234
Young Bill Hickok 80, 105, 136, 257
Young Buffalo Bill 105
Yowlachie, Chief 230

Zorro Rides Again 212
Zorro's Black Whip 212
Zorro's Fighting Legion 22

www.ingramcontent.com/pod-product-compliance
Lightning Source LLC
Chambersburg PA
CBHW051213300426
44116CB00006B/547